French Grammar

HARPERCOLLINS COLLEGE OUTLINE
French Grammar

Julio Celestin
Stuyvesant High School

HarperPerennial
A Division of HarperCollins*Publishers*

An American BookWorks Corporation Production

Project Manager: William R. Hamill

Editor: Courtenay Dodge

Library of Congress Cataloging-in-Publication Data

Celestin, Julio.
    French grammar / Julio Celestin.
       p.   cm. — (HarperCollins college outline series)
    Includes index.
    ISBN 0-06-467128-3 (pbk.) : $9.95
    1. French language—Grammar—1950- 2. French language—Textbooks
for foreign speakers—English.   I. Title.   II. Series.
PC2112.C4 1991
448.2'421—dc20   90-56018

91 92 93 94 95   ABW/RRD 10 9 8 7 6 5 4 3 2 1

Contents

1

Nouns and Articles

SINGULAR NOUNS

La **souris** mange le **fromage.**
Le **chat** guette la **souris.**
Le **garçon** chasse le **chat.**
La **jeune** mère fesse le **garçon.**

In French, all nouns have gender. They are either masculine or feminine in "gender." ("**La**" souris is a feminine noun.) Nouns that refer specifically to females are feminine in gender. ("**La**" jeune fille is a feminine noun.)

Likewise, those nouns that refer to males are masculine. ("**Le**" garçon is a masculine noun.) There are also some general patterns of meaning and spelling which can help determine the gender (masculine or feminine) of some French nouns.

Masculine nouns, for example, are sometimes acccompanied by the definite article **le** ("the," masculine form) or the indefinite article **un** ("a/an," masculine form). Feminine nouns are accompanied by the definite article la ("the," feminine form) or the indefinite article **une** ("a/an," feminine form).

When a noun begins with the unaspirated consonant "h" or a vowel, "l'" is used for either gender to translate the English definite article, "the."

1. Some masculine nouns have feminine equivalents:

Masculine		Feminine	
le beau-fils	son-in-law	la belle-fille,	daughter-in-law
l'oncle	uncle	la tante	aunt
le chat	cat	la chatte	cat
le chien	dog	la chienne	dog
le coq	rooster	la poule	hen
le dieu	god	la déese	goddess
le dindon	turkey	la dinde	turkey

le duc	duke	la duchesse	duchess
l'empereur	emperor	l'impératice	empress
le frère	brother	la soeur	sister
le garçon	boy	la fille	girl
le héros	hero	l'héroine	heroine
le male	male	la femelle	female
le mari	husband	la femme	wife
le mouton	sheep	la brebis	sheep
le père	father	la mère	mother
le roi	king	la reine	queen
le veuf	widower	la veuve	widow

2. Some nouns, whether applying to males or females, are always masculine ("**le**" = "*the*"):

le docteur	doctor
le guide	guide
le peintre	painter
le poète	poet
le professeur	professor

3. Some nouns are always feminine:

la personne	person
la sentinelle	sentry
la victime	victim

4. Feminine equivalents of masculine nouns ending in **-er** end in **-ère**:
l'étranger l'étrangère

l'ouvrier	l'ouvrière

5. Other feminine nouns are formed by adding **-sse** to the masculine noun:

le comte	la comtesse
le prince	la princesse
le traître	la traîtresse

6. The feminine equivalents of masculine nouns ending in **-eur** end in **-euse**:

le chanteur	la chanteuse
le danseur	la danseuse
le voyageur	la voyageuse

7. There are several nouns that have a different meaning for each gender: They are gender homonyms. Homonyms are nouns that have identical spelling and pronunciation, but have different meanings. The article before a homonym tells the gender and meaning of the word.

Masculine		Feminine	
l'aide	helper	l'aide	help
le bourgogne	burgundy	la Bourgogne	Burgundy
le champagne	champagne	la Champagne	Champagne
le critique	critic	la critique	criticism
le livre	book	la livre	pound
le manche	handle	la manche	sleeve
le mémoire	memoir	la mémoire	memory
le mode	method	la mode	fashion
le mort	dead person	la mort	death
l'office	duty	l'office	pantry
le page	page boy	la page	page
le livre	book	la livre	pound
le pendule	pendulum	la pendule	clock
le poêle	stove	la poêle	frying pan
le politique	politician	la politique	politics
le poste	job	la poste	post office
le somme	nap	la somme	sum
le tour	turn	la tour	tower
le vapeur	steamship	la vapeur	steam
le vase	vase	la vase	mud
le voile	veil	la voile	sail

8. The definite articles **le** or **la** must change to **l'** before a silent **h**, called the **h** ("**hache**") **muet**. However, definite articles do not change before a noun that begins with an **h** that is not silent, called the **h** ("**hache**") **aspiré.**

"h" muet		"h" aspiré	
l'habitude (f.)	the habit	la haine	the hatred
l'histoire (f.)	*the history/the story*	le hibou	*the owl*
l'homme (m.)	the man	le havre	the haven
l'horloge (f.)	the clock	**le hors-d'oeuvre**	**the appetizer**

9. Compound nouns that begin with a verb or a preposition are masculine, even when the noun is feminine.

chasser + la neige = le chasse-neige	snow blower
gagner + le pain = le gagne-pain	livelihood
chausser = le pied = le chausse-pied	shoe horn
en + la tête = l'en-tête	heading
	(of a letter)
passer + partout = le passe-partout	master key
porter + la feuille = le portefeuille	wallet
porter + la monnaie = le porte-monnaie	change purse
tourner + la vis = le tournevis	screwdriver

10. Most nouns ending with the suffixes: **-ale,-aison, -ie, -ion, -aison, -esse, -ole, -te, -tude**, and **-ure** are feminine.

la capitale	capital	la combinaison	combination
la bourgeoisie	middle class	la jeunesse	youth
la casserole	pan	la beauté	beauty
la solitude	solitude	la peinture	painting
l'action	action		

11. Most nouns ending with the suffixes: **-ment, -eur, -oir, -oce, -acle, -isme**, and **-age** are masculine.

le capitalisme	capitalism	le chanteur	singer
le tiroir	drawer	le spectacle	show
le jardinage	gardening	le négoce	trade
le commencement	beginning		

Note: Some nouns that end in **-eur** or **-age** are feminine. The endings **-eur** and **-age** are part of the root word.

la cage	cage	la douceur	sweetness
la page	page	la faveur	favor
l'image	image/picture	la fleur	flower

12. Most nouns that end in **-ce, -che, -sse**, and **-se** are feminine.

l'église	church	la fiche	index card/form
la chose	thing	la classe	class
la chance	luck/chance	la crèche	cradle/nursery
la quiche	quiche/crusted pie		

13. Most nouns referring to the sciences and to most academic disciplines are feminine.

la biologie	biology	la chimie	chemistry
l'histoire	history	la médecine	medicine
la physique	physics	la littérature	literature

Note:

a) Nouns referring to languages are masculine.

le japonais	Japanese	le français	French
l'anglais	English	l'italien	Italian

b) In French, the names of languages are not capitalized.

14. Most names of machines and mechanical devices are feminine.

l'auto	automobile	l'avion	airplane
la machine	machine	la voiture	car
la cuisinière	stove	l'arme	weapon

Note: Names of machines, using masculine suffixes (e.g. **-oir, -eur**) are masculine.

le rasoir	razor	le moteur	motor
le séchoir	dryer	l'ascenseur	elevator

15. Adding the ending **-ée, -ette, -elle** or **-ille** to nouns of either gender makes them feminine.

Masculine	Feminine	
l'an	l'année	year
le cigare	la cigarette	cigarette
le brin	brindille	sprig/ twig
la vache	vachette	cow

Exercise 1

Identify the gender of the following nouns.

Write **le**, **la** or **l'** before each noun. Then place **M** for masculine noun or **F** for a feminine noun after the word.

Examples: 1. **la viande** (F); 2. **le pain** (M)

1. page	11. solitude
2. soeur	12. médecin
3. réfrigérateur	13. homme
4. gratte-ciel	14. haine
5. hibou	15. comptoir
6. chimie	16. cigarette
7. chinoiserie	17. fraise
8. fleur	18. biologie
9. bicyclette	19. patience
10. valise	20. invitation

Exercise 2

Identify the gender of each noun by placing **M** for masculine or **F** for feminine before the noun. Then, rewrite the word with its proper article.

1. anglais	2. image
3. danseur	4. jeunesse
5. lapin	6. lion
7. tiroir	8. capitale
9. église	10. histoire
11. professeur	12. machine
13. question	14. maison
15. ordinateur	16. chimie
17. bouche	18. chemise
19.négoce	20. musée

Exercise 3

Translate into French, using the correct article.

1. classroom	2. fashion
3. pound	4. cup
5. sister	6. fork
7. musician	8. dryer
9. skirt	10. neck tie
11. bike	12. show
13. flower	14. beginning
15. bull	16. habit
17. kitchen	18. oil
19. jewelry	20. wallet

PLURAL NOUNS

Les **souris** mangent les **fromages**.

Les **chats** guettent les **souris**.

Les **garçons** chassent les **chats**.

Les **jeunes mères** fessent les **garçons**.

Several different spelling patterns form the plural of French nouns, even though the plural noun usually has the same pronunciation as the singular.

1. Nouns are normally made plural by adding -s to the singular forms. The definite article accompanying plural nouns is **les**.

Masculine

Singular	Plural
l'ami	les amis
le garçon	les garçons
le livre	les livres
le crayon	les crayons

Feminine

Singular	Plural
l'amie	les amies
la fille	les filles
la table	les tables
la voiture	les voitures

2. Some nouns ending in **-ou** add an **-s** to form the plural:

Singular		Plural
le clou	nail	les clous
le sou	penny	les sous
le trou	hole	les trous
le verrou	bolt	les verrous

Note: Other nouns ending in **-ou** add an **-x** to form the plural:

le bijou	jewel	les bijoux
le chou	cabbage	les choux
le genou	knee	les genoux
le hibou	owl	les hiboux
le joujou	toy	les joujoux
le pou	flea	les poux

3. Most nouns ending in **-au**, **-eau**, **-eu**, or **-oeu** add an **-x** to form the plural:

le bâteau	boat	les bâteaux
le feu	fire	les feux
le jeu	game	les jeux
le noyau	pit	les noyaux
la peau	skin	les peaux
le voeu	wish	les voeux

Others add **-s** for the plural:

le landau	carriage	les landaus
le pneu	tire	les pneus

4. The nouns that end in **-s**, **-x**, or **-z** remain the same in the plural:

le bras	arm	les bras
la fois	time	les fois
le prix	price	les prix
le fils	son	les fils
le vers	verse	les vers
la voix	voice	les voix
la souris	mouse	les souris

5. Most nouns that end in **-al** change to **-aux** in the plural:

l'animal	animal	les animaux
le cheval	horse	les chevaux
l'hôpital	hospital	les hopitaux
le journal	newspaper	les journaux

A few end in **-s**:

le bal	ball	les bals
le festival	festival	les festivals
le carnaval	carnival	les carnavals

6. Many nouns ending in **-ail** add **-s** to form the plural:

le détail	detail	les détails
l'éventail	fan	les éventails

Note: Some of these nouns change to an **-aux** ending:

le bail	lease	les baux
le travail	work	les travaux
l'émail	enamel	les émaux

7. Some nouns ending in **-l** preceded by more than one vowel have plurals ending in **-x**.

l'aieul	ancestor	les aieux
le ciel	sky	les cieux
l'oeil	eye	les yeux

8. The plural of a compound noun is formed according to its composition.

A. If a compound noun consists of two nouns in which one noun identifies or explains the other, make both nouns plural.

le chou-fleur	cauliflower	les choux-fleurs
le chef-lieu	county seat	les chefs-lieux

B. If a compound noun consists of a noun and an adjective, make both parts plural.

le cerf-volant	kite	les cerfs-volants
le grand-père	grandfather	les grands-pères
le procès-verbal	officail report	les procès-verbaux
le beau-frère	brother-in-law	les beaux-frères

C. If a compound noun consists of a noun and a verb, preposition, prepositional phrase or an adverb, make only the noun plural.

l'arc-en-ciel	rainbow	les arcs-en-ciel
le chemin de fer	railroad	les chemins de fer

D. Family names and proper names are not to be made plural. Only the titles of these names are pluralized.

Monsieur Dupont va au cinéma chaque dimanche.
Mister Dupont goes to the movie every Sunday.

Les Dupont vont au cinema chaque dimanche.
The Duponts go to the movie every Sunday

E. If a compound noun consists of two nouns in which one noun completes the meaning of the other, make only the first noun plural.

le chef-d'oeuvre	masterpiece	les chefs-d'oeuvre
le timbre-poste	stamps	les timbres-poste

F. Some compound nouns do not change:

l'abat-jour	lampshade	les abat-jour
l'après-midi	afternoon	les après-midi
le cache-nez	muffler	les cache-nez
le gratte-ciel	skyscraper	les gratte-ciel
le pare-brise	windshield	les pare-brise
le rendez-vous	appointment	les rendez-vous

8. Some nouns are only used in the plural:

les environs	surroundings
les frais	expenses
les fiançailles	engagement
les mathématiques	mathematics
les moeurs	customs

Exercise 4

Change the singular form of the noun to its plural form. Don't forget to change the definite article from the singular form to the plural.

1. le cahier	2. le travail
3. la chemise	4. le pardessus
5. le stylo	6. le bureau
7. le journal	8. le chandail
9. le casse-noisette	10. le chapeau
11. la fête	12. le festival
13. la bouteille	14. le tire-bouchon
15. le petit-fils	16. le lycée
17. le hors-d'oeuvre	18. le gâteau
19. le coup de grace	20. le cheval

Exercise 5

Write the plural form of the words in italics. The write the correct plural translation of the noun.

Example: **Le chandail de laine lui va bien.**

le chandail	**les chandails**	sweater

1. Pendant la pluie, l'*arc-en-ciel* était visible derrière le *gratte-ciel*.
2. Le *pou* est un insecte sans ailes.
3. Le *hibou* est un oiseau de proie nocturne.
4. Je ne pourrai pas vous accompagner, *madame*; j'ai un *rendez-vous* important.
5. Le *prisonnier* avait creusé un *trou* secret dans le mur.
6. Les pommes de terre et le *chou-fleur* frais étaient exquis.
7. Le *travail* est-il approuvé?
8. Le bruit de mon *réveille-matin* me derange.
9. La *grand-mère* et le *grand-père* gâtent toujours leur *petit-fils*.

Exercise 6

Complete the sentences, using the plural form of the words in parentheses.

1. (le beau-frère)_____avaient promis de se rejoindre pour un grand dîner en famille.
2. (l'après-midi) Les dames passaient_____à cause de leurs maris.
3. (cache-nez de laine) Quand nous faisons du ski, nous portons toujours _____de notre clubs.
4. (l'abat-jour) Comment trouvez-vous_____?
5. (le prix du repas)_____n'ont pas été changes.
6. (pneu) Ce matin ils ont du changer _____?
7. (l'animal) Ou sont _____?
8. (le gateau) Les enfants ont mangé _____.
9. (le bal) _____ont eu lieu hier.
10. (le matelas) _____sont faits aux Etats-Unis.

Exercise 7

Complete the sentences by using the plural form of the words in parentheses.

1. (le genou) Il essaya de se baisser sans plier
2. (le cheveu) Si j'ai le temps aujourd'hui, j'irai me faire couper _____.
3. (l'oeil bleu) Tous leurs enfants ont_____.
4. (le timbre-poste) Nous cherchons un bureau de tabac pour acheter _____étrangers.
5. (le cerf-volant) Mon père s'amusait plus que moi a jouer avec _____.
6. (le tire-bouchon) Il a enlevé _____.
7. (le taureau) Le jardinier approche _____.
8. (le chemin de fer) M. Dupont aime _____.
9. (le bateau) Le millionnaire a acheté _____.
10. (le chandail) Madame Dubois donne_____de laine a sa mère.

DEFINITE ARTICLES

**The = le, la, l'
and les**

La souris mange **le** fromage.
Le chat guette **la** souris.
L'homme chasse **le** chat.
La jeune femme connaît **l'**homme.

Earlier it was mentioned that all French nouns are either masculine or feminine in gender.

The definite article "**le**" precedes masculine nouns (le fromage). "**La**" precedes feminine nouns (la jeune fille). "**L'**" precedes nouns that begin with a vowel or a silent "**h.**170

"**Les**" is the definite article that precedes a plural noun, whether masculine or feminine.

The definite article has many similar uses in French and English, but it is used much more frequently in French. In English, the definite article (the) has only one form which is used with all nouns, regardless of whether the noun is singular or plural. In French, however, the form of the definite article is changed according to the gender and number (singular or plural) of the noun it introduces.

1. The definite article must agree in gender with the noun it introduces.

A. The masculine form of the definite article is used before a masculine noun:

le magasin   **le restaurant**   l'homme

B. The feminine form of the definite article is used before a feminine noun:

la chemise   **la cravate**   la robe

2. The definite article must agree in number with the noun it introduces.

A. The plural form of the definite article is used before a plural noun:

les magasins   **les cravates**   les hommes

Note: The masculine and feminine plural of the definite article are the same. (**Les**)

3. Uses of the definite article:

A. Use a definite article before a specific noun.

Le livre est sur la table.

Il n'aime pas la bière.

La souris mange le fromage.

Note: Unlike English, a French definite article comes before each noun in a series; not just before the first noun.

Il mange **le** pain et **le** chocolat.

He eats the bread and the chocolate.

B. Use a definite article before the parts of the body.

Elle se lave **les** mains et **la** figure.

She washes her hands and her face

Jean se brosse **les** dents chaque matin.

Jean brushes his teeth every morning.

4. Use the definite article before generic or collective nouns and before nouns used in an abstract sense.

La vérité est relative.   Truth is relative.

Les Américains ne tolèrent pas l'injustice.

The Americans do no tolerate injustice.

J'aime **les pommes**.   I love apples.
J'aime **la bière**.

Note: Capitalize a noun referring to a nationality.

Les Tunisiens mangent beaucoup de couscous.
The Tunisians eat a lot of couscous.

L'Américain qu'on a rencontré à la fête s'appelle George.

5. Use a definite article before the names of languages:
André comprend **le russe**.   André understands Russian.
Nous étudions **l'allemand**.   We study German.

Note: The definite article is not used with the name of a language after the verb "**parler**" (to speak), or the prepositions, "**en**" or "**de**," unless the name of the language or the verb "**parler**" is modified.

Non, il ne **parle** pas **japonais.**
No, he doesn't speak Japanese.

Pierre a traduit le roman en français.
Pierre has translated the novel in French.

Je trouve mon cours **d'espagnol** bien facile.
I find my Spanish class quite easy.

Il **parle** bien l'italien.
He speaks Italian well.

Ou parle-t-on le français le plus pur?
Where is the purest French spoken?

6. Use the definite article with titles of profession or rank, except when addressing a person directly:

Le professeur Brun arrive.   Professor Brun is coming.
Le docteur Marais est patient.   Doctor Marais is patient.
Au revoir, professeur Brun.   Goodbye, Professor Brun.

7. Use the definite article with names of places other than cities:

Nous voyagerons à travers les Etats-Unis.
We will travel through the United States.

Nous resterons à New York.
We will stay in New York.

8. Use the definite article with days of the week to translate the English word, "**on**."

> Je ne travaille pas le samedi.
> I do not work on Saturday.

> Paul ne travaille pas le samedi.
> Paul doesn't work Saturdays.

> Les écoles sont fermées le samedi et le dimanche.
> Schools are closed on Saturdays and Sundays.

> Ce restaurant offre un prix fixe tous les lundis.
> This restaurant offers a set price every Monday.

Exception: To refer to a specific day or to tell about a single event or occurence, the definite article is not used.

> Dimanche prochain, je vais chez mon oncle.
> Next Sunday I am going to my uncle's house.

> Je viendrai te voir mardi.
> I will come to see you Tuesday.

> Il était en classe lundi dernier.
> He was in class last Monday.

9. Use the definite article with colors and seasons, when discussing the season in a general sense.

> Elle n'aime pas le jaune. She doesn't like yellow.
> J'adore le printemps I love Spring.

10. Use the definite article to express "**in**" with parts of the day.

> Est-ce qu'il mange le petit déjeuner le matin?
> Does he eat breakfast in the morning?

> Le soir il boit un verre de lait avant de se coucher.
> In the evening he drinks a glass of milk before going to bed.

11. Use the definite article with dates in general and to express the word "**on**."

> C'est aujourd'hui le 10 octobre 1990.
> Today is October 10, 1990.

> L'avocat arrivera le premier février.
> The lawyer will be here on the first of February.

12. Use a definite article before expressions of quantity to express the word "**per**" or "**a**."

> Les bananes coûtent dix francs la douzaine.
> The bananas cost ten francs per dozen.

Le prix des cerises est trente francs le kilo.
The price of the cherries is thirty francs a kilo.

13. Use a definite article before most geographic names.

Continents: **l'Afrique, l'Europe, l'Asie**
Countries: **la Martinique, les Etats-Unis, l'Irlande**
Provinces: **la Bretagne, la Bourgogne, la Normandie**
Rivers: **la Mississipi, la Loire, la Seine**
Mountains: **les Alpes, les Pyrénées, les Andes**
Bodies of Water: **l'Atlantique, le Pacifique**
Islands: **la Guadeloupe, la Corse, les Antilles**

Note: Do not use the definite article before the name of a city unless the definite article is part of the name or an adjective that modifies the name.

New York est la capitale commerciale des Etats-Unis.
New York is the commercial capital of the United-States.

Madame Dupont va souvent à Moscou.
Madame Dupont goes often to Moscow

Mon correspondant français habite Le Havre.
My French penpal lives in Le Havre.

EXCEPTIONS

A. Use the article when referring to a particular aspect of the city.
Le New York des écrivains est calme et placide.
The New York of writers is calm and placid.

Le Paris que j'aime est le Paris du mois de mai.
The Paris I love is the Paris of the month of May.

B. When translating "**to**" before a feminine country.

Madame Dupont va souvent en France.
Mrs. Dupont goes to France often.

C. After the preposition "**de**" with simple (one word) names of countries.

Son mari aime beaucoup l'histoire de France.
Her husband likes the history of France very much.

Nous apprécions la culture de la République Dominicaine.
We appreciate the culture of the Dominican Republic.

14. The following are some rules governing the use of the definite article with the days, months, and seasons.

A. The days of the week are masculine and are not capitalized.

Je vais au cinema le vendredi.
I go to the movies on Fridays.

B. Never use a definite article before the name of a month. Names of months are not capitalized.

>Mai est le mois des muguets.
>May is the month of the lilies of the valley.

>Ordinairement, il pleut beaucoup en avril.
>Usually, it rains a lot in April.

C. Always use a definite article before the names of the seasons of the year. The seasons are not capitalized in French.

>L'hiver est la saison préferée des skieurs.
>Winter is the favorite season of skiers.

>Au Canada, le printemps est très doux.
>In Canada, Spring is very mild.

Note: Use the preposition "**en**" before seasons and months to translate in, to, or during. Although all the seasons are masculine, use "**au**" instead of "**en**" before *le printemps*. It is an exception.

>Madame Dupont est allée à Paris en juillet.
>Mrs. Dupont went to Paris in July.

>Son mari n'y va jamais au printemps.
>Her husband never goes there during Spring.

15. Never use an article with **monsieur, madame** and **mademoiselle**. In formal address, the article is used before the title.

>Madame Dupont est arrivée.
>Mrs. Dupont is here.

>Monsieur Dupont est absent.
>Mister Dupont is absent.

>Bonjour, monsieur le vice-président.
>Good morning, Mr. Vice-president, sir.

16. There are several contractions of the definite article:

>to, at, toward, in the   **à + le = au; à + les = aux**

A. When the preposition **à** (toward, at, in, to) precedes the masculine, singular definite article "**le**," the two words contract to form "**au**," or "**aux**."

>Je ne vais jamais au musée le lundi.
>I never go to the museum on Mondays.

>J'aime aller au cinema.
>I like to go to the movies.

>Le président du club a adressé la parole aux écrivains.
>The club president address the writers.

Le journaliste raconte l'histoire aux soldats.
The journalist relates the story to the soldiers.

Note: The preposition "**à**" never contracts with the feminine definite article, "**la**" or with "**l'**."

to, at, toward, in the   à + la = à la; à + l' = à l'

Le professeur parle á l'étudiant.
The professor speaks to the student.

Il est allé à la pharmacie.
He went to the pharmacy.

B. If the definite article "**le**" or "**les**" is part of the name of a city, the preposition "**à**" contracts with the definite article "**le**" to form "**au**," or "**les**" to form "**aux**."

Nous arrivons au Havre.   We arrive at Le Havre.

Il fait chaud aux Etats Unis en été.
It is warm in the United States during summer.

of, from, about, belonging to the de + le = du; de + les = des

C. When the preposition **de** (of, from, about, belonging to) precedes the masculine, singular definite article "**le**," the two words contract to form "**du**," or "**des**."

C'est l'anniversaire du médecin.
It is the doctor's birthday.

Il parle du lycée français.
He speaking about the French high school.

C'est la mère des enfants.
This is the mother of the children.

Quels sont les noms des écrivains?
What are the names of writers?

Note: The preposition "**de**" never contracts with the feminine definite article, "**la**" or with "**l'**."

of, from, about, belonging to the
de + la = de la; de + l' = de l'

Madame Dupont sort de la maison.
Mrs. Dupont leaves (from) the house.

Son fils revient de l' école de bonne heure.
Her son returns from (the) school early.

Exercise 8

Fill in the blanks with the correct form of the definite article, if one is needed. Then translate the sentences into English. Look back to the appropriate section to refresh your memory.

1. _____garçon achète_____chemise blanche.
2. _____banane est sur_____table.
3. _____boîtes sont dans_____tiroir.
4. Monsieur Dupont, aimez-vous_____thé avec ou sans _____lait?
5. Vas-tu manger_____pommes?
6. _____jeune-fille aime_____petite voiture.
7. _____cerises coûtent 20 francs_____kilo.
8. Madame Dupont voyage_____été.
9. Elle est allée_____Moscou_____année dernière.
10. _____oeufs coûtent 10 francs_____douzaine.
11. _____enfants couvrent_____livre?
12. _____mademoiselle se lave_____cheveux.
13. Elle achète les tomates à 10 francs_____livre.
14. _____Mardi est le deuxième jour de la semaine.
15. _____Martinique est_____île charmante.

Exercise 9

Translate into French:

1. I visit the museum on Tuesdays.
2. She brushes her teeth every morning and night.
3. We are learning Russian now.
4. I like apples.
5. Sugar costs 10 francs a pound.
6. The books are in her arms.
7. Tell me the story in French.
8. Today is Monday.
9. I like to go the movies on Sunday.
10. Madame Dubois has long hair.
11. I visited the university Friday.
12. Do you want your coffee with or without sugar.
13. I am going home.
14. She likes New York in the spring.
15. Africa is a vast continent.

Exercise 10

Complete the following sentences, using the preposition "**a,**" and the correct definite article or contraction.

Example: **Marie dîne souvent_____restaurant.**
Marie often dines in a restaurant.

1. Pierre va_____aéroport.
2. Je parle_____garçon.
3. Qui est allé_____bibliothèque?
4. La jeune fille va_____cinéma.
5. Nous voulons aller_____parc.
6. Elle porte la lampe_____table.
7. Ils sont allés_____lycée.
8. Le professeur dit bonjour_____élèves.
9. J'ai parlé_____professeur.
10. Je pose une question_____écrivains.

Exercise 11   Complete the following sentences using the preposition **"de"** and the correct form of the definite article or a contraction.

Example: **Le directeur parle_____élèves absents.**
              Le directeur parle des élèves absents.

1. J'ai les cahiers_____enfants.
2. Elle admire l'architecture_____musée.
3. Monsieur Dupont revient de_____gare.
4. Madame Dupont mange_____salade.
5. Le président_____Méxique aime la démocracie.
6. La couleur_____chemise est blanche.
7. Qui veut_____thé?.
8. On ne parle que_____événements récents.
9. Elle ne parle que_____Guadeloupe.
10. Pierre est arrivé_____Restaurant.

THE INDEFINITE ARTICLES

a, an = un, une;
***some, any* = des**

Une souris mange le fromage.
Un chat guette la souris.
Un garçon chasse le chat.
Une jeune mère fesse le garçon.

The indefinite article has three forms: **un, une,** and **des.**

Masculine, singular	**un** (a, an)
Feminine, singular	**une** (a, an)
Masculine, plural	**des** (some, any)
Feminine, plural	**des** (some, any)

un garçon - a boy	**des garçons** - some boys
une jeune fille - a girl	**des jeunes filles** - some girls

Uses of the Indefinite Article

1. The indefinite article (un, une or des) is used before a noun to indicate "a" or "an" in the singular and "some" or "any" in the plural. The indefinite article must agree in number and gender with the noun it precedes.

Jean a **une** voiture neuve.
Jean has a new car.

Son ami a **un** vase en porcelaine.
His friend has a porcelain vase.

2. "**Des**," the plural form of the indefinite article may mean "*some*" or "*any*." Its meaning is determined from the context of the sentence.

J'ai des nouvelles pour vous.
I have some news for you.

Prenez-vous des cerises?
Are you having any cherries?

3. Use the indefinite article before each in a series.

Il prend un sandwich et une tasse de thé.
He has a sandwich and a cup of tea

Jean a une maison et une voiture.
Jean owns a house and a car.

4. Do not use the indefinite article before an unmodified noun that follows the verb "**être**."

Il est Américain.	He is an American.
Etes-vous artiste?	Are you an artist?
Mon frère est devenu médecin.	My brother became a doctor.

Note: The indefinite article must be used if the predicate noun is modified.

C'est un repas délicieux!	It's a delicious meal!

Mon frère est devenu un médecin célèbre.
My brother became a famous doctor.

Ce sont des pommes vertes.	Those are (some) green apples.

5. The indefinite article is not used after the exclamation **quel** (**quelle, quels, quelles**).

Quel beau jour!	What a beautiful day!
Quelles belles vaches!	What beautiful cows!

Exercise 12

Write the correct indefinite article before each of the following nouns. Then translate both the article and the noun into English.

1. crayon 2. craie
3. musée 4. école
5. image 6. écriture
7. idées 8. hommes
9. pêche 10. chaise
11. cravate 12. chemises
13. Anglais 14. couteau
15. fourchette 16. enfants
17. restaurants 18. fiancés
19. photo 20. invitation

Exercice 13 Translate the following sentences into French. Use the correct form of the indefinite article.

1. Does she want a sandwich?
2. She has a plate and some cherries.
3. Here are a pen and a pencil.
4. He is a very good lawyer.
5. I eat some fruit and vegetables.
6. She is wearing sunglasses.
7. They have some messages for Jean.
8. She needs a new car.
9. I would like a glass of milk, please.
10. It is a hard job.

THE PARTITIVE ARTICLES

**some, of the =
du, de la, de l',
des**

La souris mange du fromage

A. The partitive article has four forms: du, de la, de l' and des.
 Masculine, singular **du (de + le)**
 Feminine, singular **de la (de + la, no contraction)**
Masculine or feminine, singular (before a vowel) **de l'**
 Feminine, plural **des (de + les)**
 Masculine, plural **des (de + les)**
Masculine or feminine, after a verb in the negative de
du pain = some bread (some of the bread)
des pains = some loaves of bread (some "breads")

de la viande = some meat (some of the meat)
des viandes = some meats (some different kinds of meats)

Uses of the partitive article

1. Use the partitive article before a noun to express the idea of "*some*" "*some of the*" or "*any*" in both the singular and plural. A partitive article is used before a noun referring to an undetermined quantity. In English it is not necessary to use an article before nouns such as water, energy, patience. In French, however, a partitive article must be used.

Monsieur Dupont mange du pain et de la viande
Mister Dupont eats (some) bread and (some) meat.

Y a-t-il encore de l'eau?
Is there *any* more water?

2. Omission of the partitive article:
Des become "**de**" or "**d'**" (before a vowel) before a noun modified by a preceding adjective.

Ce quartier a de beaux arbres.
This neighborhood has some lovely trees.

Monsieur Dupont porte de jolies cravates.
Mister Dupont wears some attractive neckties.

C'est agréable de boire du bon vin.
It is pleasant to drink (some) good wine.

3. The partitive article becomes "de" or "d'" (before a vowel) when the statement expresses a general negation.

Elle n'a pas d'enfants.
She does not have any children.

Je ne veux pas de thé.
I do not want (any) tea.

4. Some of the negative expressions in French are:

ne ... pas (de)	not any
ne ... guère (de)	hardly any
ne ... jamais (de)	never any
ne ... plus (de)	no more/longer, any
ne ... rien (de)	nothing, not at all

Elle **n'a pas** d'amis.	She does not have any friends.
Elle **ne** mange **jamais** de pommes.	She never eats (any) apples.
On **ne** voit **plus** d'oiseaux.	One no longer see birds.

5. When the nouns in a negative statement are specific, a partitive article must be used.

Nous n'avons pas de la soie que vous voulez, madame.
We do not have any of the silk that you want.

6. Either a partitive article or an indefinite article may be used after the negative form of the following verbs: être (to be), devenir (to become), rester (to stay). With any of these verbs, the negative is specific, not general.

Non, ce ne sont pas des photos du paysage francais.
No, these are not pictures of the French countryside.

7. A definite article is never affected by a preceding negative verb. It does not change.

J'aime le fromage de chèvre.   I like (the) goat cheese.

Je n'aime pas le fromage de chèvre.
I do not like (the) goat cheese.

8. Do not omit the singular indefinite article (un, une) after the preposition "**de**" when "**de**" is part of the verbal expression.

Nous n'avons pas besoin d'une chambre luxueuse.
We do not need a luxurious room.

Madame Dupont n'a pas envie d'une tarte aux pommes
Mrs. Dupont does not feel like having a apple pie.

9. When a noun or an adverb of quantity modifies a noun, "**de**" is used without an article before the modified noun.

Nous avons acheté une douzaine d'oeufs et une bouteille de vin.
We have bought a dozen (of) eggs and a bottle of wine.

La jeune fille voudrait avoir un morceau de papier.
The girl would like to have a piece of paper.

10. The partitive becomes "de" after expressions of quantity such as:

assez	enough	une boite	a box
beaucoup	a lot	une bouteille	a bottle
peu	a little	ne verre	a glass
trop	too much	un kilo	a kilogram
tant	so many	un litre	a liter
autant	as much	une livre	a pound
moins	less	une douzaine	a dozen
une tranche	a slice		

Note: The definite article is used, however, before a noun following these expressions of quantity:

bien de	a lot of
la plupart de	most of
la majorité de	the majority

Monsieur Dupont s'est donne bien du (de +le) mal pour payer les voyage de sa femme.
Mr. Dupont took great pains to pay off his wife's trips.
La plupart des (de + les) étudiants vont au concert.
Most of the students are going to the concert.
La majorité de la population de New York a voté pour le président.
The majority of the New York population voted for the president.

Note: Whenever it is appropriate to use the expression "*of the*" in English, use **de** plus the definite article in French.

11. When a noun modifies another noun, the definite article is not used before the modifying noun. (Use "**de.**")

Monsieur Dupont a une cravate de soie.
Mister Dupont has a silk necktie.

Il voyage souvent en chemin de fer.
He travels often by railroad.

Note: The partitive is used when the adjective is an integral part of the idea.

Ce sont des jeunes filles intelligentes.
These are (some) intelligent girls.

Madame Dupont mange des petits pois pour le déjeuner.
Madame Dupont eats (some) peas for lunch.

2. The partitive article is not used with another adjective of quantity.

Je vois quelques jeunes gens dans la classe.
I see a few young people in the classroom.

Il y a plusieurs assiettes dans la cuisine.
There are several plates in the kitchen.

13. The partitive article is not used before the noun after certain verbal expressions ending with "**de.**" Some of these are:

être couvert de	to be covered with
être débordé de	to be up to one's ears
être entouré de	to be surrounded by
être rempli de	to be filled with
se passer de	to get along without
s'occuper de	to take care of
se regaler de	to feast on

Monsieur Dupont se passe de cigarettes.
Mr. Dupont does without cigarettes.

La route est couverte de boue.
The road is covered with mud.

14. After "**ne que**" (only), the partitive is used.

Madame Dupont ne mange que de la viande et de la salade.
Mrs. Dupont eats only (some) meat and (some) salade.

Monsieur Dupont ne boit que de l'eau minérale.
15. With sans (without) and ne . ni ni
(neither...nor), the partitive is omitted.

Il boit son café sans sucre.
He drinks his coffee without sugar.

Elle n'a ni argent ni carte de credit.
She has neither money nor credit card.

Exercise 14

Fill in the blanks with the correct form of the partitive article or "**de**."
Example: **Il y a _____ vin sur la table**
Il y a du vin sur la table
Je voudrais un verre ____ eau, s'il vous plaît.
Je voudrais un verre d'eau, s'il vous plaît.
1. Monsieur Dupont n'a pas ____ patience.
2. Tous les matins, il boit ____ cafe sans sucre.
3. A midi, il mange ____ haricots verts.
4. Il mange ____ pommes frites avec ____ viande.
5. Il mange aussi ____ bons petits pains et beurre.
6. Toute de suite après le repas, il aimerait avoir confiture.
7. Il laisse toujours ____ monnaie sur la table.
8. Avant de rentrer chex lui, il prend billets de théâtre.
9. Parfois, il achète ____ fleurs pour sa femme.
10- A la maison, il ne mange pas ____ gâteau.

Exercise 15

Complete the following sentences with the correct form of the partitive, if necessary.
1. Madame Dupont ne peut pas se passer ____ nourriture.
2. Au petit déjeuner, elle mange ____ pain et confiture.
3. Elle mange aussi ____ oeufs.
4. Elle boit ____ jus d'orange.
5. Elle boit aussi café avec ____ sucre et creme.
6. Au dejeuner, elle mange ____ soupe et ____ salade verte.
7. Elle boit un verre ____ vin.
8. Au dîner, elle mange ____ poulet et ____ légumes.
9. Elle mange aussi ____ riz blanc et ____ petits pois.
10. Elle ne fume jamais ____ cigarettes.

Exercice 16

Complete the following sentences with the appropriate definite article (le, la, l', les) or contraction (au, du, des or de), as necessary.

1. Monsieur Dupont travaille _____ bureau.
2. Madame Dupont reste à _____ maison.
3. Elle adore faire _____ emplettes.
4. Il y a plusieurs _____ supermarchés dans son quartier.
5. Monsieur Dupont n'aime pas _____ pommes.
6. Elle achete toujours une douzaine _____ pommes.
7. Monsieur Dupont n'aime pas _____ beurre.
8. Elle achète toujours _____ livre _____ beurre.
9. Elle a quelques _____ amis qui aiment _____ bonnes pommes.
10. Ils aiment aussi _____ beurre sur une tranche _____ pain.

LE CAHIER FRANÇAIS: MASTERY DRILLS

Before doing the following exercises, remember:
1. The definite articles le, la, l' and les must agree in gender and number with the noun they introduce.
2. French nouns are either masculine or feminine. There are no neuter nouns.
3. A silent (unpronounced) final "s" is added to the singular to form the plural of most nouns.
4. A definite article introduces (a) a specific noun, (b) collective or generic nouns, (c) nouns used in an abstract or general sense, (d) parts of the body, (e) most geographic place names, (f) expressions of quantity, (g) names of languages.
5. The indefinite article (un, une = a, an, one) introduces singular nouns of undetermined aspect. The plural indefinite article (des = some, any) must be used with plural nouns of undetermined number.
6. The partitive article (du, de la, or de l' = of the, some) must be used with singular nouns that refer to an indefinite quantity.
7. Indefinite and partitive articles are not used after expressions of quantity or after negatives indicating a lack of something.

Les articles:

Exercices	Sujet
1. 2. 3.	Formes de l'article
4. 5. 6. 7.	Emploi des trois articles
8.	Révision 1
9. 10. 11.	Modifications des articles indéfinis et partitifs
12. à 20.	Omission de l'article
21.	Révision 2

Exercice 1

Compléter les phrases suivantes par:

A.   L'article indéfini
   1. Ils ont deux enfants: ＿＿＿ garçon et ＿＿＿ fille.
   2. J'ai ＿＿＿ meubles anciens dans mon salon.
   3. Elle a acheté ＿＿＿ sandales blanches pour l'été.

B.   L'article défini
   1. Mets ＿＿＿ assiettes dans ＿＿＿ lave-vaisselle!
   2. Ferme ＿＿＿ fenêtre!
   3. J'ai rencontré M. Berteau dans ＿＿＿ escalier.
   4. ＿＿＿ abeille est un insecte qui fait du miel.
   5. ＿＿＿ Déjeuner sur ＿＿＿ herbe est un célèbre tableau de Manet.
   6. Tout le monde se plaint de ＿＿＿ hausse des prix.
   7. ＿＿＿ haut de la montagne est couvert de neige.
   8. ＿＿＿ cerisiers que j'ai plantes il y a cinq ans donnent déjà des fruits.
   9. J'aime beaucoup ＿＿＿ haricots verts.

C.   L'article partitif
   1. Les tartines beurrées sont encore meilleures avec ＿＿＿ confiture.
   2. En general, les Français boivent ＿＿＿ vin aux repas.
   3. Il faut avoir ＿＿＿ patience pour faire un puzzle.
   4. Elle a ＿＿＿ goût et elle s'habille très bien.
   5. Dans le Nord, on trouve ＿＿＿ charbon et ＿＿＿ fer avec lesquels on fait ＿＿＿ acier.
   6. Cette centrale nucléaire fournit ＿＿＿ énergie à toute la region.
   7. J'ai préparé ＿＿＿ épinards à la crème pour ce soir.

Exercice 2

Compléter par l'article défini (contracté ou non avec les prepositions "a" ou "de"):

A. 1. Le livre ＿＿＿ professeur.
    2. Les portières de ＿＿＿ voiture.
    3. La cloche ＿＿＿ église.
    4. La lecture de ＿＿＿ journaux.
    5. Les branches de ＿＿＿ arbres.
    6. L'entrée de ＿＿＿ tunnel.
    7. Le musée de ＿＿＿ Homme.

B. 1. Téléphonez à ＿＿＿ médecin.
    2. Je vais à ＿＿＿ banque!
    3. Pensez à ＿＿＿ avenir!
    4. Elle s'interesse à ＿＿＿ autres!
    5. Jouons à ＿＿＿ cartes!
    6. Allons à ＿＿＿ hotel!
    7. Soyez à ＿＿＿ heure!

Mettre les noms soulignés au singulier et faire des accords necessaires:
1. M. et Mme. Leroy ont parlé aux professeurs de leur fils.
2. Le chef du Personnel a demandé l'avis des syndicats.
3. Les résultats des examens seront affichés demain.
4. Elle a raconté une histoire aux enfants.
5. Catherine a accroché des tableaux aux murs, et elle a mis des rideaux aux fenêtres.
6. Ils ont parlé des derniers films de Godard.
7. Elle n'a pas besoin des autres dictionnaires.

Exercice 4

Compléter les phrases suivantes par l'article qui convient:
1. "Pour la table 6, ____ thé au lait et ____ chocolat chaud!" a crié le serveur.
2. J'ai acheté . . . the de Chine.
3. J'ai commandé au boucher ____ poulet pour six personnes.
4. A la cantine, on sert ____ poulet aux enfants une fois par semaine.
5. Dans le bac à légumes du réfrigerateur, il reste ____ chou-fleur et trois artichauts.
6. Veux-tu encore ____ chou-fleur?

Exercice 5

Compléter les phrases suivantes par l'article qui convient:
1. Il y a ____ station de metro tout près d'ici; c'est ____ station Concorde.
2. ____ café m'empêche de dormir.
3. J'aime bien prendre ____ tasse de café après ____ déjeuner.
4. Mathilde fume ____ cigarettes blondes.
5. Mathilde n'aime que ____ cigarettes blondes.
6. ____ dimanche, nous allons souvent à ____ cinéma.
7. Ma fille est née ____ dimanche.
8. Feriez-vous lire ce livre à ____ enfant de huit ans?
9. Dans ____ écoles primaires, on fait faire ____ travaux manuels à ____ enfants.
10. En general, ____ villes de province offrent moins d'activités culturel-les que Paris; cependant, il y a ____ villes tres vivantes qui organisent ____ concerts, ____ expositions, ____ représentations théâtrales et ____ festivals en été.

Exercice 6

Compléter les phrases suivantes par l'article qui convient:
A. 1. ____ soleil éclaire la terre.
2. Hier, il y a eu ____ soleil presque toute la journée.
3. Ce jour-la, il faisait ____ soleil magnifique.
4. On dit souvent que ____ argent ne fait pas le bonheur.
5. Il a demandé ____ argent à son père.
6. Cet homme gagne ____ argent fou!
7. ____ fromage est riche en calcium.
8. Nous mangeons souvent ____ fromage.
9. Le munster est ____ fromage fort.
10. Denis a trouvé ____ travail très bien payé.
11. Le professeur nous a donné ____ travail pour demain.
12. Cécile aime beaucoup ____ travail qu'elle fait.

B. Imiter les phrases de l'exercice 6. A en employant les noms suivants:
(a) eau (b) bruit (c) vent

Exercice 7

Indiquer la nature des mots soulignés (article indéfini, défini contracté, partitif ou préposition + article défini):

Exemple: **Il s'est servi du magnétoscope.**

du = article contracté   Il boit du thé.   du = article partitif

1. Il joue du violon.
2. Le bâteau s'éloigne du port.
3. Elle fait du sport tous les dimanches.
4. Nous avons parlé des examens du semestre dernier.
5. Nous avons passé des examens.
6. Il s'est approché de la fenêtre pour voir ce qui se passait dans la rue.
7. Nous avons reçu des nouvelles de notre fille.
8. Je me souviendrai toujours des vacances que nous avons passées en Crête.
9. Le feu va s'éteindre. Remets du bois dans la cheminée.

Exercice 8

Compléter le texte suivant par les articles qui conviennent:

Alexis et Genèvieve ont _____ très joli salon. Sur _____ sol, ils ont fait poser _____ moquette et, sur _____ murs, _____ papier peint. Dans _____ angle de _____ piece, ils ont installé _____ canapé et, en face, _____ fauteuils. Entre _____ canapé et _____ fauteuils, sur _____ table basse, ils ont disposé _____ bibelots qu'ils ont rapportés de leurs voyages.

Exercice 9

Mettre les phrases suivantes à la forme negative:

A. 1. Il ya une lampe sur la table.
   2. On voyait de la lumière aux fenêtres.
   3. J'ai acheté des oeufs au marché.
   4. Les Berger ont un jardin.
   5. Les étudiants avaient des questions à poser.
   6. On a trouve de l'uranium dans cette région.
   7. Il avait du travail à faire.
B. 1. C'est du thé de Ceylan.
   2. C'est un film en version originale.
   3. Ce sont des touristes étrangers.
   4. C'est de l'or pur.
   5. Ce sont des bonbons à la menthe.

Exercice 10

Répondre négativement aux questions suivantes (ne pas employer de pronom personnel):

1. Avez-vous un ordinateur chez vous?
2. Regardez-vous regulierment le journal télévise?
3. Est-ce que les enfants peuvent boire du vin?
4. Faites-vous la cuisine tous les jours?
5. Y a-t-il des feuilles sur les arbres en mai?
6. Avez-vous peur des araignées?

7. Mettez-vous du sucre dans votre café?

8. Mme Lebrun s'occupera-t-elle encore de la bibliothèque de l'école l'an prochain?

9. Portez-vous des lentilles de contact?

10. Est-ce que ce sont des fleurs naturelles?

11. Y a-t-il un distributeur automatique de billets de banque dans le quartier?

12. Est-ce que quelqu'un s'est servi des ciseaux? Je ne les retrouve plus.

Exercice 11

Mettre au pluriel les mots en italique et faire les accords necessaires:

1. J'ai acheté *une affiche* au Centre Pompidou.

2. J'ai acheté *une belle affiche* au Centre Pompidou.

3. Il a *un ami américain.*

4. Il a *un très bon ami américain.*

5. On a construit *un nouveau quartier* à la périphérie de la ville.

6. A cette réunion, j'ai rencontré *un ancien camarade* d'école.

7. David a invite *un petit ami* à faire du camping.

8. C'est *un jeune homme très sympathique.*

9. J'ai lu *une petite annonce intéressante* dans Le Figaro.

10. A quatorze ans, vous n'êtes plus *une petite fille,* vous êtes déjà *une jeune fille.*

11. Excusez-moi! J'ai oublié de vous donner *une petite cuillère.*

12. La mère a grondé l'enfant qui avait dit *un gros mot.*

13. J'ai fait tomber *un petit pois* par terre.

Exercice 12

Imiter l'exemple suivant:

Mes enfants font du ski. (beaucoup)
Mes enfants font beaucoup de ski.

1. N'allons pas à la plage aujourd'hui! Il y a du vent. (trop)

2. Cette année, Jean-Christophe a du temps pour faire du piano. (plus)

3. Rajoute de la crème dans les épinards! (un peu)

4. Les Forestier ont-ils des enfants? (combien)

5. Y a-t-il des verres pour tout le monde? (assez)

6. A Dijon, on rencontre des étudiants étrangers. (peu)

7. Jean-Michel a des amis. (beaucoup)

Exercice 13

Utiliser les mots kilo, livre, litre, mètre, heure et imiter selon l'exemple:

J'ai acheté du sucre.   **J'ai acheté un kilo de sucre.**

1. Pour faire cette crème au chocolat, il faut du lait.

2. Donnez-moi des pêches, s'il vous plait, monsieur!

3. J'ai commande du tissu pour faire des rideaux.

4. Il y a encore du beurre dans le congélateur!

5. A quatre-vingts ans, il faisait du tennis une fois par semaine.

Exercice 14

Relier les éléments de la colonne de gauche aux éléments de la colonne de droite en inscrivant les lettres correspondantes dans les cases:

1. Un paquet de _____ aspirine
2. Un bol de _____ sucre en poudre
3. Un bouquet de _____ pain
4. Un pot de _____ dentifrice
5. Une carafe de _____ cigarettes
6. Une tranche de _____ eau
7. Une goutte de _____ café au lait
8. Un cachet de _____ vin
9. Une cuillerée de _____ tulipes
10. Un morceau de _____ confiture
11. Un tube de _____ jambon

Exercice 15

Relier les éléments de la colonne de gauche aux éléments de la colonne de droite en inscrivant les lettres correspondantes dans les cases:

1. Un verre de/en _____ cristal
2. Une robe de/en _____ cuir
3. Un pantalon de/en _____ métal argenté
4. Un chapeau de/en _____ soie
5. Une veste de/en _____ paille
6. Des couverts de/en _____ velours

Exercice 16

Compléter les phrases suivantes par un article défini, si necessaire:

1. Il y a des clefs de _____ voiture sur la table. A qui sont-elles?
2. Les clefs de _____ voiture de Jean-Baptiste sont dans le tiroir.
3. Quelles sont les dates de _____ vacances de Noël cette année?
4. Quelles sont vos dates de _____ vacances?
5. Ce plan indique tous les arrêts de _____ autobus.
6. L'arrêt de _____ autobus 63 a été déplacé.
7. Ce professeur a écrit une histoire de _____ France au Moyen Age.
8. Ce livre d'histoire de _____ France est utilisé dans beaucoup d'écoles.

Exercice 17

Compléter les phrases suivantes:

1. Il a perdu sa carte de _____ dans le métro.
2. J'ai acheté un livre de _____
3. Mes parents ont une maison de _____ à 60 kilometres de Paris.
4. N'oublie pas d'emporter ton maillot de _____
5. Charlie Chaplin est un acteur de _____ très connu.
6. Il m'a donne un billet de _____
7. Dans ce magasin de _____ on trouve tout pour le ski, le tennis, etc.

Exercice 18
Mettre au pluriel les groupes de mots soulignés:
1. Elle s'occupe de l'enfant de sa soeur le mercredi.
2. Cette jeune femme s'occupe d'un enfant handicapé.
3. Paul et Christine ont parle d'une actrice que je ne connais pas.
4. Ils ont parlé de l'actrice qui vient d'obtenir un "**César**".
5. Pour dessiner, l'enfant se sert d'un crayon feutre.
6. Il s'est servi du crayon de son frère.
7. J'ai besoin d'une pile neuve pour ma radio.
8. Il se plaint d'un mal de tête.
9. Je ne me souviens plus du nom de cette personne.

Exercice 19
Compléter les phrases suivantes par un article si cela est necessaire:
1. Le chateau de Chambord est entouré de _____ mur de 32 kilometres de long.
2. Une île est un morceau de terre entouré de _____ eau.
3. La célèbre actrice entra, entourée de _____ eau.
4. La table était couverte de _____ nappe blanche.
5. Le bureau était couvert de _____ livres et de _____ documents.
6. C'etait l'hiver; tout était couvert de _____ neige.
7. Ce tiroir est plein de _____ photos.
8. L'alcoolisme est responsable de _____ mort de nombreuses personnes.
9. Derrière l'école, il y a une cour plantée de _____ arbres.
10. Le verbe "ressembler" est toujours suivi de _____ préposition "à".
11. Ce verbe est toujours suivi de _____ complément d'objet direct.

Exercice 20
Relier les éléments de la colonne de gauche aux éléments de la colonne de droite en inscrivant les lettres correspondantes dans les cases:
1. Une boîte à_____ _____ ongles
2. Un sac à_____ _____ dents
3. Une corbeille à _____ _____ main
4. Du rouge à _____ _____ outils
5. Du vernis à _____ _____ papiers
6. Une brosse à _____ _____ pain
7. Du papier à _____ _____ lèvres
8. Un couteau à _____ _____ lettres

Exercice 21
Compléter par un nom precedé d'un article défini:
1. Du café à _____   3. Un croissant à _____
2. Une tarte à _____   4. Une glace à _____
5. Un poulet à _____

2

Verbs

PRESENT INDICATIVE

La souris **mange** le fromage.
Le chat **guette** la souris.
Le garçon **chasse** le chat.
La jeune mère **fesse** le garçon.

1. *To conjugate a verb*, appropriate endings to denote person, number, tense and mood are added to the verb stem or, in some cases, directly to the infinitive. To denote the person and the number, a subject is essential. A subject pronoun often functions as the subject of a sentence.

A. Forms of the subject pronoun:

Person	Singular	Plural
1st	**je** = I	**nous** = we
2nd	**tu** = you, fam.	**vous** = you, formal
3rd-masc.	**il** = he/it	**ils** = they
3rd-fem.	**elle** = she/it	**elles** = they

3rd, s. - impersonal **on** = one, they, we, people

Examples:

Je parle russe.	I speak Russian.
Tu parles allemand.	You speak German.
Il parle bien l'italien.	He speaks Italian well.
Elle parle à voix basse.	She speaks with a low voice.
On parle espagnol au Méxique.	People speak Spanish in Mexico.
Nous parlons anglais.	We Speak English.
Vous parlez trop, mon ami.	You speak too much, my friend.
Ils parlent tous à la fois.	They speak all at once.
Elles parlent, et elles parlent.	They talk and talk.

Note: a) Both **"tu"** and **"vous"** mean *"you."* Use **tu** when addressing a relative, friend, classmate, a child, people with whom one is familiar. Use vous when addressing a stranger, an adult, more than one person, people with whom one should be more formal.

Pierre, mon enfant, **tu** manges trop!
Pierre, my child, you eat too much.

Ma cherie, que tu es belle ce soir.
My darling, how lovely you look tonight.

Monsieur Dupont, **vous** travaillez trop dur.
Mr. Dupont, you are working too hard.

Monsieur et Madame Dupont, vous perdez votre temps.
Mr. and Mrs. Dupont, you are wasting your time.

b) When the subject of a sentence is indefinite, **on** is used with the verb in the third person singular. **On** can mean, "we", "they", "you" or "people."

On chante bien dans cette église.
People sing well in this church.

On dit qu'il va pleuvoir.
They say that it is going to rain.

On dîne le dimanche chez nos grand parents.
We have dinner every Sunday at our grandparents'.

c) When the subject of a sentence is a noun rather than a pronoun, the third person form of the verb—singular or plural—is used.

L'oiseau vole d'un arbre à un autre.
The bird flies from one tree to another.

Les enfants ne regardent jamais la television.
The children never watch television.

Exercise 1

Fill in the blank with the correct subject pronoun.

1. _____ marchons vite.
2. _____ parles trop.
3. _____ dînez au restaurant.
4. _____ chantent bien, ces garçons.
5. _____ aide sa mère, cette fille.
6. _____ parle espagnol à Porto-Rico.
7. _____ causons au téléphone.
8. Moi, _____ porte un chapeau sur la tête.
9. _____ fument beaucoup, ces belles dames.
10. _____ habite à Paris avec son mari.

Exercise 2

Write the plural form of the following subject pronouns. Then translate the sentence into English.

Example: **Elle casse le verre.**
            Elles cassent le verre. (They break the glass.)

1. Tu fermes la fenêtre.
2. J'arrive en retard.
3. Il explique la leçon.
4. Je reste à la maison.
5. Il tombe sur le trottoir.
6. Tu quittes la maison à sept heures.
7. Je danse mal.
8. Elle commence le travail.
9. Tu demandes le billet d'avion.
10. J'aime les pommes frites.

2. *First Conjugation.* The present indicative tense (le present) of regular verbs is formed by dropping the infinitive ending (-er) and adding the personal endings.

Person	Singular	Plural	
1st	(je)	e	(nous) ons
2nd	(tu)	es	(vous) ez
3rd	(il, elle, on)	e	(ils, elles) ent

chanter, to sing

Affirmative	*Interrogative*
Je chante bien.	Est-ce que je chante bien?
I sing well.	Do I sing well?
Tu chantes bien.	Chantes-tu bien?
You sing well.	Do you sing well?
Il chante bien.	Chante-t-il bien?
He sings well.	Does he sing well?
Elle chante bien.	Chante-t-elle bien?
She sings well.	Does she sing well?
On chante bien.	Chante-t-on bien?
One sings well.	Does one sing well?
Nous chantons bien.	Chantons-nous bien?
We sing well.	Do we sing well?
Vous chantez bien.	Chantez-vous bien?
You sing well.	Do you sing well?
Ils chantent bien.	Chantent-ils bien?
They (m.) sing well.	Do they (m.) sing well?
Elles chantent bien.	Chantent-elles bien?
They (f.) sing well.	Do they (f.) sing well?

Common -er Verbs

accompagner, to escort
aider, to help
aimer, to love
ajouter, to add
allumer, to light
apporter, bring
arrêter, to stop
attraper, to catch
baigner, to bathe
baisser, to lower
bavarder, to chat
blâmer, to blame
blesser, to hurt
briller, to shine
briser, to break
brosser, to brush
bruler, to burn
cacher, to hide
casser, to break
causer, to chat
cesser, to stop
chanter, to sing
chasser, to hunt
chauffer, to warm
chercher, to look
commander, to order
compter, to count
conseiller, to advise
couper, to cut
coûter, to cost
crier, to shout
danser, to dance
déchirer, to tear
déjeuner, to lunch
demander, to ask
demeurer, to live
dépenser, to spend
désirer, to wish
déssiner, to draw
dîner, to dine
diviser, to divide
donner, to give

enchanter, to delight
enseigner, to teach
entourer, to surround
entrer, to enter
envelopper, to wrap
épouser, to marry
éternuer, to sneeze
étonner, to astonish
étudier, to study
éveiller, to wake
éviter, to avoid
expliquer, to explain
éxprimer, to express
fabriquer, to produce
fatiguer, to tire
féliciter, to pride
fermer, to close
frapper, to knock
frotter, to rub
fumer, to smoke
gagner, to earn
garder, to keep
gaspiller, to waste
gâter, to spoil
glisser, to slide
goûter, to taste
gronder, to scold
habiter, to live in
hésiter, to hesitate
ignorer, be unaware of
intéresser, to interest
jouer, to play
jurer, to swear
laisser, to leave
laver, to wash
louer, to rent, hire
manquer, to lack, miss
marcher, to walk, go
mêler, to mix
mériter, to deserve
monter, to go up
nommer, to name

peigner, to comb
penser, to think of
pleurer, to cry
porter, to carry, wear
poser, to put, place
pousser, to push, grow
présenter, to introduce
prêter, to lend
prier, to pray, beg
prouver, to prove
quitter, to leave
raconter, to relate
ramasser, to pick up
regarder, to look (at)
regretter, to be sorry
remarquer, to notice
remercier, to thank
rencontrer, to meet
rentrer, to return
repasser, to review,
rester, to remain, stay
retourner, to go back
retrouver, to find
réveiller, to wake (up)
rêver, to dream
saluer, to greet
sauter, to jump
sauver, to save
sembler, to seem
siffler, to whistle
signifier, to mean
soigner, to take care
sonner, to ring
souhaiter, to wish
souligner, to underline
tâcher, to try
téléphoner, to telephone
terminer, to end, finish
tirer, to pull
tomber, to fall
tourner, to turn
tousser, to cough

douter, to doubt	ordonner, to order	travailler, to work
durer, to last	oser, to dare	traverser, to cross
échouer, to fail	ôter, to take off	tremper, to soak, dip
éclater, to burst	oublier, to forget	tromper, to deceive
écouter, to listen	pardonner, to forgive	trouver, to find
embrasser, to kiss	parler, to talk	tuer, to kill
empêcher, to prevent	passer, to spend time	voler, to fly, steal
emprunter, to borrow	patiner, to skate	voyager, to travel

Exercise 3

Choose the correct form of the verb to match the subject:

1. Ils (enseignons, enseignons, enseignes, enseignent) l'espagnol.
2. Tu (racontent, racontes, racontez) une histoire drôle.
3. Les billets d'avion (coûte, coûtes, coûtent) cher.
4. Vous (accompagnes, accompagne, accompagnez) vos amis à la gare.
5. Elles (trouves, trouvons, trouvent) le parapluie.
6. Elles (habites, habite, habitent) à New York.
7. Je (gagne, gagnes, gagner) beaucoup d'argent.
8. M. Dupont (invites, invite, invitent) ses amis à la campagne.
9. Nous (traversez, traversent, traversons) Paris en auto.
10. Madame Dupont (ramassons, ramasse, ramasses) les assiettes.

Exercise 4

Repeat each sentence using each of the subjects in parenthesis:

1. Je mange au restaurant. (Paul et Jacques, Nous, Qui)
2. Il aide le docteur. (Nous, Les étudiants, Je)
3. Voyages-tu souvent? (vous, je, le bébé)
4. Ils ne fument pas beaucoup. (On, Vous, Tu)
5. Ne causer-ils pas avec eux? (vous, elle, vos amis)

Exercise 5

Answer the following questions in French:

1. Qui proteste quand vous sortez le soir?
2. Qui porte une robe, un homme ou une femme?
3. Travaillez-vous beaucoup?
4. Qu'est-ce que vous détestez?
5. Quelle page regardez-vous maintenant?
6. Où les élèves étudient-elles?
7. Ecoutes-tu la musique classique en travaillant?
8. Où étudiez-vous?
9. Est-ce que vos parents passent l'été à la campagne?
10. Demeurez-vous au Canada?

Exercise 6

Write the proper form of the present tense:

1. chercher: Je _____ mes amis.
2. monter: _____ -il l'escalier ?
3. causer: Nous ne _____ pas en classe.
4. apporter: Ils _____ les fleurs à Madame Dupont.
5. chanter: Elle ne _____ pas la chanson.
6. emprunter: _____ -tu le livre de poesie?
7. couper: Le boucher_____ la viande.
8. dîner: Ne _____ -vous pas à six heures?
9. marcher: _____ -on sur le trottoir?
10. aimer: Nous _____ la musique classique.

Exercise 7

Write the following sentences in the plural:

1. Il quitte la maison de campagne.
2. Je n'arrive pas en retard à la gare.
3. Tu remarques les fautes.
4. Rencontre-t-elle l'avocat?
5. L'enfant tombe par terre.
6. Elle marche vite.
7. Je parle anglais.
8. Tu fumes trop.
9. Il achète des souvenirs de Paris.
10. Je voyage souvent au Canada.

3. Second Conjugation. The present indicative tense (le present) of regular verbs is formed by dropping the infinitive ending (-ir) and adding the personal endings.

Person	Singular	Plural
1st	(je) is	(nous) issons
2nd	(tu) is	(vous) issez
3rd	(il, elle, on) it	(ils, elles) issent

obéir, *to obey*

Affirmative	Interrogative
J'obéis à la loi.	**Est-ce que j'obéis à la loi?**
I obey the law.	Do I obey the law?
Tu obéis à la loi.	**Obéis-tu à la loi?**
You obey the law.	Do you obey the law?
Il obéit à la loi.	**Obéit-il à la loi?**
He obeys the law.	Does he obey the law?
Elle obéit à la loi.	**Obéit-elle à la loi?**
She obeys the law.	Does she obey the law?
On obéit à la loi.	**Obéit-on à la loi?**
One obeys the law.	Does one obey the law?

Nous obéissons à la loi.   Obéissons-nous à la loi?
We obey the law.   Do we obey the law?
Vous obéissez à la loi.   Obéissez-vous à la loi?
You obey the law.   Do you obey the law?
Ils obéissent à la loi.   Obéissent-ils à la loi?
They (m.) obey the law.   Do they (m.) obey the law?
Elles obéissent à la loi.   Obéissent-elles à la loi?
They (f.) obey the law   Do they (f.) obey the law?

Common -ir Verbs

accomplir, to accomplish	jouir (de), to enjoy
agir, to act	nourrir, to feed
applaudir, to applaud	obéir (a), to obey
bâtir, to build	punir, to punish
bénir, to bless	ravir, to delight
choisir, to choose	réfléchir, to think
désobeir (a), to disobey	remplir, to fill
établir, to establish	reussir, to succeed
finir, to finish	rougir, to blush
grandir, to grow	saisir, to seize
guérir, to cure	trahir, to betray

Exercise 8

Complete each of the following French sentences by using the correct form of the present tense:

1. Réussir: Tu _____ toujours.
2. Remplir: Nous _____ le verre.
3. Choisir   Qui _____ ce beau vase?
4. Finir   Elles _____ le livre.
5. Punir   _____ -vous le chien?
6. Obéir   _____ -tu à la loi?
7. Grandir   Les enfants_____ bien.
8. Guérir   _____ la maladie.
9. Bâtir   L'architecte_____un bel hôpital.
10. Réflechir _____ -ils avant de parler?

Exercise 9

Complete each sentence with the correct verb form:

1. (bâtir)   Que _____ -ils? Qui _____ ce beau musée?
2. (obéir)   J' _____ au lieutenant. Nous _____ à ses ordres.
3. (punir)   _____ _ -nous les voleurs? Qui _____ -elle?
4. (remplir) Les touristes _____ l'hôtel.
              Pourquoi _____ -vous cette boîte?
5. (choisir) Quel sport _____ -vous?
              Combien de cartes _____ -tu?

Exercise 10

Answer the following questions in French, in the affirmative or in the negative, as indicated:

1. Choisissez-vous ces fleurs? Non, nous _____ces vases.
2. Remplissez-vous la tasse? Oui, nous _____.
3. Est-ce que le garçon obéit à sa mère? Oui, il _____.
4. Est-ce que j'obeis au professeur? Oui, vous _____.
5. Choisis-tu cette route? Oui, je _____.
6. Est-ce que je choisis un cadeau? Oui, vous _____.
7. Obeissez-vous à l'homme? Non, je _____.
8. Remplissent-ils le stylo? Non, ils _____.
9. Est-ce que les femmes choisissent les robes?
   Non, elles _____ les jupes.
10. Remplissez-vous le verre? Non, je _____ les tasses.

Exercise 11

Choose the correct verb form:

1. Nous (bâtissent, bâtis, bâtissons) un garage.
2. Ils (punissent, punit, punissons) l'assassin.
3. Elle (choisir, choisit, choisis) la voiture rouge.
4. M. Dupont (bâtir, bâtit, bâtis) une bibliothéque.
5. Je (finissez, finit, finis) le travail à temps.
6. Mon cousin (reussit, reussir, reussis) à l'éxamen.
7. Elles (guérissons, guérissent, guérit) l'animal.
8. (Remplis, Remplit, Remplir)-tu la tasse?
9. On ne (réussissons, réussissez, réussit) pas toujours.
10. Ils (obéit, obéissons, obéissent) à l'avocat.

Exercise 12

Complete each sentence with the French equivalent of the English words:

1. Do I finish _____ le roman?
2. to finish J'aime _____ mon travail.
3. Are you finishing _____ les devoirs?
4. I am finishing _____ le dîner.
5. We are not finishing _____ le livre.
6. He finishes _____ la page.
7. Don't I finish _____ tous les exercices?
8. Aren't they finishing _____ la soupe?
9. She is finishing _____ la leçon.
10. They finish _____ l'histoire.

4. Third Conjugation. The present indicative tense (le present) of regular verbs is formed by dropping the infinitive ending (-re) and adding the personal endings.

Person	Singular	Plural
1st	(je)s	(nous) ons
2nd	(tu)s	(vous) ez
3rd	(il, elle, on)-	(ils, elles) ent

attendre, to wait for

Affirmative	Interrogative
J'attends mon ami.	Est-ce que j'attends mon ami?
I wait for my friend.	Do I wait for my friend?
Tu attends ton ami.	Attends-tu ton ami?
You wait for your friend.	Do you wait for your friend?
Il attend son ami.	Attend-il son ami?
He waits for his friend.	Does he wait for his friend?
Elle attend son ami.	Attend-elle son ami?
She waits for her friend.	Does she wait for her friend?
On attend son ami.	Obéit-on son ami?
One waits for one's friend.	Does one wait for one's friend?
Nous attendons notre ami.	Attendons-nous notre ami?
We wait for our friend.	Do we wait for our friend?
Vous attendez votre ami.	Attendez-vous votre ami?
You wait for your friend.	Do you wait for your friend?
Ils attendent leur ami.	Attendent-ils leur ami?
They (m.) wait for their friend.	Do they (m.) wait for their friend?
Elles attendent leur ami.	They (f.) wait for their friend?
Attendent-elles leur ami?	Do they (f.) wait for their friend?

Common -re Verbs

attendre, to wait (for)
confondre, to confuse
défendre, to defend
dépendre, to depend
descendre, to descend
entendre, to hear
étendre, to spread out
interrompre, to interrupt

mordre, to bite
pendre, to hang
perdre, to lose
rendre, to give back
répondre, to answer
rompre, to break
tendre, to tighten, draw tight
vendre, to sell

Exercise 13   Choose the correct subject pronoun:

1. Entendez- (nous, vous, ils) le bruit de la voiture?
2. (elles, Il, Nous) rendent les gants jaunes.
3. Attendent-(elle, vous, ils) un taxi?
4. (Vous, Tu, Elles) répondez au president.
5. N'entends- (il, tu, vous) pas la sirene?
6. (Elle, Tu, Ils) descend par les escaliers.
7. (Je, Il, Elles) perd son billet d'avion.
8. (Il, Elle, Je) réponds à la lettre.
9. (Nous, Vous, Ils) défendons la vieille dame.
10. (Elle, Vous, Je) vends la maison de campagne.

Exercise 14   Rewrite each sentence, using the subjects indicated:

1. Il perd la clef de sa chambre d'hotel. (Nous, Ils, Je)
2. Vous ne rendez pas l'addition. (Les enfants, Nous, Tu)
3. Nous descendons du train. (Je, I, Elles)
4. Attends-tu M. Dupont ? (elle, vous, ils)
5. Ils entendent l'oiseau. (Paul, Je, Vous)

Exercise 15   Answer in complete French sentences:

1. Entendez-vous les voitures dans la rue?
2. Rends-tu les livres que tu empruntes?
3. A quelle heure descendons-nous à la salle à manger?
4. Est-ce que tu défends ta patrie ?
5. Attendent-ils une lettre de leurs parents?
6. Qui répond aux questions en classe?
7. Qui vend de la viande?
8. Qui attendez-vous?
9. Qu'est-ce qu'on vend dans la boulangerie?

Exercise 16   Give the equivalent in French:

1. Mr. and Mrs. Dupont are coming down.
2. The lady sells the newspaper to the man.
3. Who is returning the map?
4. They lose their time.
5. Does he always wait for the girls?

Exercise 17

Translate the following sentences into English:

1. Madame Dupont ne perd jamais son temps.
2. L'épicier vend du sucre.
3. Monsieur Dupont n'aime pas attendre.
4. Quand elle monte, elle ne descend pas.
5. Les soldats défendent leur pays.
6. Ne répond-il pas à la question.
7. Le garçon attend la commande.
8. Nous répondons à la lettre tout de suite.
9. Entends-tu le bébé?
10. Rendez-vous les livres à la bibliothèque?

Reminders

A. The subject pronouns of conjugated verbs are: je, tu, il, elle, on, nous, vous, ils, or elles. The subject pronoun and its verb must agree in person and number.

B. On is an indefinite subject pronoun used with a third person singular verb.

C. When the subject of a sentence is a noun rather than a subject pronoun, the third person form of the verb (singular or plural) is used.

D. The present indicative of regular -er verbs is formed by adding the following endings: (je) e, (tu) es, (il) e, (elle) e, (on) e, (nous) ons, (vous) ez, (ils) ent, and (elles) ent to the stem of the infinitive.

E. The present indicative of regular -ir verbs is formed by adding the following endings: (je) is, (tu) is, (il) it, (elle) it, (on) it, (nous) issons, (vous) issez, (ils) issent, and (elles) issent to the stem of the infinitive.

F. The present indicative of the regular -re verbs is formed by adding the following endings: (je) s, (tu) s, (il) — or t, (elle) — or t, (on) — or t, (nous) ons, (vous) ez, (ils) ent, and (elles) ent to the stem of the infinitive.

G. An affirmative sentence becomes negative when ne precedes the verb and pas follows it.

H. When there is more than one verb in a simple sentence, all but the first verb remain in the infinitive.

THE PRESENT TENSE OF IRREGULAR VERBS

La souris **a** le fromage.

Elle **craint** le chat.

Le garçon ne **comprend** pas la souris.

La jeune mère **voit** le garçon.

1. All irregular verbs—except **aller**, to go —have infinitives that end in **-oir**, **-ir**, or **-re**. Although many common verbs besides **être** and **avoir** are irregular, most of them follow some general pattern.

A. The verb **être** (to be) is one of the most frequently used French verbs. It is an irregular verb which has a different present tense form for each of the six persons.

1. The present indicative of the verb être:

Singular		Plural	
je suis	I am	nous sommes	we are
tu es	you are	vous êtes	you are
il/elle/on est	he/she/one is	ils/elles sont	they are
(on = we, you, people are)			

2. Uses of the verb être:

a) The verb **être** is used as the main verb in a sentence to identify or describe the subject.

Jean est un garçon brillant.	Jean is a brillant boy.
Ces fleurs sont charmantes.	Those flowers are lovely.

Le bureau de poste est juste en face de la boulangerie.

The post office is right in front of the bakery.

b) The verb être is also used as an auxiliary to form a compound tense. (See Chapter 3 on the compound tenses.)

B. The verb **avoir** is also one of the most frequently used verbs in French. Like the verb **être**, it is very irregular.

1. The present indicative of the verb **avoir**:

Singular		Plural	
j'ai	I have	nous avons	we have
tu as	you have	vous avez	you have
il/elle/on a	he/she/one has	ils/elles ont	they have
(on= we, you, people have)			

2. The uses of the verb **avoir**:

a) The verb avoir is used as a main verb to indicate the relationship between a noun or noun phrase and the subject of the sentence.

Le professeur **a** une pipe.
The teacher has a pipe.

Nous **avons** des amis sympathiques.
We have nice friends.

Les élèves **ont** quelque chose à dire.
They students have something to say.

b) The verb avoir is used with a noun to form many idiomatic expressions in French. These expressions are idiomatic because no article introduces the noun, and the entire phrase forms a single unit of meaning. They are often translated in English with a form of the verb, to be and an adjective. The following is a list of the most common of these expressions.

avoir _____ ans	to be_____ years old
avoir besoin de	to need
avoir chaud	to be warm
avoir de la chance	to be lucky
avoir envie de	to feel like/doing or having something
avoir faim	to be hungry
avoir froid	to be cold
avoir honte	to be ashamed
avoir mal	to hurt
avoir mal à la tête	to have a headache
avoir peur	to be afraid
avoir raison	to be right
avoir soif	to be thirsty
avoir sommeil	to be sleepy
avoir tort	to be wrong

Je n'ai pas faim, mais j'ai froid.   I am not hungry, but I am cold.

Monsieur Dupont a toujours soif.   Mister Dupont is always thirsty.

Madame Dupont a envie d'un morceau de chocolat.
Mrs. Dupont feels like having a piece of chocolate.

Notes:
a) The personal expressions avoir chaud (to be warm) and avoir froid (to be cold) are used when referring to how someone feels.

However, when referring to the weather, the impersonal expression **il fait** must be used.

Les enfants ont froid ici parce qu'il fait très froid dehors.
The children are cold here because it is very cold outside.

Il fait beau. Il fait du soleil. Nous avons chaud.
It is nice. Il is sunny. We are warm.

b) The same impersonal expressions are also used to talk about the weather.

Il fait beau (temps) aujourd'hui.
It is nice out today.

Il fait mauvais (temps).
It is bad out. It's nasty out. The weather is bad.

Il fait du vent.
It is windy.

c) The third person of the verb avoir is used in the invariable expression il y a (there is; there are) simply to express that something exists.

Il y a de la neige dans les rues.
There is snow in the streets.

Il y a du pain et du fromage sur la table.
There isbread and cheese on the table.

d) The third person of the verb avoir is used in the invariable expression il y a to mean *ago, for,* or *since.*

Le film a commence il y a dix minutes.
The movie began ten minutes ago.

Il y a un mois que j'attends la réponse.
I have been waiting for the answer for a month.

e) The third person of the verb avoir is used in the invariable expression il y a to form some idiomatic expressions.

Il n'y a pas de quoi. Don't mention it.
Qu'est-ce qu'il y a? What is the matter?

C. The pattern of some irregular verbs:

1. Most irregular verbs end in -s, -s, -t in the three singular forms.

a) Some verbs like conduire, croire, courir, dire, écrire, faire, lire, produire, and voir add these endings directly to the infinitive stem.

conduire	*to drive*
je conduis	I drive
tu conduis	you drive
il/elle/on conduit	he/she/one drives
croire	*to believe*
je crois	I believe
tu crois	you believe
il/elle/on croit	he/she/one believes
courir	*to run*
je cours	I run
tu cours	you run
il/elle/on court	he/she/one runs

dire	*to say*
je dis	I say
tu dis	you say
il/elle/on dit	he/she/one says
écrire	*to write*
j'écris	I write
tu écris	you write
il/elle/on écrit	he/she/one writes
faire	*to do/ to make*
je fais	I do
tu fais	you do
il/elle/on fait	he/she/one does
lire	to read
je lis	I read
tu lis	you read
il/elle/on lit	he/she/one reads
produire	*to produce*
je produis	I produce
tu produis	you produce
il/elle/on produit	he/she/one produces
voir	*to see*
je vois	I see
tu vois	you see
il/elle/on voit	he/she/one sees

b) Verbs like admettre, battre, comprendre, convaincre, coudre, and mettre whose infinitive stem ends in -d or -t and verbs based on vaincre (to conquer) do not add the final -t in the third person singular form.

admettre	*to admit*
j'admets	I admit
tu admets	you admit
il/elle/on admet	he/she/one admits
battre	*to hit*
je bats	I hit
tu bats	you hit
il/elle/on bat	he/she/one hits
comprendre	*to understand*
je comprends	I understand
tu comprends	you understand
il/elle/on comprend	he/she/one understands
convaincre	*to convince*
je convaincs	I convince
Tu convaincs	you convince
il/elle/on convainc	he/she/one convinces

coudre	*to sew*
je couds	I sew
tu couds	you sew
il/elle coud	he/she sew
mettre	*to put*
je mets	I put
tu mets	you put
il/elle/on met	he/she/one puts

D. Some irregular verbs drop the final stem consonant before adding -s, -s, -t.

1. A few of these verbs are battre, dormir, mettre, partir, savoir, and servir.

battre	*to beat*
je bats	I beat
tu bats	you beat
il/elle/on bat	he/she/one beats
dormir	to sleep
je dors	I sleep
tu dors	you sleep
il/elle/on dort	he/she/one sleeps
mettre	*to put*
je mets	I put
tu mets	you put
il/elle/on met	he/she/one puts
partir	*to leave*
je pars	I leave
tu pars	you leave
il/elle/on part	he/she/one leaves
savoir	*to know* (something)
je sais	I know
tu sais	you know
il/elle/on sait	he/she/one knows
servir	*to serve*
je sers	I serve
tu sers	you serve
il/elle sert	he/she serves

2. All verbs ending in -indre also drop the final stem consonant before adding **-s, -s, -t**.

craindre	*to fear*
je crains	I fear
tu crains	you fear
il/elle/on craint	he/she/one fears

joindre	*to join*
je joins	I join
tu joins	you join
il/elle/on joint	he/she/one joins

3. Some verbs undergo a vowel change when the last vowel of the stem is stressed.

acquerir	*to acquire*
j'acquiers	I acquire
tu acquiers	you acquire
il/elle/on acquiert	he/she/one acquieres
mourir	*to die*
je meurs	I die
tu meurs	you die
il/elle/on meurt	he/she/one dies
venir	*to come*
je viens	I come
tu viens	you come
il/elle/on vient	he/she/one comes
tenir	*to hold*
je tiens	I hold
tu tiens	you hold
il/elle/on tient	he/she/one holds

4. The verbs **devoir** and **savoir** change vowels as well as drop the final stem consonants in the singular.

devoir	*must, ought to, should*
je dois	I must
tu dois	you must
il/elle/on doit	he/she/one must
savoir	*to know*
je sais	I know
tu sais	you know
il/elle/on sait	he/she/one knows

5. The verbs **pourvoir** and **vouloir** also change vowels and drop the final stem consonants. In addition, they use an old spelling for the final **-us/-ux**.

pouvoir	*to be able*
je peux	I am able
tu peux	you are able
il/elle/on peut	he/she/one is able

vouloir	*to want*
je veux	I want
tu veux	you want
il/elle/on veut	he/she/one wants

6. The verb **cueillir** (to pick), its compounds, and verbs whose infinitives end in **-vrir** or **-frir** follow the pattern of regular **-er** verbs.

ouvrir	*to open*
j'ouvre	I open
tu ouvres	you open
il/elle/on ouvre	he/she opens
offrir	*to offer*
j'offre	I offer
tu offres	you offer
il/elle/on offre	he/she offers
accueillir	*to welcome*
j'accueille	I welcome
tu accueilles	you welcome
il/elle/on accueille	he/she/one welcomes

Note: Three irregular verbs, être, avoir, and aller, follow no predictable pattern in the present tense singular form.

être	*to be*
je suis	I am
tu es	you are
il/elle/on est	he/she/one is
avoir	*to have*
j'ai	I have
tu as	you have
il/elle/on a	he/she/one has
aller	*to go*
je vais	I go
tu vas	you go
il/elle/on va	he/she/one goes

E. The plural forms of certain irregular verbs in the present indicative.

1. The most common endings for the plural of the present tense are **-ons**, **-ez**, and **-ent**. Only **être**, **avoir**, **aller**, **dire**, and **faire** are irregular in the present tense plural forms.

a) Verbs like **battre, courir, couvrir, croire, découvrir, dormir, mettre, offrir, partir, savoir, sentir, souffrir, vaincre, voir, sortir** add the plural endings directly to the infinitive stem.

battre - *to beat*
nous battons
vous battez
ils/elles battent

couvrir - *to cover*
nous couvrons
vous couvrez
ils/elles couvrent

découvrir - *to discover*
nous découvrons
vous découvrez
ils/elles découvrent

mettre - *to put*
nous mettons
vous mettez
ils/elles mettent

savoir - *to know*
nous savons
vous savez
ils/elles savent

souffrir - *to suffer*
nous souffrons
vous souffrez
ils/elles souffrent

voir - *to see*
nous voyons
vous voyez
ils/elles voient

courir - *to run*
nous courons
vous courez
ils/elles courent

croire - *to believe*
nous croyons
vous croyez
ils/elles croient

dormir - *to sleep*
nous dormons
vous dormez
ils/elles dorment

offrir - *to offer*
nous offrons
vous offrez
ils/elles offrent

sentir - *to feel*
nous sentons
vous sentez
ils/elles sentent

vaincre - *to conquer*
nous vainquons
vous vainquez
ils/elles vainquent

sortir - *to go out*
nous sortons
vous sortez
ils/elles sortent

Note: 1. The **-y-** of the first person, plural forms of verbs like voir and croire is an alternate spelling for the -i- in non-final syllables.

2. The **-qu-** in the plural forms of vaincre maintains the hard **-c** sound of the infinitive.

b) Verbs like **coudre, craindre, connaître, écrire, lire, produire** change or add a final consonant of the infinitive stem in forming the present tense, plural forms.

coudre - to sew
nous cousons
vous cousez
ils/elles cousent

craindre - to fear
nous craignons
vous craignez
ils/elles craignent

connaître - to be familiar with
nous connaissons
vous connaissez
ils/elles connaissent

lire - to read
nous lisons
vous lisez
ils/elles lisent

écrire - to write
nous écrivons
vous écrivez
ils/elles écrivent

produire - to produce
nous produisons
vous produisez
ils/elles produisent

Note: a) Most verbs ending in **-uire** add an **-s** following the pattern of **produire**.

b) Most verbs ending in **-indre** add **-gn-** following the pattern of craindre.

c) Verbs like prendre and resoudre drop the final infinitive stem consonant before the plural endings are added.

prendre - *to take*
nous prenons
vous prenez
ils/elles prennent

résoudre - *to resolve*
nous résolvons
vous résolvez
ils/elles resolvent

Note: a) All compounds of prendre follow the same pattern.

b) All verbs ending in **-oudre** follow the same pattern of résoudre.

c) For certains verbs, when there is a vowel change in the singular, the vowel in the third person plural form (**ils/elles**) maintains the same change as that of the singular forms. The first and second person plural verb forms of such verbs are regular.

The verb **savoir** is an exception to that rule. Its third person plural form is regular.

acquérir - to acquire
(j'acquiers)
nous acquérons
vous acquérez
ils/elles acquièrent

mourir - to die
(je meurs)
nous mourons
vous mourez
ils/elles meurent

devoir - *must*
(je dois)
nous devons
vous devez
ils/elles doivent

boire - *to drink*
(je bois)
nous buvons
vous buvez
ils/elles boivent

venir - *to come*
(je viens)
vous venez

nous venons
ils/elles viennent

Notes: a) The verb boire is the only verb whose present tense first and second person plural forms (nous and vous) contain a vowel which does not occur in the infinitive or in the singular forms.

b) Venir, tenir, prendre and all their compounds take a double **-nn-** spelling in the third person plural of the present tense.

Elles ne comprennent pas le ruse.
They do not understand Russian.

Elles obtiennent leurs visas de sortie.
They obtain their exit visas.

Ils reviennent à l'heure.
They come back on time.

3. The verb **être** is the only verb whose present tense first person plural form does not end in **-ons**. The nous form for the verb **être** is "nous sommes."

4. The verbs **être**, **faire**, and dire are the only verbs whose present tense second person plural forms do not end in **-ez**.

être/*to be*	vous êtes
faire/*to do*	vous faites
dire/*to say*	vous dites

5. The verbs **être**, **faire**, **avoir**, and **aller** are the only verbs whose present tense third person plural forms do not end in **-ent**.

être/*to be*	ils sont
faire/*to do*	ils font
avoir/*to have*	ils ont
aller/*to go*	ils vont

2. The present indicative tense of the most common irregular verbs are:
aller, to go: vais, vas, va, allons, allez, vont
s'asseoir, to sit (down): m'assieds, t'assieds, s'assied, nous asseyons, vous asseyez, s'asseyent
avoir, to have: ai, as, a, avons, avez, ont
battre, to beat: bats, bats, bat, battons, battez, battent. Like battre: se battre, to fight
boire, to drink: bois, bois, boit, buvons, buvez, boivent
conduire, to lead, drive: conduis, conduis, conduit, conduisons, conduisez, conduisent. Like conduire:
construire, to construct; produire, to produce; traduire, to translate connaître, to know, be acquainted with: connais, connais, connait, connaissons, connaissez, connaissent. Like connaître:
reconnaître, to recognize; paraitre, to appear; disparaitre, to disappear.
courir, to run: cours, cours, court, courons, courez, courent
craindre, to fear: crains, crains, craint, craignons, craignez, craignent.
Like craindre: **plaindre**, to pity;
atteindre, to reach, attain; éteindre, to extinguish, turn off;
peindre, to paint; joindre, to join

croire, to believe: crois, crois, croit, croyons, croyez, croient

devoir, to owe, have to, be (supposed) to: dois, dois,
doit, devons, devez, doivent

dire, to say, tell: dis, dis, dit, disons, dites, disent

dormir, to sleep: dors, dors, dort, dormons, dormez,dorment. Like dormir:
s'endormir, to fall asleep;

mentir, to lie; partir, to leave; sentir, to feel, smell;
servir, to serve; sortir, to go out

écrire, to write: écris, écris, écrit, écrivons,
écrivez, écrivent. Like écrire: décrire, to describe

envoyer, to send: envoie, envoies, envoie, envoyons, envoyez, envoient

être, to be: suis, es, est, sommes, êtes, sont

faire, to do, make: fais, fais, fait, faisons, faites, font

falloir, to be necessary: il faut

lire, to read: lis, lis, lit, lisons, lisez, lisent

mettre, to put, put on: mets, mets, met, mettons, mettez, mettent. Like mettre:
permettre, to permit;

promettre, to promise; remettre, to put back, postpone

mourir, to die: meurs, meurs, meurt, mourons, mourez, meurent

ouvrir, to open: ouvre, ouvres, ouvre, ouvrons, ouvrez, ouvrent. Like
ouvrir: couvrir, to cover;

découvrir, to discover; offrir, to offer; souffrir, to suffer

plaire, to please: plais, plais, plait, plaisons, plaisez, plaisent

pleuvoir, to rain: il pleut

pouvoir, to be able: peux (puis), peux, peut pouvons, pouvez, peuvent

prendre, to take: prends, prends, prend, prenons, prenez, prennent. Like
prendre:

apprendre, to learn, teach; comprendre, to understand, include;
reprendre, to take back; surprendre, to surprise

recevoir, to receive: reçois, reçois, reçoit, recevons, recevez, reçoivent

rire, to laugh: ris, ris, rit, rions, riez, rient. Like rire: sourire, to smile

savoir, to know: sais, sais, sait, savons, savez, savent

suivre, to follow: suis, suis, suit, suivons, suivez, suivent

se taire, to be silent, keep quiet: me tais, te tais, se tait, nous taisons, vous
taisez, se taisent

tenir, to hold: tiens, tiens, tient, tenons, tenez, tiennent. Like tenir:
appartenir à, to belong to; **devenir**, to become; **obtenir**, to obtain;
retenir, to hold back; **revenir**, to come back; **venir**, to come

valoir, to be worth: vaux, vaux, vaut, valons, valez, valent

vivre, to live, be alive: vis, vis, vit, vivons, vivez, vivent

voir, to see: vois, vois, voit, voyons, voyez, voient. Like voir: **revoir**, to
see again

vouloir, to wish, want: veux, veux, veut, voulons, voulez, veulent

Exercise 18

Rewrite the following sentences by replacing the subjects with those given in the parentheses.

Example: **je ne ment jamais (vous)**
Vous ne mentez jamais

1. Nous dormons tard le weekend. (je)
2. Elle lit tous les romans de Stephen King. (elles)
3. Tu attends le petit dejeuner. (Les enfants)
4. Jean écrit à ses parents. (nous)
5. Ils veulent sortir malgres la neige. (tu)
6. J'éteins la lumiere avant de sortir. (ils)
7. Crois-tu à cette histoire? (vous)
8. Le guide nous conduit à travers le jardin. (vous)
9. Le monsieur nous accueille le bras ouvert. (elles)
10. Tu dois arriver à l'heure. (nous)
11. Je bois du café noir le matin. (vous)
12. Monsieur Dupont ne sait pas danser. (Pierre et Jean)
13. Le garçon cueille les pommes. (les jardiniers)
14. Prend-il du sucre? (vous)
15. Elles font de la bonne cuisine. (je)
16. L'avocat convainc les clients. (nous)
17. Ils ont beaucoup d'argent. (tu)
18. Il est en bonne santé (nous)
19. Le jeune homme ouvre la porte pour la dame. (ils)
20. Pourquoi ne resoud-il pas le problème? (vous)

Exercise 19

Rewrite the following sentence in the plural.

1. J'envoie une carte postale à mon amie.
2. Que veux-tu?
3. L'artiste peint des potraits de valeur.
4. Elle veut acheter une robe neuve.
5. Aie la bonté de fermer la porte en sortant.
6. L'étudiant prend ses couurs au serieux.
7. Tu lis le journal en mangeant ton petit déjeuner.
8. Souffres-tu souvent de maux de tete?
9. Je n'en peux plus. Je suis crêve.
10. Elle connait bien cette route.

Exercise 20

Complete each sentence with the verb in parentheses.

1. (admettre) Elle _____ d'avoir menti.
2. (construire) Qu'est-ce qu'ils _____ là bas.
3. (boire)   Nous _____ du jus d'orange chaque matin.
4. (s'endormir) L'enfant _____ tout habille.

5. (plaire)   Le film ne lui _____ pas.
6. (servir)   Le garçon _____ la salade.
7. (recevoir) Vous _____ une lettre importante.
8. (prendre)   Ils _____ un grand repas.
9. (avoir)   _____ ils encore de l'appetit?
10. (être)   _____ vous prests mes amis?
11. (connaître) Nous _____ bien ce peintre.
12. (sortir)   Les enfants _____ sans la permision.
13. (aller)   Ou _____ ils?
15. (éteindre) Vous _____ la lumière avant de vous coucher.

IMPERATIVES: FORMAL AND INFORMAL COMMANDS

Mange le fromage, mon enfant.
Chantons la chanson, mes amis.
Parlez plus fort, s'il vous plaît.

1. The imperative of regular verbs:

The forms of the imperative (l'impératif) of regular verbs are the same as the corresponding forms of the present indicative except that the subject pronouns, tu, vous, and nous are omitted.

chanter: chante, chantez, chantons
obéir: obéis, obéissez, obéissons
répondre: réponds, répondez, répondons

Note: One exception is found in the familiar form of **-er** verbs, which drops the final **-s:chante.**

2. The imperative of irregular verbs:

The imperative of irregular vebs generally follows the same pattern as regular verbs. The pronouns **tu, vous** and **nous** are omitted.

aller: va, allez, allons
dire: dis, dites, disons
ouvrir: ouvre, ouvrez, ouvrons
recevoir: recois, recevez, recevons

Note: a) Irregular **-er** verbs, and verbs conjugated like **-er** verbs in the present indicative, drop the final **-s** in the familiar, singular imperative.

However, when linked to the pronouns y and en, all regular and irregular verbs retain the -s.

Manges-en la moitié.	Eat half of it.
Vas-y vite.	Go there quickly.

b) The object pronoun of a reflexive verb follows the verb in the affirmative imperative but precedes it in the negative imperative.

s'asseoir

Affirmative Imperative	Negative Imperative
Assieds-toi!	Ne t'assieds pas!
Asseyez-vous!	Ne vous asseyez pas!
Asseyons-nous!	Ne nous asseyons pas!

3. The Imperative of the Most Common Irregular Verbs

aller, to go: **va, allez, allons**

s'asseoir, to sit (down): assieds-toi, asseyez-vous, asseyons-nous

avoir, to have: aie, ayez, ayons

battre, to beat: bats, battez, battons

boire, to drink: bois, buvez, buvons

conduire, to lead, drive: conduis, conduisez, conduisons

connaître, to know, be acquainted with: connais, connaissez, connaissons

courir, to run: cours, courez, courons

craindre, to fear: crains, craignez, craignons

croire, to believe: crois, croyez, croyons

devoir, to owe, have to, be (supposed) to:

dois, devez, devons

dire, to day, tell: dis, dites, disons

dormir, to sleep: dors, dormez, dormons

écrire, to write: écris, écrivez, écrivons

envoyer, to send: envoies, envoyez, envoyons

être, to be: sois, soyez, soyons

faire, to do, make: fais, faites, faisons

lire, to read: lis, lisez, lisons

mettre, to put, put on: mets, mettez, mettons

mourir, to die: meurs, mourez, mourons

ouvrir, to open: ouvre, ouvrez, ouvrons

plaire, to please: plais, plaisez, plaisons

pouvoir, to be able: peux, pouvez, pouvons

prendre, to take: prends, prenez, prenons

recevoir, to receive: recois, recevez, recevons

rire, to laugh: ris, riez, rions

savoir, to know: sais, savez, savons

suivre, to follow: suis, suivez, suivons

se taire, to be silent, keep quiet: tais-toi, taisez-vous, taisons-nous

tenir, to hold: tiens, tenez, tenons
valoir, to be worth: vaux, valez, valons
vivre, to live, be alive: vis, vivez, vivons
voir, to see: vois, voyez, voyons
vouloir, to wish, want: veux, voulez, voulons

Exercise 21

A. Give the equivalent in French:
1. Let's see the pictures.
2. Let us not forget.
3. Let's have some ice cream.
4. Let us succeed.
5. Let us do the homework.
6. Let us not break the cup.
7. Let's open the door.
8. Let us leave/go away.
9. Let us drink the tea.
10. Let's be reasonable.

Exercise 22

Complete the sentences in English:
1. Apportez le livre à l'école. _____ the book to school.
2. Courez au magasin. _____ to the store.
3. Sortons tout de suite. _____ at once.
4. Remplis cette bouteille. _____ that bottle.
5. Ne rougissez pas, mes enfants. _____ children.
6. Apprenez ce proverbe. _____ this proverb.
7. Lavons le plancher. _____ the floor.
8. Soyez donc plus actifs! _____ more active!
9. Ne rions pas tant. _____ so much.
10. Ne casse pas l'assiette. _____ the plate.

Exercise 23

Rewrite, giving the plural (**vous**) imperative:
1. réflechir bien
2. ne pas attendre l'avion
3. ne pas rire
4. parler moins haut
5. traduire la paragraphe
6. apprendre le poème
7. se dépécher
8. dire la vérité
9. ouvrir les fenêtres
10. dormir bien

Exercise 24

Rewrite, giving the familiar, singular (tu) imperative:
1. traverser le jardin
2. se taire
3. boire le lait
4. être sage
5. obéir à sa soeur
6. jouer à la balle
7. revenir vite
8. remplir la tasse
9. aller à l'école
10. prendre un taxi

Exercise 25

Replace the sentence verb by the correct form of the verb in parentheses:
1. (écrire)   Etudie la lettre.
2. (voir)   Regardons la télé.
3. (vendre)   Ne perdez pas votre billet.

4. (choisir)   Prenez une de ces chemises.
5. (croire)   Ne racontez pas cette histoire.
6. (dire)   Expliquez-nous son point de vue.
7. (chercher)   Faites le travail.
8. (envoyer)   Ouvre la lettre.
9. (manger)   Ne cours pas si vite, mon enfant.
10. (traduire)   Lisons la phrase.

REFLEXIVE VERBS

Je **me lève** le matin a sept heures.

Nous **nous lavons**.

Mes frères **se brossent** les dents.

1. In a reflexive verb, the action is performed by the subject upon itself. Thus, the subject and the object pronoun refer to the same person(s): he hurt himself; we will enjoy ourselves.

se laver	to wash oneself
Present Indicative	
je me lave	I wash myself
tu te laves	you wash yourself
il se lave	he washes himself
elle se lave	she washes herself
nous nous lavons	we wash ourselves
vous vous lavez	you wash yourselves
ils se lavent	they (m.) wash themselves
elles se lavent	they (f.) wash themselves
s'amuser	to enjoy oneself

Imperatives:	
Affirmative	
Amuse-toi.	Enjoy yourself.
Amusez-vous.	Enjoy yourself(-selves).
Amusons-nous.	Let's enjoy ourselves.
Negative	
Ne t'amuses pas.	Do not enjoy yourself.
Ne vous amusez pas.	Don't enjoy yourself(-selves).
Ne nous amusons pas.	Let's not enjoy ourselves.

Note: A verb that is reflexive in French need not be reflexive in English.

Vous vous trompez.	You are mistaken.
Qu'est-ce qui se passe?	What's happening?

2. Reflexive verbs used in the plural may show reciprocal force, that is, mutual action of two parts of the subject on each other.

Nous **nous aidons**.	We help one another.
Ils ne **s'écrivent** pas.	They don't write to each other.

3. Common Reflexive Verbs

s'amuser, to enjoy oneself, have a good time
s'appeler, to be called
s'arrêter, to stop
s'asseoir, to sit (down)
se battre, to fight
se blesser, to hurt oneself, get hurt
se brosser, to brush oneself
se coucher, to lie down, go to bed, set
se dépécher, to hurry
se déshabiller, to get undressed
s'en aller, to go away
s'endormir, to fall asleep
s'ennuyer, to get bored
se fâcher, to get angry
s'habiller, to dress (oneself), get dressed
se laver, to wash (oneself), get washed
se lever, to get up, rise
se marier, to marry, get married
se passer, to happen
se plaindre, to complain
se porter, to feel (of health)
se promener, to take a walk
se rappeler, to recall, remember
se raser, to shave (oneself)
se reposer, to rest
se réveiller, to wake up
se sentir, to feel
se souvenir de, to remember
se taire, to be silent, keep quiet
se tromper, to be mistaken, make a mistake
se trouver, to be, be situated

Exercise 26

Give the correct form of the present.

1. (se lever) Les étudiants _____ de bonne heure.
2. (se réveiller) _____ -ils avant vous?
3. (se coucher) Je _____ quand j'ai sommeil.
4. (se porter) Il _____ comme le Pont Neuf.
5. (se dépécher) Pourquoi _____ -elles?
6. (se promener) Qui _____ devant ce batiment?
7. (s'habiller) Nous _____ pour la soirée.
8. (s'appeler) Comment _____ vos amis?
9. (se trouver) Vous _____ à la place de l'Opera.
10. (s'ennuyer) On ne _____ pas chez lui.

Exercise 27

Complete the sentences in French.

1. I usually wake up before nine. D'habitude, _____ avant neuf heures.
2. I do not remember your address. _____ votre adresse.
3. I take a walk every evening. _____ tous les soirs.
4. Do not brush yourself in the living room. ____ dans la salle de séjour.
5. Is she feeling better? _____ mieux?
6. I do not want to get up. Je ne veux pas _____
7. Let's hurry to get there. _____ pour y arriver.
8. I'm lying down because I'm tired. _____ si je suis fatigué.
9. Get washed at once! _____ tout de suite!
10. They are going to get hurt if they stay there. _____ s'ils y restent.

Exercise 28

Use a complete sentence in French to ask the following questions to your neighbor.

1. at what time he (she) gets up in the morning
2. if he (she) washes quickly
3. why he (she) is hurrying
4. what his (her) father's name is
5. where New York is situated
6. when he (she) is going to rest
7. if he (she) falls asleep early
8. how his (her) mother is feeling
9. if he (she) gets bored easily
10. if he (she) is mistaken

Exercise 29

Complete the sentences in English.

1. Je me trouve devant le magasin. ____ in front of the department store.
2. Je crois que vous vous trompez. I think _____.
3. Les étudiants, se levent-ils avant six heures? _____ before six?
4. Ne s'amusent-ils pas le weekend? _____ on weekends?

5. Nous nous réveillons a sept heures. _____ at seven.

6. Tu te brosses les cheveux. You _____.

7. Je ne m'ennuie pas a Paris _____ in Paris.

8. Ils se lavent avant de manger _____ before eating.

9. Elles ne se depechent jamais. They never _____.

10. Tout à coup, le professeur se fâche. Suddenly, _____.

11. Ne vous portez-vous pas bien? _____ well?

12. La malade se promene quand il fait beau. _____ when it is nice.

13. Je me rase avec de l'eau froid. I_____ with cold water

14. Elle se lave la figure. She _____ her face.

15. Ils se brosse les dents. They_____ their teeths.

Exercise 30   Repeat each sentence by replacing the words in italics by the correct form of the expression in parenthesis.

1. Nous *travaillons dur* ce matin-là. (s'amuser bien)

2. Nous allons *essayer nos nouvelles lunettes*. (se brosser les dents)

3. *Courront*-ils autour du lac? (se promener)

4. Non, nous *n'habitons pas au cinquième étage*. (s'appeler Durand)

5. *Attends* ici, mon petit. (se coucher)

6. Elles *sont plus contentes*. (se sentir mieux)

7. Attention! Ne *tombez* pas. (se blesser)

8. J'*écoute la radio* a sept heures chaque jour. (s'habiller)

9. *Mange les légumes,* Pierre (se laver)

10. *Partons* vers huit heures. (se lever)

THE PASSE COMPOSE

La souris **a mangé** le fromage.

Le chat **a guetté** la souris.

Le garçon **a chassé** le chat.

La jeune mère **a fessé** le garçon.

1. The passé composé (past indefinite) of most verbs is formed by combining the present tense of avoir and the past participle of the verb. (La souris **a mangé** le fromage.) **"A"** is the present tense of the verb avoir and serves as an auxiliary to the past participle **"mangé"** to denote an action that took place in the past. The past participle by itself does not convey the past meaning.

The auxiliary verb must be used with the past participle to express a past meaning. It is the same principle for transitive verbs — verbs that are followed directly by a noun phrase without an intervening preposition, that is, verbs that can take a direct object.

A. Past participles of -er verbs are formed by dropping the infinitive ending (-er) and adding -é.

chanter = to sing	(chanté = sung)
J'ai chanté	nous avons chanté
tu as chanté	vous avez chanté
il a chanté	ils ont chanté
elle a chanté	elles ont chanté

B. Past participles of -ir verbs are formed by dropping the infinitive ending (-ir) and adding -i.

obéir = to obey	(obéi = obeyed)
j'ai obéi	nous avons obéi
tu as obéi	vous avez obéi
il a obéi	ils ont obéi
elle a obéi	elles ont obéi

C. Past participles of -re verbs are formed by dropping the infinitive ending (-re) and adding -u.

répondre = to answer	(répondu = answered)
jai répondu	nous avons répondu
tu as répondu	vous avez répondu
il a répondu	ils ont répondu
elle a répondu	elles ont répondu

D. Past participles are derived from verbs, but are not used as verbs since they do not have tense or personnel endings.

1. The past participles of all -er verbs end in -é.

Infinitive	Past Participle
chanter to sing	chanté sung
parler to speak	parlé spoken
arriver to arrive	arrivé arrived
aller to go	allé gone

Note: The irregular verbs **être** and **naître** also have past participles ending in -é.

Infinitive	Past Participle
être to be	été been
naître to be born	né (been) born

2. The past participles of regular -ir verbs and many irregular verbs ending in -ir end in -i.

Infinitive	Past Participle
choisir to choose	choisi chosen
grandir to grow	grandi grown
sortir to go out	sorti gone out
dormir to sleep	dormi slept
cueillir to gather/pick	cueilli gathered/picked
faillir to almost	failli almost

Note: The past participles of the verbs **rire** and **suivre** and all their compounds also end in **-i**.

Infinitive	Past Participle
rire to laugh	ri laughed
sourire to smile	souri smiled
suivre to follow	suivi followed
poursuivre to pursue	poursuivi pursued

3. Many verbs have past participles ending in **-u**. All regular **-re** verbs and most irregular verbs have past participles ending in **-u**.

Infinitive	Past Participle
apparaître to appear	apparu appeared
avoir to have	eu had
apercevoir to notice	aperçu noticed
boire to drink	bu drunk
connaître to know	connu known (about)
concevoir to conceive	conçu conceived
décevoir to disappoint	déçu disappointed
émouvoir to move/touch	emu moved/touched
devoir to owe/ought to/must	du owed/had to
falloir to be necessary	fallu been necessary
percevoir to perceive	perçu perceived
plaire to please	plu pleased
pouvoir to be able/can	pu been able
savoir to know	su known (as fact)
valoir to be worth	valu valued
vouloir to want/wish	voulu wanted/wished

Note: The infinitive stem of these verbs is always shortened. Irregular verbs whose infinitives end in **-oudre** have irregular past participle stems and the **-u** ending.

Infinitive	Past Participle
résoudre to resolve	resolu resolved
moudre to grind	moulu ground
coudre to sew	cousu sewn

4. The past participles of a few irregular verbs ending in **-ir** and **-ire** and their compounds end in **-u**.

Infinitive	Past Participle
courir to run	couru run
devenir to become	devenu become
élire to elect	élu elected
lire to read	lu read
parcourir to run through	parcouru run through
retenir to retain	retenu retained
tenir to hold, grasp	tenu held/grasped
venir to come	venu come

5. Some irregular verbs have past participles ending in consonants. The irregular verbs **prendre**, **mettre**, **asseoir**, their compounds, and verbs ending in **-quérir** have past participles ending in **-is**.

The infinitive stem is shortened.

Infinitive	Past Participle
acquérir to acquire	acquis acquired
s'asseoir to sit down	assis sat down
commettre to commit	commis commited
comprendre to understand	compris understood
conquérir to conquer	conquis conquered
prendre to take	pris taken

6. Verbs whose infinitives end in **-frir** or **-vrir** have past participles ending in **-ert**.

Infinitive	Past Participle
couvrir to cover	couvert covered
offrir to offer	offert offered
ouvrir to open	ouvert opened
souffrir to suffer	souffert suffered

7. The common irregular verbs **faire**, **dire**, and **écrire**, their compounds, and all verbs ending in **-indre** and **-uire** have past participles which are identical to their third, person, singular present tense form.

Present Tense Infinitive	3rd Person, Singular Past Participle
conduire to drive	il conduit conduit driven
craindre to fear	il craint craint feared
décrire to describe	il décrit décrit described
dire to say	il dit dit said
écrire to write	il écrit écrit written
faire to do, make	il fait fait done, made
joindre to join	il joint joint joined
peindre to paint	il peint peint painted
produire to produce	il produit produit/produced

Note: The past participle of mourir, to die, is mort, died/dead.

Remember: A past participle cannot be used alone as the verb in the sentence. A verb has personal endings and a specific tense. (A participle has neither).

E. A past participle can be used as an adjective when it modifies a noun. Then, it follows the noun and agrees with it in gender and number.

Les feuilles mortes ...   The dead leaves ...

2. Passive sentences:

A. In a passive sentence, the direct object of a transitive verb becomes the subject of the sentence. Only transitive verbs can be used passively.

Les garçons lavent les voitures.
The boys wash the cars.

Les voitures sont lavées par les garçons.
The cars are washed by the boys.

B. A passive sentence is formed with the appropriate person and tense of être plus the past participle of the main verb. In a passive sentence, the past participle is an adjective and agrees in gender and number with the subject of the sentence.

On apprend la leçon.   They learn the lesson.
La leçon est apprise.   The lesson is learned.

Note: A passive sentence is not always a past tense sentence. The verb **être** indicates the tense of the sentence.

Les robes sont mouillées par la tempette de pluie.
The dresses are wet from the rainstorm. (present)

Hier, les robes ont été mouillées par la tempette de pluie. (past)
Yesterday, the dresses got wet from the rainstorm.

3. The following irregular verbs and verbs conjugated like them have irregular past participles:

asseoir, assis	**mettre**, mis
avoir, eu	**ouvrir**, ouvert
boire, bu	**plaire**, plu
conduire, conduit	**pleuvoir**, plu
connaître, connu	**pouvoir**, pu
courir, couru	**prendre**, pris
craindre, craint	**recevoir**, reçu
croire, cru	**rire**, ri
devoir, du (f.-due; pl.-dus, dues)	**savoir**, su
	suivre, suivi
dire, dit	**taire**, tu
écrire, écrit	**tenir**, tenu
être, été	**valoir**, valu
faire, fait	**vivre**, vécu
falloir, fallu	**voir**, vu
lire, lu	**vouloir**, voulu

4. Sixteen common verbs are conjugated with **être**, instead of avoir in the passé composé. In such cases, the past participle must agree with the subject in number and gender. For example, the past participle, "**parti**" of the verb, "**partir**" has four forms: masculine, singular = **parti**; feminine, singular = **partie**; masculine, plural = **partis**; feminine, plural = **parties**.

partir, to leave   (parti, ie, is, ies = left)

Masculine Subjects	Feminine Subjects
je suis parti	je suis partie
tu es parti	tu es partie
il est parti	elle est partie
nous sommes partis	nous sommes parties
vous êtes parti(s)	vous êtes partie(s)
ils sont partis	elles sont parties

VERBS CONJUGATED WITH ETRE IN THE PASSÉ COMPOSÉ

Infinitive	Past Participle
aller, to go	allé, -é, -s, -és
venir, to come	venu, -e, -s, -es
arriver, to arrive	arrivé, -é, -s,-és
partir, to leave, go away	parti, -e, -s, -es
entrer, to go/come in, enter	entré, -e, -s, -es
sortir, to go out, leave	sorti, -e, -s, -es
monter, to go/come up	monté, -e, -s, -es
descendre, to go/come down	descendu,-e,-s,-es
revenir, to come back, return	revenu, -e, -s,-es
retourner, to go back, return	retourné,-é,-s,-és
rentrer, to go back in	rentré, -é, -s,-és
tomber, to fall	tombé, -é, -s, -és
rester, to remain, stay	resté, -é, -s, -és
devenir, to become	devenu, -e, -s,-es
naître, to be born	né, -é, -s, -és
mourir, to die	mort, -e, -s, -es

Remember: Like adjectives, past participles of verbs conjugated with être agree in number and gender with the subject.

Quand sont-ils sortis?	When did they go out?
Sa femme est née en Afrique.	His wife was born in Africa.

Notes: In the passé composé, the present tense of the auxiliary verb (**avoir** or **être**) is conjugated as the main verb, while the past participle accompanying it conveys the action. Thus,

a. In the negative, the auxiliary verb is made negative.

Elles ne sont pas venues.	They didn't come.

b - In the interrogative, the auxiliary verb is inverted.

A-t-il plu hier?	Did it rain yesterday?

5. All reflexive verbs are conjugated with être in the passé composé.
   se laver, to wash oneself

je me suis lavé(e)	nous nous sommes lavé(e)s
tu t'es lavé(e)	vous vous êtes lavé(e)(s)
il s'est lavé	ils se sont lavés
elle s'est lavée	elles se sont lavées

6. Translation of the passé composé:

A. The passé composé is often translated into English by a simple one word past tense.

Monsieur Dupont a mangé du poulet hier.
Mr. Dupont ate chicken yesterday.

Le weekend dernier j'ai vu un beau film.
Last weekend I saw a beatiful film.

B. The passé composé may be also translated in English by the present perfect tense (has or have + the past participle)if the event has taken place recently.

Les garçons ont lavé les voitures.
The boys have washed the cars.

7. Use of the passé composé:

The passé composé always refers to a situation or turn of events that took place in the past. It is used to express completed action.

Jean est arrivé a New York hier soir à 18 heures.
Jean arrived in New York last night at 6 o'clock.

(This sentence implies that Jean was not in New York before that time.)

Jean a ouvert la porte de l'appartement, et il est entré a l'interieur.
Jean opened the appartment door and went inside.

(Here, there are two events, one after the other.)

Note: The passé composé also describes a series of repeated, but not continuous, actions in the past.

Le train s'est arrêté plusieurs fois.
The train stopped several times.

8. Use of the pronouns in the passé composé:

A. All personal object pronouns and **y** and **en** precede avoir in the passé composé.

Je lui ai donné l'argent.
I gave him the money.

Les cravates? Il me les a vendues.
The neckties? He sold them to me.

Les pommes? J'en ai mangé deux.
The apples? I have eaten two of them.

9. Agreement of the past participle in the passé composé:

A. When a direct object precedes the past participle, the past participle agrees with the direct object in number and gender. (The past participle modifies the direct object.)

Quelle chemise a-t-il choisie?   What shirt has he chosen?

Les fleurs que nous avons achetées sont fanées.
The flowers that we have bought are withered.

B. In the passé composé, when the preceding direct object is a pronoun, the past participle must agree with it in number and gender.

La viande? Monsieur Dupont l'a cuisinée.
The meat? Mr. Dupont has cooked it.

Le pain? Madame Dupont l'a mangé.
The bread? Mrs. Dupont has eaten it.

NOTE: A past participle does not agree with an indirect object or with a direct object that follows a verb.

Il nous a écrit une longue lettre.   He wrote us a long letter.

(Nous is an indirect object of the verb **écrit**. Therefore, the past participle is unchanged. There is no agreement.)

Les pommes? J'en ai mangé deux. The apples? I have eaten two.

(**En** is the indirect object pronoun, replacing "**pommes**," a feminine plural noun. Therefore, the past participle remains unchanged. There is no agreement.)

Exercise 31

Complete each sentence with the correct form of the past participle.

1. (laisser) Son grand-père lui a _____ une jolie maison.
2. (savoir) Nous n'avons pas _____ la date.
3. (venir) Elle est _____ nous voir.
4. (dormir) J'ai _____ pendant huit heures.
5. (taire) En voyant sa femme, le mari s'est _____.
6. (défendre) L'armée a-t-elle _____ la patrie?
7. (retourner) Les voyageurs sont _____ au Mexique.
8. (ravir) Cela m'a _____ .
9. (asseoir) Il s'est _____ devant la classe.
10. (pouvoir) N'ont-ils pas _____ y arriver à l'heure?

Exercise 32

Translate the following sentences in English:

1. Ne sont-ils pas revenus du Canada?
2. Nous sommes restés dans la salle d'attente.
3. La cuisine lui a plu.
4. J'en ai eu assez.
5. Vous êtes arrive à temps.

6. Elle est devenue infirmière.
7. N'a-t-il pas plu hier soir?
8. Il n'a pas voulu entrer tout seul.
9. Le paysan a vécu longtemps.
10. As-tu apporte ta carte de crédit?

Exercise 33

Write the following in the passé composé:

1. Je dois partir toute de suite.
2. Epouse-t-il son amie d'enfance?
3. Nous saisissons l'occasion de lui envoyer une note.
4. Que craignez-vous?
5. Sa grande-mère meurt l'année dernière.
6. Connaissez-vous sa nouvelle adresse?
7. Les enfants tombent?
8. Il faut écrire la lettre en vitesse.
9. La mère conduit son fils au musée.
10. Le peintre découvre sa nouvelle peinture.
11. Elles font un voyage en Californie.
12. Bien entendu, nous arrivons en retard.
13. Cette église vaut une visite.
14. Les plantes ne meurent pas.
15. A quelle heure rentrez-vous, Marie?

Exercise 34

Translate into French:

1. Where did they (f.) go?
2. They went to Paris.
3. I had his plane ticket.
4. Who came into the restaurant?
5. I put the car keys on the desk.
6. Which book did you (fam.) take?
7. We opened the window.
8. How much have they understood?
9. How did he do it?
10. When did they go down to the café?
11. Why didn't you run last night?
12. At what time did Monsieur Dupont go out?
13. Why didn't they (f.) go to the movies?
14. We didn't see the sign.
15. Whom did the priest bless?

Exercise 35

Answer the following questions in French:

1. Qu'est-ce que vous avez pris ce matin pour le petit déjeuner?
2. Qui a écrit les phrases sue cette feuille de papier?
3. Est-ce que la nuit est déjà tombée?
4. As-tu suivi les nouvelles à la télé?
5. Quand ont-ils reçu l'argent?
6. Avez-vous couvert le lit?
7. Est-ce que vous êtes sorti hier soir?
8. Dans quel pays êtes-vous né(e)?
9. A quelle heure as-tu quitté la maison ce matin?
10. A-t-on ri quand le comédien a raconté une histoire amusante?

THE IMPERFECT TENSE

La souris **mangeait** le fromage.
Le chat **guettait** la souris.
Le garçon **chassait** le chat.
La jeune mère **fessait** le garçon.

1. The imperfect tense is used for two kinds of past action: continous and repeated or habitual. The imperfect is also used to set the background of a story. It is frequently translated in English as *"was/were...ing"* or *"used to ..."*

Il **pleuvait** ce soir là.
Il was raining that night.

Elle **dormait** et je lisais.
She was sleeping and I was reading.

L'été passé, nous **allions** souvent à la plage.
Last summer, we used to go to the beach often.

2. Forms of the Imperfect Tense:

A. The imperfect (l'imparfait) indicative of regular verbs is formed by dropping the -ons from the first person, plural ("nous" form) of the present tense and adding the personal endings: -ais, -ais, -ait, -ions, -iez, -aient.

travailler: je travaillais, tu travaillais, il/elle/on travaillait, nous travaillions, vous travailliez, ils/elles travaillaient

finir: je finissais le travail, tu finissais, il/elle/on finissait, nous finis-
sions, vous finissiez, ils/elles finissaient

attendre: j'attendais la reponse , tu attendais, il/elle/on attendait, nous
attendions, vous attendiez, ils/elles attendaient

B. The imperfect of irregular verbs, with few exceptions, is formed in the same way. For example:

Infinitive	First Person	Plural Imperfect
("nous" form) of Present Tense		
boire	buvons	je buvais
craindre	craignons	je craignais
faire	faisons	je faisais
voir	voyons	je voyais

C. The imperfect tense forms of être and the impersonal verbs are as follows:

être: j'étais, tu étais, il/elle/on était, nous étions, vous étiez, ils/elles étaient

falloir: il fallait   **pleuvoir**: il pleuvait

D. Verbs that end in **-ions** in the present indicative have forms ending in **-iions** and **-iiez** in the imperfect:

étudier: nous étudiions, vous étudiiez

rire: nous riions, vous riiez.

Exercise 36

Answer the following questions in complete sentences in French:

1. Où étais-tu pendant qu'il neigeait?
2. Quand vous étiez jeune, obeissiez-vous a votre père?
3. Quelle roman lisaient les étudiants?
4. Que faisaient-ils pendant que vous travailliez?
5. Où alliez-vous, hier soir ?
6. Y avait-il beaucoup de gens dans le théâtre?
7. Pouvait-on croire tout ce que vous racontiez?
8. Quel temps faisait-il ce matin lorsque vous avez quitté la maison?
9. Pourquoi dormiez-vous?
10. Qu'est-ce que tu faisais pendant que j'écivais la lettre?

Exercise 37

Translate into English:

1. Il était fois.
2. Elle ne pouvait pas revenir a l'heure.
3. Nous suivions toujours ses conseils de notre avocat.
4. Ecrivait-il une deuxieme roman?
5. Ils avaient un beau magnétophone.
6. Fallait-il boire cette vieille bouteille de vin?
7. Il perdait souvent son portefeuille.
8. Ce pays produisait beaucoup de ble.
9. Nous causions quand le professeur est arrivé.
10. Mme. Dupont voulait faire la connaissance de cette dame?

Exercise 38	Write in the Imperfect Tense:

1. Il met la lettre dans la boite à lettre.
2. N'a-t-il pas un nouveau stylo?
3. Les étudiants causent beaucoup.
4. Etudiez-vous tout seul?
5. Nous recevons la réponse de notre dernière lettre.
6. Ne connais-tu pas cette rue?
7. Qu'est-ce que tu fais?
8. Je la tiens dans mes bras.
9. Monsieur Dupont porte un belle cravate en soie.
10. Ils boit de l'eau mineral.

Exercise 39	Translate into French:

1. they were waiting
2. was she reading?
3. you used to owe
4. we used to laugh
5. who used to send?
6. we were choosing
7. you (fam.) used to see
8. he was hot translating
9. weren't they learning?
10. I was not succeeding

Exercise 40	Translate the English words into French:

1. You used to help votre mari.
2. Tout le monde knew qu'ils étaient fiancés.
3. They were accomplishing beaucoup.
4. A qui were you writing?
5. Chaque nuit one could voir les etoiles dans le ciel.
6. We believed qu'elle avait raison.
7. Le matin they used to run à l'ecole.
8. Quelle heure was it?
9. A l'âge de quinze ans, she would blush fréquemment.
10. It was not raining quand nous sommes revenus.

CONTRASTING USES OF PAST TENSE FORMS

Le Passé Composé v. L'imparfait

La souris **mangeait** le fromage quand le chat **est arrivé**.

La souris **mangeait** le fromage et le chat **guettait** la souris.

Le garçon **a chassé** le chat et la mère **a fessé** le garçon.

1. Whether the passé composé or the imparfait is used depends on the event or the situation. The imperfect tense is used to describe an action that was taking place and continuing to take place in the past when something else happened. The latter action must be expressed in the passé composé. However, if the two actions occurred simultaneously, the two actions must be expressed in the same tense. The imperfect is sometimes used to describe the background setting of an event in the passé composé. While the imperfect tense relates the condition, or the state of actions that were going on, the passé composé relates the completed actions of the events; it tells what happened.

A. Use the passé composé to describe an event whose entire duration (including its beginning) falls within the past time frame spoken about.

Quand il a ouvert l'enveloppe, la lettre est tombée.
When he opened the envelope, the letter fell out.

(Two events, each begin and end during the time under consideration.)

B. Use the imparfait to describe an event which was already under way at the past moment spoken about.

Il dormait pendant que je jouais au tennis.
He was sleeping while I was playing tennis.

(Two simultaneous occurrences, neither necessarily beginning at the moment under consideration.)

C. Use the passé composé to say that something new took place or that the situation changed. Otherwise, use the imparfait.

Les étudiants causaient quand le professeur est entré.
The audience was applauding when the actor entered.

(Continuing state of affairs which began at some unspecified time before the moment under consideration, followed by a new event which began at that moment.)

Il a neigé hier.   It snowed yesterday.
(It began and stopped snowing yesterday.)
Il neigeait hier.   It was snowing yesterday.
(It was snowing yesterday, but it is not known when it began.)

D. In French the expressions **venir de + infinitive** (to have just done something) and **aller + infinitive** (to go to do) indicate the immediate past or future. Do not use these expressions in the passé composé. **Venir** and **aller** are expressed in the imparfait when a past tense is required.

J'allais te demander ce que tu voulais dire.
I was going to ask you what you meant.

Il venait de terminer son travail quand je l'ai rencontré.
He had just finished his work when I met him.

Exercise 41

Write the following sentences either in the passé composé or the imperfect, as required.

Example: Les étudiants causent quand le prof rentre.
Les étudiants causaient quand le prof. es rentré.

1. Je parle au moment elles rentrent.
2. Le chien aboie quand des visiteurs arrivent.
3. Ils lisent et nous regardons la télé.
4. Je dors et puis le téléphone sonne.
5. Il fait froid quand il commence a neiger.
6. La dame regarde le titre du livre que je lis.
7. Quand ils partent je mange le petit dejeuner
8. Comme il fait beau nous allons a la pêche.
9. Je mange et je regarde la télé.
10. Madame Dupont nettoie la chambre, son fils dort.

Exercise 42

Tell why the following people did the actions indicated.

Example: Pierre/prendre/des medicaments/ avoir/un rhume/
Pierre a pris des médicaments parce qu'il avait un rhume.

1. Jean/porter/un parapluie/ pleuvoir/
2. Monsieur Dupont/boire de la bierre/soif
3. Elle/se dépêcher/être en retard
4. L'enfant/aller chez le médecin/être malade
5. Il/ouvrir la fenêtre/avoir chaud
6. Je/visiter mon ami/devoir/un livre
7. Renée/rester à la maison/ne se sentir pas bien
8. je/aller à la gare/mes amis/ y attendre
9. Faire chaud/elle/aller à la plage
10. Elle/rougir/le garçon/ la regarder

Exercise 43

Write the following sentences either in the passé composé or the imperfect, as required.

C'est le trois janvier. Il est sept heures du matin. Il fait froid. Je vais a l'école pour la première fois après les vacances de Noël. Je prends le métro. Il ne marche pas bien. Il fait chaud à l'intérieur des wagons. Les gens se bousculent. Le train s'arrête plusieurs fois. Je change de train. Je prends un autre train. Je fais la correspondance à Manhattan. Malgrés tous mes efforts j'arrive quand même à l'école en retard. Je passe une journée désagreable.

THE FUTURE TENSE

La souris **mangera** le fromage.

Le chat **guettera** la souris.

Le garçon **chassera** le chat.

La jeune mère **fessera** le garçon.

1. In formal French the future is indicated by adding future tense endings to the infinitive or future stem of a verb.

2. Formation of the future tense: To form the future tense of all but a few irregular verbs, add the following endings to the complete infinitive ("**-re**" verbs drop the final "**-e**"): **-ai, -as, -a, -ons, -ez, -ont.**

travailler

je travaillerai	nous travillerons
tu travailleras	vous travaillerez
il/elle/on travaillera	ils/elles travailleront

finir

je finirai	nous finirons
tu finiras	vous finirez
il/elle/on finira	ils/elles finiront

attendre

j'attendrai	nous attendrons
tu attendras	vous attendrez
il/elle/on attendra	ils/elles attendront

3. The future tense of some irregular verbs: Some verbs have an irregular stem in the future. They are:

Infinitive	Future Stem	Future
aller	ir-	j'irai
s'asseoir	assier-	je m'assierai (je m'assoirai)
avoir	aur-	j'aurai
courir	courr-	je courrai
cueillir	cueiller-	je cueillerai
devoir	devr-	je devrai
envoyer	enverr-	j'enverrai
être	ser-	je serai
faire	fer-	je ferai
falloir	faudr-	il faudra
mourir	mourr-	je mourrai
pleuvoir	pleuvr-	il pleuvrai
pouvoir	pourr-	je pourrai
recevoir	recevr-	je recevrai

savoir	saur-	je saurai
tenir	tiendr-	je tiendrai
valoir	vaudr-	je vaudrai
venir	viendr-	je viendrai
voir	verr-	je verrai
vouloir	voudr-	je voudrai

4. Uses of the future tense:

A. Use the future tense to express what will take place in the future.

Il y aura un examen la semaine prochaine.
There will be an exam next week.

Nous visterons Paris cet été.
We will visit Paris this summer.

B. Use the future tense in a subordinate clause introduced by one of the following time conjunctions when the verb of the subordinate clause implies or refers to a future action, event or situation.

quand (when); lorsque (when); dès que (as soon as);
tant que (as long as); aussitôt que (as soon as);
pendant que (while); après (after).
Je bois un verre d'eau quand j'ai soif.
I drink a glass of water when I am thirsty.
(Habitual situation, the present is used.)
Quand ils arriveront, on se mettra à table.
When they (will) arrive, we will sit down at the table.
Lorsque je verrai le directeur, je lui donnerai la lettre.
When I (will) see the principal, I will give him the letter.

Exercise 44

Complete each sentence by following the model in the example.

Example: Il ne va pas danser; il ne dansera pas.

1. Vous allez savoir sa reponse; _____
2. Ils vont recevoir le candidat; _____
3. Tu vas courir avec moi; _____
4. Colette ne va pas être en retard; _____
5. Nous n'allons pas avoir tort; _____
6. Elle va lui envoyer une carte postale; _____
7. Je vais aller en France; _____
8. Elles vont faire des achats; _____
9. Nous allons voir la pièce; _____
10. Les acteurs ne vont pas jouer; _____

Exercise 45 Write in the future:

1. Dans quel pays demeure-t-il?
2. Vous me devez mille francs.
3. Savons-nous son opinion?
4. Il y a plusieurs statues dans le village.
5. Ils voient les étoiles du drapeau.
6. Quand finis-tu le roman?
7. Elle vous invite à la soirée.
8. Je lis le conte.
9. Cela lui fait plaisir.
10. Il ne pleut pas.
11. Ne vont-ils pas en ville?
12. Quel collège choisissent-ils?
13. Il prend le petit déjeuner à huit heures.
14. Répondez-vous à la question?
15. Qui coupe la viande?

Exercise 46 Write the verbs in parentheses in the future tense:

1. (être) Pourquoi _____ -vous absent demain?
2. (accompagner) Qui vous _____ à la gare?
3. (envoyer) Elles _____ leurs billets aujourd'hui.
4. (pouvoir) Je ne _____ pas le terminer.
5. (vendre) Ils ne _____ pas leur appartement.
6. (faire) Que _____ -nous ce soir?
7. (vouloir) Je _____ voir la chambre.
8. (guerir) Le médecin _____ le garçon.
9. (avoir) Quand _____ -vous la nouvelle voiture?
10. (falloir) Il _____ partir à sept heures du matin.

Exercise 47 Translate into French.

1. I shall ask for a sandwish and a beer.
2. Will I see you this weekend?
3. We shall not have enough money for the trip.
4. Who will return my pen?
5. Will they come to see us on Sunday?
6. She will fill your glass.
7. Will you send Mr. Dupont the silk ties?
8. They will never do the work on time.
9. Won't the ladies be ready at noon?
10. When will I arrive in Paris?

THE PRESENT CONDITIONAL TENSE

La souris **mangerait** le fromage.

Le chat **guétterait** la souris.

Le garçon **chasserait** le chat.

La jeune mère **fesserait** garçon.

1. The conditional is not associated with any particular time or tense. Therefore, it may be used in both present and past time. The meaning of the conditional depends upon the context in which it is used.

2. Formation of the present conditional: To form the present conditional of regular verbs, add the imperfect (imparfait) tense endings to the entire infinitive. ("**-re**" verbs drop the final "**-e**".)

Singular	Plural
-ais	**-ions**
-ais	**-iez**
-ait	**-aient**
travailler	
je travaillerais	nous travaillerions
tu travaillerais	vous travailleriez
il/elle/on travaillerait	ils/elles travailleraient
finir	
je finirais	nous finirions
tu finirais	vous finiriez
il/elle/on finirait	ils/elles finiraient
attendre	
j'attendais	nous attendrions
tu attendrais	vous attendriez
il/elle/on attendrait	ils/elles attendraient

Infinitive	Conditional	
préférer	je préfererais	I would prefer
établir	tu établirais	you would establish
rompre	il romprait	he would break
danser	nous danserions	we would dance
comprendre	vous comprendriez	you would understand
finir	ils finiraient	they would finish

3. Verbs that have an irregular stem in the future tense have the same stem in the conditional. Add the imperfect (imparfait) tense endings to the irregular future stems to form the present conditional.

Infinitive	Conditional	
aller	j'irais	I would go
apercevoir	j'apercevrais	I would perceive
s'asseoir	tu t'assierai	you would sit down
avoir	il aurait	he would have
courir	nous courrions	we would run
accueillir	vous accueilleriez	you would welcome
devoir	ils devraient	they ought to/should

Note: Although *"should"* is sometimes used to translate the conditional, in American English *"should"* usually means *"ought to"*. The conditional "would" is used to translate the present conditional in French.

J'aurais peur d'y aller tout seul.
I would be afraid to go there all alone.

Nous devrions respecter nos parents.
We should/ought to respect our parents.

Infinitive	Conditional	
être	je serais	I would be
faire	tu ferais	you would do
falloir	il faudrait	it would be necessary
mourir	nous mourrions	we would die
pleuvoir	il pleuvrait	it would rain
pouvoir	vous pourriez	you would be able/could
recevoir	ils recevraient	they would receive
savoir	je saurais	I would know
tenir	tu tiendrais	you would hold
venir	elle viendrait	she would come
voir	nous verrions	we would see
vouloir	vous voudriez	you would want

Note: In some English sentences *"would"* means *"used to."* In those cases, *"would"* is translated by the imperfect (imparfait) tense in French because it implies repeated, habitual action.

We would often take walks after dinner.
Nous faisions souvent des promenades après diner.

4. Uses of the present conditional:

A. Use the present conditional tense in present time to ask a polite question or make a request.

Voudriez-vous une tasse de café?
Would you like a cup of coffee?

J'aimerais t'inviter a dîner ce soir.
I would like to invite you for dinner to night.

B. Use the present conditional tense in present time to make contrary-to-fact statements - what would happen if something imaginary were true.

S'il était malade, on appellerait le médecin.
If he were sick, we would call the doctor.

J'irais à la fête s'ils m'invitaient.
I would go to the party if they invited me.

Note: Even though the imaginary situation is expressed in the imperfect (imparfait) tense, it is referring to time in the present or future.

C. Use the present conditional tense in past narration to tell about things that were supposed to happen later. It is the future in a narration in the past.

Il a dit qu'il aurait le devoir le lendemain.
He said he would have the homework the next day.

Le météo a annoncé qu'il pleuvrait ce soir.
The meteorologist annonced that it would rain tonight.

5. In addition to the usual translation, certain conditional forms frequently have other translations.

je devrais = I ought/should (in the sense of obligation)
je pourrais = I could
je voudrais = I would like

Exercise 48

Write the following sentences in the conditional:

1. (voir) Il croyait que je ne _____ pas sa bague.
2. (bâtir) Où est-ce qu'on _____ la nouvelle église?
3. (recevoir) Si je vous envoyais la lettre ce matin, quand la ____ - vous?
4. (devenir) Sa mère pensait qu'elle _____ avocate.
5. (avoir) Y _____ -il assez de café pour tout le monde?
6. (revenir) Nous ne savions pas qu'elles _____ bientôt.
7. (falloir) Pourquoi _____ -il cacher l'addition?
8. (savoir) _____ -tu reparer cette machine?
9. (devoir) Nous _____ encourager les jeunes artists.
10. (neiger) On a dit qu'il _____ ce soir.

Exercise 49

Translate into English:

1. Il n'aurait pas assez de sucre.
2. Nous vendrions la voiture.
3. Je voudrais une tasse de café, s'il vous plaît.
4. Vous devriez partir tout de suite.
5. Nous viendrions à la maison de bonne heure.

6. Que feriez-vous ce weekend?
7. Je lui enverrais une carte postale.
8. Je courrais vite à la poste.
9. Nous pourrions essayer de voir la pièce.
10. Les connaîtriez-vous?

Exercise 50

Complete the following sentences with the correct form of the conditional tense of the indicated verb.

1. Vous_____ le faire. Il faut essayer. (pouvoir)
2. Elles_____ dans l'eau, mais elle n'a pas de maillot de bain. (nager)
3. Je _____ un verre d'eau, s'il vous plaît. (vouloir)
4. Nous _____ à Paris, si nous avions de l'argent. (aller)
5. Tu _____ à table, mais le dîner n'est pas encore prêt. (asseoir)
6. Vous _____ faim bientôt. Il faut manger quelque chose. (avoir)
7. Nous _____ tous nos amis, si nous avions une grande maison. (recevoir)
8. Il _____ l'addition, mais il n'est pas la. (payer)
9. Nous _____ le devoir tout de suite, mais nous n'avons pas le livre. (faire)
10. Nous _____ de faim. Mangeons un morceau de fromage. (mourir)

Exercise 51

Replace the present tense by the conditional:

1. Nous allons au théâtre.
2. Avez-vous le temps de le faire?
3. Qui reçoit le grand prix?
4. Qu'est-ce que vous écrivez?
5. Il veut vous accompagner.
6. Ne dînent-ils pas au restaurant?
7. Pourquoi le font-ils?
8. Vous n'êtes pas impoli.
9. Nous choisis la meilleure bouteille.
10. Elle tient la tête haute.
11. Elle peut se défendre.
12. Savez-vous l'heure?
13. Que voient-ils?
14. Nous prend un bon repas.
15. Tu dois réfléchir.

Exercise 52

Translate into French the English expressions:

1. She would do it si elle pouvait.
2. Would you send la lettre par avion?
3. We would succeed si nous travaillions dur.
4. J'ai dit que I would come to see you.
5. Si je le lui disais, she would laugh.
6. Wouldn't they help le malade?
7. I should go a la Martinique si j'avais l'argent.
8. Ils savaient que we would not be mistaken.
9. Il pensait que you would see his point of view.
10. Si je portais mon costume blanc, it would rain.

THE PASSE SIMPLE

La souris **mangea** le fromage.

Le chat **guetta** la souris.

Le garçon **chassa** le chat.

La jeune mère **fessa** le garçon.

1. For most regular verbs, the forms of the passé simple (past definite) tense are formed by dropping the infinitive ending and adding the following personal endings:

A. For all "**-er**" verbs: **-ai, -as, -a, -âmes, -âtes,-èren**t.

B. For regular "**-ir**" and "**-re**" verbs: **-is, -is, -it, -îmes, -îtes, -irent**.

chanter: je chantai, tu chantas, il/elle/on chanta, nous chantâmes, vous chantâtes, ils/elles chantèrent

obéir: je obéis, tu obéis, il/elle/on obéit, nous obéîmes, vous obéîtes, ils/elles obéirent

répondre: je répondis, tu répondis, il/elle/on répondit, nous répondîmes, vous répondîtes, ils/elles répondirent

2. Irregular Verbs in the Passé Simple:

Verbs with irregular stems in the passé simple have the following endings: **-s, -s, -t, -^mes, -^tes, -rent**.

Their stems generally end in "**-i**" or "**-u**."

For example: **faire**: fis, fis, fit, fîmes, fîtes, firent

boire: bus, bus, but, bûmes, bûtes, burent

tenir: tins, tins, tint, tînmes, tîntes, tinrent

3. The following irregular verbs and verbs conjugated like them have irregular stems in the passé simple:

Infinitive	Passé Simple
s'asseoir	je m'assis
avoir	j'eus
boire	je bus
conduire	je conduisis
connaître	je connus
construire	je construisis
courir	je courus
craindre	je craignis
croire	je crus
devoir	je dus
dire	je dis
écrire	j'écrivis
être	je fus
faire	je fis
falloir	il fallut
joindre	je joignis
lire	je lus
mettre	je mis
mourir	il mourut
naître	je naquis
paraître	je parus
plaindre	je plaignis
plaire	je plus
pleuvoir	il plut
pouvoir	je pus
prendre	je pris
recevoir	je reçus
rire	je ris
savoir	je sus
suivre	je suivis
se taire	je me tus
tenir	je tins
traduire	je traduisis
valoir	je valus
venir	je vins
vivre	je vécus
voir	je vis
vouloir	je voulus

Note: The passé simple is used in historical and literary writing to express an action completed in the past. (In conversation and informal writing, such past action is expressed by the passé composé.)

Jeanne d'Arc naquît en Lorraine.
Joan of Arc was born in Lorraine.

Les Américains arrivèrent en Normandie.
The Americans arrived in Normandy.

Exercise 53

Complete each sentence with one of the following verbs: **coururent; demandai; écrivit; regardâmes; mourut; racontèrent; quittas; devinrent; chercha; fîtes.**

1. Victor Hugo _____ "Les Misérables."
2. Nous les _____ en silence.
3. On _____ l'assassin dans toutes les rues.
4. Ils _____ une histoire amusante.
5. Tu _____ ta ville pour traverser la mer.
6. Je lui _____ce qu'elle voulait.
7. La Fontaine _____ en 1695.
8. Washington et La Fayette _____ amis.
9. Vous _____ sur lui une impression trés forte.
10. Les enfants _____ plus vite.

Exercise 54

Put the italicized verbs in the style required by the conversation:

1. Ils *reussirent* à la faire.

2. Je *remarquai* sa beaute.

3. Nous *vîmes* l'ennemi.

4. Ils *burent* le vin rouge.

5. Qui lui *donna* les fleurs?

6. Les soldats *perdirent* la bataille.

7. Les nobles *firent* la guerre.

8. L'actrice *naquît* en Italie.

9. Elle *lut* le conte.

10. Je le *reconnus* immédiatement.

11. Ce soir-la, il *plut*.

12. Les feuilles *tombèrent*.

13. Il *tint* le chapeau sous le bras.

14. Il *rit* en voyant mon expression.

15. Qui *sut* le faire?

Exercise 55

Complete in the simple past (au passé simple):

1. (passer) Les semaines _____ lentement.
2. (être) L'opera "Carmen" _____ composé par Bizet.
3. (faire) Je _____ un grand effort pour ne pas rire.
4. (venir) Il _____ tard à l'ecole.
5. (prendre) Les Parisiens _____ la Bastille le 14 juillet 1789.
6. (écrire) Nous _____ des poemes.
7. (traverser) Je _____ le jardin du Luxembourg.
8. (dire) "Bonjour," _____ -elle.
9. (vouloir) Ils ne _____ pas vivre dans ce climat.
10. (avoir) Louis XIV _____ un grand ministre, Colbert.
11. (parler) L'ambassadeur _____ de paix.
12. (finir) Enfin, elles _____ leurs devoirs.
13. (traduire) Je _____ le passage difficile.
14. (partir) Le roi _____ pour son palais.
15. (voir) Ils _____ Jeanne d'Arc dans la cathédrale.

Exercise 56

Write the correct form of the simple past (passé simple).

1. craindre: elle _____
2. suivre: nous _____
3. plaire: il _____
4. ajouter: elle _____
5. courir: nous _____
6. conduire: ils _____
7. s'asseoir: je _____
8. reconnaître: il _____
9. marcher: ils _____
10. tenir: je _____
11. savoir: je _____
12. connaître: tu _____
13. traduire: qui _____ ?
14. se taire: elle _____
15. plaindre: on _____
16. pleuvoir: il _____
17. ramasser: je _____
18. aller: vous _____
19. valoir: il _____
20. construire: je _____

Exercise 57

Translate into English:

1. Tout à coup, elle ouvrit les yeux.
2. Les ouvriers recurent la nouvelle offre avec joie.
3. Ils entrerent dans la forêt.
4. Je dus rester chez moi.
5. La reine ne voulut pas accepter les réformes.
6. Le voleur mit les bijoux dans la boîte.
7. Il y eut quarante-cinq années de guerre.
8. Nous ne crûmes pas un seul mot.
9. Molière na7uit en 1633 et mourut en 1673.
10. Nous causâmes avec nos voisins.
11. Il prit son parapluie et sortit.
12. Les ennemis arrivèrent sous les murs de Paris.
13. François Ier fut un des meilleurs rois de France.

14. Ils entendirent le bruit de la foule.
15. Rouget de Lisle composa "la Marseillaise."
16. Ils aidèrent le pays à gagner son independance.
17. Pasteur fit beaucoup pour aider l'humanité.
18. Vous ne dîtes pas la verité.
19. On me conduisit dans une grande salle.
20. Napoléon donna à la France un bon systeme de lois.
21. Elle vit une enfant qui la regardait.
22. Tu ne pus pas voir tes fautes.
23. Paris devint le centre de la culture française.
24. Beaucoup de personnes apprirent à lire.
25. Au XVIe siècle on bâtit de beaux châteaux en France.

SPELLING CHANGES IN CERTAIN VERBS

Mangeons le fromage, mes amis.
Il **espère** danser le rock 'n' roll.
Madame Dupont **paiera** l'addition.

Some regular **-er** verbs change the spelling of their stems to preserve a particular sound in the infinitive.

1. Verbs ending in **-cer** change the **-c** to **-ç** before an **-a** or an **-o** to keep the soft **-c** sound of the infinitive.

prononcer, to pronounce

Present Indicative: prononce, prononces, prononce, prononçons, prononcez, prononcent

Imperfect Indicative: prononçais, prononçais, prononçait, prononcions, prononciez, prononçaient

Passé Simple: prononçai, prononças, prononça, prononçâmes, prononçâtes, prononcèrent

Some verbs whose spelling changes in this way are:

annoncer	to announce/to declare
avancer	to advance /to promote
effacer	to efface / to erase
exercer	to exercise/ to practice
lancer	to throw
menacer	to threaten
placer - remplacer	to place/ to put - to replace
renoncer	to give up

2. Verbs ending in **-ger** insert a mute **-e** between the **-g** and the **-a** or the **-o** to keep the soft **-g** sound of the infinitive.

voyager, to travel

Present Indicative: voyage, voyages, voyage, voyageons, voyagez, voyagent

Imperfect Indicative: voyageais, voyageais, voyageait, voyagions, voyagiez, voyageaient

Passé Simple: voyageai, voyageas, voyagea, voyageâmes, voyageâtes, voyagèrent

Some other verbs whose spelling changes in this way are:

arranger	to arrange
bouger	to move
changer	to change
corriger	to correct
deranger	to bother/disturb
exiger	to require
infliger	to inflict
nager	to swim
neiger	to snow
obliger	to oblige
partager	to share
plonger	to dive/ plunge
protéger	to protect
songer	to imagine
soulager	to ease

3. Verbs ending in **-yer** change **-y** to **-i** before a mute **-e**: employer, to use

Present Indicative: emploie, emploies, emploie, employons, employez, emploient

Future: emploierai, emploieras, emploiera, emploierons, emploierez, emploieront

Conditional: emploierais, emploierais, emploierait, emploierions, emploieriez, emploieraient

Some other verbs whose spelling changes in this way are:

ennuyer, to bore	noyer, to drown/to flood
essuyer, to wipe	nettoyer, to clean

Note: However, verbs ending in **-ayer** may or may not change the **-y** to **-i**. Both forms of spelling are correct.

payer, to pay   elle paye or elle paie, she pays

4. Verbs with a mute **-e** in the next to last syllable in the infinitive change the mute **-e** to **-è** when the next syllable contains another mute **-e**. (**-e** —consonant— **-er**)

mener, to lead

Present Indicative: mène, mènes, mène, menons, menez, mènent
Future: mènerai, mèneras, mènera, mènerons, mènerez, mèneront
Conditional: mènerais, mènerais, mènerait, mènerions, mèneriez, mèneraient
Some other verbs whose spelling change in this way are:

acheter, to buy	**achever**, to achieve
élever, to raise/ bring	**lever**, to raise
peser, to weigh	**emmener,** to take (someone) away

5. Two verbs with a mute **-e**, **appeler** and **jeter,** and compounds of these verbs, double the consonant instead of adding the "accent grave" when the next syllable contains another mute **-e**. (**-e** —consonant— **-er**)

appeler, to call

Present Indicative: appelle, appelles, appelle, appelons, appelez, appellent
Future: appellerai, appelleras, appellera, appellerons, appellerez, appelleront
Conditional: appellerais, appellerais, appellerait, appellerions, appelleriez, appelleraient

However: **geler**, to freeze

je gèle	nous gelons
tu gèles	vous gelez
il/elle gèle	ils/elles gèlent

6. Verbs with -e in the next to last syllable in the infinitive change the -e to -e only before the mute endings -e, -es, -ent. (-e —consonant— -er) The verb forms of the future and the conditional remain unchanged.

espérer, to hope

Present Indicative: espère, espères, espère, espérons, espérez, espèrent
Some other verbs whose speling changes in this way are:

celébrer to celebrate	**compléter** to complete
exagérer to exaggerate	**interpréter** to interpret
préférer to prefer	**posséder** to possess
protéger to protect	**répéter** to repeat
révéler to reveal	

REMEMBER:

Common **-cer** Verbs

annoncer, to announce	**lancer**, to hurl, launch
avancer, to advance; be fast (of clocks and watches)	**menacer**, to threaten
	placer, to place, set
commencer, to begin	**prononcer**,to pronounce
effacer, to erase, efface	**remplacer**, to replace

Common **-ger** Verbs

arranger, to set in order	**neiger,** to snow
ranger, to set in order	**obliger**, to oblige, compel

changer, to change   partager, to share, divide
corriger, to correct   plonger, to plunge, dive
déranger, to disturb   songer, to think
manger, to eat   voyager, to travel
nager, to swim

Common **-yer** Verbs

employer, to use   essuyer, to wipe
ennuyer, to bore   nettoyer, to clean
essayer, to try, try on   payer, to pay, pay for

Common Verbs with Mute -e in the Stem

Mute -e changes to -è: **Consonant doubles:**
acheter, to buy   appeler, to call
achever, to complete   jeter, to throw
amener, to bring, lead to   rappeler, to recall
élever, to bring up, raise
emmener, to lead away, take away
enlever, to remove, take off
geler, to freeze
lever, to raise, lift
mener, to lead, take
peser, to weigh
se promener, to take a walk

Common Verbs with **-e** in Stem

célébrer, to celebrate   préférer, to prefer
espérer, to hope   protéger to protect
posséder, to possess, own   répéter, to repeat

Exercise 58

Form present tense and future tense sentences using the subjects in the parentheses.

Example: déjeuner sur l'herbe (ils)
           Ils déjeunent sur l'herbe.
           Ils déjeuneront sur l'herbe.

1. employer un transistor (je)
2. appeler le coiffeur (vous)
3. ne pas répéter ce qu'il a dit (nous)
4. mener a la ville (tous ces chemins)
5. jeter la balle (tu)
6. préférer une maison comfortable (tout le monde)
7. corriger ce que nous avons écrit (nous)
8. ne pas enlever nos privilèges (ils)
9. nettoyer bien les escaliers (nous)
10. posséder un bon système de communication (vous)

Exercise 59

Form imperfect tense (l'imparfait) and past definite tense (passé simple) sentences using the subjects in the parenthesis.

    1. annoncer des programmes tres variés (ils)
    2. partager leur opinion (je)
    3. prononcer toutes les syllabes (nous)
    4. changer après la guerre (ces conditions)
    5. avancer de l'argent a ses fils (M. Leger)

Exercise 60

Repeat each sentence by substituting the correct form of the verb in parentheses.

    1. Elle vendrait la maison. (acheter)
    2. Je mange des croissants. (preferer)
    3. Ils mettaient la table. (lever)
    4. Regardons la phrase entière. (effacer)
    5. Voient-ils les pierres? (jeter)
    6. Elle allumera la lampe. (nettoyer)
    7. Qui m'aidera demain? (appeler)
    8. Cela m'amuse. (ennuyer)
    9. On chercherait du bois. (employer)
   10. Ses parents dansaient souvent. (voyager)

Exercise 61

Write the underlined verbs in the plural.

    1. Je jette le papier dans la corbeille.
    2. J'essaie de nager.
    3. Tu effaçais la faute.
    4. Tu n'espères pas le retrouver.
    5. Il voyagea en Afrique.
    6. Je commence à étudier.
    7. Achète des cerises.
    8. Elle corrigeait l'exercice.
    9. Nettoies-tu le tapis?
   10. Je mène la danse.

Exercise 62

Complete in French:

    1. Qui efface le tableau noir? Nous _____ le tableau noir.
    2. Jetez-vous la première balle? Non, le président la _____
    3. Employez-vous tous ces mots? Oui, je les _____
    4. Est-ce que je paie l'addition? Oui, vous la _____
    5. Qui commenca à chanter? Les messieurs _____ à chanter.
    6. Qui annonçait les nouvelles? Les _____ -vous?
    7. Esperez-vous aller en Europe? Bien entendu, j' _____ y aller.
    8. Comment vous appelez-vous? Je m' _____ Berthe.
    9. Est-ce que je nageais bien? Oui, vous _____ très bien.
   10. Achèteriez-vous ce complet? Non, nous ne l' _____ pas.

THE PRESENT SUBJUNCTIVE

1. The subjunctive (le subjonctif) is the mood of uncertainty and emotion. Verbs in the subjunctive mood are generally used in a dependent clause introduced by "**que**" (that).

2. The present subjunctive is formed by dropping the **-ant** of the present participle and adding the following endings: **-e, -es, -e, -ions, -iez, -ent**. These endings are the same for all verbs except **avoir** and **être**.

3. **Regular Verbs**

chanter: que je chante, que tu chantes, qu'il chante, qu'elle chante, qu'on chante, que nous chantions, que vous chantiez, qu'ils chantent, qu'elles chantent

obéir: que j'obéisse, que tu obéisses, qu'il obéisse, qu'elle obéisse, qu'on obéisse que nous obéissions, que vous obéissiez, qu'ils obéissent, qu'elles obéissent

répondre: que je réponde, que tu répondes, qu'il réponde, qu'elle réponde, qu'on réponde, que nous répondions, que vous répondiez, qu'ils répondent, qu'elles répondent

4. Verbs with certain spelling changes, such as nettoyer, acheter, appeler, and préférer, have the same changes in the present subjunctive as in the present indicative. For example:

que j'emploie	qu'il appelle
qu'elle mène	qu'elles espèrent

5. **Irregular Verbs**

The stem of most irregular verbs, as with regular verbs, can be found by dropping the **-ant** of the present participle. For example:

Infinitive	Present Participle	Present Subjunctive
s'asseoir	s'asseyant	je m'asseye
conduire	conduisant	je conduise
connaître	connaissant	je connaisse
courir	courant	je coure
craindre	craignant	je craigne
écrire	écrivant	j'écrie
rire	riant	je rie
vivre	vivant	je vive

6. A few irregular verbs have a single irregular stem: **faire**: je fasse, tu fasses, il fasse, nous fassions, vous fassiez, ils fassent.

falloir: il faille

pouvoir: je puisse, tu puisses, il puisse, nous puissions, vous puissiez, ils puissent

savoir: je sache, tu saches, il sache, nous sachions, vous sachiez, ils sachent

7. A number of irregular verbs have two stems in the present subjunctive, one stem for the nous and vous forms (which is identical with the stem of the nous and vous forms of the present indicative), and one for the other forms:

aller: j'aille, tu ailles, il aille, nous allions, vous alliez, ils aillent

boire: je boive, tu boives, il boive, nous buvions, vous buviez, ils boivent

croire: je croie, tu croies, il croie, nous croyions, vous croyiez, ils croient

devoir: je doive, tu doives, il doive, nous devions, vous deviez, ils doivent

envoyer: j'envoie, tu envoies, il envoie, nous envoyions, vous envoyiez, ils envoient

mourir: je meure, tu meures, il meure, nous mourions, vous mouriez, ils meurent

prendre: je prenne, tu prennes, il prenne, nous prenions, vous preniez, ils prennent

recevoir: je reçoive, tu reçoives, il reçoive, nous recevions, vous receviez, ils reçoivent

tenir: je tienne, tu tiennes, il tienne, nous tenions, vous teniez, ils tiennent

valoir: je vaille, tu vailles, il vaille, nous valions, vous valiez, ils vaillent

venir: je vienne, tu viennes, il vienne, nous venions, vous veniez, ils viennent

voir: je voie, tu voies, il voie, nous voyions, vous voyiez, ils voient

vouloir: je veuille, tu veuilles, il veuille, nous voulions, vous vouliez, ils veuillent

8. The only verbs with irregular endings are avoir and être:

avoir

j'aie	nous ayons
tu aies	vous ayez
il/elle/on ait	ils/elles aient

être

je sois	nous soyons
tu sois	vous soyez
il/elle/on soit	ils/elles soient

9. The subjunctive is also used after impersonal expressions other than those that show certainty or probability. Common impersonal expressions followed by the subjunctive are:

il faut, it is necessary, must	il est nécessaire, it is necessary
il est bon, it is good	il est important, it is important
il est juste, it is right	il est possible, it is possible
il se peut, it may be	il est impossible, it is impossible
il est temps, it is time	il semble, it seems
il vaut mieux, it is better	il est (c'est) dommage, it is a pity/shame

10. Some examples are:

Il faut que vous veniez à l'heure.
You must (It is necessary that you) come on time.

Est-il impossible qu'elle le fasse?
Is it impossible for her to do it?

Il se peut que tu aies raison.
You may be right.

Il vaut mieux que nous travaillions.
It is better for us to work.

11. After impersonal expressions of certainty or probability, the indicative is used. Some common expressions of this type are:

Il est certain, it is certain   Il est clair, it is clear
Il est évident, it is evident   Il est probable, it is probable
Il est vrai, it is true   Il paraît, it appears

12. Some examples are:

Il est évident que vous savez la leçon.
It is evident that you know the lesson.

Il est probable qu'ils viendront demain.
It is probable that they will come tomorrow.

13. However, when these expressions are used negatively or interrogatively, they generally express doubt and take the subjunctive.

Il n'est pas certain qu'il vienne demain.
It is not certain that he will come tomorrow.

Est-il vrai qu'on bâtisse une nouvelle école?
Is it true that they are building a new school?

Notes: 1. There is no future tense in the subjunctive. The present subjunctive is used to express both present and future actions.

2. The subjunctive in French is often translated by an infinitive in English.

Exercise 63

Choose the correct response:

1. (Combien de temps, Depuis quand) a-t-il plu?
2. As-tu besoin de lunettes lorsque tu (lis, liras)?
3. Vos cousins habitent en Provence?
   (Combien de temps, Depuis quand) y habitent-ils?
4. Ils y habitent (depuis, pendant) longtemps.
5. Ou habiteront-ils après qu'on (vend, vendra) la maison?
6. Portez-vous un parapluie quand il (pleut, pleuvra)?
7. J'ouvrirai mon parapluie (s'il, quand il) pleut.

8. Depuis quand (a-t-il plu, pleuvait-il)?
9. Il a lu la revue (pendant, pour) une heure.
10. (Depuis quand, Combien de temps) faites-vous du judo chaque jour?
11. (Combien de temps, Combien de temps y a-t-il que) vous faites du judo?
12. Aussitôt que vous vous (laverez, lavez), nous nous mettrons en route.

Exercise 64

Give the French equilavent:
1. How long have you been working? I have been working for three weeks.
2. How long do they study? They study for two hours.
3. How long did he stay in Europe? He stayed there for six months.
4. How long had she been singing? She had been singing for ten minutes.
5. How long will you swim? I will swim for a half hour.

Exercise 65

Respond to each question with a complete French sentence:

1. Combien de temps y avait-il que vous écriviez quand la cloche a sonné?
2. Que feras-tu des que les grandes vacances seront arrivées?
3. Combien de temps y a-t-il que le mécanicien répare votre automobile?
4. Qui lui dira la mauvaise nouvelle quand il reviendra?
5. Combien de temps ont-elles parlé au téléphone hier soir?
6. Depuis quand cette jolie infirmière travaille-t-elle dans cet hôpital?
7. Ou irez-vous apres que nous partirons?
8. Combien de temps est-ce que je pourrai garder ce livre?
9. Est-ce que le soleil se leve ou se couche quand la journée commence?
10. Depuis quand l'attendiez-vous lorsqu'elle est rentrée?

Exercise 66

Give the question posed which resulted in the following questions:

Example: Elle attend le médecin depuis dix minutes. Depuis quand attend-elle le médecin?
1. Ils écoutent la radio une demi-heure chaque matin.
2. Ils écoutent la radio depuis une demi-heure.
3. Il y a une demi-heure qu'ils écoutent la radio.
4. Ils écoutaient la radio depuis une demi-heure.
5. Ils ont écoute la radio pendant une demi-heure.

Exercise 67

For each one of the following sentences, give an equivalent sentence, using "depuis."
1. Combien de temps y a-t-il que vous lisez le journal?
2. Il y avait une heure que nous mangions.
3. Il y a quinze jours que je suis ici.
4. Voilà longtemps que les deux garçons patinent.
5. Combien de temps y avait-il qu'ils suivaient cette route?

3

Verbs: Complex Tenses and Forms

COMPOUND TENSES: AGREEMENT OF PAST PARTICIPLES

La souris **eut mangé** le fromage. (passé anterieur)

Le chat **a guetté** la souris. (passé composé)

Le garçon **avait chassé** le chat. (plus-que-parfait)

La mère **aura fessé** le garçon. (futur antérieur)

C'est domage que la souris ait mangé le fromage. (subjonctif passé)

1. Compound tenses are formed with the auxiliary verb **avoir** or **être** and the past participle.

2. Passé Composé

A. With the auxiliary verb, **avoir**:

The passé composé is formed by using the present tense of the auxiliary **verb + the past participle**.

chanter, to sing

j'ai chanté	nous avons chanté
tu as chanté	vous avez chanté
il/elle/on a chanté	ils/elles ont chanté

B. With the auxiliary verb, **être**:

The passé composé is formed by using the present tense of the auxiliary **verb + the past participle**. The past participle must agree with the subject in number and gender.

revenir, to return/to come back

je suis revenu(e)	nous sommes revenus(ues)
tu es revenu(e)	vous êtes revenus(ues)
il/elle/on est revenu(e)	ils/elles sont revenus(ues)

C. The passé composé of all reflexive verbs is conjugated with the auxiliary verb être + the past participle. The past participle must agree with the subject in number and gender.

se laver, to wash oneself

je me suis lavé(e)	nous nous sommes lavés(ées)
tu t'es lavé(e)	vous vous êtes lavé(é,s,ées)
il/elle/on s'est lavé(e)	ils/elles se sont lavés(ées)

3. Pluperfect (le plus-que-parfait)

A. The plus-que-parfait of the verbs conjugated with the auxiliary verb avoir is formed with the imperfect of the **auxiliary verb + the past participle**.

chanter, to sing

j'avais chanté	nous avions chanté
tu avais chanté	vous aviez chanté
il/elle/on avait chanté	ils/elles avaient chanté

B. The plus-que-parfait of verbs conjugated with the auxiliary verb être is formed with the imperfect of the auxiliary verb + the past participle. The past participle must agree with the subject in number and gender.

retourner, to return

j'étais retourné(e)	nous étions retournés(ées)
tu étais retourné(e)	vous étiez retourné(é,s,ées)
il/elle/on était retourné(e)	ils/elles étaient retournés(ées)

se laver, to wash oneself

je m'étais lavé(e)	nous nous étions lavés(ées)
tu t'étais lavé(e)	vous vous étiez lavé(é,s,ées)
il/elle/on s'était lavé(e)	ils/elles s'étaient lavé(es)

4. Passé Anterieur

A. The passé anterieur of verbs conjugated with the auxiliary verb avoir is formed with the simple past of the **auxiliary verb + the past participle**.

chanter, to sing

j'eus chanté	nous eûmes chanté
tu eus chanté	vous eûtes chanté
il/elle eut chanté	ils/elles eurent chanté

B. The passé anterieur of the verbs that are conjugated with the auxiliary verb **être** is formed with the auxiliary verb in the **passé simple + the past participle**. The past participle must agree with the subject in number and gender.

retourner, to return

je fus retourné(e)	nous fûmes retournés (ées)
tu fus retourné(e)	vous fûtes retourné (é,s,ées)
il/elle/on fut retourné(e)	ils/elles furent retournés(es)

se laver, to wash oneself

je me fus lavé(e)	nous nous fûmes lavés(ées)
tu te fus lavé(e)	vous vous fûtes lavé(é,s,ées)
il/elle/on se fut lavé(e)	ils/elles se furent lavé(e)s

5. Future Perfect (le futur antérieur)

A. The futur antérieur of verbs conjugated with the auxiliary verb, avoir is formed with the future of the auxiliary verb + the past participle.

chanter, to sing

j'aurai chanté	nous aurons chanté
tu auras chanté	vous aurez chanté
il/elle/on aura chanté	ils/elles auront chanté

B. The futur antérieur of verbs conjugated with the auxiliary verb être is formed with the future of the auxiliary verb + the past participle. The past participle must agree with the subject in number and gender.

retourner, to return

je serai retourné (e)	nous serons retournés(ées)
tu seras retourné (e)	vous serez retourné(é,s,ées)
il/elle/on sera retourné(e)	ils/elles furent retourné(e)s

se laver, to wash oneself

je me serai lavé(e)	nous nous serons lavés(ées)
tu te seras lavé(e)	vous vous serez lavé(é,s,ées)
il/elle/on se sera lavé(e)	ils/elles se seront lavés(es)

6. Past Conditional (le conditionnel passé)

A. The conditionnel passé of verbs conjugated with the auxiliary verb avoir is formed with the conditional of the auxiliary + the past participle.

chanter, to sing

j'aurais chanté	nous aurions chanté
tu aurais chanté	vous auriez chanté
il/elle/on aurait chanté	ils/elles auraient chanté

B. The conditionnel passé of verbs conjugated with the auxiliary verb être is formed with the conditional of the auxiliary verb + the past participle. The past participle must agree with the subject in number and gender.

revenir, to return/to come back

je serais revenu(e)	nous serions revenus(es)
tu serais revenu(e)	vous seriez revenu(e,s,es)
il/elle/on serait revenu(e)	ils/elles seraient revenus(es)

se laver, to wash oneself

je me serais lavé(e)	nous nous serions lavés (ées)
tu te serais lavé(e)	vous vous seriez lavé (é,s,ées)
il/elle/on se serait lavé(e)	ils/elles se seraient lavé(e)s

7. Past Subjunctive - Le subjonctif passé

A. The subjonctif passé of the verbs conjugated with the auxiliary verb avoir is formed with the present subjunctive of the **auxiliary verb + the past participle**.

chanter, to sing

j'aie chanté	nous ayons chanté
tu aies chanté	vous ayez chanté
il/elle/on ait chanté	ils/elles aient chanté

B. The subjonctif passé of verbs conjugated with the auxiliary verb être is formed with the present subjuntive of the **auxiliary verb + the past participle**. The past participle must agree with the subject in number and gender.

retourner , to return

je sois retourné(e)	nous soyons retournés (ées)
tu sois retourné(e)	vous soyez retourné (é,s,ées)
il/elle/on soit retourné(e)	ils/elles soient retournés(ées)

se laver , to wash oneself

je me sois lavé(e)	nous nous sommes lavés(ées)
tu te sois lavé(e)	vous vous êtes lavé (é,s,ées)
il/elle/on se soit lavé(e)	ils/elles se soient lavés(ées)

Notes:

1. **ALL** reflexive verbs are conjugated with the auxiliary verb être.

2. In forming the negative and interrogative of compound tenses, only the auxiliary verb is affected. Thus,

a. In the negative, the auxiliary is made negative.

b. In the interrogative, the auxiliary is inverted.

Nous n'avions pas joué au tennis.
We hadn't played tennis

Serait-elle partie?
Would she have left?

Ne se sont-ils pas amusés à la soirée?
Didn't they enjoy themselves at the soirée?

3. As the subjunctive equivalent of the passé composé, the past subjunctive is used to express an action that has already taken place.

C'est dommage qu'il ne soit pas venu.
It is a pity that he didn't come.

Il semble qu'ils soient sortis avec les enfants.
It seems they have gone out with the children.

Exercise 1

Choose the correct translation:
1. **il était resté**: he stayed, he had stayed, he was staying
2. **j'aurai commencé**: I had begun, I will begin, I will have begun
3. **vous avez rompu**: you broke, you would have broken, you had broken
4. **elle était morte**: she would have died, she was dying, she had died
5. **je me serais levé**: I would get up, I would have gotten up, I had gotten up
6. nous **avions connu**: we had know, we knew, we would have known
7. **ils seraient entrés:** they did enter, they would enter, they would have entered
8. **nous aurons preparé**: we shall prepare, we should have prepared, we shall have prepared
9. **elle s'était amusée**: she had had a good time, she had a good time, she was having a good time
10. **vous auriez préféré**: you did prefer, you would have preferred, you will have preferred

Exercise 2

Repeat each sentence and substitute a correct form of the verb in parenthesis:

1. Elle a couru chez elle. (rester, s'ennuyer)
2. N'aurait-il pas répondu? (mourir, boire)
3. Nous avions dine ce soir-la. (se fâcher, sortir)
4. J'étais rentré de bonne heure. (s'habiller, écrire)
5. J'aurais joué dans la rue. (entrer, être)
6. N'avons-nous pas attendu? (se blesser, revenir)
7. Ils auront fini avant six heures. (se lever, arriver)
8. Elles seront déjà parties. (se reveiller, oublier)
9. Etes-vous allée au cinéma, Julie? (étudier, s'amuser)
10. Elles n'auraient pas dormi. (retourner, s'ennuyer)

Exercise 3

Complete each sentence with the missing word:
1. I had borrowed: j' _____ emprunté.
2. he was born: il _____ né.
3. he had been born: il _____ né.
4. they got angry: ils se _____ fâches.
5. he will have done: il _____ fait.
6. they had remained: elles _____ restées.
7. she would have come: elle _____ venue.
8. they got up: elles se _____ levées.
9. we had had: nous _____ eu.
10. I will have left: je _____ sorti.
11. you had returned: tu _____ retourné.
12. she had enjoyed herself: elle s'_____ amusée.
13. they would have answered: elles _____ répondu.
14. you had washed yourself: vous vous _____ lavé.
15. I would have hurried: je me _____ dépêche.

Exercise 4

Complete these sentences in English:
1. Quelle voiture aurait-il conduite? Which car _____?
2. Elle ne s'était pas encore brossé les dents. She _____.
3. Le jour tant attendu est arrivé. The day so waited for _____.
4. Il serait devenu ingénieur. _____ engineer.
5. Où sont les cravates que tu as achetées?
   Where are the neckties that _____?
6. Qu'auraient-ils dit de moi? What _____ of me?
7. Quand vous arriverez, ils seront partis. When you arrive, _____
8. Le garçon avait garde la monnaie. The waiter _____ the change.
9. Combien d'animaux étaient morts? How many animals _____ ?
10. Auriez-vous pu le faire? _____ to do it?

THE LITERARY TENSES

C'est dommage que la souris **ait mangé** le fromage.
Le chat **guetta** la souris la nuit dernière.
Le chat **a eu été** chassé par le garçon.
Le garçon **craignait** que la mère le fessa.

1. The Literary Past Tense (le passé simple). The literary past is a one-word verb form used in formal writing where the passé composé is normally used in spoken French.

2. Formation of the literay past tense (passé simple):

A. All regular **-er** verbs form the literary past tense by adding the following "**a**" endings to the infinitive stem.

Person	Singular	Plural
1st	**-ai**	**-âmes**
2nd	**-as**	**-âtes**
3nd	**-a**	**-èrent**

Les élèves entendirent l'arrivée du professeur et ils se mirent à travailler.
The student heard the coming of the professeur and they began to work.

B. To form the passé simple of all regular **-ir** and **-re** verbs, add the following "**i**" endings to the infinitive stem.

Person	Singular	Plural
1st	**-is**	**-îmes**
2nd	**-is**	**-îtes**
3rd	**-it**	**-irent**

C. To form the literary past tense (passé simple) of irregular **-ir** verbs other than **courir, mourir, tenir, venir,** and their compounds, add the "i" endings to the infinitive stem.

dormir, to sleep, il dormit, he slept; ils dormirent, they slept
ouvrir, to open, elle ouvrit, she opened; elles ouvrirent, they opened
acquerir, to acquire il acquérit, he acquired; ils acquérirent, they acquired

D. Many irregular **-re** verbs form the passé simple by adding the "i" endings to the stem of the first person plural of the present indicative ("**nous**" form).

écrire, to write (and its compounds)
écrivons, ils écrivit, he wrote; ils écrivirent; they wrote
inscrire, to inscribe
inscrivons: elle inscrivit, she inscribed; elles inscrivirent, they inscribed
coudre, to sew (and its compounds)
cousons: il cousit, he sewed; ils cousirent, they sewed
recoudre, to restitch
recousons, je recousis, I restitched; nous recousîmes, we restitched
vaincre, to conquer (and its compounds)
vainquons, il vainquit, he conquered; ils vainquirent, they conquered
craindre, to fear (and other -indre verbs)
craignons, il craignit, he feared; ils craignirent, they feared
produire, to produce (and other -uire verbs)
produisons: je produisis, I produced; nous produisîmes, we produced

E. Many irregular verbs base the passé simple on the stem and final vowel of the past participle. If the final vowel of the past participle is "**-u**," use the following "u" endings to form the passé simple.

Person	Singular	Plural
1st	-us	-ûmes
2nd	-us	-ûtes
3rd	-ut	-urent

Infinitive/Past Participle	Passé simple
apercevoir/aperçu	il aperçut, he glimpsed
to glimpse/glimpsed	ils aperçurent, they glimpsed
croire/cru	elle crut, she believed
to believe/believed	elles crurent, they believed
dire/dit	nous dîmes, we told
to tell/told	vous dîtes, you told
devoir/du	tu dus, you must
must/must	vous dûtes, you must
falloir/fallu	il fallut, it was necessary
mettre/mis	elle mit, she put
to put/put	elles mirent, they put
plaire/plu	il plut, it pleased

to please/pleased	ils plurent, they pleased
pleuvoir/plu	il plut, it rained
pouvoir/pu	nous pûmes, we were able
able/able	vous pûtes, you were able
prendre/pris	elle prit, she took
to take/taken	elles prirent, they took
recevoir/reçu	il reçut, he received to
receive/received	ils reçurent, they received
résoudre/resolu	il résolut, he resolved
solve/solved	ils résolurent, they resolved
savoir/su	elle sut, she knew
to know/known	elles surent, they knew
vivre/vécu	il vécut, he lived
to live/lived	ils vécurent, they lived
vouloir/voulu	elle voulut, she wanted
to want/wanted	elles voulurent, they wanted

F. Some irregular verbs and their compounds have unpredictable passé simple stems and final vowels.

être: je fus, il fut, nous fûmes
to be: I was, he was, we were

avoir: elle eut, vous eûtes, ils eurent
to have: she had, you had, they had

courir: je courus, tu courus, ils coururent
to run: I ran, you ran, they ran

faire: tu fis, nous fîmes, ils firent
to do: you did, we did, they did

mourir: il mourut, ils moururent
to die: he died, they died

naître: je naquis, il naquit, elles naquirent
to be born: I was born, he was born, they were born

vivre: il vécut, nous vécûmes, ils vécurent
to live: he lived, we lived, they lived

voir: je vis, elle vit, elles virent
to see: I saw, she saw, they saw

Note: The simple past stems of the verbs tenir and venir and their compounds follow the "-i" pattern, but drop the vowel.

tenir: tu tins, vous tintes, ils tinrent
to hold: you held, you held, they held

venir: je vins, il vint, nous vîmes
to come: I came, he came, we came

3. Use of the passé simple
The simple past tells about something that began at the past moment under consideration.

La Fontaine, un grand écrivain français, mourut en 1695.
La Fontaine, a renowned French writer, died in 1695.

Note: The imparfait is used in literary French to describe events whose beginnings are not in focus—just as you use the imparfait in spoken French.

4. Le passé sur-composé
The passé sur-composé, a super compound form of the past antérior (past infinitive of the auxiliary verb + the past participle) is used in correlation with a verb in the past indefinite. This tense is used in formal letter writing whenever the past indefinite is used.

Dès que le directeur a eu signé la lettre, sa secrétaire l'a mise à la boîte à lettre.
As soon as the principal had signed the letter, his secretary put it in the mail box.
Aussitôt que les étudiants ont eu reçu le résultat de leur examen, ils sont sortis du bâtiment.
As soon as the students had received the result of their examination, they left the building.

Note: The super-compound form may not be used with the reflexive or passive verbs.

5. The Literary Past Perfect (passé anterieur)
The literary past perfect (passé anterieur) is used after certain time conjunctions—where you would use the passé sur-composé in spoken French.

A. The literary past perfect is formed by taking the passé simple of être or avoir followed by the past participle of the main verb to mean "had . . ."

Aussitôt qu'il eut lu la lettre il la déchira.
As soon as he had read the letter he tore it up.

Nous ne sortîmes de notre abri qu'après qu'il eut cessé de pleuvoir.
We came out our our shelter only after it had stopped raining.

Note: The rules for past participle agreement apply to the literary past perfect.

Dès qu'elle se fut levée, elle quitta la forêt.
As soon as she was up, she left the forest.

B. The literary past perfect (passé anterieur) is used after the following time conjunctions: quand - when; aussitôt que - as soon as; lorsque - when; après que - after; dès que - as soon as.

Lorsqu'il furent nés, ils commencèrent à crier.
When they were born, they began to scream.

Note: Like the passé sur-composé, the literary past perfect refers to a singular event and is not used to describe habitual or ongoing actions in the past.

Chaque fois qu'ils eurent reçu une mauvaise note, ils se plaingnirent.
Each time they had received a bad grade, they complained.

6. The imperfect subjunctive is the formal or literary equivalent of the subjunctive mood used in spoken French. Unlike the spoken subjunctive, the imperfect subjunctive is always translated by the past or the conditional.

A. The imperfect subjunctive of all regular verbs is formed by adding the following endings to the stem of the passé simple.

Person	Singular	Plural
1st	-sse	-ssions
2nd	-sses	-ssiez
3rd	-at/-it/-ut	-ssent

Note: Only the circumflex accent of the third person, singular distinguishes the spelling of the imperfect subjunctive from that of the passé simple.

Passé simple Stem	- Imperfect Subjunctive	
aller, to go	- que j'allasse, that I went...	
alla-	- que tu allasses	- qu'il allat
- que nous allassions	- que vous allassiez	- qu'ils allassent
grandir, to grow	- que je grandisse,	that I grew
grandi-	- que tu grandisses	- qu'il grandit
- que nous grandissions	- que vous grandissiez	- qu'ils grandissent
perdre, to lose	- que je perdisse	that I lost
perdi-	- que tu perdisses	- qu'elle perdit
- que nous perdissions	- que vous perdissiez	- qu'ils perdissent
être, to be	- que je fusse,	that I was
fu-	- que tu fusse	- qu'on fut
- que nous fussions	- que vous fussiez	- qu'ils fussent

La dame craignait que son fils ne fit pas ses devoirs.
The lady feared that her son did not do his homework.

Elle doutait qu'il travaillat quand elle est rentrée.
She doubted that he was workinbg when she returned.

Elle avait peur qu'il n'échouat.
She was afraid that he would fail.

B. Use of the imperfect subjunctive:

The imperfect subjunctive is the formal or literary equivalent of the spoken subjunctive.

Spoken French ... Literary French
(Present Subjunctive v. Imperfect Subjunctive)

Je doute qu'elle comprenne. (present subjunctive)
Je doute qu'elle comprit. (imperfect subjunctive)

Elle craignait qu'il ne fasse pas ses devoirs. (present subjunctive)
Elle craignait qu'il fit pas ses devoirs. (imperfect subjunctive)

Il aimerait qu'elle revienne. (present subjunctive)
Il aimerait qu'elle revint. (imperfect subjunctive)

Quoique nous soyons pauvres, nous étions heureux. (present subjunctive)
Quoique nous fussions pauvres, nous étions heureux. (imperfect subjunctive)

7. The pluperfect subjunctive is formed by combining the imperfect subjunctive of **être** or **avoir** with the past participle of the main verb, just as the present subjunctive of **être** or **avoir** combines with the past participle of the main verb in the spoken subjunctive.

Spoken French ...	Literary French
(Perfect Subjunctive	v. Pluperfect Subjunctive)
que je sois venu ...	que je fusse venu
qu'il ait terminé ...	qu'il eut terminé
qu'elle se soit levée ...	qu'elle se fut levée

8. Uses and meaning of the pluperfect subjunctive:

1) In subordinate clauses, the pluperfect subjunctive is the literary equivalent of the past subjunctive and corresponds to the pluperfect indicative. It is translated as "had..."

Elle craignait que son fils n'eut pas fait ses devoirs.

She was afraid that her son had not done his homework.

2) In main clauses, the pluperfect subjunctive is the literary equivalent of the past conditional and means "would have ..."

Elle doutait que son fils eut refusé de travailler si le professeur avait insisté.

She doubted that her son would have refused to work if the professor had insisted.

Exercise 5

Rewrite the following sentences using the passé composè in place of the passé simple.

1. Les soldats marchèrent dans les rues désertes.
2. Nous répondîmes aussi honnêtement que possible.
3. Le roi alla à la messe.
4. Les musiciens voulurent jouer devant l'assemblée.
5. Elle prit toutes les précautions nécéssaires.
6. Les espions furent attrapés par les soldats du roi.
7. On vendit les biens du baron.
8. Les cardinaux choisirent le nouveau Pape.
9. Les invités vinrent nombreux.
10. Nous dûmes remercier notre protecteur.
11. La petite fille vit la procession.

12. Le comte tint sa promesse au roi.
13. Qui furent ses ministres?
14. Napoléon fit construire l'Arc de Triomphe.
15. On brûla Jeanne d'Arc en 1431 à Rouen.
16. Elle mourut sans reprendre conscience.
17. Les messagers annoncèrent la mauvaise nouvelle.
18. Nous sûmes que la reine était morte.
19. La Fayette et Washington furent amis.
20. L'actrice naquit en Italie.

Exercise 6

Supply the appropriate tense of être or avoir according to whether the event represents a past single occurrence or ongoing situation.

1. Dès que les révolutionnaires _____ ouvert les portes de la Bastille, les prisonniers se sauvèrent.
2. Aussitôt que les Anglais _____ brûlé Jeanne d'Arc, elle devint un symbole de patriotisme.
3. Les nobles s'arrangeaient pour augmenter les taxes des que les récoltes _____ été bonnes.
4. Lorsque une croisade _____ annoncée les eglises commencaient toutes à demander de l'argent aux fidèles.
5. Aussitôt que les colonies américaines se _____ declarées indépendantes, la France les reconnut.
6. Quand les armées _____ chasse les Anglais de France, le peuple se rejouit.
7. Henri IV put monter au pouvoir lorsque ses ennemis_____ été répudiés.
8. Quand Balzac _____ fini un roman, il en commençait tout de suite un autre.
9. Aussitôt que le Roi se _____ levé, le public dut se lever aussi.
10. Tous les matins, quand Napoleon _____ surveillé les travaux, ils consultait ses maréchaux.

Exercise 7

Rewrite the sentences in current, informal French style, changing the passé simple and imperfect subjunctive verbs to appropriate conversational forms.

1. Il n'eut jamais admis son erreur.
2. Il fallut que nous vissions ce spectable.
3. Leurs parents ne permettaient pas qu'ils vécussent ensemble.
4. Elle cherchait un mari qui sut fire la guerre.
5. Il fut impossible que nous acceptassions ces conditions.
6. La princesse était contente que son pére fit cette célébration.
7. Le capitaine ordonna que les soldats revinssent en arrière.
8. Les propriétaires n'étaient pas contents bien qu'ils s'enrichissent.
9. S'il comprenait tout cela il se résignat.
10. Les prétés refusèrent que les impôts fussent diminués.

Exercise 8   Rewrite the following sentences in informal, conversational style, replacing the literary tenses by spoken forms.

1. L'archevêque douta qu'elle se fut compromise dans l'affaire.
2. Elle ne voulait rien entendre, quoiqu'il eut fait tout son possible.
3. Si vous nous aviez invités, nous eussions accepté avec plaisir.
4. Nous aurons voulu qu'elle eut dit franchement son opinion.
5. Avait-il été certain que vous eussiez rejeté son offre?

Exercise 9   Translate the following sentences into French, using the passé simple.

1. I took the liberty of sitting down.
2. We wrote many times to the senator.
3. Mister Dupont held his hat under his arm.
4. The officers gave evidence of great intelligence.
5. They behaved with care.
6. The armies of the goverment conquered the invaders.
7. The suppliers appropriated the stock.
8. The senator was elected.
9. That night, it poured.
10. We told all our thoughts.
11. Finally the author came!

THE PRESENT AND PAST PARTICIPLES

En mangeant le fromage la souris s'endort.

Après **avoir mangé** le fromage, la souris s'est endormie.

Tout en léchant ses lèvres, le chat guettait la souris.

Après **avoir léché** ses lèvres, le chat a guetté la souris.

Sortant de sa chambre, le garçon chasse le chat.

Après **être sorti** de sa chambre, le garçon a chassé le chat.

Se levant, la mère a fessé le garçon.

Après **s'être levée**, la mère a fessé le garçon.

1. The Present Participle

A. The present participle of all verbs - except **être, avoir,** and **savoir** - is formed by dropping the **-ons** from the first person, plural (nous) form of the present indicative tense, and then adding **-ant**.

Infinitive	1st, plural	Present Participle
(Nous) form regarder	regardons	regardant/regarding
vouloir	voulons	voulant/willing

Note: The present participles of **être**, **avoir**, and **savoir** must be memorized.

Infinitive	Present Participle
être	étant/being
avoir	ayant/having
savoir	sachant/knowing

B. Uses of the present participle:

1) You may use the present participle as an adjective which must then agree in gender and number with the noun it modifies.

une soirée dansante   an evening of dancing

2) Use a present participle as the verb in an abbreviated clause to describe a secondary event or action - in this case, the present participle is invariable.

On a vu des voleurs courant dans la rue.

3) The preposition en is the only preposition that can be used to introduce a present participle. In this case, en functions as an adverb and means "in, while, or by" doing something.

Elle s'est fait mal en descendant la pente.

Note: When a present participle follows the preposition en, it always refers to the subject of the sentence, but remains invariable.

2. **The Past Participles**

A. Past participles are derived from verbs, but are not used as verbs since they do not have tense or personal endings. They are formed as follows:

1. The past participle of all regular -er verbs, drop the infinitive endings and add **-e**.

Infinitive	Past Participle
parler, to speak	parle, spoken
manger, to eat	mange, eaten

Note: The irregular verbs être and naître also have past participles ending in **-e**.

Infinitive	Past Participle
être, to be	été, been
naître, to be born	né, (was/were) born

2. The past participles of regular **-ir** verbs and many irregular verbs ending in **-ir** end in **-i**.

Infinitive	Past Participle
choisir	choisi
grandir	grandi
dormir	dormi

Note: The past participles of the verbs rire and suivre and all their compounds also end in **-i**.

Infinitive	Past Participle
rire	ri
sourire	souri
poursuivre	poursuivi

3. Many verbs have past participles ending in **-u**:
a) All regular and many irregular **-re** verbs have past participles ending in **-u**.
b) The verb vivre and its compounds have an irregular past participle stem and the **-u** ending.
c) Irregular verbs ending in **-oire**, **-oir**, **-aire**, and **-aître** (except **faire** and **naître**) have past participles ending in **-u**.

Infinitive	Past Participle
apparaître	apparu
avoir	eu
apercevoir	aperçu
connaître	connu
concevoir	concu
décevoir	déçu
émouvoir	ému
devoir	dû
falloir	fallu
percevoir	perçu
plaire	plu
pouvoir	pu
savoir	su
se taire	tu
valoir	valu
vouloir	voulu

d) Irregular verbs whose infinitives en in **-oudre** have irregular past participle stems and the **-u** ending.

Infinitive	Past Participle
résoudre	résolu
moudre	moulu
coudre	cousu

e) A few irregular verbs ending in **-ir** and **-ire** and their compounds have past participles ending in **-u**.

Infinitive	Past Participle
courir	couru
devenir	devenu

élire	élu
lire	lu
parcourir	parcouru
retenir	retenu
tenir	tenu
venir	venu

4. Some irregular verbs have past participles ending in consonants.

a) The irregular verbs prendre, mettre, asseoir, their compounds, and verbs ending in **-querir** have past participles ending in **-is**. The infinitive stem is shortened.

Infinitive	Past Participle
acquérir	acquis
s'asseoir	assis
commettre	commis
comprendre	compris
conquérir	conquis

b) Verbs whose infinitives end in **-vrir** or **-frir** have past participles ending in **-ert**.

Infinitive	Past Participle
couvrir	couvert
offrir	offert
ouvrir	ouvert
souffrir	souffert

c) The common irregular verbs **faire**, **dire**, and **écrire**, their compounds, and all verbs ending in **-indre** or **-uire** have past participles which are identical to the third person, singular of the present tense.

Infinitive	3rd, Sing./Pres.	Past Participle
conduire	il conduit	conduit
craindre	il craint	craint
décrire	il décrit	décrit

Note: The past participle of **mourir** (to die), is **mort** (died). A past participle cannot be used alone as the verb in a sentence. A verb has personal endings and a specific tense. A past participle has neither.

Exercise 10

Replace the phrase given in parentheses with the appropriate form of the present participle.

1. Vous apprenez bien une langue (si vous la pratiquez beaucoup).
2. Les valises arrivent sur des tapis (qui roulent).
3. (A force de chercher) je trouve une bonne réponse.
4. Il s'en va sur la montagne (pendant qu'il chante et siffle).
5. Je n'ai jamais vu une soucoupe (qui vole).

6. J'écoute (en meme temps que pense à autre chose).
7. Elle n'est pas contente d'être une femme (qui obéit)!
8. Ne parle pas (pendant que tu manges).
9. Tu deviens bronze (si tu restes au soleil).
10. Ils arrivent (en train de crier) parce qu'ils ont gagné.

Exercise11

Change the verbs in the following sentences to the passé composé.

1. On offre une cigarette à la dame.
2. On vend le journal dans la rue.
3. On voit ces films à la télévision.
4. On ferme les fenêtres à cause de la pluie.
5. On peint les murs en blanc.
6. On sert les clients comme il faut.
7. On prend ces photos comme souvenir.
8. On écrit souvent ces mots incorrectement.
9. On met cette lettre à la poste.
10. On conduit l'auto pour lui.

PASSIVE VOICE

Le fromage est mangé par la souris.
La souris est guettée par le chat.
Le chat est chassé par le garçon.
Le garçon est fessé par la mère.

1. The passive is formed by combining any tense of être with he past participle of the verb. Since the past participle is conjugated with **être**, it agrees with the subject in gender and number.

La voiture a été lavée par la pluie.
The car was washed by the rain.

Toutes les pêches seront mangées avant midi.
All the peaches will be eaten before noon.

2. The passive is generally avoided in French by using an active construction: the pronoun on followed by the third person singular of the verb:

On parle français au Canada.   French is spoken in Canada.

3. The passive construction is less frequently replaced by a reflexive verb.

Est-ce que les billets se vendent ici?
Are tickets sold here?

Exercise 12

Complete the sentences in English:

1. Une école sera construite près de l'église.
   A school_____ near the church.
2. Le gâteau se fait avec de la farine.
   Cake_____ with flour.
3. Elle était étonnée de ce qu'elle voyait.
   She_____ at what she saw.
4. Rien n' a été ajouté à la soupe.
   Nothing_____ to the soup.
5. Cela s'explique facilement.
   That _____
6. La soupe est servie.
   The soup _____
7. Les assiettes avaient été posées sur la table.
   The plates_____ on the table.
8. On a paye la somme due.
   The money due _____
9. Peut-on guéir cette maladie?
   Can this disease be cured?
10. Il est défendu de stationner devant l'hotel.
    It_____ to park in front of the hotel.

Exercise 13

Replace each sentence with an equivalent impersonal sentence using "on":

1. Comment se prononce ce nom?
2. L'assassin n'a pas été condamné.
3. Les repas se preparent dans la cuisine.
4. Les malades seront guéris.
5. Ces romans ne seront jamais lus.
6. Quelle langue se parle au Méxique?
7. Le papier a été place sur le bureau.
8. Cette lettre doit être mise à la boîte à lettre.
9. Cela ne se dit pas en publique.
10. La viande est servie avec une salade verte.

Exercise 14

Translate the English words into French by using the passive voice (le passif).

1. Les Antilles had been discovered!
2. Votre temps would not have been wasted.
3. Par qui ce château has it been built?
4. La fenêtre had been closed par le professeur.
5. Ces cravates will be sold dans tous les magasins.

Exercise 15   Translate into French the English words by using the impersonal "**On.**"

1. It is said que la ville de New York ne s'endort jamais.
2. A tip was given à la serveuse.
3. Dans ce restaurant necktie is worn.
4. A prize will be offered au meilleur étudiant.
5. The ham had been divided en six tranches.

Infinitives

La souris **veut manger** le fromage.

Le chat **continue à guétter** la souris.

Le garçon **est** content **de chasser** le chat.

La jeune mère **se met à fesser** le garçon.

1. An infinitive is a verb form that has neither tense nor person; it is the basic unconjugated form of the verb. Many tenses are formed from the infinitive. When there is more than one verb in a simple sentence, the first verb is conjugated; all others are in the infinitive.

Je refuse de sortir.

2. The infinitive phrase "**de sortir**" completes the meaning of the verb refuse. The preposition "de" connects the two verbs.

3. **Infinitives introduced by "de":**

A. When the first verb of a sentence describes an activity that is independent of the activity of the following verb, use the preposition de to introduce the infinitive.

Nous décidons de partir immediatement.
We decide to leave immediately.

Je cesse de fumer.
I stop smoking.

B. Use "**de**" to introduce an infinitive following a performative verb, that is, a verb that performs the act it describes. For example, "I'm telling you to leave me alone!" Some performative verbs in French are: commander, permettre, demander, promettre, dire, ordonner, and sometimes écrire and téléphoner.

L'avocat dit à Jean de passer à son bureau.
The lawyer tells John to come to his office.

C. When an infinitive follows an adjective or a noun that is not its direct object, "de" is used to introduce the infinitive.

Le docteur n'a pas le temps de me parler.
The docteur does not have the time to talk to me.

4. Use the preposition "à" to introduce an infinitive.

A. When an intervening noun is the object of both the main verb and the infinitive:

Donnez-moi quelque chose à boire, s'il vous plait!
Give me something to drink, please.

B. When the actions of the two verbs begin at the same time:

Ils commencent à partager mes opinions.
They begin to see my points.

C. The following are some of the more common verbs which require "a" before an infinitive:

s'amuser à	to have a good time ...ing
apprendre à	to learn to
continuer à	to continue ...ing
se decider à	to get around to
s'habituer à	to get used to
s'interesser à	to get involved in ...ing
inviter (quelqu'un) à	to invite (someone) to
se mettre à	to start to
se preparer à	to get ready to
réussir à	to succeed in ...ing
tarder à	to be late in ...ing

5. **Infinitives introduced by other prepositions**

A. In French, if the object of a preposition is a verb, that object will be an infinitive, not a participle as in English. The only exception to this is the preposition "**en**" which does require a participle. Before an infinitive which follows a verb, use the preposition "**pour**" to mean "**in order to,**" and the preposition "**sans**" to mean "**without ...ing.**"

Je prends mes clés pour ne pas les oublier.
I'm taking my keys so that I don't forget them.

6. Infinitives that follow verbs directly:

A. Use an infinitive without an intervening preposition after à verb that denotes wanting, hoping, or intending to do something, but not actually doing it.

Ils veulent dîner en ville.
They want to dine in town.

Nous ne pouvons pas vous mentir, monsieur.
We can't lie to you. sir.

B. Use an infinitive without à preposition after verbs of perception such as voir, regarder, observer, entendre, écouter, and sentir. In these cases, the subject of the infinitive becomes the direct object of the entire verb phrase.

Elle voit venir la foule.　　　　She sees the crowd coming.

C. Use an infinitive without à preposition after intransitive verbs, that is, verbs that do not take an object, denoting à change of place.

Nous montons prendre nos valises.

We're going upstairs to get our suitcases.

SUMMARY

1-The following verbs are followed by the preposition a before an infinitive:

aider à	continuer à	se mettre à	se résigner à
aimer (à)	se décider à	obliger à	se resoudre à
s'amuser à	demander à	parvenir à	reussir à
apprendre à	destiner à	passer du temps à	servir à
arriver à	encourager à	penser à	songer à
s'attendre à	engager à	persister à	suffire à
avoir à	enseigner à	se plaire	tarder à
chercher à	forcer à	pouser à	tendre à
commencer à	s'habituer à	se preparer à	tenir à
condamner à	hésiter à	recommencer à	travailler à
consentir à	inviter à	renoncer à	trouver à

Exercise 16　　Combine each pair of sentences into single sentences containing à verb in the infinitive form.

1. Complete-t-il ses devoirs? Oui, il tache de le faire.
2. Aidez-vous vos parents? Oui, je jure de le faire.
3. Accompagnez-vous Marc? Oui, nous acceptons de le faire.
4. Annonce-t-on le depart? Non, on oublie de le faire.
5. Mangez-vous à midi? Oui, nous finissons de le faire.
6. Manque-t-il son autobus? Oui, il risque de le faire.
7. Est-ce que vous votez pour notre parti? Oui, je decide de le faire.
8. Est-ce qu'elle travaille des heures supplémentaires? Non, elle refuse de le faire.
9. Est-ce que tu emploies la voiture de ton père? Oui, je promets de le faire.
10. Assistent-ils aux cours le samedi? Non, ils évitent de le faire.

Exercise 17   Answer each of the following questions using the cue in the response in an infinitive form.

1. Qu'est-ce que le client commande à la serveuse? (Qu'elle apporte une bouteille de champagne.)
2. Qu'est-ce que ses parents ne permettent pas à Jeanne? (Qu'elle passe la nuit dehors.)
3. Qu'est-ce que le médecin ordonne à la malade? (Qu'elle reste une semaine au lit.)
4. Qu'est-ce qu'elle dit à son ami? (Qu'il regarde la première page du journal.)
5. Qu'est-ce que nous écrivons à nos cousins? (Qu'ils viennent à New York par le prochain avion.)

Exercise 18   Combine each pair of sentences into single sentences containing a verb in the infinitive.

1. Il est surprenant. On remarque toutes ces erreurs.
2. Elle est enchantée. Elle voyage en première classe.
3. J'ai le plaisir. Je présente mes amis à mes parents.
4. Elles sont vraiment contentes. Elles finissent leurs études.
5. Il est nécéssaire. On paie ses taxes.
6. Nous sommes bien obligés. Nous remercions nos clients.
7. Henri-Roger n'a pas le temps. Il ne déjeune pas.
8. Je n'ai vraiment pas envie. Je ne prepare pas le diner.
9. Il est impossible. On arrive à l'heure.
10. Mon médecin a l'habitude. Il soigne les malades.

Exercise 19   Answer in a complete sentence by incorporating the question.

1. Critique-t-il ses amis? Oui, mais il hesite.
2. Finissons-nous cet exercice? Oui, nous reussissons.
3. Demandez-vous votre passeport? Oui, mais je tarde.
4. Etudie-t-elle le russe? Oui, elle continue.
5. Profitons-nous du beau temps? Oui, nous commençons.

Exercise 20   Combine each pair of sentences into one with a verb in the infinitive.

1. Manges-tu maintenant? Je descends tout de suite!
2. Joue-t-elle au tennis? Tout le monde la regarde.
3. Est-ce qu'on étudie la grammaire? Il faut le faire!
4. Est-ce que vous voyagez en Europe? Je désire le faire.
5. Annoncent-ils la bonne nouvelle? Ils viennent le faire.
6. Est-ce que quelqu'un sonne à la porte? Je l'entends.
7. Parlent-elles au téléphone? Elles aiment le faire.
8. Est-ce que Paul dîne seul au restaurant? Il préfère le faire.
9. Le train arrive-t-il? On l'entend.
10. Travaillez-vous dans le jardin? Je déteste le faire.

4

Adjectives and Adverbs

DESCRIPTIVE ADJECTIVES

La souris **noire** mange le fromage **blanc**.
Le **gros** chat guette la **petite** souris.
Le **méchant** garçon chasse le **vilain** chat.
La **belle** maman fesse le garçon **stupide**.

1. Forms of the descriptive adjectives:

A descriptive adjective agrees in gender and number with the noun it modifies. Therefore, adjectives have four forms: masculine singular, feminine singular, masculine plural, and feminine plural.

Un homme heureux	masculine, singular
Une femme heureuse	feminine, singular
Des hommes heureux	masculine, plural
Des femmes heureuses	feminine, plural

2. The singular forms:

The feminine singular of all adjectives ends in **-e**. The regular feminine adjective is formed by adding an **-e** to the masculine singular.

M., Sing.	F., Sing.	English
petit	petite	small
noir	noire	black
grand	grande	big/great
élégant	élégante	elegant

3. If the masculine singular form of an adjective ends in **-e**, the adjective is invariable, that is, it stays the same in both masculine and feminine forms.

M., Sing.	F., Sing.	English
jaune	jaune	yellow
sympathique	sympathique	sympathic
utile	utile	useful

4. For masculine adjectives ending in **-el**, **-eil**, **-en**, **-on**, **-et**, **-os**, and **-as**, double the last consonant before adding -e to form the feminine.

M., Sing.	F., Sing.	English
Parisien	Parisienne	Parisian
formel	formelle	formal
gros	grosse	big
bon	bonne	good
pareil	pareille	like/similar
gras	grasse	fat
muet	muette	silent

5. A few adjectives have two masculine forms. Use the first form before nouns beginning with a consonant and the second form before nouns beginning with a vowel or mute **-h**. To form the feminine of these adjectives, double the last consonant and add a final **-e** to the second masculine form.

M., Sing.(1st form)	M., Sing.(2nd form)	F., Sing.
le nouveau livre	le nouvel an	la nouvelle mode
ce beau garçon	ce bel homme	cette belle femme
un vieux monument	un vieil homme	une vieille amie
un fou rire	un fol amour	une folle affaire

Le vieux batiment reste intact.
The old building remains whole.

Le vieil instituteur a pris sa retraite.
The old teacher is retired.

La vieille église est fermée.
The old church is closed.

6. Change masculine singular adjectives ending in **-f** to **-ve** to form the feminine.

M., Sing.	F., Sing.	English
naïf	naïve	naïve
neuf	neuve	new
sportif	sportive	athletic

7. When an adjective whose masculine singular form ends in **-eur** is derived from a present participle, the feminine ends in **-euse**. If the adjective is derived from a noun ending in **-tion**, the feminine ends in **-trice**.

M., Sing.	F., Sing.	English

moquant/moqueur	moqueuse	mocking
mentant/menteur	menteuse	lying
tentation/tentateur	tentatrice	tempting

8. Certain adjectives that imply comparison simply add **-e** in the feminine.

M., Sing.	F., Sing.	English
meilleur	meilleure	better
antérieur	antérieure	previous

9. There are some adjectives that follow no definite rules when forming the feminine.

M., Sing.	F., Sing.	English
blanc	blanche	white
franc	franche	frank
frais	fraîche	fresh/cool
sec	sèche	dry
épais	épaisse	thick
faux	fausse	false
doux	douce	sweet/soft
jaloux	jalouse	jealous
gentil	gentille	nice
nul	nulle	null
complet	complète	complète
public	publique	public
grec	grecque	Greek
sot	qsotte	silly

10. The plural forms:

A. The plural form of an adjective is formed by adding an unpronounced final **-s** to its singular form.

M., Singular	M., Plural
Le garçon est élégant.	Les garçons sont élégants.
The boy is elegant.	The boys are elegants.
L' étudiant sera actif.	Les étudiants seront actifs.
The student will be active.	The students will be active.

B. If the masculine singular adjective ends in **-s** or **-x**, there is no change in the masculine plural form.

M., Sing.	M., Pl.
Le garçon heureux	Les hommes heureux
L'enfant curieux	Les enfants curieux

C. Most masculine singular adjectives ending in **-al** have masculine plural endings in **-aux**.

M., Sing.	M., Pl.
un document légal	des documents légaux
un monument national	des monuments nationaux

Note: The common adjectives **fatal**, **final**, and **naval,** which ends in **-l** form their plurals regularly: **fatals, finals,** and **navals**.

D. Add an **-x** to masculine singular adjectives ending in **eau** or **-eu** to form the plural.

M., Sing.	M., Pl.
jumeau	jumeaux
beau	beaux

E. When two or more feminine nouns are qualified by the same adjective, the adjective is feminine, plural. When the nouns are all masculine or of two genders, the adjective is masculine, plural.

Ma femme et ma fille sont tres amusantes
My wife and my daughter are amusing

Mon frère et mon neveux seront contents.
My brother and my nephew will be happy.

Ma femme a acheté une robe et un manteau elegants.
My wife bought a stylish dress and coat.

11. Position of adjectives:

A. The position of adjectives used as predicates is the same as in English.

L'enfant est heureux.	The child is happy.
Il reste patient.	He remains patient.

Note: The position of the adjectives used as epithets is variable and may depend on such factors as euphony, emphasis, or shades of meaning. However, the position of certain adjectives is relatively fixed.

1. Adjectives which normally follow the noun:

a) Adjectives of color, shape, and other physical characteristics; nationality, religion, class, political groups, and present and past participles used as adjectives.

de l'eau bouillante	boiling water
une fenêtre ouverte	an open window

Note: Adjectives of nationality, religion, etc., which are capitalized in English, are not capitalized in French. However, nouns of nationality are capitalized: Un Italien.

b) Adjectives denoting a distinguishing quality or characteristic:

un animal cruel	cruel animal
des enfants intelligents	intelligent children
une histoire amusante	an amusing story

12. Adjectives which precede the noun:

A. Adjectives used figuratively. If these adjectives are placed after the noun, the meaning is literal.

Literal	Figurative
des chausettes chaudes	une chaude réception
(some warm socks)	(a warm reception)
une allée sombre	une sombre complot
(a dark alley)	(a dark plot)
une terre maigre	un maigre salaire
(a barren piece of land)	(a low wage)

B. Adjectives qualifying a proper name or a noun followed by a proper name.

mon brave ami Pierre	my brave friend Pierre
le malin détectif Rouen	the clever Detective Rouen
l'habile mécanicien Jean	the skillful mechanic Jean

13. The following common adjectives usually precede the noun they qualify: **beau - bon - dernier - gentil - grand- gros -jeune -joli - long - mauvais - meilleur - moindre -petit - pire - prochain - vieux - vilain**

Notes: a) **Bon**. When the adjective, "bon" precedes the nouns homme, femme, garçon, fille, it means "good-natured/easy-going," but it may also imply condescension. To mean "good" in the sense of kindhearted, "bon" is placed after these nouns. Un bonhomme is one word (plural = des bonshommes) and means "chap/fellow."

b) **Grand**. Un grand homme means "a great man." Un homme grand means "a tall man." Grand means "great" also when it is followed by such words as écrivain (writer), savant (scientist), chef (leader/chief), roi (king), etc. Followed by other nouns, grand means "big/large/tall."

c) **Jeune**. Un jeune homme means "a young man" or "a youth." The plural is des jeunes gens which may also mean "young people" (of both genders). Jeune, implying "still young" or "not yet old" is placed after the noun.

d) **Une jeune fille**. The word fille, except when it means daughter, is not used without a qualifier: une jeune fille, une belle fille, une fille sympathique, etc. Une jeune fille (plural = des jeunes filles) means a girl in her late teens or early twenties. Fille used alone is derogatory.

e) **Prochain**. In describing time, prochain follows the noun.

f) **Dernier**. Dernier also follows the noun in a description of time when "last" means "just past." However, when dernier means "last" (in a series), it precedes the noun: la semaine dernière (last week), la dernière semaine de mes vacances (the last week of my vacation).

14. Certain adjectives may precede the noun:

A. When a quality is not a distinguishing characteristic but is merely added to the noun as a descriptive epithet: une charmante femme, un excellent homme, un magnifique spectacle, un célèbre avocat.

B. When a descriptive epithet and a noun are associated in meaning through an accepted conception: un cruel tyran (tyrants are usually cruel), une violente tempête, une riche banquier (bankers are supposed to be rich), une rare occasion, les braves troupes (troops are always braves), etc.

C. Used after the noun, the above adjectives in A and B would stress the quality as a distinguishing characteristic of the subject. It is always safer to use such adjectives after the noun.

15. When a noun is modified by more than one adjective, each adjective retains its position according to the rules already explained. (When all of them must follow, the adjective immediately preceding the noun in English is the first to follow the noun in French.)

une élégante petite fille	an elegant little girl
un petit garçon intelligent	an intelligent little boy
un chapeau blanc élégant	an elegant white hat

16. Adjectives joined by a conjunction follow the general rule, except that if one must follow the noun, both must follow.

une homme habile et ingénieux	a skilfull and resourcefull man
une famille noble et généreuse	a noble and generous family
un petit garçon poli et intelligent	a polite and intelligent little boy

17. Adjectives followed by a prepositional complement must follow the noun as in English.

une leçon facile à comprendre	a lesson easy to understand
un hero digne d'éloges	a hero worthy of praise

18. The preposition de is used before an adjective after indefinite pronouns such as **quelqu'un, quelque chose, personne, rien, quelques-uns,** etc., and when the adjective refers to the pronoun **en**.

quelqu'un de serieux	someone serious
quelque chose de raisonable	something reasonable
Il n'y a rien de nouveau.	There is nothing new.
J'en ai trouvé beaucoup de cassés.	I have found many broken ones.
Il en connait une d'interessante.	He knows an interesting one.

Note: It is to be noted that de as used in these sentences has the meaning of qui+ être: quelqu'un qui est serieux, beaucoup qui ont été cassés.

19. Most French adjectives may be used as nouns by placing an article (or a possessive or demonstrative adjective) before them.

Le noir ne lui va pas.	Black does not suit her.
Cette petite est mignone.	This little one is cute.

Exercise 1
Replace the noun in the following phrases with the noun in the parentheses. Be sure to make any other necessary changes. Then change the new phrase from singular to plural.
1. la comédie interessante (roman)
2. un silence mortel (blessure)
3. l'accent italien (prononciation)
4. la belle femme (homme)
5. le gentil compliment (carte)
6. ce dessert delicieux (sucrerie)
7. le jus frais (pommes)]
8. le beau tableau ancien (peinture)
9. cette légende médievale (histoire)
10. une idée générale (plans)
11. sa soeur ainée (frere)
12. l'exercice difficile (leçon)
13. ce fruit frais (eau)
14. une vieille histoire (argument)
15. un homme calculateur (personne)
16. une photo flatteuse (portrait)
17. un mot discret (lettre)
18. cet acteur célèbre (actrice)
19. votre meilleur ami (amie)
20. un air sérieux (position)
21. la nouvelle bicyclette (velo)
22. ce cahier bleu (chemise)
23. la phrase complète (exercice)
24. une organisation active (club)
25. notre premier message (leçon)

Exercise 2
Position of descriptive adjectives: Combine the sentences by using the adjective in an emphatic manner.
Reminders:
1. In French, most adjectives follow the nouns they modify:
Le professeur a présenté une leçon importante sur la biologie moderne.
2. Some adjectives precede the nouns they modify:
a) the adjective before a noun may add emphasis or to indicate feelings:

Mr. Célestin est un docteur habile.
Mr. Célestin is a skillful doctor.

(The adjective follows the noun because it denotes a distinguishing quality or characteristic.)

L'habile docteur Célestin est mon ami.
The skillful doctor Célestin is my friend.

(The adjective preceded the noun because the adjective is qualifying a proper noun. The adjective may precede the noun when a quality is not a distinguishing characteristic but is merely added to the noun as a descriptive epithet: une excellente école, un adorable petit garçon.)

1. C'est un écrivain. Il est formidable!_____
2. Ce sont mes romans. Ils sont superbes!_____
3. Vous connaissez ces poems. Ils sont émouvants!_____
4. Prenons cette peinture. Elle est magnifique!_____
5. Voilà le gâteau! Il est sensationnel!_____

b) Some descriptive adjectives normally precede the nouns they modify, such as those on the following list:

M./F., Sing.	English
beau/belle	handsome, beautiful
bon/bonne	good
gentil/gentille	nice
gros/grosse	big, fat
jeune/jeune	young
long/longue	long
mauvais/mauvaise	bad

Elle est une gentille petite fille.

c) When these adjectives occur after a noun they accentuate the adjective's meaning.

Ce n'est pas une femme gentille.

3. An indefinite adjective, an adjective that does not specify distinct limits, usually precedes the noun it modifies. Following is a list of indefinite adjectives that precede nouns.

aucun(e)* - no one, none   autre* - other
chaque - each   divers(e) - various
maint(e)* - many a   nul(le)* - no, no one
plusieurs* - several   quelque - some
quelques-uns/unes - a few   tel(le)* - such a
tout(e)*all, whole, everything, every
tous,(toutes)* - all, whole, everything, every
un/une* - one

Note: These indefinite adjectives (*) may be used as indefinite pronouns.

Elle n'a aucune raison de se facher ainsi.
She has no reason to be so angry.

Elle n'en a aucune.
She has none. ("no reason," implied)

4. In order to intensify a noun, a form of the adjective "tout" may be used before the article or possessive adjective or pronoun that introduces the noun.

Toute la bande sera à la fête.
The whole gang will be at the party.

5. The adjective qualifying a proper noun must be placed before the noun.

le cruel dictateur Janvier
l'intelligent professeur Dupont

Exercise 3

Rewrite the following sentences, inserting the correct form of the adjective given in its correct position.
1. C'était une fille. (curieux)
2. Je regarde un film. (mauvais)
3. Les jeunes gens dansent. (tout)
4. Ce assassin a été condamne. (cruel)
5. Elle a choisi une chanson. (long)
6. C'est un bijou. (beau)
7. Personne n'est venu. (aucun)
8. Je vois les roses. (tout)
9. J'ai acheté un bureau. (anciens)
10. Il mangeait des pommes. (trois)

6. There are a number of common descriptive and indefinite adjectives whose English translation changes according to whether they come before or after a noun.

Before a Noun	After a Noun
ancien - former	old/ancient
brave - worthy/good	brave
certain - certain/distinct	sure
cher - dear (sweet)	dear/expensive
dernier - past/final	last
grand - big/great	famous/tall
maigre - scanty/meager	lean/thin
mechant - naughty	wicked
meme - same	very
pauvre - pitiable	penniless
propre - own	clean
sale - grimy	nasty
seule - only one	alone
simple - mere	not complicated
vrai - real/genuine	true

Exercise 4

Translate the following sentences into English. Be sure to note the position of the adjective.

1. Ces méchants garçons jouent dans la rue.
2. J'ai de braves amis.
3. J'ai des voisins amis.
4. Il peint avec un certain style.
5. Il peint avec un style certain.
6. J'ai de chers souvenirs de la Californie.
7. Le pauvre écrivain est devenu célèbre.
8. Je vois une seule personne.
9. Je vois une personne seule.
10. Elle est arrivée la semaine derniere.
11. Elle est arrivée la dernière semaine.
12. C'est un grand homme.
13. C'est un homme grand.
14. Le lycée est dans un ancien bâtiment.
15. Le lycée est dans un bâtiment ancien.
16. Ces violentes tempête frappent la campagne.
17. Le riche financier aiment les enfants pauvres.
18. Voilà mon propre lit.
19. Voilà mon lit propre.

Exercise 5

Answer the following questions negatively, using the adjective given in the parenthèses.

1. Les Irlandais font-ils de la mauvaise cuisine? (bonne)
2. Est-ce le temps de voir les anciens amis? (nouveaux)
3. Est-ce que c'est un frère détestable? (cher)
4. Sort-elle avec un garçon laid? (beau)
5. Jeanne a-t-elle l'autre modele de voiture? (meme)
6. Prend-on le nouvel train tous les jours? (meme)
7. Est-ce que c'est une composition enorme? (petit)
8. Est-ce que c'est une bague moderne? (ancien)
9. Ont-ils un garçon méchant? (gentil)
10. Est-ce que votre anniversaire tombe toujours à une date differente? (même)
11. Lit-elle le même poème? (autre)
12. Est-ce que ton père est un bel homme? (laid)
13. Ta mère est-elle une vieille personne? (jeune)
14. Ce magasin a-t-il des chaussures bon marche? (chères)
15. Monsieur Mendez est-il notre professeur actuel? (ancien)

7. Uses of descriptive adjectives:

a) When you have two or more adjectives of the same category following a noun, connect the adjectives with **et**.

C'est un travail sensible et ingenieux.

It's a sensitive and ingenious job.

b) When two or more adjectives describe different aspects of a noun, the conjunction is not used.

Monsieur Dupont porte un chapeau noir élégant.

Mr. Dupont is wearing an elegant black hat.

c) An adjective modifying more than one noun is plural.

Le garçon et sa soeur sont contents.

The boy and his sister are happy.

8. A series of adjectives collectively modifying a plural noun may be singular.

Il a invité les representants italien et canadien.

Exercise 6

Combine the sentenes by inserting the second adjective into the appropriate position in the first sentence.

1. Il achète une voiture anglaise. Elle est noire.
2. Prenez de ces pommes vertes. Elles sont delicieuses.
3. Qui va écouter cette musique moderne? Elle est ennuyeuse.
4. Nous nous asseyons a une table solide. Elle est lourde.
5. Vous offrez votre aide financière. Elle est considerable.
6. Ils préfèrent les costumes chics. Ils sont chers.
7. Je frequente des amis etrangers. Ils sont intéréssants.
8. Il a des leçons difficiles. Elles sont compliquées.

Exercise 7

Answer the questions affirmatively, placing the adjectives in the appropriate places.

1. Votre meilleur ami est-il jeune et sportif?
2. Est-ce que vous pensez à une profession sure et certaine?
3. Est-ce que votre oncle est pauvre et malheureux?
4. Votre chat est gros et gras, n'est-ce pas?
5. Est-ce que votre mére est charmante et riche?
6. Est-ce que votre voiture est petite et économique?
7. Est ce que votre petite amie est blonde et jolie?
8. Est-ce que votre patron est bête et méchant?
9. Votre professeur est gentil et patient, n'est-ce pas?
10. Votre chemise est-elle belle et élégante?

9. As a general rule, the partitive should be expressed by de alone before a plural adjective.

Cette rue a de beaux arbres.   This street has some beautiful trees.

Madame Dupont possède de jolies robes.

Mrs. Dupont possesses some pretty dresses.

10. However, to emphasize the quantity of a noun, the partitive **des** may be used.

Elle porte des jolies boucles d'oreilles.
She is wearing some pretty earrings.

Les enfants ont fait des petites fleurs en papier.
The children made some small paper flowers.

Note: Des autres means *"of the others"* or *"belonging to the others."* It is not the plural of un autre/une autre, *"another."* The plural form is always d'autres, *"other, some other."*

Exercise 8

Respond to the following questions and include the plural adjective in the answer.

1. Il a des plans. Sont-ils bons?
2. Cet homme a des idées. Sont - elles nouvelles?
3. Voilà des photos interessantes. Sont-elles jolies?
4. Nous faisons des exercices physique. Sont-ils bons?
5. Il y a des bijoux dans le musée. Sont-ils anciens?
6. Elle a fait des biscuits. Sont-ils petits?
7. Nous avons des amies chinoises. Sont-elles jeunes?
8. Le Louvre a des tableaux modernes. Sont-ils beaux?
9. Il y a des fleurs dans le jardin. Sont-elles grandes?
10. Jean a des peintures. Sont-elles vieilles?

COMPARATIVE AND SUPERLATIVE ADJECTIVES

La souris est **plus grande** que le fromage.
Le chat est **plus violent** que la souris.
Le garçon est **aussi méchant** que le chat.
La jeune mére est **moins cruelle** que le garçon.

1. Comparative and Superlative Adjectives. The comparative and superlative of an adjective is used to indicate degrees in quality or quantity. There are three degrees: positive, comparative, and superlative.

Positive	Comparative	Superlative
clair/clear	plus clair/clearer	le plus clair/clearest

2. The comparative adjective is formed by simply adding one of the adverbs plus, moins, or aussi before an adjective in the positive. The comparative adjective must agree in gender and number with the first noun in the

comparison. The conjunction que follows directly after the adjective and before the second noun in the comparison, which is called the complement of the comparison.

A. A comparison can be made on the basis of superiority — plus, more: Elle est plus sympatique que vous.

B. A comparison can be made on the basis of inferiority — moins, less: Elle est moins sympatique que sa soeur.

C. A comparison can be made on the basis of equality — aussi, as: Elle est aussi sympatique que son amie, Pauline.

D. The following two rules about comparative adjectives must be remembered.

1. Shorten aussi to si after a negative.

Notre usine est aussi moderne que la votre.

Notre usine n'est pas si moderne que la votre.

2. The preposition **de** must follow plus or moins before a numerical adjective.

La classe a plus de trente étudiants.

Exercise 9   Make a logical comparison of superiority, inferiority, or equality by placing the noun given in parentheses at the beginning of your new sentence. Be sure to watch for the agreement of the adjective with the first noun in the comparison; the placement of que after the adjective; the use of si after a negative; and the use of **plus** or **moins** + **de** before a numerical adjective.

1. Le lait est froid. (l'eau)
2. Le soleil est brillant. (la lune)
3. Le lait est nourrissant. (la creme)
4. Une plume n'est pas légère. (un livre)
5. Mai a plus de vingt neuf jours. (fevrier)
6. Les cravates sont chères. (les costumes)
7. Un dictateur est cruel. (un tyrant)
8. L'algèbre est difficile. (l'arithmetique)
9. La glace n'est pas solide. (l'eau)
10. Le texas est grand. (New York)
11. Le train est rapide. (l'avion)
12. Les chiens sont intelligents. (les hommes)
13. Un mois est long. (une année)
14. Les bonbons sont doux. (le sucre)
15. La glace est froide. (la pluie)

3. Formation and use of superlative adjectives. The superlative adjective is used to denote the utmost degree of quality or quantity.

A. To form a superlative adjective, the definite article **le, la,** or **les** precedes a comparative adjective. The definite article must agree in number and gender with the noun it modifies.

Positive	Comparative	Superlative
actif	plus actif	le plus actif
active	more active	most active

B. The preposition de must be used before the complement of the superlative—the word or words used to complete the sense of the superlative.

C'est le garçon le plus actif du lycée.
He is the most active boy in the school.

Note: When an adjective is used in the superlative form, it goes in its usual position, before or after the noun.

C'est le garçon le plus paresseux de la classe.

C. The following adjectives have irregular comparative and superlative forms.

Positive	Comparative	Superlative
bon	**meilleur**	**le (la) meilleur(e)**
good	better	best
mauvais	**plus mauvais**	**le (la) plus mauvais(e)**
	moins mauvais	**le (la) pire**
	pire	le (la) pire)
bad	worse	worst
petit	**plus petit**	**le (la) plus petit(e)**
	moins petit	**le (la) moins petit(e)**
small	smaller	smallest
	moindre	**le (la) moindre**
	lesser	the least

Notes: a) With concrete nouns, **plus (moins)** mauvais and **le (la)** plus **(moins)** **mauvais(e)** must be used.

Les gâteaux sont plus mauvais pour les dents que les pommes.

b) With abstract nouns pire and le (la) pire must be used.

L'avarice est le pire des péchés.

c) To compare size, **plus (moins)** grand, **plus (moins)** petit and **le (la)** plus **(moins)** **grand, le (la)** plus **(moins)** **petit (e)** must be used.

Ma voiture est plus petite que la tienne.

d) To compare quantity or importance, moindre and le (la) moindre must be used.

Les mots ont moindre importance que les actions.

4. There should not be any difficulty identifying the comparative or superlative forms for adjectives that normally follow a noun.

La voiture plus économique coûte 10 milles dollars.

Note: The comparative and superlative forms are the same for adjectives that normally precede a noun. Only the context will tell you the difference.

The best books are the most expensive.

Exercise 10

Use the elements provided to form sentences containing a superlative.

Example: Connaissez-vous/l'eleve intelligent/dans votre classe.
Connaissez-vous l'élève le plus intelligent de votre classe.

1. le Texas/grand etat/Etats-Unis
2. l'été est/une saison agréable/ dans l'année
3. c'est un/mes petits/soucis
4. l'eau/boisson chère/monde
5. Ce sont des édifices/impressionnants/dans notre ville.

Exercise 11

Rewrite the following sentences so that the adjective is in the superlative form.

1. Elle nous a donné une mauvaise excuse.
2. Je pense que notre médecin est très habile.
3. Il a mis sa vieille cravate.
4. Elle est sortie protant son chapeau elegant.
5. Le printemps est une belle saison.
6. Madame Dupont a une bonne idée.
7. Elle fait parfois des remarques moins originales.
8. C'est une des écoles anciennes du pays.

THE POSSESSIVE ADJECTIVES

La souris mange **son** fromage.
Le chat ne guette pas **sa** souris.
Le garçon ne chasse pas **son** chat.
La jeune mére fesse **ses** fils.

1. The Possessive Adjectives. In French the possessive adjective must agree in number and gender with the thing possessed—not with the possessor.

son cadeau = his gift or her gift

Note: A possessive adjective agrees in person with the possessor, even though it does not show the possessor's gender.

Singular	Plural	English
Mas. / Fem.	Mas. / Fem.	
mon / ma	mes	my
ton / ta	tes	your (fam.)
son / sa	ses	his/her/its
notre / notre	nos	our
votre / votre	vos	your
leur / leur	leurs	their

2. Use of the possessive adjective. The possessive adjective must agree in number and in gender with the object possessed and in person with the possessor.

C'est le lit de Claudette.
C'est son lit.

C'est la voiture de Pierre.
C'est sa voiture.

Marie et Jean sont les amis de Paul.
Ce sont ses amis.

Note: Possessive adjectives, like other adjectives, agree in gender and number with the nouns they modify. They must be repeated before each noun.

Nos enfants sont dans notre voiture.
Our children are in our car.

Son père et sa mère demeurent à la campagne.
Her father and her mother live in the country.

3. The forms mon, ton, and son are used instead of **ma**, **ta**, and **sa** before a feminine singular noun beginning with a vowel or silent **-h**.
Quelle est ton adresse?   Marie, est-elle ton amie?

4. If it is necessary to distinguish between his and her for the sake of clarity, à lui or à elle are added.

C'est sa chambre à lui.   It is his bedroom.
C'est son père à elle.   It is her father.

5. With parts of the body, the possessive adjective is frequently replaced by the definite article if the possessor is clear.
Je me suis cassé la jambe.   I broke my leg.

Exercise 12

Compléter chaque phrase avec la forme convenable de l'adjectif possessif:

1. L'avocat a rendu visite a _____ client.
2. Mme Dupont va repasser _____ robes.
3. Ne jouez pas avec _____ santé.
4. Les paysans ont coupe la laine de _____ moutons.
5. J'ai dit bonjour en enlevant _____ chapeau.

6. Fais-tu _____ derniere année d'études?

7. Nous avons joui d'un beau temps pendant _____ vacances.

8. Elle voudrait vivre _____ propre vie.

9. Avez-vous amené _____ amis au cinema?

10. Les femmes n'ont pas encore fini _____ thé.

Exercise 13   Complete the following sentences with the appropriate possessive adjective or definite article.

1. Personne n'a oublié _____ plume.

2. Il a levé (his) _____ main.

3. (My) _____ voiture est en panne.

4. Ils lisent (leur) _____ journal.

5. (your, formal) mère m'a écrit.

6. Elle brosse (her) _____ cheveux.

7. Il a (his) _____ main sur la table.

8. Leon et André ont écrit à _____ parents.

9. Tu as (your) chemise.

10. Pierre et Andre a telepone à _____ mère.

11. Elle adore (her) _____ père.

12. (My) amies sortent souvent avec moi.

DEMONSTRATIVE ADJECTIVES

Cette souris mange le fromage.

Ce chat guette la souris.

Ce garçon chasse le chat.

Cette jeune mère fesse le garçon.

1. Demonstrative Adjectives. The demonstrative adjectives are ce, cet, cette (this, that), and ces (these, those).

A. Ce is used before a masculine singular noun beginning with a consonant.

    ce musée   this (that) museum

B. Cet is used before a masculine singular noun beginning with a vowel or silent -h.

    cet homme   this (that) man

C. Cette is used before a feminine singular noun.

    cette robe   this (that) dress

D. Ces is used before all plural nouns.

ces moulins   these (those) mills

Note: The demonstrative adjective must be repeated before each noun.

Ce sac coûte plus cher que cette robe.

This hand bag cost more than that dress.

2. If it is necessary to distinguish between this and that, or between these and those, -ci and -la are attached to the nouns contrasted with a hyphen. To mean *"this"* or *"these,"* -ci is added; to mean *"that"* or *"those,"* -la is added.

Cette pomme-ci ou cette pomme-là coûte la même chose.

This apple here or that apple there cost the same.

Exercise 14

Fill in the blank with the correct form of the demonstrative adjective.

1. _____ faits sont importants.
2. Elle aime _____ roman.
3. Elle a écrit _____ pièce.
4. _____ automobile est dans le garage.
5. _____ amies arrivent ce soir.
6. Parlez à _____ enfant.
7. _____ garçon arrive toujours en retard.
8. Sur _____ page j'écris mon nom.
9. _____ homme défend son honneur.
10. Nous allons déjeuner dans _____ restaurant.
11. _____ route va à Paris.
12. _____ artiste travaille bien.

INTERROGATIVE ADJECTIVES

Quel fromage la souris **a-t-elle mangé**?

Quelle souris le chat **a-t-il guetté**?

Quel chat le garçon **a-t-il chassé**?

Quel garçon la jeune fille **a-t-elle fessé**?

1. **Interrogative adjectives.** The interrogative adjective, quel (which, what) agrees in gender and number with a following noun or stands in place of the noun as a pronoun when the subject noun follows a form of être.

A. Forms of the interrogative adjective

	Singular	Plural	
Masculine	quel	quels	which, what
Feminine	quelle	quelles	which, what

B. Exclamations with quel

Use quel in exclamations with the same meaning as "What (a)...!" in English. In an exclamation, quel is not followed by an article.

Quelle pagaie!	What a mess!
Quel pessimisme insense!	What a senseless pessimism!
Quel toupet!	What (a) nerve!

C. Quel as an interrogative pronoun

Quel may stand alone as an interrogative pronoun in the subject position if the subject noun follows the verb être. In this case, quel takes its gender and number from the subject noun.

| Quels seront les résultats? | What will the results be? |
| Quelle est la différence? | What's the différence? |

Exercise 15

Replace the expression il y a with the appropriate form of the verb être and a following subject.

Example: Quelle raison y a-t-il?   Quelle est la raison?

1. Quel menu y aura-t-il? _____
2. Quelles objections y aurait-il? _____
3. Quels vins y avait-il? _____
4. Quelle reponse y avait-il? _____
5. Quelle atmosphere y a-t-il? _____

Exercise 16

Create an exclamation following the model:

Regarde le garçon!   Quel garçon!

1. Regarde les livres! _____
2. Reggarde le paysage! _____
3. Regarde la peinture! _____
4. Regarde l'arbre! _____
5. Regarde les animaux! _____

Exercise 17

Form questions, using **quel**.

1. Le tableau au coin est grand.
2. Les restaurants là-bas sont bons.
3. Mon adresse est 15, rue de Prony.
4. Les robes rouges sont dans l'armoire.
5. J'aime bien ces peintures-là.

INDEFINITE ADJECTIVES

La souris a mangé **un** autre fromage.
Le chat guette **quelques** souris.
Chaque garçon a chassé **un** chat.
La jeune mère fesse **tous les** garçons.

1. Indefinite adjectives. The most common indefinite adjectives are:
A. **un(e) autre, d'autres** (another, other, different)

Je voudrais essayer une autre paire de chaussures.
I would like to try on another pair of shoes.

Avez-vous d'autres cravates?
Do you have any other neckties?

Notes: 1. The plural of un autre is d'autres.

une autre paire de chaussures   another pair of shoes
d'autres paires de chaussures   other pairs of shoes

2. In spoken language, autres is also used to reinforce a first or second person plural subject pronoun.

Nous autres étudiants, nous travaillons dur.
As for us students, we work hard.

3. Autre is also used without an article or demonstrative adjective in certain expressions.

Ca c'est autre chose.   That's something else. (That's different.)
de temps a autre   from time to time

B. **Aucun(e)...ne, nul(le)...ne, ne...aucun(e), ne...nul(le)** (no, none, not one, no one)

Aucun de ses amis n'est venu.
None of his friends came.

Nul ne lui a parlé au sujet de l'examen.
None spoke to him about the exam.

C. **certain(e), certain(e)s (certain**, some)
Certain is placed before the noun. Sometimes **certain** can mean the same thing as quelque.

Un certain monsieur a téléphoné.
A certain gentleman called.

Certains amis sont arrives en retard.
Some friends arrived late.

D. **chaque** (each, every)

Chaque homme doit suivre son destin.
Each man must live his destiny

L'enfant trébuche à chaque pas.
The child stumbles at every step.

E. **divers(es), different(e)s, maint(e)s** (several, various)

Divers étudiants ont participe a la manifestation.
Various students took part in the march.

A maintes reprises, j'ai du tout reprendre a zero.
Many times, I was compelled to begin all over again.

F. **même** (same, itself, very, even).

After a noun or a pronoun, même means *"very," "even," "same,"* *"itself," "herself," "himself," "yourself,"* etc.

Cette femme est la vertue même.   This woman is virtue itself.

Il est parti le jour même.   He left that very day.

Même ses enfants lui ont abandonne.
Even his children adandonned him.

Parle-lui toi-même.
Speak to him yourself.

Notes: 1. Même means "same" before a noun preceded by **a** definite article.

C'est la même chose.
It's the same thing.

Nous avons acheté les mêmes cravates.
We bought the same neckties.

2. **Même** is attached by a hyphen to personal disjunctive (stress) pronouns to mean, *"myself," "yourself,"* etc. (**moi-même, toi-même, lui-même, elle-même, soi-même, nous-même, vous-même, eux-même, elles-même**)

G. **n'importe** (no matter)

N'importe combines with **quel, quelle, quels, quelles,** to signify *"no matter what/which."*

Viens me voir a n'importe quelle heure.

Come to see me any time. (at any hour)

H. **plusieurs** (several)

Ils ont plusieurs petits enfants.
They have several grandchildren.

Plusieurs feuilles sont déjà tombées.
Several leaves have already fallen.

Note: Plusieurs is invariable.

I. **quelque (s)** (a little, some, any kind of, few)

1. In the singular, quelque means *"a little," "some," "any kind of."*

Il nous reste quelque temps.
We have a little time left.

Elle cherche quelque poste.
She is looking for any (some) kind of job.

2. In the plural, **quelques** means *"a few," "some,"* or *"several."*

Nous allons prendre quelques billets.
We are going to buy a few tickets.

Elle a quelques amis a Paris.
She has some (several) friends in Paris.

3. **Quelques** can be an adverb and, therefore, invariable when used before a number to mean **"environ"** (about).

Les pompiers ont attaqué une bande de feu de quelques cinquante mètres.
The fire fighters attacked a blazing fire of about fifty meters.

J. quelque... que (whatever, however) versus quel, quelle, quels, quelles... que (whatever)

1. Quelque and the interrogative adjective quel combine with the relative pronoun que to mean "whatever." The verb that follows is always in the subjunctive. Before a noun, quelque is a variable adjective.

Quelque peine que vous ayez, n'abandonnez pas la cause.
However difficult thing might be, don't give up.

2. Before a descriptive adjective, quelque is an adverb and, therefore, invariable.

Quelque méchants que soient les hommes, nous sommes tous frères.
However mean man might be, we are all brothers.

3. Before an adverb, quelque is used as an adverb and is therefore invariable.

Quelque bêtement que ses enfants agissent, elle les aime de toute sa force maternelle.
However foolishly her children behave, she loves them with all her motherly power.

4. Quel que is written as two words when it is followed by a verb (almost always the verb être). Quel que agrees with the subject in number and gender.

Quel que soit votre avis, ne parlez pas sans réfléchir.
Whatever your point of view, do not speak without thinking.

Quelle que soit la querelle, ne perdez pas votre sang froid.
Whatever the the dispute, do not lose your nerve.

Quels que soient les obstacles, restez déterminé.

Whatever the obstacles, remain determined.

K. **quelconque** (just any, any old)

Ce n'est pas un manteau quelconque. C'est un manteau en fourrure.
This is not just any coat. It's a fur coat.

L. **je ne sais quel** (le)(s)(les) (I don't know)

on ne sait quel (le)(s)(les) (one doesn't know)
Dieu sait quel (le)(s)(les) (God only knows)

These expressions are used to indicate an approximate resemblance. They are similar in meaning to "certain" in an undetermined sense.

Je ne sais quelle personne a compose cette chason.
I don't know who composed this song.

Elle arrivera Dieu sait quel jour.
She will arrive God only knows when. (which day)

Il a on ne sait quelles idées absurdes.
He has some absurd ideas or others.

M. **tel** (m. sing.), **tels** (m. pl.), **telle** (f. sing.), **telles** (f. pl.) (such, such a , like, as)

Tel est son opinion.   Such is his opinion.
Je n'ai jamais vu une telle armée. I never saw such an army.
Telle mère, telle fille.   Like mother, like daughter.

Un étudiant tel que lui mérite de bonnes notes.
A student such as he deserves good grades.

Note: Use si instead of tel in expressions containing an adjective.

Avez-vous jamais vu une si belle église?
Have you ever seen such a beautiful church?

Avez-vous jamais des idées si absurdes?
Have you ever heard such absurd ideas?

N. **tout** (m. sing.), **tous** (m. pl.), toute (f., sing.), **toutes** (fem. pl.) (all, every, the whole).

1. In the singular, tout means *"each"* or *"every"* when it is used without an article.

Tout homme doit servir son pays.
Every man must serve his country.

Elle a perdu tout espoir.
She lost all hope.

en tout cas   in any case (at any rate)

2. When followed by an article, tout means *"the whole," "the entire part/thing."*

La jeune fille sourit tout le temps.

The young lady smiles all the time.

Tout le pays chante les louanges du président élu.
The whole country sings the praises of the elected president.

Note: In certain expressions, tout means "only."

Pour toute réponse, elle secoua la tête.
Her only answer was to shake her head.

3. In the plural, tout means "all" or "every."

Tous nos enfants sont au lit.
All our children are in bed.

4. Tout is invariable when using before the name of an author to mean the ensemble of his or her works; (all of the works of):

J'ai lu tout Colette.   I've read all Colette's work.

5. Tout is an invariable adverb when used to mean "quite," "entirely."

ma jeunesse tout entière.   my entire youth.
Nous sommes tout heureux.   We are quite happy.

6. Tout is also invariable before a feminine word beginning with a vowel or silent **h**.

Elle est tout souriant, tout heureuse.
She is all smiles, altogether happy.

However, the adverb tout must agree in gender and number before a feminine adjective beginning with a consonant or an aspirated h.

Les jeunes filles sont toute honteuses.
The young ladies are quite ashamed.

7. Some common expression formed with tout are:

tous (toutes) les deux both, both of them

en tout cas	in any case
pas du tout	not at all
a moi tout seul	all by myself
tout à l'heure	just now, presently
tout de suite	right away
tout de même	just the same
tout à fait	entire, completely
tout à coup	all of a sudden

Exercise 18

Change the sentences, using the words that follow the sentence. Make all necessary changes.

Example: Jean a des voitures. (plusieurs). Jean a plusieurs voitures.

1. Jeanne a des mouchoirs. quelque
2. Paul a beaucoup de copains. plusieurs
3. La jeune fille a du temps. quelque
4. Ces décisions sont difficiles. certain

5. Elle a vu des personnes. divers
6. Une peine mérité salaire. tout
7. Avez-vous des pommes? autre
8. Nous avons visité les maisons. tout
9. Il n'y a pas de verre dans la cuisine. aucun
10. L'enfant a mangé les bonbons. tout
11. Son père le déteste. même
12. Je n'ai jamais entendu de bétises. tel
13. C'est mon opinion. tel
14. Nous avons confiance en lui. tout
15. Des robes sont chères. autre
16. Nous avons parcouru cent mètres. quelque
17. Ils sont arrivés en hâte. tout
18. Prenez une cravate. quelconque.
19. Il a perdu l'envie de vivre avec sa femme. tout
20. L'équipe était prête. tout.

ADVERBS

La souris mange le fromage rapidement.
Le chat guette la souris malveillamment.
Le garçon chasse le chat malicieusement.
La mère fesse le garçon malignement.

1. Formation. An adverb is an invariable word that usually modifies a verb; but an adverb may also be used to modify other adverbs or adjectives.

Jean arrive souvent en retard à l'école.
Jean arrives often late to school.

C'est très mauvais.   It's very bad.

A. Most adverbs in French are formed from adjectives by adding **-ment**:
1. to the masculine singular form of the adjective when it ends in a vowel.

Adjective	Adverb
facile	facilement, easily
poli	poliment, politely
probable	probablement, probably
rapide	rapidement, rapidly/ quickly
rare	rarement, rarely, seldom
triste	tristement, sadly

vrai   vraiment, truly/really

2. to the feminine singular form of the adjective when the masculine adjetival form ends in a consonant.

Adjective (M. / F.)	Adverb
actif / active	activement, actively
attentif / attentive	attentivement, attentively
certain / certaine	certainement, certainly
correct / correcte	correctement, correctly
cruel / cruelle	cruellement, cruelly
distinct / distincte	distinctement, distinctly
doux / douce	doucement, sweetly/mildly
fier / fière	fièrement, proudly
général / générale	généralement, generally
heureux / heureuse	heureusement, happily
immédiat / immédiate	immédiatement, immediately
léger / légère	légèrement, lightly
lent / lente	lentement, slowly
malheureux/malheureuse	malheureusement, unfortunately
naturel / naturelle	naturellement, naturally
seul / seule	seulement, only

B. The other common adverbs are:

alors, then	mal, badly
assez, enough	moins, less
aujourd'hui, today	partout, everywhere
aussi, too, also	peu, little
autant, as much	peut-être, perhaps, maybe
beaucoup, much	plus, more
bien, well	près (de), near
bientôt, soon	presque, almost
déjà, already	quelquefois, sometimes
demain, tomorrow	si, so
encore, still, yet	souvent, often
ensemble, together	surtout, especially
ensuite, next	tant, so much
hier, yesterday	tard, late
ici, here	toujours, always
là, there	très, very
loin, far	trop, too much
longtemps, a long time, vite, quickly	
maintenant, now	

2. Position of adverbs. In simple tenses, the adverb is usually placed immediately after the verb it modifies. If the verb is negative, the adverb follows the complete negative.

Elle boit lentement son café.	She drinks her coffee slowly.
Ils ne voyagent pas beaucoup.	They don't travel much.

A. In compound tenses, most adverbs follow the past participle, but a few common ones, such as bien, mal, toujours, beaucoup, déjà, and encore, usually precede the past participle.

Elle a bu lentement son café.

Ils n'avaient pas beaucoup voyagé.

3. Comparative and superlative adverbs. Comparative and superlative adverbs indicate degrees in quality, quantity, or manner. There are three degrees: positive, comparative, and superlative.

Positive	Comparative	Superlative
facilement	plus facilement	le plus facilement
tôt	moins tôt	le moins tôt

4. Formation and use of comparative adverbs. The comparative of an adverb is formed exactly as the comparative adjective. One of the adverbs plus, moins, or aussi (si, after a negative verb) is used before the adverb in a comparison. The conjunction que follows directly after the adverb and precedes the second noun in the comparison (the complement of the comparison).

Jean lit plus vite que moi.	Jean reads more quickly than me.
Il parle moins vite que moi.	He speaks less quickly than me.
Il écrit aussi vite que moi.	She write as quickly as you.

Note: The second term in a comparison can be implied, but not mentioned, just as in English.

Il marche plus doucement.	He sings more slowly.

5. Formation and use of superlative adverbs. The superlative adverb denotes the utmost degree of quality, or manner.

A. To form the superlative adverb, place the definite article le before the comparative adverb. Because an adverb is invariable, the masculine singular form of the definite article is always used.

Positive	Comparative	Superlative
facilement	plus facilement	le plus facilement
easily	more easily	most easily
souvent	moins souvent	le moins souvent
often	less often	least often

B. Always use the preposition de before the complement of the superlative.

Dans la classe de français, c'est Jean qui est le plus intelligent de tous les étudiants.
In the French class, Jean is the most intelligent.

C'est le couple qui dance le plus doucement de tous les danseurs.
That is the couple who dances the slowest of all the dancers.

C. The following adverbs form their comparatives and superlatives irregularly.

Positive	Comparative	Superlative
bien, well	mieux, better	le mieux, best
beaucoup, much	plus, more	le plus, most
mal, bad	plus mal, worse	le plus mal, worst
peu, little	moins, less	le moins, least

C'est Jean qui chante le mieux.
It is Jean qho sings the best.

Il est l'étudiant qui s'amuse le moins.
He is the student who enjoys himself the least.

Notes: a) Some English adverbs have the same form as the corresponding adjective: better, best, worse, worst, little. In translating into French, it is important to distinguish between the adjective and the adverb.

Ces cravates-ci sont meilleures que ces adj. cravates-la.
These ties are better than those ties adj.

Jean travaille mieux que moi. adv.
Jean works better than me. adv.

b) Before numerals, "than" is translated by de.

J'ai passé plus de deux mois à la Guadeloupe.
I spent more than two months in Guadeloupe.

Cette chemise vaut plus de 50 dollars.
This shirt is worth more than 50 dollars.

6. Adverbs of quantity. The common adverbs of quantity are:

assez, enough	guère, hardly
aussi, so	moins, fewer, less
autant, as many	peu/un peu, little, a few
autrement, otherwise	plus, more
beaucoup, many/a lot of	presque, almost
bien, very, a lot of	si, so much
combien, how many	tant, so many, so much
comme, as, like	tellement, so/so many/so much
davantage, more	très, very
encore, still, yet	trop, too much, too many

La soupe est tellement bonne.   The soup is so good.

Il voudrait davantage.
He would like to have some more.

7. Uses of adverbs of quantity are:

A. The preposition de must be used after the adverbs of quantity and nouns of quantity when they introduce a noun.

Il y a assez de café.
There is enough coffee.

Vous consumez trop de sucre, mon ami.
You consume too much sugar, my friend.

B. Peu de used as an adverb of quantity is translated as "few or little."

J'ai très peu d'argent.
I have very little money.

Elle a peu d'ami.
Elle has few friends.

C. Si is used to modify an adjective. Un, une, or de comes before si if the adjective precedes the noun.

Madame Dupont a de si beaux cheveux.
Mrs. Dupont has such beautiful hair.

Note: If si modifies an adjective that follows the noun, un, une, and de remain in their normal position—before the noun.
Elle a un chapeau si grand qu'on voit à peine sa figure.
She has such a large hat that one can hardly see her face.

D. De plus en plus. The expression de plus en plus is translated as "more and more."

Elle sort de plus en plus ces jours-ci.
She goes out more and more these days.

Notes: a) De plus en plus is also used before an adverb or adjective to translate expressions such as faster and faster, blacker and blacker, etc.

Il danse de plus en plus vite.
He dances faster and faster.

b) The expression de moins en moins is translated as "less and less."

E. Beaucoup must not be modified by another adverb of quantity.

Jean mange beaucoup.
Jean eats a lot.

F. Bien instead of très can be used to modify an adjective or adverb. Bien de can be followed by le, la, or les instead of beaucoup de.

A New York, il fait bien chaud en été.
In New York, it is very hot in the summer.

La chanteuse avait bien du succès.

The singer had a lot of success.

G. The French language does not distinguish between *"much"* and *"many."* Therefore, autant, beaucoup, combien, moins, peu, tant, tellement, or trop are translated as *"much"* with a singular noun, and as *"many"* with a plural noun.

autant de livres	as many tickets
autant de sucre	as much sugar

Exercise 19

Translate into French:

1. actively, more actively, most actively
2. more naturally than, not so naturally as
3. as politely as, least politely
4. more politely than, less politely
5. very cruelly, too cruelly, so well
6. more than five, less than ten
7. truly, also, maybe
8. more slowly than, as much as
9. as sweetly as, least mildly
10. much, more, most

Exercise 20

Complete with the missing word.

1. Hier il a fait beau, et aujourd'hui il fait très beau. On dit qu'il fera beau _____ aussi.
2. Quels fruits frais avez-vous aujourd'hui? Y a-t-il des pommes ou des pêches? - Non, madame, malheureusement. Nous avons _____ des oranges.
3. Sont-ils retournés tout de suite? -Oui, ils ont du retourner _____.
4. Il y avait plus _____ vingt voitures dans la rue.
5. Jean écoutait avec attention le chant des oiseaux. Oui, il l'écoutait très _____.
6. Monsieur et Madame Célestin, sont-ils arrivés séparément? Non, ils sont arrivés _____
7. Mes chers amis, je crois que vous chantez mieux _____ jamais.
8. Pourquoi dites-vous que Jean est parfait? -Parce qu'il fait _____ tout ce qu'il fait.
9. Parlez plus_____, s'il vous plait. Quelquefois il est difficile de vous comprendre.
10. Ont-ils recu la lettre avec joie? En effet, ils les ont reçues _____.

Exercise 21

Answer the following questions, using the cues given in parentheses.

1. Ecrivez-vous beaucoup? (non, peu)
2. Ce déjeuner est-il bon? (oui, bien)
3. Dépense-t-elle dans les grands magasins? (beaucoup)
4. Le professeur parle-t-il autant que les étudiants? (davantage)
5. Cet employé est-il aussi intelligent que son collègue? (plus que)
6. Le climat devient-il moins agréable? (de moins en moins)
7. Le travail est-il difficile? (de plus en plus)
8. A-t-elle une jolie robe qu'on admire? (si jolie)
9. Le directeur fait-il des cadeaux aux employés? (si beaux)
10. Avez-vous des devoirs à l'école? (peu de)

Exercise 22

Translate into English.

1. Ce sera bientôt l'hiver.
2. Ils m'ont rendu visite plus de dix fois.
3. Elles se sont levées immédiatement; ensuite elles sont sorties.
4. Jean s'est habillé plus vite que nous.
5. Marianne va au cinéma aussi souvent que possible.
6. Il y avait des fleurs presque partout dans le jardin.
7. Comment vont vos parents? Ils vont beaucoup mieux.
8. Les étudiants, étudient-ils assez? Ils étudient trop, surtout Jean.
9. Les meilleurs étudiants n'écrivent pas toujours le mieux.
10. Il est le plus brillant de tous les sénateurs.

Exercise 23

Translate into French.

1. They have traveled much through Europe.
2. There are more than thirty passengers in this bus.
3. Do you read as much as your friend?
4. They have spoken of you often.
5. He made fewer than five mistakes in his composition.
6. Jean has rarely told the truth.
7. We looked for him everywhere.
8. Pierre studies more than André but less than Jean.
9. Henry has not yet left.
10. Who works least? Pierre, André or Jean?

LE CAHIER FRANÇAIS: MASTERY DRILLS

LEÇON 1: L'IDENTIFICATION ET LA DESCRIPTION

Exercices	Sujet
1.	Emploi de c'est / il est
2.	Identification
3. à 8.	Description
9.	Localisation
10. 11. 12.	Mesures

Exercice 1

Imiter l'exemple suivant: "Est-ce que vous connaissez ce monsieur?
- Oui, c'est mon voisin, il est très sympathique, il est informaticien."

1. "Connaissez-vous Le Rouge et le Noir?
   - Oui, _____ est un roman de Stendhal, _____ est passionnant."
2. "Est-ce que vous connaissez M. Raimondi? -Oui, _____ est un de nos amis,_____ est chirurgien, _____ est italien."
3. "Qui est cette jeune fille? _____ est une étrangère, _____ est jeune fille au pair chez ma soeur et _____ est charmante."
4. "Cet appareil, qu'est-ce que c'est?_____ est un magnétoscope, _____ est très perfectionné."
5. "Vous connaissez ce oiseau? - _____ est un merle, _____ est très courant dans cette region."
6. "Qui est cette dame qui parle si fort? - _____ est notre vieille concierge, _____ est un peu sourde."
7. "Qui sont ces enfants? - _____ sont les petits Barsac, _____ sont des amis de ma fille, _____ sont très mignons."
8. "Delacroix, qui est-ce? _____ est un peintre du XIXe siècle, _____ est français; _____ était contemporain de Charles Baudelaire."
9. "Cette crème, qu'est-ce que c'est? - _____ est une crème pour les mains, _____ est hydratante; _____ est la meilleure que je connaisse."
10. "Qu'est-ce que la Bourgogne? - _____ est une province de France, _____ est très célèbre pour ses églises romanes et ses vins."
11. "Qui est Yves Montand? - _____ est un chanteur et un acteur de cinéma; _____ est d'origine italienne, est grand et brun."

Exercice 2 - A

Répondre aux questions suivantes:

1. Qui est Hector Berlioz?
2. Qui a decouvert le vaccin contre la rage?
3. Qu'est-ce qu'un cordonnier?
4. Qui a dit: "Je pense donc je suis"?
5. Qui a peint le plafond de l'Opera de Paris?

6. Qui était roi de France en 1789?

7. Qu'est-ce qu'un égoiste?

8. Quelle est votre actrice préferée?

9. Quels sont les écrivains les plus célèbres de votre pays?

10. Quels sont les peuples qui parlent français hors de France?

Exercice 2 - B

1. Qu'est-ce qu'une peniche?

2. L'ONU, qu'est-ce que c'est?

3. Qu'est-ce qu'une synagogue?

4. Qu'est-ce qu'une harpe?

5. Qu'est-ce que l'équitation?

6. Qu'était le Louvre avant d'être un musée?

7. Quelle est votre couleur préférée?

8. Est-ce que le champagne est un vin?

9. Quels sont les cinq sens?

10. Quel est le contraire de "maigrir"?

11. Quel est le futur du verbe "envoyer"?

12. Qu'est-ce qui à deux longues oreilles, un nez qui remue et qui aime les carottes?

Exercice 3

Répondre aux questions suivantes:

1. Comment est vote chambre à Paris?

2. Comment sont les tours de Notre-Dame?

3. Est-ce que les Alpes sont plus hautes que les Pyrénées?

4. Est-ce que les citrons sont sucres?

5. Quelles sont les caractéristiques du diamant?

6. En quoi est votre montre?

7. En quoi sont généralement les statues?

8. Comment a été l'hiver dernier dans votre pays?

Exercice 4

Répondre aux questions suivantes:

Exemple: "Quelle est la forme d'un ballon de rugby?

 - Il est ovale."

"De quelle forme est un ballon de rugby?

 - Il est ovale."

1. Quelle est la couleur de vos cheveux?

2. De quelle couleur sont vos yeux?

3. Quelle était la nationalité de l'acteur Orson Welles?

4. De quelle nationalité êtes-vous?

5. Quel est le style de la Sainte-Chapelle?

6. De quel style est le château de Versailles?

Exercice 5

Répondre aux questions suivantes:

1. Quelle est la profession de votre père?
2. Que fait le mari de Mme Hubert?
3. Jeremie est-il médecin comme son père?
4. Votre mère est-elle infirmière?
5. Que voulez-vous faire plus tard?
6. Que faisait Antoine de Saint-Exupéry tout en écrivant des romans?
7. Quel était le métier de votre grand-père?

Exercice 6

Répondre aux questions suivantes:

Exemple: "Comment trouvez-vous le restaurant en bas de chez moi?
- Il est très agreable."
"Comment trouvez-vous le restaurant Maxim?
- C'est très bon et très cher."

1. Comment trouvez-vous ce tableau?
2. Comment trouvez-vous La Ronde de nuit de Rembrandt?
3. Que penses-tu de ce film?
4. Que penses-tu de West Side Story?
5. Comment est la ville ou vous êtes né(e)?
6. Comment est Paris?
7. Comment trouvez-vous votre quartier?
8. Comment trouvez-vous Montmartre?

Exercice 7

Compléter les phrases suivantes:

Exemple: C'est bon, les tartes aux pommes!
Elle était excellente, ma tarte aux pommes!

1. _____ est difficile, les dictées!
2. _____ était vraiment très difficile, la dictée d'hier!
3. "Tu aimes la fourrure? - Oui, mais _____ est trop cher pour moi."
4. "Tu aimes ce manteau de fourrure? - Oui, mais _____ est trop cher pour moi."
5. Une voiture à Paris, _____ n'est pas indispensable.
6. _____ est quand même bien pratique, ma petite Renault!
7 "Comment est le café italien? _____ est très fort."
8. Trop de café _____ est mauvais pour la santé!
9. _____ est presque toujours clair, un appartement au cinquième étage.
10. _____ est malheureusement très sombre, mon appartement!

Exercice 8

Imiter le modele donne avec chacun des sujet donnes ci-dessous.

(N'employer que le verbe être):
Exemple: Sir Winston Churchill

C'était un homme politique anglais. Il était Premier ministre pendant la Seconde Geurre mondiale. Il était très gros. C'était un homme remarquable. C'était un grand fumeur de cigares.

1. Venise	2. Le général de Gaulle
3. La pizza	4. L'éléphant
5. La Sorbonne	6. Votre meilleur(e) ami(e)

Exercice 9 - A

Répondre aux questions suivantes:

1. Où est la clé de votre appartement?
2. Où est votre passeport?
3. Où sont vos parents en ce moment?
4. Où est le Pape?
5. Où sont Joelle et Christine?

Exercice 9 - B

1. Où est Genève?	2. Où est Le Mans?
3. Où est la Finlande?	4. Où est le Nigéria?
5. Où est l'Ecosse?	6. Où est la Lorraine?
7. Où est Monaco?	8. Où est Cuba?

Exercice 10 - A

Répondre aux questions suivantes en imitant le modèle donne:

Exemple: Quelle est la hauteur de la tour Eiffel?
La hauteur de la tour Eiffel est de 300 mètres.
Elle à 300 mètres de haut/hauteur. Elle mesure 300 mètres.
Elle fait 300 mètres de haut. (langue courante)

1. Quelle est la longueur de l'avenue des Champs-Elysées?
2. Quelle est la largeur de la rue ou vous habitez?
3. Quelle est la hauteur du mont Everest?
4. Quelles sont la largeur et la longueur d'un lit d'une personne?

Exercice 10 - B

Exemple: Quelle est l'épaisseur de ce livre?

L'épaisseur de ce livre est de 5 centimetres.
Il à 5 centimetres d'épaisseur.
Il fait 5 centimetres d'épaisseur. (langue courante)

1. Quelle est l'épaisseur de votre livre d'exercices?
2. Quelle est la profondeur normale d'un réfrigérateur?
3. Quelle est la profondeur du petit bain d'une piscine?
4. Quelle est l'épaisseur d'une belle moquette comfortable?

Exercice 11

Répondre aux questions:

1. Combien mesurez-vous?
2. Si vous achetez des chaussures, quelle est votre pointure?
3. Combien pesez-vous?
4. Si vous achetez des vêtements, quelle est votre taille?

Exercice 12

Imiter l'exemple suivant:

Ce livre coûte 100 francs. Le prix de ce livre est de 100 francs.
1. Aujourd'hui, il fait 30 degrés.
2. Munich est à 800 kilomètres de Paris environ.
3. En 1983, la France avait 54,8 millions d'habitants.
4. Les vacances de Noël durent généralement deux semaines.
5. Je gagne 10 000 francs par mois.
6. En novembre 1985, 100 yens valaient 3,85 francs.
7. Le mois prochain, le prix de l'essence augmentera de 3%.
8. En 1981, la Colombie a produit 724 millions de tonnes de café.
9. Je loue mon appartement 3.000 francs par mois.
10. Cette voiture consomme 10 litres au cent.

2. Les adverbes

Exercices	Sujet
1.	Formation des adverbes de manière
2.	Emploi de l'adverbe de manière
3.	Emploi de l'adjectif comme adverbe
4.	Place de l'adverbe

Exercice 1

Former l'adverbe à partir de chacun des adjectifs suivants:

Exemple: lent —->   lentement
1.   doux   _____
2.   premier   _____
3.   net   _____
4.   facile   _____
5.   complet   _____
6.   sérieux   _____
7.   certain   _____
8.   franc   _____
9.   vif   _____
10.   exceptionnel   _____

Exemple: prudent —-->   prudemment
11.   évident   _____
12.   constant   _____
13.   courant   _____
14.   violent   _____

15.	suffisant	_____
16.	fréquent	_____
17.	inconscient	_____
18.	patient	_____
19.	bruyant	_____
20.	récent	_____

Exercice 2

Compléter les phrases suivantes par l'adjectif ou l'adverbe selon le cas:

Exemple: lent/lentement
Le vieillard marchait à pas _____ —->
Le vieillard marchait à pas lents.
Le vieillard marchait _____ —->
Le vieillard marchait lentement.

1. confortable/confortablement
Ce fauteuil ancien n'est pas _____
Il était _____ installé dans un fauteuil et lisait le journal.

2. gratuit/gratuitement
Aujourd'hui, notre magasin vous remet _____ un paquet de lessive.
Aujourd'hui, notre magasin vous remet un paquet de lessive.

3. objectif/objectivement
Ce journaliste a présenté un rapport très _____ des faits.
Ce journaliste a présenté les faits très _____.

4. bref/brièvement
Résumez _____ cet article.
Vous ferez un résume très _____ de cet article.

5. rapide/rapidement
Dans cette brasserie, le service est très _____
Passez me prendre à 12 h 30! On déjeunera _____
avant d'aller aux courses à Longchamp.

6. sec/sèchement
Il a répondu d'un ton _____ que cela ne l'intéressait pas.
Il a répondu _____ que cela ne le concernait pas.

Exercice 3

Compléter les phrases suivantes par les adjectifs donnés, employés soit comme adjectifs, soit comme adverbes:
Exemple: bas
Parlez à voix _____! Parlez à voix basse!
Parlez tout _____! Parlez tout bas!

1. bon: Ces éclairs au chocolat sont _____.
   Ces roses sentent _____.
2. cher: Un voyage en avion Concorde coûte _____.
   Les perles fines sont plus _____ que les perles de culture.
3. haut: Quelle est la montagne la plus _____ d'Europe?
   Les aigles volent très _____.
4. dur: Le diamant est le plus _____ des mineraux.
   Elle à travaillé _____ pour entrer au Conservatoire national de musique.
5. fort: Dans ce magasin de vêtements, il y à un rayon "femmes_____"
   Ne criez pas si _____! On ne s'entend plus!
6. faux: Elle chante _____ comme une casserole!
   La police a découvert un important stock de _____ pièces de dix francs.
7. droit: La route était _____ bordée de platanes. "Où est la rue de l'Eglise?
   - Continuez tout _____! C'est la première à gauche."

Exercice 4

Mettre les phrases suivantes au passé composé:

1. Il neige déjà.
2. Il pleut beaucoup.
3. Elle porte toujours des lunettes.
4. Ce plombier travaille très bien.
5. Vous ne mangez pas assez.
6. Je comprends mal votre explication.
7. M. Girodet parle peu.
8. Cet enfant apprend vite à lire.
9. Grâce à ce médicament, je dors mieux.
10. Il arrive sûrement à 8 heures.
11. Cet expert se trompe rarement dans ses estimations.
12. Il avoue enfin la vérité.

5

Pronouns

PERSONAL PRONOUNS

La souris, mange-t-**elle** le fromage?
Le chat, guette-**il** la souris?
Le garçon, chasse-t-**il** le chat?
La mère, fesse-t-**elle** le garçon?

1. Subject Pronouns

A subject pronoun functions as the subject of a sentence.
1st person: the speaker (je) or the speakers (nous)
2nd person: the one spoken to (tu) or the ones spoken to (vous)
3rd person: the one/thing spoken about (il, elle, on)
                or the ones/things spoken about (ils, elles)

A. Forms of the Subject Pronouns

Person	Singular	Plural
1st	je: I	nous: we
2nd	tu: you (familiar)	vous: you (formal, singular; informal and formal, plural)
3rd-masc.	il: he/it, m.	ils: they, m.
3rd-fem.	elle: she/it, f.	elles: they, f.
	on: one/they/we/people	

Je suis fatigué.	I am tired.
Tu es heureux.	You are happy.
Il est malin.	He is shrewd.
Nous sommes Parisiens.	We are Parisian.

B. Comments about the subject pronouns

1. Both tu and vous mean you. Tu is used when speaking to a relative, friend, classmate, child, or to an animal. Vous is used when speaking to an adult, a stranger, or to more than one person.

> Julie, ma chérie, veux-tu dîner maintenant?
> Julie, my dear, do you want to have diner now?

2. When the subject of a sentence is someone indefinite, *on* must be used with a verb in the third person singular. *On* can be used to mean we, they, you, or people.

> On ne peut pas faire autrement.
> One (we, people) cannot do otherwise.

> On dit qu'il vaut mieux tard que jamais.
> People say it is better late than never.

3. The third person subject pronouns il(s) and elle(s) are the only subject pronouns that show gender, as well as person and number.

> Les pommes? Elles ne sont pas très douces.
> The apples? They are not very sweet.

> Où est ta clef? Elle est dans ma poche.
> Where is your key? It is in my pocket.

> Madame Dupont est journaliste, et elle a deux enfants.
> Mrs. Dupont is a newspaper reporter, and she has two children.

2. Direct Object Pronouns

me (m')	me	nous	us
te (t')	you (fam.)	vous	you
le (l')	him/it, m.	les	them, m. & f.
la (l')	her/it, f.		
se (s')	himself/herself se (s') themselves		

3. Indirect Object Pronouns

me (m') me/	to or for me	nous us/	to or for us
te (t') you/	to or for you	vous you/	to or for you
lui him/	to or for him	leur them/	to or for them
lui her/	to or for her		
se (s')	to or for himself/herself	se (s')	to or for themselves

Notes:

a) The subject pronoun *on* refers to an indefinite person or persons and always takes a third person singular verb.

b) Personal direct and indirect object pronouns are placed immediately before the verb of which they are the object, except in affirmative commands.

> Je vous écoute.　　　　　I am listening to you.
> Je peux pas le faire.　　　I cannot do it.

3. In affirmative commands (the affirmative imperative) only the object pronoun is placed directly after the verb and is linked to it by a hyphen. The pronouns me and te change to moi and toi when they are the last pronouns attached.

Affirmative	Imperative
Ecoutez-moi.	Listen to me.
Lève-toi.	Get (yourself) up.
Essayez-le.	Try it.
Parlons-leur.	Let us speak to them.
Negative	Imperative
Ne m'écoutez pas.	Don't listen to me.
Ne te lève pas.	Don't get up.
Ne l'essayez pas.	Do not try it.

4. a) The verbs écouter, regarder, chercher, attendre, and demander take a direct object in French.

Où est ton amie? Je l'attends encore.
Where is your friend? I am still waiting for her.

As-tu la clef de la chambre? Non, je la cherche.
Do you have the bedroom key? No, I am looking for it.

b) The verbs répondre, obéir, and désobéir take an indirect object in French.

je réponds au professeur/Je lui réponds.
Nous obéissons au professeur/ Nous lui obéissons.

5. Past participles of verbs conjugated with avoir and past participles of reflexive verbs agree in gender and number with their preceding direct object (if there is one).

Les vaches? Il les a vendues. (f.,pl.)
Elles se sont levées. (f.,pl.)

Exercise 1

Translate the pronoun in parentheses into French:

1. (them)   Mettons- _____ dans la voiture.
2. (to him) Je _____ ai expliqué le problème.
3. (to me) _____ montreront-ils leur chef-d'oeuvre?
4. (it) Prenez ce journal et portez- _____ chez vous.
5. (us) _____ ont-ils vus?
6. (to you) Je crois qu'elle _____ dit la vérité.
7. (to them) Ne _____ parlons pas maintenant.
8. (me) Donnez- _____ une livre de jambon, s'il vous plaît.
9. (to her) Sa mère _____ lit un conte.
10. (yourself) Habille- _____ vite, Theodore.

Exercise 2

Complete with the missing object pronoun:

1. A-t-elle lu le roman? Non, elle ne _____ a pas encore lu.
2. Ou sont les oranges? _____ voici.
3. Qui a enseigné la grammaire aux étudiants? Le professeur _____ a enseigné le français.
4. Achetons une pomme et mangeons- _____
5. Vous a-t-il montré le gâteau? Oui, il _____ a montré le tableau.
6. Où ont-ils rencontré leurs amis? Ils _____ ont rencontrés à la gare.
7. Qui va couper le gâteau? Philippe va _____ couper.
8. M'aimes-tu? Oui, je _____ aime.
9. Comment se portent-ils? Ils _____ portent bien.
10. Est-ce que le médecin vous a guéris? Oui, il _____ a guéris.

Exercise 3

Complete the sentence in English:

1. Il refuse de leur répondre. He refuses to _____.
2. Amusons-nous ce soir. Let's _____ tonight.
3. Quand on est malade, on envoie chercher le médecin. When _____ sick, _____ send for the doctor.
4. On nous a invités au bal _____ to the dance.
5. Nous ne leur donnerons pas un cadeau _____ a gift.
6. Comment traduit-on ce proverbe? How _____ this proverb?
7. Il a fait une faute, mais il l'a corrigée _____ made a mistake, but he _____
8. Rendez-lui le savon; il veut se laver _____ the soap; he _____.
9. En France on mange bien. In France _____ well.
10. Ne vous ont-ils pas donné la machine ordinateur? Didn't _____ the computer?

Exercise 4

Answer each question with a complete sentence in French. In the answers, replace the nouns by pronouns:

1. Votre mere, a-t-elle deja termine ses etudes?
2. Comprend-on l'allemand ici, aux Etats-Unis?
3. Téléphonez-vous souvent à vos amis?
4. Les pauvres? Voulez-vous les aider?
5. Pouvez-vous entendre les oiseaux?
6. Est-ce qu'on a fermé la porte à clef?
7. Votre père, fait-il attention à sa santé?
8. M'écoutes-tu?
9. Vos amis, vont-ils vous répondre tout de suite?
10. Votre sœur, quand s'est-elle levée?

Exercise 5

Give the equivalent in French:

1. I cannot forget you. _____
2. He is washing himself. _____
3. We brushed our teeth. _____
4. We brushed ourselves. _____
5. They do it. _____
6. They didn't do it. _____
7. Didn't they do it? _____
8. Do it. _____
9. Don't do it. _____
10. I know her. _____
11. She knows me. _____
12. I spoke to her. _____
13. Will she speak to me? _____
14. She wants to speak to you. _____
15. Didn't she speak to him? _____
16. I'm going to speak to them. _____
17. Look at her. _____
18. Let's not look at her. _____
19. Wait for me. _____
20. Let us wait for them. _____

4. Reflexive Pronouns

A reflexive pronoun repeats the subject noun or pronoun in the form of a second pronoun. The reflexive pronoun is the direct or indirect object of the verb and refers to the same person or thing as the subject of the verb.

A. Forms of the reflexive pronoun

Person	Singular	Plural
1st	me (m')/moi	nous
2nd	te (t')/toi	vous
3rd	se (s')	se

Il se lève; il se lave, et il s'habille.
He gets (himself) up; he washes (himself) and he dresses (himself).

Il se rase. (direct object)
Il se rase la figure. (indirect object)

B. Use of the reflexive pronoun

1. The reflexive pronoun must agree in person and number with the subject of the sentence.

Nous nous dépêchons pour arriver à l'heure.
We hurry ourselves up to arrive on time.

Je m'occupe de mes affaires; je n'aime pas
m'occuper des affaires des autres.

I take care of my business; I don't like to take care of other
people's business.

2. The refexive pronoun comes before the verb except in affirmative
commands.

Elle se l'offrent.   She buys it for herself.
(She gets/"offers" it to herself.)

Vous vous levez à six heures du matin.
You get (yourself) up at six o'clock in the morning.

BUT

Assieds-toi, je t'en prie.   Sit (yourself) down, please!

Note: Although the reflexive pronoun is sometimes understood in
English without expressing it, it must always be expressed in French.

La pluie s'est arrêtée.   The rain stopped (itself).

3. Elide me, te, and se before a verb beginning with a vowel or a mute
h. (m', t', and s')

Je m'ennuie si tu ne m'écris pas.
I get bored if you do not write to me.

Note: A verb that has no reflexive equivalent can sometimes be translated
in English using the word, "get."

Ils s'ennuient quand il pleut.
They get bored when it rains.

Nous nous lavons, et nous nous rasons avant de sortir.
We get washed, and we get shaved before going out.

4. When the action of the verb is performed by the subject on itself, a
reflexive pronoun is used with the definite article instead of the possessive
adjective. Therefore, the definite article is used instead of a possessive
adjective before parts of the body. However, if the part of the body is
modified by an adjective other than droit (right) or gauche (left), the reflexive
pronoun is not used. The possessive adjective is used in this case.

Elle se brosse les dents.   She brushes her teeth.

Il se casse la jambe gauche.   He breaks his left leg.

Elle se lave ses beaux cheveux blonds.
She washes her beautiful blond hair.

5. The basic infinitive of reflexive verbs is expressed with the third
person, singular reflexive pronoun. For example, se lever = to get (oneself)
up. However, when using an infinitive in a sentence, the reflexive pronoun
must refer to the person being spoken about. Infinitives of reflexive verbs
are listed in the dictionary under the spelling of the verb. "Se lever" is found
in alphabetical order in the "L" section.

Je sais que vous allez vous marier.
I know you are going to get married.

Elle nous dit de nous laver les mains avant le repas.
She tells us to wash our hands before the meal.

6. Many verbs can be made reflexive with only a slight change in meaning. The reflexive pronoun is either the direct or indirect object.

Il regarde la jeune fille.	He looks at the young lady.
Il se regarde dans le miroir.	He looks at himself in the miroir.
Il achète une belle voiture.	He buys a beautiful car
Elle s'achète une belle voiture.	He buys (himself) a beautiful car.

7. Idiomatically reflexive verbs are verbs which change their meaning when they become reflexive. These verbs are idiomatic in meaning in their reflexive form.

amuser - to amuse	s'amuser to - have a good time
appeler - to call	s'appeler - to be named
attendre - to wait for	s'attendre (à) - to expect
demander to ask for	se demander - to wonder
douter (de) - to doubt	se douter (de) - to suspect
élever - to raise	s'élever - to rise
lever - to raise up	se lever - to get up
mettre - to put	se mettre (a) - to begin
passer - to pass	se passer (de) - to do without
plaindre - to pity	se plaindre - to complain
rappeler - to call back	se rappeler - to remember
se rendre compte (de)	to give an account of
rendre compte (de)	to realize/become aware of
sauver - to save	se sauver - to run away
servir - to serve	se servir (de) to use
tromper - to deceive	se tromper - to be mistaken
trouver - to find	se trouver - to be situated

8. Some verbs are essentially or exlusively reflexive. These verbs are referred to as "reflexive verbs" and must always be used with a reflexive pronoun. Following is a list of some of the more common reflexive verbs.

s'abstenir (de) - to abstain (from)	s'évader - to escape
s'écrier - to exclaim	s'évanouir - to faint/vanish
s'écrouler - to tumble down	se fier à - to trust
s'éffondrer - to cave in	se méfier de - to mistrust
s'efforcer de - to strive to	se moquer de - to make fun of
s'emparer de - to grab	s'en aller - to leave/go away
s'enfuir - to flee	s'envoler - to fly off

se repentir - to repent   se soucier de - to care about
se suicider - to commit suicide   se taire - to keep silent/be quiet

C. Reciprocal verbs

1. A reflexive verb has a reciprocal meaning when two or more subjects act upon one another, not upon themselves. Ils se blâment. <u>Reflexive</u>: They blame themselves. <u>Reciprocal</u>: They blame each other.

2. If the verb does not show clearly whether the action is reciprocal or reflexive, to avoid ambiguity, add **l'un l'autre**, each other, or **les uns les autres**, one another.

Ils se blâme l'un l'autre.   They blame each other.
Mes amis s'écrivent les uns aux autres. My friends write to each other.

3. With a verb that requires a prepositional complement, that is, a verb that must be followed by **a** or **de**, insert the preposition between **l'un** and **l'autre** or between les uns and les autres. Contract à and de with the article **l'** or **les**.

Ils se comprennent les uns des autres.   They understand one another.

Exercise 6

Write a complete sentence to say the following in French. (Directions are given in French.)

1. dire ou vous vous trouviez quand il a commence à neiger.
2. demander à quelqu'un ou el se promenarait s'il faisait beau cet après-midi.
3. dire à des amis de ne pas s'en aller si tôt.
4. dire que vous et Françoise, vous vous voyez souvent.
5. dire à Mme Lejeune que vous ne vous facherez pas si elle se trompe.
6. demander à un ami s'il ne se porte pas bien aujourd'hui.
7. demander à M. Martin s'il va se marier en juin ou en juillet.
8. demander à une connaissance si elle s'enuie quand il n'y rien à faire.
9. dire à un(e) camarade de classe de se taire quand le professeur parle.
10. dire que vous vous dépêcheriez si vous étiez en retard.

Exercise 7

Replace the infinitive by the correct form of the verb in the tense indicated.

1. (présent) Se souvenir-vous de ce qu'il vous a dit?
2. (imparfait) Ne se raser-il pas chaque matin?
3. (futur) Je s'en aller tout à l'heure.
4. (présent) Cette femme se plaindre sans cesse.
5. (conditionnel) Tu s'ennuyer si tu étais tout seul.
6. (passé simple) Elle se regarder dans la glace.
7. (impératif) Se dépêcher, mes enfants!
8. (futur) Nous s'habiller vite.
9. (present) Elle ne se rappeler pas le nom du livre.
10. (impératif) Se reposer avant de te laver.

Exercise 8

Answer each sentence with a complete sentence in French.
1. Vous sentez-vous triste ou heureux (heureuse) aujourd'hui?
2. Dans quel continent se trouvent les Etats-Unis?
3. Préferez-vous vous promener en été au soleil ou à l'ombre?
4. Lequel se plaindrait des devoirs, l'élève paresseux ou l'élève travailleur?
5. Te souviens-tu de la date de la prise de la Bastille?
6. Est-ce que je m'amuserai si je vais en France?
7. Vous brossez-vous les dents avant ou après le petit déjeuner?
8. Comment s'appelle votre professeur d'anglais?
9. A quelle heure est-ce que le soleil se couche?
10. Pourquoi vous dépêchez-vous, mes amis?

Exercise 9

Complete the following sentences in English.
1. Qu'est-ce qui se passait? What _____?
2. Le vieillard s'assied dans le fauteuil pour se reposer. The old man _____ in the arm chair to _____.
3. Te laves-tu les mains avec de l'eau chaude et du savon? _____ _____ with warn water and soap?
4. Il ne se blessera pas s'il ne se bat pas. _____ if _____.
5. Il me semble que vous vous trompez. It seems to me that _____.
6. Va-t'en, méchant garçon! _____ naughty boy!
7. Nous nous lèverions de bonne heure s'il faisait beau. _____ _____ early if the weather was nice.
8. Le petit se deshabilla, se coucha, et s'endormit tout de suite. The child _____ and immediately.
9. Je m'arretais chaque jour devant le kiosque. _____ each day in front of the newsstand.
10. Pourquoi les deux soeurs se grondaient-elles? Why _____?

Exercise 10

Write the follwing sentences in French.
1. Do not get angry. _____
2. I was getting up. _____
3. What is her name? _____
4. Aren't they taking a walk? _____
5. Aren't they taking a walk? _____
6. Enjoy yourselves. _____
7. He would not be mistaken. _____
8. Let's not stop. _____
9. Do not get hurt. (fam.) _____
10. She was washing her face. _____

PRONOUNS Y AND EN

Du fromage? La souris **en** a mangé.

Le chat **y** guette la souris.

Le garçon **y** chasse le chat.

Le garçon **en** parle à la jeune fille.

1. THE PARTITIVE PRONOUN EN

The partitive pronoun en replaces a direct object used in a partitive sense.

A. Like other object pronouns, en comes before the verb except in affirmative commands.

Il y a de la viande.	There is some meat.
Il en mangé.	He eats some of it.
Nous en mangeons.	We are eating some of it.
Prenez-en!	Take some (of it)!

B. The partitive pronoun en may be used to refer both to people and to things, especially when the noun is preceded by (**de**) (**du**) or (**des**).

De cet enfant, qu'est ce qu'on en fera?
About this child, what will we do?

De cette affaire, il en tirera un joli bénéfice.
From this business, he will get a handsome profit.

S'il y a encore du rôti, j'en reprendrai.
If there is any more roast, I will take some again.

Note: When there is more than one verb in the same clause, the pronoun goes before the verb it is the object of.

Posséder un objet, c'est pouvoir en user.
Possessing an object is being able to use it.

But:

Les bâteaux? Nous en voyons partir tous les jours.
The ships? We see some of them leave every day.

C. When a direct object is a number or an expression of quantity, the partitive pronoun en must be used before the verb to replace the noun, but not the number.

Les Dupont, ont-ils deux voitures?
Do the Duponts have two automobiles?

Oui, ils en ont deux.
Yes, they have two (of them).

D. The partitive pronoun en must be used with the indefinite pronouns plusieurs (several) and quelques-uns/unes (a few), even though it is not translated into English.

Avez-vous des cigarettes?	Do you some cigarettes?
J'en ai plusieurs.	I have several (of them).
Elle en a quelques-unes.	She has a few (of them).

2. THE ADVERBIAL PRONOUN "EN"

A. The adverbial pronoun en refers to a place from which someone leaves or something is taken.

Quand êtes-vous revenu d'Italie?
When did you return from Italy?

J'en suis revenu hier.
I returned (from there) yesterday.

B. The adverbial pronoun **en** refers to a prepositional phrase beginning with **de** and whose object is usually not a person.

Jean parle de son voyage en Italie.
Jean is speaking about his trip to Italie.

Jean en parle.
Jean is speaking about it.

3. THE PRONOUN "Y"

A. The adverbial pronoun y refers to a previously mentioned location which is the object of a preposition of places such as **à, chez, dans, en, sous,** or **sur**. In these cases, **y** is translated as there.

Jean, est-il chez lui?	Is Jean at home?
Oui, il y est.	Yes, he is there.

B. Y often refers to a prepositional phrase whose object is other than a person or place. In these cases, y has the sense of "concerning it" or "about it."

Le pouvoir de penser a une chose ou de n'y pas penser.
The ability to think about something or not to think about it.

Que voulez-vous que j'y fasse?
What do you want me to do about it?

Nous croyons au progres.	We believe in progress.
Y croyez-vous?	Do you believe in it?

Note: The pronoun y must not be used to mean "about or to a person." Instead a disjunctive pronoun or the appropriate indirect object pronoun must be used.

Elle répond mal à son frère.
She talks back to her brother.
Elle lui répond mal.
She talks back to him.

Exercise 12

Write **y** or **en** to complete the following sentences:

1. Va-t-il à la station-service? Oui, il _____ va.
2. Auras-tu besoin d'essence? Non, je n' _____ aurai pas besoin.
3. Vont-ils bientôt en Italie? Oui, ils _____ vont la semaine prochaine.
4. Vous servez-vous de savons pour vous laver? Oui, je m'_____ sers.
5. Se souvient-il de mon nom? Bien entendu, il s' _____ souvient.
6. Je cherche des cravates noires. _____ avez-vous?
7. Sont-elles allées au supermarche? Non, elles n'_____ sont pas allées.
8. Combien de langues parle-t-il? Il _____ parle quatre.
9. Voici des bananes. Prenez-_____.
10. Les enfants etaient-ils dans la rue? Oui, ils _____ étaient.
11. Qui frappait à la porte? Mon frère _____ frappait.
12. Avez-vous pris du fromage? Oui, j' _____ ai assez pris, merci.
13. Votre oncle demeure-t-il encore en Afrique? Non, il n' _____ demeure plus.
14. Je dois achétér des oeufs. Je vais _____ achétér une douzaine.
15. Les cigarettes sont-elles sur la table? Oui, elles _____ sont.

Exercise 13

Complete the sentences in English:

1. Voilà les oranges. Combien y en a-t-il? Here are then oranges. How many _____ ?
2. Aimait-elle les bottes? Oui, elle en a choisi plusieurs. Did she like the boots? Yes, she _____.
3. Va-t-il à la gare en voiture? Non, il y va à bicyclette. Is he going to the station by car? No, _____ by bicycle.
4. J'ai votre dictionnaire. En avez-vous besoin? I have your dictionary. Do you _____?
5. Si vous avez tant de crayons, prétéz-en à vos amis. If you have so many pencils, _____ to your friends.
6. Etes-vous dans la cour, mes enfants? Oui, Papa, nous y sommes. Are you in the courtyard, children? Yes, Dad, _____.
7. Voici une lettre. Répondez-y immediatement , s'il vous plaît. Here is a letter _____, please.
8. Regardez ces taxis. Il y en au moins à cent! Look at those taxis. There are _____!
9. Venez-vous de Moscou? Non, je n'en viens pas. Do you come from Moscow? No, I _____.
10. Est-ce que le vase est sur le piano? Oui, il y est. Is the vase on the piano? Yes, it _____.
11. Donnez-moi des allumettes. En voici. Give me some matches. Here are _____.
12. Les Dupont, sont-ils allés chez eux? Oui, ils y sont allés. Have the Duponts gone home? Yes, they _____.

13. Nous venons d'achétér cette machine à laver. Qu'en pensez-vous?
We just bought this washing machine. What _____ ?

14. Combien de poems a-t-elle recites? Elle en a recité cinq. How many poems did she recite? She _____.

15. Vous souvenez-vous de ce jour-là? Oui, je m'en souviens. Do you remember that day? Yes, I _____.

Exercise 14

Give the equivalent in French:

1. Let's speak of it. _____
2. You have so many! _____
3. Didn't they sell any? _____
4. Buy some. _____
5. Do not borrow any. _____
6. I need it. _____
7. He found some. _____
8. We will speak of it. _____
9. Have you any? _____
10. I have twenty. _____
11. We have none. _____
12. Eat some. _____
13. Don't eat any. _____
14. I don't want any. _____
15. Choose three. _____

16. Was he born in Spain? Yes, he was born there.

_____

17. Is Jean at home? Yes, he is (there).

_____

18. Are you answering the questions? Yes, I'm answering them.

_____

19. I'm going to the park. Don't stay there long.

_____

20. Did he go to the movies? Yes, he did (go there).

_____

Exercise 15

Answer each question with a complete sentence in French. Use y or en in the answer:

1. Combien de copains avez-vous?
2. Allez-vous souvent au concert?
3. A quelle heure du matin sortez-vous de la maison?
4. Répondez à toutes les lettrès que vous recevez?
5. Marches-tu sur le trottoir?

6. Quand avez-vous besoin d'un parapluie?
7. Mangez-vous trop de sucrerie parfois?
8. Allez-vous chez le dentiste quand on a mal aux dents?
9. Est-ce que votre famille sera en Europe cette année?
10. Venez-vous de la Russie?

4. WORD ORDER OF OBJECT PRONOUNS

A. The basic word order of object pronouns is as follows. First and second person object pronouns, direct or indirect, and reflexive pronouns are always placed first. Then, for third person object pronouns (le, la, les, lui, leur), the rule is that direct object pronouns are expressed before indirect object pronouns.

1. Priority of reflexive pronouns

Reflexive pronouns (me, te, se, nous, vous) or any pronouns that also function as reflexive pronouns (me, te, nous, vous) are used first.

La voiture? Il se l'a achetée.
The car? He bought it for himself.

Nous ne t'en pardonnerons pas.
We will not forgive you. (en = "for it")

La bicyclette? Nos cousins nous l'ont donnée.
The bicycle? Our cousins gave it to us.

Jean et Marie me les ont presentes.
John and Mary introduced them to me.

Note: The preposition "a" is used with a disjunctive pronoun, in place of the indirect object pronoun, after me, te, se, nous and vous.

B. Direct before indirect object pronouns. For object pronouns other than reflexive pronouns and y or en, the direct object pronoun precedes the indirect object pronoun.

Il les leur achété frequemment. (direct object - indirect object)
He buys them for them frequently.

C. Word order of pronouns y and en

The pronouns y and en are not used together and are always in the last position before the verb.

Ils les y attendent.　　　　　They wait there for them.
(attendre/to wait for - direct object)
Il ne faut pas lui en parler.　　You must not speak to him about it.

D. Summary of the word order of object pronouns:

1. Pronouns that can be either direct or indirect objects are placed first. (First and second person personal object pronouns and reflexive pronouns.)

2. Then, other object pronouns are used. Direct object pronouns come before indirect object pronouns. (Third person personal object pronouns.)

3. Lastly, y or en (not together) are used.

4. The following order is thus produced:

me			
te	le		
se	la	lui	y
nous	les	leur	en
vous			

E. Pronouns in affirmative commands

1. Object pronouns follow the verb in an affirmative command in the same order as in English. Direct object pronouns are placed before indirect object pronouns, including first and second person object pronouns (me, te, nous, vous).

Montrez-le-nous!	Show it to us!
Donnez-m'en!	Give me some!
Ecris-moi souvent!	Write to me often!
Envoyez-les-moi!	Send them to me!
Prépare-toi!	Get (yourself) ready!
Explique-la-lui!	Explain it to him!

Note: a) All object pronouns are attached to the verb in positive commands.

b) First and second person singular object pronouns (me and te) become "moi" and "toi" in affirmative commands when they are the last pronoun attached to the verb.

2. Object pronouns in negative commands precede the verb and follow the normal order.

Ne me la donnez pas!	Don't give it to me!
Ne te dépêche pas!	Don't hurry!
Ne m'en donnez pas!	Don't give me any!
N'y allez pas!	Don't go there!

Exercise 16

Copy the following sentences replacing the highlighted words with pronouns.

Example: Passez le sucre à Henri.
             Passez-le lui.

1. L'argent a arrêté **le voleur** dans la rue.
2. Lisez **ce conte** aux enfants.
3. Je te félicite de **tes notes exellentes**.
4. La domestique nous a apporté **les haricots verts**.
5. Envoyons-lui **son cadeau**.
6. Le journaliste se souvient-il **de la question**?
7. Porte **ces livres** à la bibliothéque.
8. Voulez-vous bien me réciter **le poème**?
9. **La Garonne** se jette dans l'ocean Atlantique.
10. Donnez-nous **un demi-killo** de beurre.

Exercise 17   Write the following commands in the affirmative imperative form.

1. Ne la lui vendez pas.
2. Ne nous les envoyez pas.
3. Ne t'en va pas.
4. Ne me la dites pas.
5. Ne les leur rendons pas.

Exercise 18   Write the following sentences in French.

1. Lend it to me.
2. Do not lend them to her.
3. I will lend them to you.
5. Aren't there any?
6. Lend him some.
7. I cannot lend you any.
8. Lend them to us.
9. Do not lend it to us.
10. I lent them to you (fam.,s.).

Exercise 19   Answer the following questions in complete sentences in French. In the answer replace the highlighted words by pronouns.

1. Avez-vous offert *du pain au mendiant*?
2. Le professeur enseignera-t-il *la biologie à ces étudiants*?
3. Qui a accompagné *vos amis en France*?
4. Combien *de timbres* vous a-t-il empruntés?
5. Quand allez-vous m'expliquer *le problème*?
6. Y a-t-il assez *d'argent* pour realiser *le projet*?
7. Messieurs, voulez-vous que je vous écrive *ma reponse*?
8. Qui a donné *le pourboire au garçon*?
9. Depuis quand m'attendais-tu dans *la salle d'attente*?
10. Quand vous enerra-t-on *les chapeaux*, madame?

DISJUNCTIVE (STRESS) PRONOUNS

La souris? Elle, **elle** mange le fromage.
Le chat? **Lui**, il guette la souris.
Le garçon? **Lui**, il chasse le chat.
La jeune fille? Elle, **elle** fesse le garçon.

1. A disjunctive pronoun always refers to a person, unlike direct and indirect object pronouns which may refer either to persons or to things. Furthermore, unlike other object pronouns, a disjunctive or *"stress"* pronoun does not have to come immediately before or after the verb. They may stand alone, that is, without a verb structure... disconnected from a verb ("dis-juncted").

The stress pronouns or *"disjunctive pronouns"* are:

moi I, me	nous we, us
toi you (fam.)	vous you
lui he, him	eux they, them (m.)
elle she, her	elles they, them (f.)

2. The stress pronouns are used:

A. After a preposition:

pour toi for you	chez elle at her house
avec lui with him	sans vous without you

B. When the pronoun is not followed by an expressed verb:

Qui l'a dit? Elle.	Who said it? She (did).
Il est plus malin que moi.	He is shrewder than I.

C. In a compound subject:

Toi et moi, nous sommes de bons amis.
You and I, we are good friends
Elle et eux sont dans le salon.
She and they are in the livingroom.

D. For emphasis:

Moi, je l'acheterai.	I shall buy it.
Toi, tu viendras!	you will come!

Nous, nous lisons; lui, il fait la cuisine.
We are reading; he is cooking.

E. After c'est and ce sont:

Qui est-ce? C'est lui.	Who is it? It is he.
Ce n'est pas elle.	She is not the one. (It's not she.)

Note: Some French verbs take the preposition à with a stress pronoun rather than an indirect object. Among them are penser à (to think of), songer à (to think of), and être à (to belong to).

Elle pensait à toi.	She was thinking of you.
Ce portefeuille est à vous, madame?	Is this wallet yours, madame?

Exercise 20   Complete the sentences in English:

1. Cet homme dort moins que toi. That man sleeps less than _____.
2. Ce n'est pas vous que je cherche. _____ I'm looking for.
3. Vous souvenez-vous d'elles? Do you remember _____ ?
4. Ce sont eux qui l'ont merité. _____ who deserved it.
5. Toi et moi, nous acheterons le chateau. _____ will buy the castle.
6. Elle va chez elle. She is going _____
7. Est-ce vous qui parlez anglais? _____ who speak English.
8. Qui va les chercher à l'aéroport? Moi. Who is going pick them up at the airport? _____
9. Toi, tu es un bon student! _____ are a good étudiant!
10. Les musées étaient devant nous. The museums were in front _____.

Exercise 21

Translate into French the expressions in English:

1. Ils ont reçu des lettres de us.
2. He is one qui devrait travailler dur.
3. Mon ami est plus gentil que you (fam.).
4. Qui va nous l'expliquer ? I vous l'expliquerai.
5. Cette clef est pour you, monsieur.
6. Sortirez-vous avant votre fiancee? Oui, je sortirai avant her.
7. You and I, nous paierons l'addition.(fam)
8. La jeune fille parle mieux que I.
9. Qui l'a entendu? We.
10. Leurs amis jouent au tennis, mais they étudient.
11. Elle chante; we dansons.
12. Ils courent vers them. (f.)
13. Vous êtes arrivé avant them.
14. Elle demeure loin de him.
15. Are they the ones que nous avons rencontrés à la gare?

Exercise 22

Write the proper pronoun:
1. Demeure-t-elle pres de vous, Jean? Oui, elle demeure près de _____.
2. Est-ce Marie qui a écrit? Oui, c'est _____.
3. Sont-ils plus riches que vous, messieurs? Non, ils sont moins riches que _____.
4. J'aimera la voir mon amie Carole. J'irai chez _____ demain.
5. Pierre et _____, nous allons au cinema chaque vendredi.
6. Est-ce à moi qu'on parle, madame? Oui, c'est _____
7. Pensez-vous souvent à vos parents? Naturellement, je pense souvent à _____.
8. Veux-tu dîner avec moi ce soir? Je voudrais bien dîner avec _____.
9. Etes-vous arrives après les jeunefilles? Oui, nous sommes arrivés après _____.
10. _____, je ne l'oublierai jamais, le jour de mon premier baiser.

Exercise 23

Translate into French:

1. Is she the one?
2. He is richer than you (fam.).
3. They were seated in front of us.
4. Who has just arrived? He.
5. Do it for her.
6. Jean eats more than you and I together.
7. Is it you, madame?
8. Come with me, please.
9. They are the ones who bought the house next door.
10. They are sad, but I am happy.
11. I do not smoke!
12. He and I are working together.
13. There is an exit near you.
14. He never goes out without her.
15. I am not the one.

Exercise 24

Answer each question with a complete sentence in French. Use an emphatic (stress) pronoun in each response.

1. Bonjour, monsieur. Vous souvenez-vous de moi?
2. Est-ce vous qui parle si fort dans la classe?
3. Quand renderez-vous visite à vos parents?
4. Est-ce que le train est arrivé avant nous?
5. Iriez-vous en Europe sans vos amis?
6. Pourrez-vous jouer au tennis avec nous demain?
7. Est-ce que cette voiture neuve à vous, mon ami?
8. C'est Monsieur Dupont qui n'aime pas parler en public, n'est-ce pas?
9. Est-ce que l'equipe de football de New York était plus fort ou moins fort que l'équipe de Miami?
10. A qui penses-tu plus souvent? A lui ou à moi?

POSSESSIVE PRONOUNS

La souris noire mange **son** fromage.
La souris blanche mange **le sien**.
Le chat noir guette **sa** souris.
Le chat blanc guette **le sien**.

1. THE POSSESSIVE PRONOUNS

A possessive pronoun refers to a previously mentioned noun and must agree in gender and number with that noun. Like the possessive adjective, the possessive pronoun agrees in person with the possessor, although not showing the gender of the possessor.

A. Forms of the possessive pronoun

Singular	Masculine	Feminine	Meaning
1st (je)	le mien	la mienne	mine
2nd (tu)	le tien	la tienne	yours (fam.)
3rd (il/elle)	le sien	la sienne	his/hers/its
1st (nous)	le nôtre	la nôtre	ours
2nd (vous)	le vôtre	la vôtre	yours (form.)
3rd (ils/elles)	le leur	la leur	theirs
Plural	Mas.	Fem.	Meaning
1st (je)	les miens	les miennes	mine
2nd (tu)	les tiens	les tiennes	yours (fam)
3rd (il/elle)	les siens	les siennes	his/hers/its
1st (nous)	les nôtres	les nôtres	ours
2nd (vous)	les vôtres	les vôtres	yours (form.)
3rd (ils/elles)	les leur	les leurs	theirs

Notes: a) Unlike the possessive adjectives, notre and votre, the 1st and 2nd person plural possessive pronouns have a circumflex accent (^) over the o: le nôtre/les nôtres, le vôtre/les vôtres.

b) The possessive pronoun replaces a possessive adjective and a noun. The pronoun agrees in gender and number with the noun it replaces.

Marie a son billet d'avion. As-tu le tien, Jean?

Marie has her airplane ticket. Do you have yours, Jean?

("Son billet" is masculine, singular; therefore, le tien is masculine, singular.)

Voici vos gants et les miens.

Here are your gloves and mine.

("Vos gants" is masculine, plural; therefore, les miens is masculine, plural.)

Il a sa clef. Elle a la sienne.

He has his key. She has hers.

("Sa clef" is feminine, singular; therefore, la vôtre is feminine, singular.)

2. The definite article, a regular part of the possessive pronoun, contracts with the prepositions a and de in the usual way.

Nous avons donné une voiture à nos enfants; ils ont donné une maison de campagne aux leurs. (a + **les** leurs cannot be expressed in French. Therefore, *a* + *les* are combined to form "**aux leurs.**")

We have given a car to our children; they have given a country house to theirs.

Je vous parle souvent de mes études; **vous, vous ne parlez jamais** des vôtres. Pourquoi? (**de + les** vôtres cannot be expressed in French. Therefore, **de + les** are combined to from "**des vôtres**.")

I often speak to you about my studies; you, you never speak of yours. Why?

Exercise 25

Express each sentence in another manner using a possessive pronoun introduced by "**C'est**" ou "**Ce sont**":

Examples: Cette voiture est à moi. C'est la mienne.

Ces cahiers sont à lui. Ce sont les siens.

1. Ces bijoux sont à Madame Dupont. _____
2. Cet impermeable est à toi. _____
3. Ces bicyclettes sont à nous. _____
4. Cette chemise est à moi. _____
5. Ce téléphone est à elle. _____
6. Ces champs sont à moi. _____
7. Cette monnaie est à nous. _____
8. Ces cravates de soie sont à lui. _____
9. Cet appareil de photo est à vous. _____
10. Cet bel enfant est à eux. _____

Exercise 26

Translate the boldface words into French.

1. Il préfère ma solution **to his**.
2. Ces avenues sont plus larges que **ours**.
3. J'ai pris mon ordinateur et **hers**.
4. Vos enfants travaillent-ils aussi dur que **theirs**?
5. Tu as mes lunettes de soleil et **yours**.
6. Cherchez votre route et nous chercherons **ours**.
7. Votre mère et **mine** travaillent bien ensemble.
8. Voici mes bagages. Où sont **yours**?
9. Parlez-vous de nos photos ou **of his**?
10. Ma mère est aussi jeune que **theirs**.

Exercise 27

Give the equivalent in French.

1. Their room and yours are on the first floor.
2. His songs or ours have received a prize.
3. This castle belong to her father and mine.
4. My friends and yours (fam.) went to the movies.
5. His cat and ours fight often.
6. Their children and mine have returned from a long trip.
7. My neighbor and yours talk a lot.
8. Our city and theirs are clean.
9. Your tickets and his are expensive
10. Her good reputation and mine have helped our children.

11. The principal speaks well of your sisters and of theirs.
12. Fill my cup and his, please.
13. His school and yours offer a good summer program.
14. His letters and mine were not very long
15. Their family and ours always spend the summer together.

Exercise 28

Answer each question with a complete sentence in French. Use a possessive pronoun in the response.
1. Si je réponds à vos lettres, répondrez-vous aux miennes?
2. Avez-vous pris vos valises ou les nôtres, Monsieur?
3. Ont-ils achete leurs livres et les nôtres?
4. Avez-vous vu ma serviette et la vôtre?
5. J'ai mes lunettes avez-vous les vôtres?
6. Votre maison de campagne est-elle belle que la nôtre?
7. Ma chambre donne sur la rue et le tienne?
8. J'ai perdu mon mouchoir, pouvez-vous me prêter le vôtre?
9. Si je te montre mes photos, me montreras-tu les tiennes?
10. Est-ce que ta voiture est plus economique que la mienne?

DEMONSTRATIVE PRONOUNS

La souris mange le fromage de Madame Dupont et celui de Monsieur Dupont.

Le chat guette la souris à droite et celle à gauche.

1. The demonstrative pronouns, celui/celle/ceux/celles, take the place of nouns and function as nouns. There are two types of demonstrative pronouns. Variable demonstrative pronouns indicate gender and number, but neuter demonstrative pronouns do not indicate gender and number.

2. A variable demonstrative pronoun must agree in number and gender with the noun it replaces. Carefullly study the following table of variable demonstrative pronouns:

Masculine singular

| celui | the one | this one | that one |

Masculine plural

| ceux | the ones | these ones | those ones |

Feminie singular

| celle | the one | this one | that one |

<u>Femine plural</u>

celles   the ones   these ones   those ones

3. A variable demonstrative pronoun never stands alone. It is always followed by a prepositional phrase or a relative clause beginning with que or qui, or the attached adverb **-ci** or **-là**.

A. A variable demonstrative pronoun followed by a prepositional phrase:

Ces maisons et celle de ma famille ont été vendues.
These houses and the one (house) of my daughter were sold.

Celui à droite est très cher. (le veste, e.g.)
The one on the right is very expensive.

B. A variable demonstrative pronoun followed by a relative clause beginning with que or qui:
<u>Singular</u>

celui/celle qui   the one that/who (subject)
celui/celle que   the one that/whom (object)
celui/celle dont   the one of which

<u>Plural</u>

ceux/celles qui   the ones/those that/who (subject)
ceux/celles que   the ones/those that/whom (object)
ceux/celles dont   the ones of which

On dit que ceux qui travaillent dur reussissent.
People say that those who work hard succeed.

La voiture rouge est celle qu'il a achetée.
The red car is the one that he bought.

C. **-ci** or **-là** may be added to a variable demonstrative pronoun: **-ci** may be added to a demonstrative pronoun to indicate that the person or object is close to the speaker. The demonstrative pronoun plus **-ci** is translated as *"this one"* or *"these."* **-là** may be added to a demonstrative pronoun to indicate that the person or object is at a dlistance from the speaker. The demonstrative pronoun plus **-là** is translated as "that one" or *"those."*
<u>Singular</u>

celui/celle-ci   this one, the latter
celui/celle-la   that one, the former

<u>Plural</u>

ceux/celles-ci   these, the latter
ceux/celles-la   those, the former

Madame Dupont préfère celle-là.
Mrs. Dupont prefers that one.

Ceux-ci sont plus chers que celui-là.
These are more expensive than that one.

Note: A variable demonstrative pronoun sometimes means *"the former"* or *"the latter."* When two nouns are mentioned, *"the former"* is the first noun. It is translated as celui-là, celles-là, etc. *"The latter"* is the second noun mentioned. It is translated as celle-ci, ceux-ci, etc.

Monsieur Dupont écrit des articles pour son journal et des revues pour enfants; ceux-la ont plus succes que celles-ci.
Monsieur Dupont writes articles for his newpaper and magazines for children; the former are more successful than the latter.

4. A neuter demonstrative pronoun does not have gender or number. Therefore, it does not agree in gender or number with the noun it replaces. The neuter demonstrative pronouns are:

ceci	this, it
cela (ça)	that, it
ce	he, she, it, this, that, these, those

Note: Use of ça: ça, a contraction of cela, is used informally in spoken French, or to emphasize an exclamation.

Ça m'étonne!	This surprises me!
Ça va?	How's it going?

5. Neuter demonstrative pronouns usually refer to event, ideas, or indefinite concepts. The neuter demonstrative pronoun always stands alone, that is, it does not need another noun or phrase to complete it.

Remember: Variable demonstrative pronouns - **celui, ceux, celle(s)** - never stand alone. Neuter demonstrative pronouns - **ceci, cela (ça), ce** - always stand alone.

A. Ceci or cela can be used as the subject or object of any verb but être, to be. Ceci or cela is used to point out something that has not been previously mentioned.

Note: **Ceci** usually refers to something near, and cela to something far away; however, sometimes cela may be used in either case, unless drawing a contrast.

Ceci me dérange.	This disturbs me.
Cela m'est égal.	It doesn't matter to me.
Avez-vous jamais vu ça (cela)?	Have you ever seen that (anything like that)?

B. Ce may be used to mean he, she, or it when the subject noun phrase follows the verb être. Ce does not replace the noun phrase, but merely occupies the subject position. Ce has no gender or number.

Ce sont Jules et Jim.	It's Jules and Jim. (They are Jules and Jim.)
C'est mon meilleur ami.	He's my best friend.
C'étaient des musées modernes.	They were modern museums.

Notes: a) When a word referring to nationality, religion, or profession follows **être**, that word functions as an adjective and an appropriate subject pronoun must be used - **il, ils, elle,** or **elles.**

    Elle est professeur.   She's a doctor.

    Il est catholique.   He is Catholic.

    Ils sont Japonais.   They are Japanese.

    b) When a word referring to nationality, religion, or profession is modified and forms a noun phrase which functions as the subject of the sentence, ce must be used.

    Ce sont des chauffeurs habiles.   They are skillful drivers.

    C'est mon infirmière.   She's my nurse.

Exercise 29

Replace the phrase given in parentheses with the appropriate neuter demonstrative pronoun.

Example: Il n'aime pas (nager dans l'eau froid). Il n'aime pas cela.

1. (Cette demande) a choqué ses parents.
2. (Le socialisme) est un système politique.
3. (voyager seul dans un petit avion) est mon seul reve.
4. Il déteste (dîner tout seul).
5. (Le fait qu'il a reçu un prix noble) est très impressionant.
6. (Ce que vous venez d'entendre dire) est faux.
7. Il lui a donné (la petite voiture rouge).
8. (Leur note de paiement mensuel) est due demain.
9. (Voir quelqu'un pleure) me rend fou de tristesse.
10. (Qu'elle a laissé passer cette opportunité) était suprennant.
11. (Jean et Pierre) sont des étudiants intelligents.
12. (Cette femme) est une avocate douee.
13. Elle attend (son arrivée avec impatience).
14. (L'Angleterre) est une des grandes puissances du monde.
15. Il ne voulait pas accepter (le fait qu'il avait échoué).

Exercise 30

Replace the noun phrase given in parentheses with the appropriate form of the variable demonstrative pronoun.

1. Qui t'a suggéré (cette robe)?
2. Regarde (ce beau costume) que j'ai.
3. (Cette explication) met en relief le même point.
4. Marie verra (ces photos-ci) et elle m'écrira.
5. (Cette bouteille de vin-là) n'est plus bonne à boire.
6. (Ces rivières) sont les plus longues de l'Afrique.
7. Qui aurait pensé qu'il aurait acheté (ces cravates)
8. Donnez-moi (ce cadeau) que vous m'avez promis.
9. (Cet avion décole à 15 heures et (l'autre) part à 20 heures.
10. (Ces chaussures-ci) sont bon marchés.

Exercise 31

Answer the following questions incorporating the suggestions given in parentheses and using either ceci or cela.
1. Comment ça va? (bien)
2. Est-ce que ceci vous plaît? (non)
3. Tout va bien? (très bien)
4. Que pensez-vous de cela? (c'est formidable)
5. Est-ce que ça vous dit quelque chose?

Exercise 32

Translate the following sentences into French using either il, elle est or c'est.
1. He is Peruvian.
2. It's a country house.
3. They are clever businessmen.
4. They are young.
5. She is a good friend.
6. It's a beautiful city.
7. She is an excellent doctor.
8. He is a secretary.
9. She is a lawyer.
10. She is a tall African American.

Exercise 33

Translate the following sentences into French using a neuter demonstrative pronoun.
1. It is too cheap.
2. It must be easy.
3. It will be expensive.
4. It doesn't matter to me
5. It will be up to her.
6. The demonstrative pronouns, ceci, cela and ce refer to things indicated but not named.
A. **ceci**, this
Donnez-lui ceci de ma part.   Give him this for me.
Qui a fait ceci?   Who did this?
B. **cela (ça)**, that
Cela (Ça) me fera plaisir.   That will please me.
Qu'est-ce que c'est que cela (ça)? What is that?

Note: The form ça often replaces cela in conversation.
C. **ce**, (**c'** before a vowel), **it, he, she, this, that, they, these, those**
Ce is used only with the verb être. Ce replaces il, elle, ils, and elles in the following cases:
1. Before a modified noun:
C'est un mouton.   It is a sheep.
C'est une affaire grave.   That's a serious matter.

Ce sont de vrais amis.　　　　They are real friends.

But unmodified:

Il est pompier.　　　　　　　He is a fireman.

2. Before a proper noun:

Qui m'appelle? C'est Jeanne.

Who is calling me? It is Joan.

Quelle est la capitale de l'Angleterre? C'est Londres.

What is the capital of England? It's London.

3. Before a pronoun:

Je doute que ce soit elle.　　　I doubt that it is she.

Est-ce vous qui avez toussé?　　Are you the one who coughed?

Ce sont les vôtres.　　　　　They (These, Those) are yours.

C'était celui de son père.　　　It was his father's.

4. Before a superlative:

C'est la plus belle de la famille. She is the best looking in the family.

C'est le moindre de ses soucis. That's the least of his worries.

5. In dates:

C'est aujourd'hui lundi.　　　Today is Monday.

Ce sera demain le deux fevrier. Tomorrow will be February 2nd.

Note: In expressions denoting the hour of the day, il is used.

Il est 14 heures.　　　　　　It is two o'clock.

6. Before masculine singular adjectives to refer to ideas or actions previously mentioned. In this case, the English equivalent of **ce** is *it* or *that*, However, in referring to a preceding noun, il and elle are used.

Tony est Italien.　　　　　　C'est évident.

Tony is Italien.　　　　　　That's obvious.

Puis-je vous aider?　　　　　C'est inutile.

May I help you?　　　　　　It's useless.

but:

Regardez cette vase.　　　　Elle est mignonne.

Look at that vase.　　　　　It is pretty.

7. Before an adjective + a + an infinitive.

C'est bon à savoir.　　　　　That's good to know.

C'est impossible à faire.　　　That's impossible to do.

Note: The impersonal pronoun, il (it) is used with être and an adjective before de + infinitive and before a clause beginning with que.

Il est impossible de faire cela.　It is impossible to do that.

Il est impossible que je le fasse. It is impossible for me to do it.

Exercise 34　　　　Complete the following sentences in French:

1. (that) Partira-t-il malgré _____ ?
2. (It) _____ n'est pas une methode nouvelle.
3. (They)_____ sont en guerre.
4. (They) _____ sont des bateaux à moteur.
5. (it) Est-_____ un aliment qui donne des forces?
6. (This) _____ vous donnera la meme impression.
7. (These) _____ sont les miens.
8. (She) _____ est la seule qui reçoive tant de lettres.
9. (She) _____ est actrice.
10. (It) _____ est mon tour.
11. (that) Qu'est-ce que _____ prouve?
12. (He) _____ est un savant illustre.
13. (they) Achetez ces roses; _____ sont très jolies.
14. (That) _____ n'est pas de la science-fiction.
15. (this) Regardez _____.
16. (It) _____ est New York.
17. (They) A qui sont ces gants? _____ ne sont pas à moi.
18. (This) _____ est la plus difficile des questions.
19. (It) _____ est la fete de maman.
20. (Those) _____ sont les resultats de plusieurs années de recherches.

Exercise 35

Complete with the most suitable pronoun (ce, c', il, elle, ils, elles):

1. _____ est le musee d'histoire naturelle.
2. _____ sont revenues tard.
3. _____ est lui qui le fera.
4. _____ est ecrivain.
5. _____ sont des climats froids.
6. _____ est Henri.
7. _____ n'était pas sa faute.
8. _____ est probable qu'elle m'a reconnu.
9. _____ est du sable blanc.
10. Est-_____ une machine à laver?
11. Connaissez-vous Albert? _____ est très timide.
12. _____ est celui de l'avocat.
13. _____ sont les meilleurs du monde.
14. _____ est utile de savoir nager.
15. _____ etait la marine française.
16. _____ sont toujours heureuses.
17. L'Etat, _____ est moi.
18. _____ est cela.
19. La paix est précieuse. Qui, _____ est précieuse.
20. _____ est le Rhone.

21. _____ sera demain vendredi.
22. Tout le monde aime le beau temps. _____ est vrai.
23. _____ était M. Sorel.
24. De quelle couleur sont les arbres? _____ sont verts.
25. _____ est le dos du livre.
26. _____ est neuf heures et demie.
27. _____ est le plus intelligent de la classe.
28. Quel est ce oiseau? _____ est un aigle.
29. Ou sont vos fils à présent? _____ sont en Europe.
30. _____ est un projecteur de cinéma sonore.

Exercise 36

Answer the following questions, using the indicated vocabluary. Begin each sentence with one of the following expressions: **il est, ils sont, elle est, elles sont, c'est, ce sont.**

Exemple: M. Lefort est mal habillé? (bien)
Non, il est bien habillé.

1. Quelle est cette fleur? (violette)
2. Est-ce que l'air de "La Marseillaise" est beau? (très)
3. Qu'est-ce qu'elle bat? (des oeufs)
4. Ou sont les autres oeufs? (dans le réfrigerateur)
5. Va-t-il pleuvoir cet après-midi? (possible)
6. Est-ce que Mme Duval entend bien? (un peu sourde)
7. Qu'est-ce qui tourne autour de la terre? (lune)
8. Ces étudiantes sont faibles en mathématiques? (fortes)
9. Quel est le metier de cet homme? (coiffeur)
10. Qu'est-ce que tu manges? (une glace à la vanille)
11. Ces patins appartiennent à Pierre? (les notres)
12. Tu peur l'accomplir? (impossible que)
13. Ce gratte-ciel est très haut, m'est-ce pas ? (le plus haut de la ville)
14. Ces langues sont faciles à comprendre? (très)
15. Qui frappe à la porte, Leon? (nos voisins)
16. Qu'est-ce qu'on joue ce soir au theatre? (pièce de Molière)
17. Sommes-nous en retard? (midi précis)
18. Quelles sont ces montagnes? (Pyrénées)
19. Cette voiture est bien construite? (construite pour durer)
20. Est-ce que Paulette est la soeur de Jacques? (de Bernard)

Exercise 37

Write in French:

1. She is my grandmother.
2. Who gave you this?
3. He is a sculptor.
4. He is a well-known sculptor.
5. Today is June 10th.

6. Those are beautiful leaves.
7. He came back? That's interesting!
8. Do you prefer this or that?
9. It is easy to read that.
10. That is easy to read.

RELATIVE PRONOUNS

La souris a mangé le fromage qui était sur la table.
Le chat guette la souris dont je parle.
Le garçon chasse le chat contre lequel il est fâché.
La jeune mère fesse le garçon que nous connaissons.

1. THE RELATIVE PRONOUNS

A relative pronoun introduces a relative clause: a subordinate clause which modifies a noun in the main clause. The most frequent relative pronouns are:

Relative pronoun	Meaning	Function
qui	who/ which/that	subject of a verb
que	whom/which/that	direct object of a verb
quoi	whom/which	object of a preposition
lequel/ laquelle	whom/which	object of a preposition
lesquels/ lesquels	whom/which	object of a preposition
dont	whose/of whom/ of which	indirect object of a verb

A. Relative pronouns with adjectival clauses. An adjectival clause describes an immediately preceding noun. The form of the relative pronoun that introduces that adjectival clause depends on its function.

1. The relative pronoun qui (who/which/that) introduces an adjectival clause and is the subject of that clause. Qui is invariable and stands for persons or things, masculine or feminine, singular or plural.

Donnez-moi le stylo qui est sur le bureau.
Give me the pen that is on the desk.

Connaissez-vous la femme qui chante?
Do you know the woman who is singing?

Note: The relative pronoun **qui** is usually placed directly before its verb.

Nous avons manqué le train qui est parti a huit heures.
We missed the train that left at eight o'clock.

2. The relative pronoun **que** (who/which/that) introduces an adjectival clause and is the direct object of that clause.

Voilà la viande que j'ai achetée.
There is the meat (that) I bought.

L'histoire, qu'il la lue en français, est intéressante.
The story, which he read in French, is interesting.

C'est la cravate que je vous ai recommandée.
This is the necktie that I recommended to you.

Notes: 1. Never omit que in French, even though the English *"that"* is often omitted.

2. The subject of the adjectival clause usually—but not always—follows the relative pronoun **que**.

Ce sont les mêmes robes que ma mère a achetées.
These are the same dresses that my mother bought.

Ce sont les mêmes robes qu'a achetées ma mère.
These are the same dresses that my mother bought.

3. The relative pronoun lequel/laquelle/lesquels/lesquelles intoduces an adjectival clause preceded by a preposition.

Où est le stylo avec lequel j'écrivais?
Where is the pen with which I was writing?

Voici la rue dans laquelle se trouve notre hotel.
Here is the street on which our hotel is located.

4. The relative pronoun **qui** (who/whom), **dont** (whose, of whom, of which), or the adverb **où** (where/when, as), are equally correct alternatives to lequel (etc.) in certain instances.

5. The relative pronoun **qui** may be used after a preposition to introduce an adjectival clause describing a person.

Le monsieur pour qui il travaille est son beau-père. (pour lequel)

The man for whom he works is his father-in-law.

C'est le seul enfant à qui je n'ai rien donné. (auquel)
This is the only child to whom I have given nothing.

6. The relative pronoun **dont** (whose/of whom/of which) is a synonym for the relative pronouns **de laquelle/duquel/desquels/desquelles,** or **de qui**. However, since dont is invariable, it is used more frequently than the longer forms.

Les garçons dont elle parle sont ses fils. (de qui)
The boys of whom she is talking are her sons.

Nous avons apporté le dictionnaire dont nous avons besoin. (duquel)
We have brought the dictionary (that) we need.

7. The adverb of time and place, où (where/when), may be used in place of a relative pronoun before an adjectival clause referring either to time or place.

C'est la rue où se trouve notre hotel.
This is the street where our hotel is located.

Voilà la maison où je suis né.
Here is the house where I was born.

2. RELATIVE PRONOUNS WITH NOUN CLAUSES

A relative clause that is not preceded by a noun functions as a noun phrase. In this case, the demonstrative pronouns, **ce/celui/ceux/celle(s)** is used before the relative pronoun in place of the noun, unless the relative pronoun means who.

A. The relative pronoun qui is followed by a singular verb to introduce a noun clause referring to an indefinite person or persons.

Je ne sais pas qui viendra à la fête.
I do not know who will come to the party.

Il est impossible de prédire qui sera élu president.
It is difficult to predict who will be elected president.

B. The demonstrative pronoun **ce** is used before the relative pronoun if the noun clause refers to something indefinite.

Je ne comprends pas ce que tu veux dire.
I do not understand what you mean.

Ce qui est sur la table est à vous.
What is on the table is for you.

Avez-vous decidé ce dont vous aurez besoin?
Have you decided what you will need?

C. The demonstrative pronoun **celui/ceux/celle/celles** of the appropriate gender and number is used before a relative pronoun if the noun refers to a person or thing whose gender and number is specified.

Ce travail est celui dont tout le monde parle.
This work is the one everyone is talking about.

Ceux qui m'aiment me suivent.
Those who love me follow me.

Notes: a) The relative pronoun **qui** may be used alone to introduce a noun clause with a broader meaning.

Qui vivrà, verrà.	Whoever will live, will see.
Qui que tu sois.	Whover you might be.

b) Que becomes qu' before a word beginning with a vowel; the **i** of qui is never dropped.

c) Since **que** is a direct object pronoun and precedes the verb, the past participle of a compound verb agrees with it (**que**).

> La lettre que j'ai écrite était très courte.
> The letter that I wrote was very short.

> Les cadeaux qu'il a achetés coûtent une fortune.
> The presents that he bought cost a fortune.

d) **Lequel** and its forms agree in gender and number with the nouns to which they refer.

e) The relative pronoun must always be expressed in French, although it is sometimes omitted in English.

Exercise 38

Choose the correct response within the parentheses:

1. Il y a beaucoup de feuilles (qui, que) sont tombées.
2. Je ne peux guère croire (ce qui, ce qu') est arrivé.
3. Montrez-moi les pages sur (lesquelles, qu') elle a écrit son nom.
4. Je n'ai pas vu l'addresse (qui, que) vous cherchez.
5. Elle ne comprend pas (ce que, ce qui) vous dites.
6. Les camarades avec (qui, lequel) Paul parle sont très gentils.
7. C'est la troisième leçon (ce qu', qu') elle doit étudier.
8. Ne nous dites pas (qu', ce qu') il a fait.
9. Claudette est la petite (dont, de ce qui) je vous ai parlé.
10. Voivi la chambre dans (laquelle, ou) je dors.
11. Ce sont les dames (que, lesquelles) nous avons aidees.
12. Quel est le soldat (lequel, dont) la femme est morte?
13. Ramassez (ce qui, ce qu') est sous la chaise.
14. Voila la jeune fille pour (qu', qui) il a écrit le poème.
15. L'agent (que, qui) lui a parlé est son ami.

Exercise 39

Complete the sentences in English:

1. Les oeufs que j'ai mangés étaient très frais. The eggs _____ were very fresh.
2. Voici la bouteille de vin dont j'ai parlé. Here is the bottle of wine _____.
3. Quelle est la personne à qui vous écrivez? Who is the person _____
4. Dites-nous ce qu'on a fait. Tell us _____ they did.
5. Donnez-moi les choses dont j'ai besoin.
   Give me the things _____.
6. C'est le bateau dans lequel j'ai fait un long voyage.
   That's the boat _____ I took a long trip.

7. Voici les cahiers dans lesquels (ou) j'écris mes devoirs. Here are the notebooks _____ I write my homework.

8. Il y a beaucoup d'Européens qui parlent anglais. There are many Europeans _____ English.

9. Où est l'enfant dont le pere vient d'arriver?
Where is the child _____ has just arrived?

10. Savez-vous ce que j'ai oublié? Do you know _____ I forgot?

Exercise 40

Give the correct pronoun:

1. Un boulanger est un homme _____ vend du pain.
2. Voici l'atelier dans _____ l'artiste travaille.
3. Le lait _____ j'ai bu était delicieux.
4. Voici _____ elle m'a envoyé.
5. Montre-moi les chapeaux _____ vous avez achetés.
6. La ville a _____ nous sommes arrives était tout à fait moderne.
7. Avez-vous lu l'anecdote _____ nous avons parlé?
8. C'est mon oncle _____ est avocat.
9. Dites-moi _____ est dans la voiture.
10. La femme avec _____ elle est partie est ma mère.
11. C'est l'ingénieur _____ j'ai fait la connaissance.
12. Ou est la lampe _____ il a cassée?
13. C'est la porte par _____ ils sont sortis.
14. Je comprends _____ vous avez dit.
15. Voila l'église _____ la cloche a sonné.

Exercise 41

Give the equivalent in French:
1. The desk on which there is a ruler belongs to me.
2. What I received is very dear to me.
3. The mother whose son succeeded is my friend.
4. The Frenchman to whom I spoke is rude.
5. The meat that was on the table cost a lot.
6. The dog he has is not a Saint Bernard.
7. What we chose were not expensive.
8. The man who left is a celebrated writer.
9. The house that they built has three floors.
10. What is on the roof will not fall down.
11. The restaurant of which everyone is speaking is located on Rue Saint Honoré.
12. The hat you will wear is very elegant.
13. The friends with whom I study live downtown.
14. What she bought does not please her.
15. The train that is leaving will arrive on time.

Exercise 42

Form one sentence using a relative pronoun:
    Examples: Les gens sont sympathiques. Nous les avons invités.
                    Les gens que nous avons invités sont sympathiques.
Ramassez la robe. La robe est tombée.
Ramassez la robe qui est tombée.

1. Prenez cet argent. Vous avez gagne l'argent.
2. J'ai écoute le poète. Il parle bien.
3. Le train est parti. Nous l'avons manqué.
4. Voila l'appartement. Pierre y demeure.
5. Ouvrez le sac. J'ai mis mes pierres dans le sac.
6. C'est notre cousin. Nous avons dîné chez notre cousin.
7. Voici les romans. Elle les a lus.
8. Elle nous montrait les vetements. Elle avait parlé des vêtements.
9. Donnez-lui les timbres. Les timbres sont sur le bureau.
10. Jean est l'ami. Je joue avec Jean chaque jour.

INTERROGATIVE PRONOUNS

Qui a mangé le fromage? La souris.
Lequel des deux chats guette le souris?
Que fait le garçon? Il chasse le chat.
Qui est-ce qui fesse le garçon? La jeune mère.

1. Interrogative pronouns can be divided into three distinct groups: the short indefinite interrogatives, the long indefinite interrogatives, and the accentuated interrogative pronouns. An indefinite interrogative is a word that serves as a subject, object or object of a preposition in a question that concerns someone or something not yet introduced into the conversation. The interrogative is neutral in gender and takes a third person singular verb.
    A. The short interrogatives are:

Interrogatives	Meaning
qui	who/whom
que	what
quoi	what

1. **Qui** is used whenever the question concerns a person.

Qui est à la porte? (subject)
Who is at the door?

Qui aimeriez-vous voir? (direct object)
Whom would you like to see?

A qui voulez-vous parler? (indirect object)
To whom do you want to speak?

Avec qui joue-t-il? (object of a preposition)
With whom is he playing?

Note: "Whose" showing possession or relationship is expressed by the preposition à or de plus the indefinite interrogative qui.

à qui - to show possession	de qui - to show relationship
A qui est cette clef?	Whose key is this? (possession)
De qui est-elle la mère?	Whose mother is she? (relationship)

2. **Que** is used to ask a question concerning something other than a person. **Que** is always the direct object of a verb.

Que voulez-vous dire?	What do you mean?
Que faites-vous là, mes amis?	What are you doing there, my friends?

Note: **Que** should never be used as the subject of a sentence or as the object of a preposition.

3. **Quoi** is used as the object of a preposition and in one word questions or exclamations.

Avec quoi voulez-vous que je fasse ce travail?
With what do you want me to do this work?

Quoi! Que veut-il faire?
What! What does he want to do?

B. The long indefinite interrogative

Interrogatives	Function	Meaning
qui est-ce qui (person)	subject	who
qu'est-ce qui (things)	subject	what
qui est-ce que (person)	object	whom
qu'est-ce que (things)	object	what

Qui est ce qui est arrivé?	Who has arrived?
Qu'est-ce qui est arrivé?	What has happened?

Qui est-ce qu'il a choisi comme vice-president?
Qui a-t-il chosi comme vice-president?
Whom did he choose as vice-president?

Qu'est ce que vous avez dit?	
Qu'avez-vous dit?	What did you say?

Notes: a) The order of subject and verb should never be inverted after a long interrogative.

b) Qu'est ce qui is always the subject of a sentence.

Qu'est ce qui s'est passé?　　　What happened?

3. Even though people take poetic license, saying casually, **"Que dois-je dire?"** or **"Que vais-je faire?"** it is recommended to use **"Qui est-ce qu(e)"** and **"Qu'est-ce que"** when je is the subject of the sentence.

C. The accentuated interrogative pronouns

1. When a question is asked about something already mentioned, already referred to by a specific noun, a form of the interrogative pronoun lequel (which/which one) must be used. Unlike the interrogative adjective quel, the interrogative pronoun lequel may function as a subject, a direct object, an indirect object, or the object of a preposition.

a) Formation of the accentuated interrogative pronouns

The interrogative pronoun lequel is a combination of the definite article, le, la, or les and the interrogative adjective, quel.

Singular	Plural	Meaning
m. lequel	lesquels	which/which one(s)
f. laquelle	lesquelles	which/which one(s)

The preposition à or de immediately preceding lequel or lesquel(le)s forms the following contractions:

a + lequel	=	auquel
a + lesquels	=	auxquels
a + lesquelles	=	auxquelles
de + lequel	=	duquel
de + lesquels	=	desquels
de + lesquelles	=	desquelles

b) Use of the accentuated interrogative pronouns.

The accentuated interrogative pronoun is used to ask a question concerning someone or something referred to by a specific noun.

i. **as a subject**

Sur la table il y a deux clefs. Laquelle t'appartient?

On the table there are two keys. Which one belongs to you?

ii. **as a direct object**

De ces deux cravates, laquelle voulez-vous?

Of those two neckties, which one do you want?

iii. **as the indirect object**

Auquel de tes amis as-tu ecrit?

To which one of your friends have you written?

iv. **as the object of a preposition**

Il y a trois chaises dans la salle d'attente; sur laquelle voulez-vous vous asseoir?

There are three chaise in the waiting room; on which one do you want to sit down?

Exercise 43

Choose the word in parenthesis that correctly completes the sentence:

1. Avec (quoi, que) le ferez-vous?
2. (A quel, Auquel) de ses amis répond-elle?
3. (Quoi, Que) me donneront-elles?
4. (A Qui, De qui) sont ces chaussures noires?
5. (Qu'est-ce que, Que) cela veut dire?
6. (Qu', Qu'est-ce qu') ont-ils perdu?
7. (Que, Quelles) cravates a-t-il choisies?
8. (Quel, Qui) joue du piano?
9. (De qui, A qui) êtes-vous le fils?
10. (Lequel, Quel) temps fait-il aujourd'hui?
11. (Quoi, Qui) cherchez-vous?
12. (Qu'est-ce qui, Qu'est-ce qu') est sur le bureau?
13. De (qui, que) parlez-vous?
14. (Lesquelles, Laquelle) de vos amies est la plus intelligente?
15. Pour (qu'est-ce qui, qui) a-t-il acheté cette voiture?

Exercise 44

Make a question for each of the responses given replacing the boldfaced words by an interrogative:

Example: J'ai vu **Philippe**. Qui avez-vous vu?

1. Je cherche mon **maillot**. _____
2. Elle est partie avec son **fiancé**._____
3. **Tout le monde** sera à la fête. _____
4. Nous avons rencontré **l'avocat**._____
5. Elle a trouvé **un roman** interessant. _____
6. Ses **gants** sont tombés. _____
7. J'ai peur du **bruit**. _____
8. Il a demandé un **verre de vin rouge**._____
9. **Jean-Claude** s'est blessé. _____
10. A quel **étudiant** donneront-ils le cadeau? _____

Exercise 45

Give the equivalent in French:

1. Which day is the shortest? _____
2. Whose daughter is she? _____
3. Which of these flowers is the prettiest? _____
4. What time is it? _____
5. What are you drinking? _____
6. Which one is the shortest? _____
7. Whom do you know? _____
8. Who came in? _____
9. What did she see? _____
10. To which children was he reading?_____

11. To which ones was he reading? _____

12. For whom does he work?   _____

13. What is on the chair?   _____

14. Whose handkerchief is this?   _____

15. With what will he cut the cake? _____

Exercise 46

Donnez l'intérrogatif convenable:

1. _____ portez-vous? Je porte un parapluie.

2. _____ est à la porte? C'est Marianne.

3. _____ êtes-vous le père? Je suis le père de Marianne.

4. A _____ parliez-vous? Nous parlions au profésseur de français, monsieur Martin.

5. _____ vous avez acheté? J'ai acheté du pain et du jambon.

6. _____ age as-tu? J'ai six ans.

7. _____ vous faites? Je prends un bain de soleil.

8. _____ sont ces belles chemises? Elles sont à mon oncle.

9. De _____ parlez-vous? Je parle de la paix.

10. _____ il y a dans cette tasse? C'est du café au lait.

11. _____ ont-ils choisi? Ils ont choisi M. De Latour.

12. De _____ a-t-elle besoin? Elle a besoin de soie.

13. Chez _____ allez-vous? Nous allons chez nos copains.

14. _____ de ces langues ont-ils étudiées? Ils ont étudié l'anglais et le français.

15. _____ a-t-il mangé? Il a mangé des pommes de terre.

Exercise 47

Completez la phrase en anglais:

1. Desquels parliez-vous? _____ were you speaking?

2. De qui est-elle la tante? _____ is she?

3. Qui vous a donné ce caniche? _____ this poodle?

4. Que regardait-il? _____ was he looking at?

5. Dans quel pays va-t-il voyager? _____ is he going to travel?

6. Avec quoi écrit-elle? _____ is she writing?

7. Qu'est-ce qui est tombé? _____ fell?

8. A qui est ce billet? _____ is this?

9. Qu'avez-vous reçu? _____ did you receive?

10. Laquelle voulez-vous chanter? _____ do you wish to sing?

THE INDEFINITE PRONOUNS

Quiconque a mangé le fromage sera malade.
La jeune mère fesse **n'importe qui**.
Le garçon chasse **n'importe quoi.**
La souris ronge **tout ce qu'**elle trouve.

1. The indefinite pronouns are:

A. **aucun(e)** anyone, none / **aucun(e)** ... ne none

Aucun de mes ami ne partira cet été.
None of my friends will go away this summer.

Aucune de mes soeurs n'est arrivée.
None of my sisters has arrived.

Y a-t-il aucun de vous qui puisse manger autant que Jean?
Is there anyone of you who can eat as much as Jean?

Avez-vous de l'argent? Aucun!
Do you have any money? None!

B. **l'autre** the other, the other one / **les autres** the others, the other ones

L'un est pauvre, l'autre est riche.
One is poor, the other is rich.

Elle a raté l'autobus, mais il y aura d'autres.
She missed the bus, but there will be others (other ones).

Je prendrai seulement ce petit chapeau; les autres ne m'intéressent pas.
I'll take only this little hat; I'm not interested in the others.

Y a-t-il quelque chose d'autre à dire?
Is there something else to add?

Note: **D'autre** means *"else"* in the last sentence above.

C. **l'un (l'une)...l'autre / the one .... the other / les uns (les unes)...les autres /** the ones (some)... the others

Les uns jouaient de la guitare; les autres dansaient.
Some were playing the guitar; the others were dancing.

L'un écoutait pendant que l'autre parlait.
One listened as the other spoke.

D. **l'un (l'une) et l'autre** both, both of them

l'un (l'une) ou l'autre	either one
ni l'un (l'une) ni l'autre	neither one
l'un (l'une) à l'autre	to each other
l'un (l'une) pour l'autre	one for the other

Ils sont partis l'un et l'autre.   Both of them went away.

Vous avez deux verres. Passez-moi l'un ou l'autre.
You have two glasses. Give me either one.

Ni l'une ni l'autre n'est allée à la fête.
Neither one went to the party.

Ils s'aident l'un à l'autre.   They help each other.

E. **autre(s)** - other(s)

Voici deux pommes: je prends celle-ci; prenez l'autre.
Here are two apples: I'll take this one; (you) take the other.

Note: When an adjective modifies autre chose, the adjective is always masculine and is always preceded by de.

F. **autrui** others, other people

Il est toujours emudevant la misère d'autrui.
He is always moved by the pain of others.

G. **certain, certaine**   a certain one; **certains, certaines** certain ones, some

Certains de mes vetements sont completement abimés.
Some of my clothes are completely ruined.

H. **chacun, chacune**   each one, everyone

Chacun rentrera chez lui à minuit.
Everyone will go home at midnight.

Chacune d'elles s'en est allee avec une amie.
Each one of them went away with a friend.

I. **grand-chose**, much

Elle n'a pas grand-chose à faire.
She does not have much to do.

Note: **Grand-chose** is always used in the negative.

J. Je ne sais qui, I don't know who / Je ne sais quoi, I don't know what

Je ne sais qui a envoyé ce colis.
I don't know who sent this package.

Il a un certain je ne sais quoi.
He has a certain something about him.

K. **le même, la même** — the same (one) / les mêmes the same (ones)

C'est le même.
It's the same thing.

L. **n'importe qui** — anyone, anybody, just anyone, just anybody

N'importe qui pourrait faire cela.
Anyone could (would be able to) do that.

Mes enfants jouent avec n'importe qui.
My children play with anybody. (everybody)

M. **n'importe quoi** - anything, just anything

Il ne faut pas dire n'importe quoi sans réfléchir, ma chérie.
You must not say just anything without thinking, my darling.

N. **nul** - no one

Nul ne viendra à son secours.   No one will help her.
Note: Nul is used in the sense of personne ("no one").

O. **on** - one, they, people, we, "you" (in general sense)

On a construit cette église en 1804.
They built this church in 1804.

On ne fait pas cela en publique.   One doesn't do that in public.
Note: On can be replaced by l'on after et, ou, ou, que, qui, quoi, and si.

Si l'on veut, on peut tout arranger.   If one wants, one can fix anything.

P. **Personne ne ... no one / ne ... personne** anyone

Personne n'a compris son discours. No one understood his speech.

Je n'ai rendu visite à personne.   I have not visited anyone.

Q. **plusieurs** - several

J'ai vu plusieurs voitures dans la rue.
I saw several cars in the street.

Plusieurs d'entre elles sont très belles.
Several of them are very good looking.

R. **qui que** - whomever / qui que ce soit qui - whoever / quoi que - whatever / **quoi que ce soit que** - whatever

A qui que vous parliez, ne mentionez pas mon nom.
To whomever you speak, do not mention my name.

Qui que ce soit qui mange ce fruit tombera malade.
Whoever eats this fruit will get sick.

Quoi que nous disions, elle a fait à sa tête.
Whatever we said, she did as she pleased.

Note: The above expressions are followed by a verb in the subjunctive mood.

S. **quelqu'un** someone

Quelqu'un est au telephone.   Someone is on the telephone.

T. **quelqu'un** d'autre someone else

Quelqu'un d'autre peut préparer la salade.
Someone else can prepare the salade.

U. quelques-uns, quelques-unes   some

Avez-vous des cigarettes? Oui, j'en ai quelques-unes.
Do you have any cigarettes? Yes, I have some.

Voudriez-vous manger des abricots? Non, merci, j'en ai déjà mangé quelques-uns.

Would you like to have some apricots? No, thank you, I have already eaten some.

Note: En is used when quelques-uns and quelques-unes are used as direct objects.

V. **quelque chose** something

Voudriez-vous voir quelque chose, madame?

Would you like to see something, Madam?

Je voudrais voir quelque chose de joli.

I'd like to see something pretty.

Note: De precedes the adjective which refers to quelque chose. The adjective is always masculine.

W. **quiconque** anyone

Quiconque practique beaucoup, aprendra.

Anyone who practices hard will learn.

X. **Rien ne... nothing / ne ... rien**, anything

Rien n'est reste. Nothing is left.

Il ne fait rien pour m'aider.   He's not doing anything to help me.

Y. **tel, telle** (designates an undetermined person)

Monsieur (M.) un tel	Mr. So-and-so
Madame (Mme.) une telle	Mrs. So-and-so
Madamoiselle (Mlle.) une telle	Miss So-and-so

The form **un tel** is used when one doesn't want to or is unable to name the person spoken about.

Tel qui arrive en retard sera puni.	He who arrives late will be punished.
Z.tout, toute, tous, toutes	all, everything
tout ce qui, tout ce quoi	everything, all that
Tout est parfait.	Everything is perfect.

Elle a toutes les enveloppes. Elles les a toutes.

She has all the envelopes. She has all of them.

Il a vu toutes les peintures. Il les a toutes vues.

He saw all the paintings. He saw all of them.

Notes: a) **De** is never used with tout, although in English we say, *"all of them"* or *"all."*

b) The -s is pronounced in the pronoun, tous.

c) The pronoun, tout precedes the past participle in compound tenses.

Il les a tous lus.	He read them all. (He read "all of them.")
d) **tout ce qui, tout ce quoi**	everything, all that

On a vu tout ce qui est dans cette ville.

We saw everything in this city.

Tout ce que nous faisons est intéressant.
Everything we do is interesting.

Tout ce qu'elle dit est intéressant.
Everything she says is interesting.

Note: tout le monde means *"everyone"* and is used with a singular verb.
Tout le monde est ici.   Everyone is here.

Exercise 48

Translate the English to complete the following sentences in French.

1. _____ (Anyone) peut faire une faute.
2. _____ (Someone) viendra.
3. _____ (Everyone) voudrait vivre en paix.
4. _____ (One) peut manger dans ce restaurant.
5. Elle a fait _____ (something) de bon à manger?
6. Nous n'avons pas _____ (everything) entendu.
7. _____ (The others) sont déjà partis.
8. Elle a écrit les phrases. elles les écrit _____ (all).
9. As-tu des timbres? Oui, j'en ai _____ (some).
10. ils partiront _____ (both of them).
11. Nous ne voulons pas _____ (either one).
12. _____ (Certain ones) d'entre elles aimeraient y aller.
13. Ce garçon _____ (anything).
14. Veux-tu _____ (something else), ma chérie?
15. _____ (All that) Jean dit est amusant.
16. Nous avons _____ (several) voitures.
17. Avez-vous des cravates rouges? Oui, j'en ai _____ (some).
18. _____ (Each one) des enfants apportera quelque chose.
19. _____ (Someone else) m'accompagnera à la gare.
20. _____ (Some) chantaient; _____ (the others) jouaient de la guitare.
21. Elles se telephonent _____ (to each other).
22. Vous avez deux crayons. Donnez-moi _____ (either one).
23. _____ (Anyone) peut obtenir un permis de conduire.
24. Est-ce que c'est une autre chemise? Non, c'est _____ (the same).
25. _____ (None) d'elles ne partira avant midi.
26. _____ (No one) ne sait le numero de téléphone de Jean.
27. _____ (Everything) est charmant dans ce petit village.
28. _____ (Nothing) n'est absolu.
29. Allez voir _____ (Mr. So-and-so).
30. _____ (Whoever) sortira sans manteau, aura froid.
31. Il ne faut pas dire _____ (anything).
32. Ont-ils _____ (something else)?

6

Prepositions

PREPOSITIONS

La souris mange le fromage **avec** hésitation.
Le chat guette la souris **depuis** une heure.
Le garçon chasse le chat **pour** s'amuser.
La mère fesse le garçon **dans** la cusine.

1. **Uses of certain prepositions**

Prepositions can establish many kinds of connections or relationships between various parts of a sentence. They can indicate place, time, cause, goal, means, possession, and so on. A preposition is an invariable word which introduces an element of a sentence that it unites or subordinates in a certain way to another element of the sentence.

Elle va chez le docteur.
She goes to the doctor's office.

Nous attendons ici depuis deux heures.
We have been waiting here for two hours.

La voiture de mon père est rouge.
My father's car (the car of my father) is red.

La machine à écrire est en panne.
The typewriter (the machine for writing) is not working.

La mère de Jean parle d'une voix douce.
John's mother speaks in a sweet voice.

Jean fait ses devoirs avec soin.
John does his homework carefully.

2. A prepositional locution or phrase is a group of words that have the same role as a preposition. Notice the comparison examples.

PREPOSITIONS

Nous sommes **devant** le batiment.

Il gagne de l'argent **pour** payer ses dettes.

Prepositional locution

L'hôtel est **en face** de l'église.

Jean gagne de l'argent **afin de** payer ses dettes.

3. Prepositions and prepositional locutions are generally followed by a noun or noun groups, a pronoun or an infinitive.

Madame Dupont cuisine pour son mari et son fils.

Madame Dupont cuisine pour eux.

Elle va au marcher pour faire des achats.

4. A difficulty for English-speakers is that often a preposition in English has several French counterparts, and the correct translation depends on the meaning in the sentence. For example, the preposition "with" in English can be translated in various ways in French, depending on the context.

Marie danse avec François.
Mary dances with François

Elle écrit avec un stylo.
She writes with a pen.

Elle écrit de la main gauche.
She writes with her left hand.

Elle écrit à l'encre rouge.
She writes with red ink.

M. Dupont embrasse son fils avec joie.
Mr. Dupont embraces his son with joy.

Il danse de joie.
He dances with joy.

Il parle d'une voix forte.
He speaks with a strong voice.

Sa voiture est couverte de neige.
His car is covered with snow.

Jean sort, la tête haute. (no preposition)
John walks out with his head held high.

Note: The correct use of various prepositions are learned through practice. In most cases there are no rules. Each expression needs to be learned individually. This discussion is not exhaustive. Therefore, consult a good dictionary for further examples of the uses of various prepositions.

5. Prepositions to indicate location or direction or place:

à, de, dans, en, chez = to, in, at

A. With names of places, à can indicate location or direction in, at or to some place:

Jean eats à l'école.
John eats in (at) school.

M. Dupont est allé à New York.
Mr. Dupont went to New York.

Jean va au cinéma tous les vendredi.
John goes to the movies every Friday.

M. Célestin arrive à l'université à l'heure.
M. Célestin arrives at the university on time.

Il retourne à la maison à cinq heures.
He returns home at five o'clock.

6. de / from, about

De indicates the place of origin with the verbs venir, sortir, arriver, s'éloigner, partir, etc.

Jean reviens du bureau.
John returns from the office.

Il est revenu de Paris.
He came from Paris.

7. dans, en / in, into

A. Dans is always used with the article. En is rarely used with an article.
Le colis est dans la voiture.

Madame Dupont est allée en ville.

B. **Dans** is used to indicate place more precisely than **a** or **en** and often means **à l'intérieur de (inside)**.

en ville - in town, to town
dans la ville - in the town, inside the town

en classe - in class
dans ce bâtiment - in this building

Est-ce que Jean est à l'école?
Is Jean in school?

Oui, il est en classe maintenant.
Yes, he is in class now.

Oui, il est dans la classe de français.
Yes, he is in the French class.

Jean y est? Non, il n'est pas à la maison.
Is John there? No, he is not at home.

Où est M. Dupont? Il est dans la salle à manger.
Where is Mr. Dupont? He is in the dining room.

C. **Dans** can indicate the place in which a thing can be found.

Le client tient l'argent dans la main.
The client holds the money in his hand.

Il met la lettre dans l'enveloppe.
He puts the letter in the envelope.

D. **Dans** is used with the names of streets and avenues, but **sur** is used with the names of rural routes and boulevards.

Nous habitons dans l'avenue B.
We live on Avenue B.

Les Dupont habitent dans la rue de Fulton.
The Duponts live on Fulton Street.

Marie habite sur la route 13.
Marie lives on Route 13.

L'église se trouve sur le boulevard Kennedy.
The church is located on Kennedy boulevard.

8. chez / to, at the house of, at someone's place
A. **Chez** is used with a person, a person's name, a pronoun, a person's profession or business, a group or society.

Marie est allée chez sa mère.
Mary went over to her mother's house.

Elle ira chez elle samedi prochain aussi.
She will go to her house next Saturday also.

Je dois aller chez le dentiste.
I must go to the dentiste.

Chez Bernard, on joue du jazz le jeudi soir.
Over at Bernard's, they play jazz every Thursday.

B. **Chez** can also mean "in a person's work," figuratively speaking.

Chez Ronsard il y a beaucoup de métaphores.
In Ronsard's works, there are a lot of metaphors.

C. **Chez** is also used in the following expressions.

Faites comme chez vous.
Make yourself at home. (Do as you do at home.)

Chez lui tout va bien.
Everything is well with him.

Exercise 1   Complete the following sentences with the preposition **a, de, dans, en, chez** or **sur** plus the definite article when necessary.

1. Madame Dupont est _____ bureau. Elle est _____ salle de conférence à dix heures du matin.
2. Elle est _____ lycée à midi. Elle est _____ classe. Elle est _____ classe de rédaction.
3. Elle sort_____ l'école à trois heures de l'après midi.
4. Elle va_____ville. Elle va_____ le boulanger. Elle marche _____ le boulevard Saint Michel. Elle rentre _____ elle tard le soir.
5. Elle range ses achats _____ le placard.
6 Elle met ses livres, et ses papiers _____ un tiroir.
7. Monsieur Dupont _____ bureau à six heures et il retourne _____ maison à sept heures.
8. Lui aussi, il marche _____ le boulevard Saint-Michel. Souvent il y a beaucoup d'etudiants _____ la rue.
9. Il ne va _____ ville pour faire des courses. Il rentre _____ et il dîne avec sa femme _____ la salle _____ manger.
10. Le matin, Madame Dupont travaille _____ bureau; l'après-midi elle enseigne _____ lycée. Le soir elle prepare à manger _____ la cuisine.

9. Prepositions with geographical names

A. The preposition **à** is used before the names of most cities.

Je vais à Londres.   I am going to London.
Ma femme est à Paris.   My wife is in Paris.

but:

Ils sont arrivés au Havre.   They arrived in Le Havre.

B. The preposition **en** is used with names of feminine countries or continents. Almost all names of countries ending in a mute **e** are feminine. (Exception: le Méxique.)

Nous allons en Italie.   We are going to Italy.
Elle est allée en Afrique.   She is in Africa.

Nous sommes en Europe depuis un mois.
We have been in Europe for a month.

Note: A few countries are used without the article. For example: **Israel / en Israel, d'Israel**

C. The preposition **au** is used with masculine countries.

Nous allons au Méxique chaque année.
We go to Mexico each year.

Ma soeur habite au Canada.   My sister lives in Canada.
Ma tante va au Japon.   My aunt is going to Japan.

D. The preposition **aux** is used with Etats-Unis since the word is plural.

La Californie est aux Etats-Unis.
California is in the United States.

E. The preposition dans is used before names of continents qualified by another expression.

Elle a fait un long voyage dans l'Amerique du Sud.
She made a long trip through South America.

F. In spoken language, **en** may be used with names of continents.

Allons en Amérique du Sud.
Let's go to South America.

When the name of a city or country is accompanied by the complement or an adjective, dans le (l', la, les) is used instead of en.

Ronsard a vécu dans la belle France du XVIe siècle.
Ronsard lived in the beautiful France of the sixteenth century.

Nous allons voyager dans toute l'Europe Occidentale.
We are going to travel all over Western Europe.

G. The preposition used before names of islands varies.

en Islande	à Cuba	à la Guadeloupe
en Nouvelle-Guinée	à la Réunion	à la Martinique
en Sardaigne	à Chypre	à Madagascar
en Haiti		

H. With names of American states and Canadian provinces, en is used if the French form of the noun ends in **-e** or **-ie**. Otherwise, **dans le** or **dans l'Etat de** is used.

en Californie	dans l' Ontario
en Floride	dans le Colorado
en Columbie-Britanique	dans le Vermont
en Nouvelle-Ecosse	dans l'Etat de Vermont
en Pennsylvanie	dans le Montana

but:

au Nouveau-Méxique	au Nouveau-Brunswick
à Terre-Neuve	à New York

I. **De** is used to mean *"from"* or *"of"* and is used without the definite article before the names of cities, feminine countries and states and masculine countries beginning with a vowel.

Il est de Rome.   He is from Rome.
Je reviens d'Angleterre.   I am back from England.

Il est passioné par l'histoire des Etat-Unis.
He loves United States history.

J. **De** is used to mean *"from"* or *"of"* and is used with the definite article before the names of masculine countries, provinces or states except those beginning with a vowel.

Ces produits viennent de Suisse.
These products come from Switzerland.

Nous revenons du Méxique.
We are back from Mexico.

K. One always says **partir pour, en route pour** or **passer par** with the name of a place.

Ils sont partis pour Israel.   They have left for Israel.

En route pour Paris, nous nous sommes arrêtés à une charmante petite auberge.
On the way to Paris, we stopped at a charming small inn.

Il a passé par la Belgique.   He passed through Belgium.

Exercise 2   Complete the following sentences with the correct preposition plus the definite article, if required.

1. Elle revient _____ Italie.
2. Elle est passée _____ France.
3. Je suis _____ New York et ma femme est _____ Japon.
4. Mr Dupont est _____ Afrique et _____ Afrique du Nord.
5. Sa femme demeure _____ Paris.
6. Ils ont à voyage _____ Mexique et _____ Amerique du Sud.
7. En route _____ l'Angleterre, ils ont passé _____ la Belgique.
8. L'accident à lieu _____ Espagne.
9. Pendant ses sejours _____ Etats-Unis Jean à demeuré _____ Floride, _____ Vermont et _____ Nouveau-Méxique.
10. Le train part_____ Bruxelles.
11. Il revient _____ Québec.
12. Ils sont débarqués _____ Havre.
13. M. Dupont va _____ San Francisco _____ Californie.
14. _____ Russie, ils sont allés_____ Israel.

10. Prepositions with modes of transportation

A. The prepositions **à** and **en** and sometimes **par** are used with means of travel when you wish to describe by what means someone is travelling.

à	en	par
à bicyclette*	en auto	par le train
à cheval	en autobus	
à motocyclette	en avion	
à pied	en bateau	
à velo*	en métro	
	en taxi	
	en voiture	

Notes: a) You may also hear **en biclyette** and **en velo**.

b) à and en are used without the definite article and par is used with the definite article.

B. To describe how someone enters or leaves a vehicle, use monter dans or descendre de, or embarquer dans or débarquer de.

monter dans un autobus	descendre d'un autobus
monter dans une voiture	descendre d'une voiture
monter dans un train	descendre d'un train
embarquer dans un bateau	débarquer d'un bateau

C. When referring to mailing a letter or a package, you use the preposition par with the means of transportation.

envoyer le paquet par avion ou par bateau

Exercise 3

Complete the following sentences with the correct preposition to indicate how the people travel and mail things.

1. Les officiers paradent _____ cheval.
2. M. Dupont va au travail _____ métro.
3. Les enfants voyagent de Paris à Tokyo _____ avion.
4. Les enfants font à l'église _____ pied.
5. Les jeunes marriés voyagent _____ train.
6. Les touristes américains aiment voyager _____ bateau.
7. Madame Célestin va en ville _____ voiture.
8. Son mari va au cinema _____ autobus.
9. Il n'aime pas voyager _____ bicyclette.
10. La compagnie va nous envoyer le colis _____bateau.
11. Prepositions with expressions of time

A. à / at

Chaque matin j'arrive à l'école à huit heures.
Every morning I arrive in school at eight o'clock.

B. dans, en / in

1) **Dans** can indicate the time after which a certain thing can be done. It can mean **après** (after) or **à la fin de** (at the end of).

> Le docteur vous verra dans une heure.
> The doctor will see you in one hour. (one hour from now)

> Le train arrive dans trois heures.
> The train arrives in three hours. (three hours from now)

> Les étudiants seront ici dans deux jours.
> The students will be here in two days.

2) **En** indicates the time necessary for the accomplishment of an action, that is, the duration of an action.

> Je lirai ce document en deux heures.
> I will read this document in two hours.
> (It will take me two hours to read it.)

> L'avion voyage de New York à Paris en huit heures.
> The air plane travels from New York to Paris in eight hours.
> (within eight hours)

C. avant, before / après, after

Avant is used to mean, *"before"* (in time), and après is used to mean, "after" (in time).

> Jean s'est réveillé avant six heures.
> Jean woke up before six o'clock.

> André s'est réveillé après Jean.
> André woke up after Jean.

Note: The prepositions, **devant** (before) and **derrière** (after or behind) are used with places.

> Jean est devant le bâtiment.
> Jean is in front of the building.

> La voiture est derrière la maison.
> The car is behind the house.

Exercise 4   Complete the following with the prepositions **à**, **dans**, **en**, **pendant**, **durant**, **avant** or **après**.

1. Ma mère rentrera à la maison à six heures. Je terminerai mes devoirs à sept heures. Donc, je les aurai terminés _____ son arrivée.
2. Ce travail prend beaucoup de temps. Je ne peux pas le terminer _____ une heure.
3. L'autobus arrive _____ huit heures précises.
4. Les étudiants rentrent dans la salle de classe à huit heures et demie. Le professeur arrive à neuf heures moins le quart. Les étudiants sont arrivés _____ le professeur, et le professeur est arrivé _____ les étudiants.

Exercise 5   Complete the following sentences with the preposition **dans** or **en**. Follow the models.

Examples: Ma famille arrivera à New York _____ une semaine.
Ma famile arrivera à New York dans une semaine.

Elle termine le repas _____ un quart d'heure.
Elle termine le repas en un quart d'heure.

1. Le mécanicien a reparé la voiture _____ une demi heure.
2. L'avocat est en conference, il pourra vous parler _____ une heure.
3. Marie arrivera _____ une semaine.
4. _____ dix ans elle sera déjà mariée.
5. La soupe sera prête _____ une demi-heure.
6. Je peux lire ce roman _____ deux jours.
7. Il faudra prendre une decision _____vingt quatre heures.
8. ILs ont vayage de Paris à New York _____ quelques heures.

12. Prepositions that join two nouns are used to indicate function or to join a noun that modifies another noun.

The prepositions **à** and **de** can introduce a noun that modifies another noun and indicates the function of the preceding noun. In French a noun with a complement is often the same as an English expression composed of two nouns written either as two words or as a single compound word. The first noun in English is the complement in French. Study the following:

A.   **à** (for)

une verre à eau - a water glass (a glass for water)
une tasse à café - a coffee cup (a cup for coffee)
une lime à ongles - a nail file
une brosse à dents - a toothbrush
une cuiller à soupe - a soupspoon
une cuiller à thé - a teaspoon

B. **de** (of)

    un verre d'eau - a glass of water
    une tasse de cafe - a cup of coffee
    mon professeur de maths - my math teacher
    une agencie de voyage - a travel agency
    une robe de chambre - a dressing gown
    une salle de bains - a bathroom

C. **à / avec** (with)

Used with the article, **à** can mean *"with."* When you wish to indicate that the second noun is a distinct part of the first one, **à** replaces **avec**.

    de la soupe à l'oignon/onion-soup (soup with onions)
    de la soupe aux pois/pea soup (soup with peas)
    du café au lait/coffee with milk
    le garçon aux yeux bleus/the boy with the blue eyes
    le bâtiment au toit rouge/the building with the red roof
    la glace à la vanille/vanilla ice cream (ice cream made with vanilla)
    la dame à la figure ovale/the lady with the oval face
    une tarte aux pommes/an apple pie (a pie made with apples)
    une peinture à l'huile/an oil painting (a painting made with oil)

13. To introduce the material from which an object is made, **de** and **en** are used.

    une robe de soie   des bas de nylon
    un porte en cuir   un bracelet en or

A. Usage determines whether you should use **de** or **en**.

Often, either preposition is possible. De is usually used to indicate the type of object one is talking about and en emphasizes the material from which the object is made.

    un sac de cuir   a leather bag
    un sac en cuir   a bag made of leather

14. **Prepositions of cause**

De can also indicate a relationship of cause between the verb and the noun complement. It is translated by *"with,"* *"of,"* *"for"* or *"from."*

    Elle danse de joie.   She dances with joy.
    je meurs de faim.   I'm dying of hunger.
    L'enfant écrit de la main gauche.   The child writes with her left hand.
    La voiture est couverte de boue.   The car is covered with mud.

15. Prepositions after indefinite pronouns

When **quelque chose, rien, quelqu'un** and personne are modified by an adjective, the adjective is introduced by **de**.

C'est quelqu'un de très adroit.   He's someone skillful.
Il ne dit rien d'interessant.   He says nothing interesting.

Nous avons mangé quelque chose de bon.
We ate something good.

Il n'y a eu personne de blessé dans l'accident.
No one was hurt in the accident.

Exercise 6   Complete the following sentences with the correct preposition a, de or en. Combine with the definite article when necessary.

1. Il faut mettre de l'eau dans les verres _____ eau.
2. Donnez-moi une tasse _____ café, s'il vous plait.
3. La dame a pleuré _____ joie quand on a annonces qu'il n'y avait personne _____ blessé dans le naufrage.
4. Nous avons mange de la soupe_____petits pois.
5. Il mange de la soupe _____ tomates, une tarte _____ pomme at de la glace _____ chocolats.
6. La jeune fille n'a pas mangé depuis ce midi. Elle meurt_____ faim.
7. Elle refuse de cuisiner. Elle prend soin des mains avec une lime_____ongles.
8. Allons à la classe _____ français.
9. La femme aux cheveux blonds dîne avec le monsieur _____ blanc.
10. Il vient de lui donner une bague _____ or.
11. La dame s'habille bien. Elle porte une robe_____soie.
12. Elle porte ausi un sac _____ cuir, et un manteau _____ laine.
13. Cette dame est quelqu'un ____ très intelligent.

16. Prepositions in adverbial clauses of manner.

A. In many adverbial phrases where *"in," "by"* or *"on"* are used in English, **à** is used in French.

Il parle à voix basse.
He speaks in a low voice.

Il parle à haute voix.
He speaks aloud (with a loud voice, loudly).

Mettez les vêtements au soleil pour les faire sécher.
Put the clothes in the sun to make them dry.

Ce chandail est fait à la main.
This sweater is made by hand.

Il a les papiers à la main.
He has the papers in hand.

Le train est arrivée à l'heure.
The train arrived on time.

Ce château a été construit au temps de Napoléon Ier.
This castle was built in the time of Napoleon I.

Les officiers marchent à grand pas.
The officers march with big steps.

B. In an adverbial clause of manner, **de** introduces the noun modified by the indefinite article.

La dame parle d'une voix faible.
The lady speaks with a weak voice.

Elle regarde le monsieur d'une air furieux.
She looked at the gentleman with a furious expression (furiously).

Elle le fait d'une manière adroite.
She does this skillfully.

C. When the noun is not modified by an indefinate article, **avec** is used.

Elle lui regarde avec fureur.
She looks at him with a furious expression (furiously).

Il lui parle avec douceur.   He speaks to her sweetly.

Il le fait avec adresse.   He does this skillfully.

Exercise 7   Complete the following sentences with the prepositions **a**, **de** or **avec**.

1. Il lui a parlé _____ tendresse.
2. Elle lui a regardé _____ un air curieux.
3. Quand elle lui parle, elle parle _____ haute voix.
4. Elle lui a questionne _____ dureté.
5. Il a tenu le colis _____ la main. Enfin il le lui donne en pleurant _____ de joie.

17. Prepositions that introduce infinitives that define a noun or adjective indicate function, result or tendency.

A. The preposition à can introduce an infinitive that indicates the function of the preceding noun or the use to which an object is destined. Often à has the meaning, "*for*." The infinitive complement is often the equivalent of an expression with "*-ing*" in English:

du papier à écrire - writing paper (paper for writing)

une machine à écrire/à laver/à coudre - a typewriter (a machine for writing)/ a washing machine (a machine for washing)/ a sewing machine (a machine for sewing)

une salle à manger - a dining room (a room for dining)

une chambre à coucher - a bedroom (a room for sleeping)

un fer à repasser - an iron

de l'eau à boire - drinking water (water for drinking)

une maison à vendre/à louer - a house for sale/ for rent

B. à can introduce an infinitive phrase that describes a preceding noun in terms of a possible result.

C'est un bruit à reveiller tout le monde.
It's a noise that could wake everyone up.

C'est une tâche à rendre fou.
This is a task that can drive you crazy.

Ce sont des cris à rendre sourd.
These are shouts that can make you deaf.

Ce sont des larmes à faire pitié.
These are tears that can make you feel pity.

C'est un exercice à recopier.
This is an exercise to be recopied.

C. à can also introduce an infinitive phrase that intensifies the meaning of an adjective.

une histoire triste à en pleurer
a story sad enough to make you cry

un animal laid à faire peur
an animal ugly enough to make you afraid

D. After an adjective, à introduces an infinitive that indicates the action to which the adjective applies.

C'est facile à apprendre.   It' s easy to do.
C'est difficile à comprendre.   It's difficult to understand.
C'est bon à manger.   It's good to eat.

E. After expressions of duration, length of time and position of the body à introduces an infinitive after certain expressions indicating duration, length of time and position of the body; à plus the infinitive is used to describe what the subject does during this time or in this position.

Elle passe son temps à écrire. (duration)
She spends her time writing.

Le tailleur reste assis à coudre. (position)
The tailor remains seated while sawing.

Elle met longtemps à comprendre cela. (time)
She takes a long time to understand that.

18. Generally, infinitives following an adjective or noun are followed by **de**.

Je suis enchanté de faire votre connaissance.
I am please to make your acquaintance.

La dame est étonnée d'apprendre cette nouvelle.
The lady is surprised to hear this news.

Je suis content de vous voir.   I am happy to see you.

Elle a envie d'aller au cinéma.   She feels like going to the movies.

19. After the impersonal **il** + **être** + **adjective**, **de** precedes the infinitive.

Il est bon de manger trois repas par jour.
It is good to have three meals a day.
Il est nécessaire de dormir.   It is necessary to sleep.

Note: When an infinitive depends on another verb, it is often introduced by **à** or **de**.

Exercise 8

Complete the following sentences with the correct preposition à or de.

1. Ce sont des voitures _____ louer.
2. Elle a honte _____ avoir fait une bétise.
3. Ce problème est difficile _____ résoudre.
4. Pourquoi hésitez-vous _____ répondre.
5. Il n'est pas nécessaire _____ mentir.
6. Vous avez l'air _____ ennuyer.
7. Ce travail est difficile _____ faire.
8. Ayez la bonté _____ entrer.
9. C'est facile _____ à laver.
10. Soyez sur _____ le féliciter.

Exercise 9

Translate the following sentences into French.

1. a French teacher
2. an appartment for sale
3. the lady with red hair
4. an apple pie
5. tomato soup
6. a cup of tea
7. vanilla ice cream
8. a travel agency
9. a tie made of silk
10. a silk tie
11. a glass of water
12. a water glass
13. an apple pie
14. a soup spoon

Exercise 10

Complete the following with the correct preposition or preposition plus the definite article.

D'habitude, Madame Dupont va _____ bureau _____ lundi _____ mercredi. Elle y va _____ voiture. Elle revient _____ bureau _____ cinq heures du soir.

Mais aujourd'hui, c'est vendredi et elle ne travaille pas. Son mari est _____ vacances. Leur fils Jean est _____ l'université. Il est maintenant dans sa classe _____ geographie. Monsieur Dupont est _____ la Martinique. Madame Dupont est _____ la maison maintenant. Elle est _____ la cuisine parce que son fils Jean qui va rentrer _____ lui à midi pour le déjeuner.

Comme elle ne travaille pas! Le matin, elle passe son temps _____ faire le ménage. Elle met les vêtements sales dans la machine _____ laver; elle range les verres _____ eau et les tasses _____ café, les cuillers _____ soupe, etc. _____ les placards. Elle époussette les meubles et elle passe l'aspirateur.

A midi elle prend son dejeuner _____ son fils Jean. Ils mangent de la soupe _____ légumes, un sandwich _____ jambon, et comme dessert une tarte _____ fraises. Comme boisson, elle boit du café _____ lait. Son fils Jean boit du jus _____ pommes.

Il est maintenant cinq heures du soir. Jean est _____ sa chambre. Madame Dupont est _____ la cuisine en train de préparer le dîner. Elle porte un tablier _____ coton. Le dîner qu'il prepare va être bon _____ manger. Elle fait la cuisine _____ une manière professionnelle, _____ l'adresse d'un grand chef. Pendant qu'elle prépare elle chante _____ haute voix. Elle peut finir la préparation du dîner _____ que son fils termine ses devoirs. Elle peut compléter cette tâche_____ une heure. Elle n'a pas envie_____ suivre un programme à la télé. Elle préfère lire livre. Elle le lira _____ deux heures. Quand elle aura ni le roman, il sera l'heure de se coucher.

_____les Dupont, tout est bien organisé grace aux efforts de Dupont. Elle, c'est quelqu'un _____ extraodinaire.

7

Negatives

NEGATIVES

La sourit **ne** mange **pas** le fromage.
Le chat **ne** guette **point** la sourit.
Le garçon **ne** chasse **jamais** le chat.
La jeune mère **ne** fesse **plus** le garçon.

1. Simple negation

A. Make an affirmative sentence negative by saying ne before the verb and pas after it.

Je **ne** comprends **pas** ce problème. I don't understand this problem.

B. **Ne** is a negative particle which alerts the listener to the eventual negative meaning of the sentence.

Pas, "*not*" is the negative **completer**. It is used when there is no other negative word in the sentence.

Pas follows a verb that has a person and tense ending or a present participle, but precedes an infinitive.

Je vous prie de **ne pas** garer votre voiture devant la voie de sortir.
I beg you not to park your car in front of the driveway.

Vous faites une erreur en **n'allant pas consulter un medecin**.
You're making a mistake by not consulting a medical doctor.

Note: **Ne** alone does not make a sentence negative. It sometimes indicates a degree of negative feeling which is not completely expressed. In these cases, the ne (called an "*expletive*" or "*pleonastic*" **ne**) is optional.

Il a peur que je (ne) voit son erreur.
He is afraid I will see his mistake. (Heaven forbid!)

Allez vite, avant qu'il (ne) pleuve!
Go quickly, before it rains!

C. **Ne** before the verb in the adverbial expression, **"ne ... que"** suggests a negative idea, but the sentence itself remains affirmative.

Nous n'avons qu'à repartir à zéro.
All we have to do is to begin all over again.

Exercise 1

Answer negatively in a full sentence in French.

1. Est-ce que quatre précède trois?
2. Est-ce qu'il neige en été?
3. Mangeons-nous le dessert avant la salade?
4. Etudiez-vous le chinois ce semestre?
5. Fermons-nous les fenêtres en juillet?
6. Est-ce que nous déjeunons à quatre heures?
7. Fume-t-on en atterrissant en avion?
8. Préférez-vous échouer aux examens?
9. Arrivez-vous en retard à toutes vos classes?
10. Les professeurs apprecient-ils les erreurs des élèves?

2. **Negative adverbs**. The particle ne must be used before the verb in a sentence containing a negative adverb. Negative adverbs follow a conjugated verb, but may precede infinitives. The negative adverbs are:

point - not at all	**plus** - no (not any) more
jamais - not ever, never	**guère** - hardly
nulle part - nowhere (follows an infinitive)	

Cela **ne** me plaît **point**.	That doesn't please me at all.
Nous **ne** voyons **plus** films-là.	We don't see those movies anymore.
Ne buvez **jamais** sans manger!	Never drink without eating!

Il est préférable de **ne plus manger** ces fraises.
It's better not to eat those strawberries anymore.

Note: **Pas** is not used in a sentence with a negative adverb.

Exercise 2

Answer the following questions in the negative by replacing the positive adverbs given in parentheses with their negative opposites.

1. Réponds-tu (toujours) en français?
2. Est-ce que tu demeures (encore) ou tu es né?
3. L'assassin, regrette-il (beaucoup) son crime?
4. Est-ce que vous fumez (quelquefois) des cigarettes?
5. Votre petite amie, travaille-t-elle (continuellement)?

3. Negative nouns and pronouns

A negative noun or pronoun may be the subject or object of the verb, or the object of a preposition. The particle ne must be used before the verb if a sentence contains one of the following negative nouns or pronouns.

rien	not anything, nothing
personne	not anyone, no one
aucun/aucune	not one (of them)

Nous n'avons **rien** trouvé.	We did not find anything.
Rien ne me plaît.	Nothing pleases me.
Je **n'**accuse **personne**!	I am not pointing my finger at anyone!

Aucun (nul) de ses amis n'est venu à la fête.
None of his friends came to the party.

Aucune (pas une) de ces cravates ne me convient.
None (not one) of these neck ties suits me.

Je **n'**en ai pris **aucune**.
I didn't take a single one of them.

Note: Aucun(e) may also function as a negative adjective meaning "*none*" or "*not one*" (of something). When a noun phrase is introduced with **aucun**, the sentence becomes negative and **ne** must be used before the verb.

Exercise 3

Answer the following questions negatively, using **rien, personne,** or **aucun(e)** in place of the words given in parentheses.

1. (Qui) parle cinq langues dans votre famille?
2. (Qu'est-ce qui) precede la lettre A dans l'alphabet?
3. (Qui) regardez-vous en ce monent?
4. (Quel) pays est plus grand que la Russie?
5. (Que) mange-t-on parlant?
6. (Quelle) lettre précède la lettre A dans l'alphabet?
7. (Que) refusez-vous dans un restaurant de luxe?
8. (Qui) proteste quand vous sortez le soir?
9. (Qui est-ce que) vous détestez?
10. (Qui) ressemble à Asterix?

4. Negative conjunctions

A. **Ni ... ni**, used in a pair or in a series, is a negative conjunction meaning *"neither ... nor."* Use the particle ne before the verb in a sentence containing **ni ... ni**. [ni ... ni ... ne... or ne ... ni ... ni...]

> Ni ma mère ni mon père ne me comprennent.
> Neither my mother nor my father understands me.

> Cela ne me fait ni froid ni chaud.
> That doesn't affect me in the least.

> Je ne le ferais ni par amour ni par haine.
> I wouldn't do it for love or spite.

B. Do not use a quantifier (**du, de la, des, un, une**) after the negative conjunction **ni**.

> Je n'ai ni voiture ni bicyclette.
> I have neither a car nor a bicycle.

> Mes amis ne mangent ni viande ni poisson.
> My friends eat neither (any) meat nor (any) fish.

Note: Always use the particle **ne** before a verb in a sentence containing one or more negative adverbs, conjunctions, or noun phrases.

> Yves **ne** prend **plus jamais rien**.
> Yves never drinks anything anymore.

> Personne **ne** va **nulle** part.
> Nobody goes anywhere.

Exercise 4

Make the following sentences negative by replacing the conjuctions (**ou**) **... ou**, *"(either) ... or,"* and (**et**)**...et**, *"(both) ... and,"* with **ne ... ni ... ni** or **ni ... ni ... ne ....**

1. Il abandonne et famille et foyer.
2. La mer et le soleil ne suffisent.
3. On offre du thé ou du café.
4. Vous écoutez avec intérêt et avec attention.
5. Les Américains prennent un apéritif et un digestif.

5. Summary:
An affirmative sentence becomes negative with any of the following combination:

ne...pas, not	**ne...rien**, nothing
ne...pas, du tout, not at all	**ne...personne**, no one, nobody
ne...point, not, not at all	**ne...ni...ni**, neither...nor
ne...jamais, never	**ne...que**, only
ne...plus, no more, no longer	**ne...aucun (aucune)**, no, none
ne...guerre, hardly, scarcely	**ne...nul (nulle)**, no, none

8

Verbal Usage

VERBAL USAGE

La souris **vient de** manger le fromage.
Depuis quand le chat guette la souris?
Le garçon **est en train** de chasser le chat.
La jeune mère **doit** fesser le garçon.

1. Personal expressions with avoir are used to explain how someone feels, either physically or emotionally.

Nous avons froid.	We are cold.
Il a honte.	He is ashamed.
Avez-vous peur?	Are you afraid?

2. The impersonal expression, "il fait" is used to refer to the weather.

Il fait froid dehors.	It's cold outside.
Il fait mauvais aujourd'hui.	It's nasty out today.

3. The verb être is used to refer to the days of the week, the time of the day and the seasons.

Quel jour de la semaine est-ce aujourd'hui?
What day (of the week) is today?

C'est aujourd'hui mardi.
Today is Tuesday.

Quel jour (du mois) sommes-nous aujourd'hui?
What day of the month is it today?

Quelle heure est-il?
What time is it?

Il est dix heures du matin.
It is ten o'clock in the morning.

En quelle saison sommes-nous maintenant?
In what season are we now?

Nous sommes en hiver.   We are in winter.

A. Dates are written as follows:

**Quel jour est-ce aujourd'hui? or
Quel jour sommes-nous aujourd'hui?**
What day is it today?

C'est aujourd'hui vendredi le premier février.
Today is Friday, February first.

**C'est aujourd'hui jeudi, trois janvier
mille neuf cents, quatre-vingt-onze.**
Today is Thursday, January 3rd, 1991.

Note these expressions:

au mois de juin	in the month of June
en juin	in June
le premier juin	June 1st the first of June
le deux juin	June 2

B. Seasons are written as follows:

le printemps - spring	**l'été** - summer
l'automne - fall	**l'hiver** - winter

Notes: a) The seasons are all masculine.

b) The preposition used with the seasons is **en**,
except for spring (au printemps).

au printemps in spring	**en** été in summer
en automne in fall	**en** hiver in winter

C. The time of day is written as follows:

Quelle heure est-il?	What time is it?
Il est une heure	It is one o'clock.
Il est neuf heures vingt	It is twenty after nine.
Il est huit heures et quart	It is a quarter after eight.
Il est onze heures et demie	It is half past eleven.
Il est trois heures moins dix	It is ten (minutes) to three.
Il est deux heures moins le quart	It is a quarter to two.
Il est midi	It is twelve o'clock (noon).
Il est minuit	It is twelve o'clock (midnight).
Il est midi (minuit) et demi	It is half past twelve.

Note: a) To express time after the hour, the number of minutes is added. The word et is used only with quart and **demi(e)**. To express time before the hour, moins is used.

b) **Midi** and **minuit** are masculine.

D. Other time expressions are:

a quelle heure?	at what time?
a midi précis	at exactly noon
a cinq heures précises	at five o'clock sharp
trois heures du matin	3 o'clock in the morning
quatre heures de l'après-midi	4 o'clock in the afternoon
sept heures du soir	7 o'clock in the evening
midi vingt-cinq	12:25 P.M.
minuit et quart	12:15 A.M.
vers neuf heures	about nine o'clock
un quart d'heure	a quarter hour
une demi-heure	a half hour

Quelle heure est-il à votre montre?
What time is it on your watch?

Ma montre avance/retarde de dix minutes.
My watch is ten minutes fast/slow.

Notes: a) In public announcements, such as timetables, the twenty-four hour system is commonly used, with midnight as the zero hour.

00.20 = 12:20 A.M.　　　**14 heures** = 2:00 P.M.　　**20 h. 45** = 8:45 P.M.

b) When it is more than 30 mimutes past the hour, the number of minutes is subtracted from the next hour.

Il est minuit moins vingt cinq.　It is 11:35.
Il est sept heures moins vingt.　It is 6:40.

c) The word demi agrees with the noun when it follows.

midi et demi	**minuit et demi**
une heure et demie	**trois heures et demie**

d) When demi precedes the noun, it is hyphenated and does not agree.

Je vous verrai dans **une demie-heure**.
I will see you in half an hour.

4. **Numbers, dates and time**

A. Cardinal Numbers

	0 zero
1 un/une	11 onze
2 deux	12 douze
3 trois	13 treize
4 quatre	14 quatorze
5 cinq	15 quinze
6 six	16 seize
7 sept	17 dix-sept
8 huit	18 dix-huit
9 neuf	19 dix-neuf
10 dix	20 vingt
21 vingt et un	80 quatre-vingts
23 vingt-trois	81 quatre-vingt-un
30 trente	88 quatre-vingt-huit
31 trente et un	90 quatre-vingt-dix
34 trente-quatre	91 quatre-vingt-onze
40 quarante	99 quatre-vingt-dix-neuf
41 quarante et un	100 cent
47 quarante-sept	101 cent-un
50 cinquante	200 deux cents
51 cinquante et un	316 trois cent seize
52 cinquante-deux	500 cinq cents
60 soixante	580 cinq cent quatre-vingts
61 soixante et un	1.000 mille
70 soixante-dix	1.001 mille un
71 soixante et onze	1.100 mille cent
75 soixante-quinze	3.000 trois mille
77 soixante-dix-sept	100.000 cent mille

Notes: a) The word et replaces the hyphen in 21, 31, 41, 51, 61, and 71. In all other compound numbers through 99, the hyphen is used.

b) **Quatre-vingts** and the plural of **cent** drop the **-s** before another number.

quatre-vingts bateaux	80 boats
quatre-vingt-deux bateaus	82 boats
quatre cents mots	400 words
quatre cent cinquante mots	450 words

c) **Cent** and **mille** are not preceded by the indefinite article.

cent mouchoirs	a (one) hundred handkerchiefs
mille fois	a thousand times

d) **Mille** does not change in the plural.

six mille plantes	six thousand plants

e) In French numerals, periods are used where

English uses commas.

    4.000 (French)   =   4,000 (English)

f) Arithmetic operations:

Cinq et sept font douze	$(5 + 7 = 12)$
Trois fois quatre font douze	$(3 \times 4 = 12)$
Huit moins six font deux	$(8 - 6 = 2)$
Douze divise par trois font quatre	$(12 / 3 = 4)$

B. Ordinal Numbers

1st premier/première	9th neuvième
2nd deuxième; second(e)	10th dixième
3rd troisième	11th onzième
4th quatrième	16th seizième
5th cinquième	20th vingtième
6th sixième	21st vingt et unième
7th septième	34th trente-quatrième
8th huitième	100th centième

Notes: a) Except for first and second, the ordinal numbers are formed by adding **-ième** to the cardinal numbers. Silent **-e** is dropped before **-ième.**

b) Originally, second referred to the second of a series of only two, while deuxième referred to the second of more than two. Today, however, this distinction is generally not observed.

c) Observe the **-u** in **cinquième** and the **-v** in **neuvième.**

d) The final **-a** or **-e** of the *preceding* word is not dropped before huit, huitième, onze, and onzième.

e) Cardinals precede ordinals in French.

    les trois premières semaines   the first 3 weeks

C. Nouns of Number

Certain numerals are used as collective nouns to express a round number. The most frequent are:

une dizaine	about ten
une douzaine	a dozen
une quinzaine	about fifteen
une vingtaine	about twenty, a score
une cinquantaine	about fifty
une centaine	about a hundred
un millier	(about) a thousand
un million	a million
un milliard	a billion

D. Fractions

½	la moitié; un demi	¼	un quart
⅓	un tiers	¾	trois quarts
⅕	un cinquième	3/7	trois septièmes
7/8	sept huitièmes	1/100	un centième

Notes: a) Fractions in French are formed, as in English, by combining cardinal and ordinal numbers.

Only **moitié, tiers**, and **quart** are irregular.

b) **Moitié** is a noun and must have an article. **Demi**, generally used as an adjective, is invariable when used with a hyphen before the noun; otherwise, it agrees with its noun.

la moitié de la classe	half the class
une demi-bouteille	a half bottle
une bouteille et demie	a bottle and a half

E. Dates

1. Days:

lundi	Monday	**vendredi**	Friday
mardi	Tuesday	**samedi**	Saturday
mercredi	Wednesday	**dimanche**	Sunday
jeudi	Thursday		

2. Months

janvier	January	**juillet**	July
février	February	**août**	August
mars	March	**septembre**	September
avril	April	**octobre**	October
mai	May	**novembre**	November
juin	June	**décembre**	December

Exercise 1

Complete the sentence by giving the French equivalent of the cue words provided.

1. **twenty-first** C'était le _____ anniversaire de la victoire.
2. **two dozen** Elle avait acheté _____ serviettes.
3. **Francis the First** _____ encouragea les lettres et les arts.
4. **five thousand** Le pilote descend a _____ pieds.
5. **half** J'ai mangé _____ du pain.
6. **ninety-one** Ce palais compte _____ pieces.
7. **Thousands** _____ de personnes visitaient l'exposition chaque jour.
8. **a half bottle** Qui a bu _____ de ce vin?
9. **a cup and a half** L'Anglaise a bu _____ de the.
10. **a hundred ten** On faisait _____ kilomètres a l'heure.

Exercise 2   Write out completely in French.

1. in the summer   _____
2. April 1, 1923   _____
3. in 1831   _____
4. November 30, 1670   _____
5. 4:30 P.M.   _____
6. about 2:00 A.M.   _____
7. 12:25 A.M.   _____
8. at 1:00 sharp   _____
9. in February   _____
10. on the twelth of October   _____

Exercise 3   Complete each sentence in French.

1. Le jour qui suit dimanche est _____
2. _____ est la saison où il fait le plus chaud.
3. Il est vraiment six heures et quart, mais a ma montre il est six heures
   précises. Ma montre _____ de quinze minutes.
4. Généralement il pleut beaucoup _____ printemps.
5. J'ai commencé mon travail à onze heures du matin et j'ai travaille
   pendant une heure. J'ai fini le travail à _____ précis.
6. Le _____ , c'est le Nouvel An.
7. L'independance des Etats-Unis a été declare le _____ 1776.
8. Nous aimons faire du ski _____ hiver.
9. C'est aujourd'hui jeudi. Je vous verrai jeudi prochain, c'est-a-dire,
   d'aujourd'hui. _____ _____.
10. Le _____ est le dernier jour de l'année.

5. Idiomatic meanings of verbs

Some tenses and combinations of verbs have unpredictable or idiomatic
meanings that cannot be deduced from the root meaning of the verb and its
tense ending.

A. Idiomatic Use of Present and Imparfait

French and English both use the present tense to describe situations that
are connected with the present but take place in the future. However, the two
languages differ in their treatment of situations that begin in one past time
period and continue into another, or that begin in the past and continue into
the present.

1) Past events continuing in the present

In French the present tense must be used to refer to situations that begin
in the past and continue in the present - where English uses a perfect tense.

Les Dupont **habite** a Paris depuis les années 60.
The Duponts have been living in Paris since the sixties.

Notes: a) **Depuis** (since, for) indicates the beginning of a situation or the length of time it has been going on. **Il y a + time + que** (for) always indicates the length of time. **Combien de temps or combien de temps y a-t-il** (how long) indicates the sum of time.

Je suis a New York **depuis cinq ans; depuis 1985.**
I've been in New York for five years, since 1985.

b) In casual spoken French, the expression **cela fait** or **ça fait + que** is used in place of il y a **+ an** expression of time.

Cela (ça) fait un moment **qu'on** attend ici.
We've been waiting here for a while.

Exercise 4

Answer the following questions affirmatively, substituting **il y a ... que** for depuis, and **depuis** for **il y a**. Then translate your sentence into English.

1. Est-ce qu'il y a an que nous avons cette maison?
2. Est-ce que le restaurant est fermé depuis un mois?
3. Est-ce qu'il y a plusieurs jours qu'ils viennent regulièrement?
4. Prends-tu ces medicaments depuis que tu es enrhume?
5. Y a-t-il longtemps que personne n'habite cet appartement?
6. Est-ce qu'on ne voit plus ces gens depuis trois semaines?
7. Est-ce qu'il y a quelque temps que ce film se joue en ville?
8. Est-ce qu'ils étudient le français depuis un mois?
9. Etes-vous fiancés depuis six mois?
10. Y a-t-il longtemps qu'ils se connaissent?

B. **Remote past situations continuing in the past**

The **imparfait** is used to refer to situations that begin in the remote past and were continuing at the past moment under consideration. English uses a past perfect tense.

Ils se connaissaient depuis deux ans quand ils se sont mariés.
They had known each other for two years when they got married.

Note: When il y a is used with a time expression in the passé composé or the imparfait, without **que**, **it means** *"ago"* rather than *"for."*

Ils se sont rencontrés il y a deux ans.
or
Il y a deux ans qu'ils se sont rencontrés.
They met two years ago.

Exercise 5

Answer the following questions in the affirmative, substituting depuis for **il y a ... que**, and **il y a ... que** for **depuis**.

Then translate your sentence into English.

1. Se connaissaient-ils depuis un mois quand ils sont partis en vacances d'été?
2. Y avait-il longtemps que vous attendiez cette lettre?
3. Y avait-il quelques mois qu'ils voyagaient quand l'accident a eu lieu?
4. Est-ce que vous mangiez depuis des heures quand le téléphone a sonné?
5. Est-ce qu'il y avait longtemps qu'elle dormait quand on frappe a la porte?

6. Aspectual Idioms

A. Combinations of verbs as well as verb endings may be used to indicate certain aspects of time or tense such as progressivity, or finality.

1) Progressive aspect

In French there are no progressive tenses equivalent to those formed with be + **ing** in English. The idiomatic verb phrase **(être) en train de** + infinitive may be used to emphasize the ongoing nature of a situation.

Jean est en train d'écrire une lettre d'amour.
Jean is writing a love letter.

Note: Etre en train de is most often used in the present or imparfait.

Exercise 6

Emphasize the ongoing nature of the following events or situations.

1. Il mourait de faim.
2. Nous dépensions tout notre energy.
3. Ils racontent une histoire drôle.
4. Ce monsieur perd son temps.
5. Les travailleurs transportaient des marchandises sur leurs épaules.
6. Ils annoncent le départ de notre train.
7. Le pays subit de grands changements.
8. Pourquoi faisaient-elles toutes ces grimaces?
9. Les professeurs résolvent les problèmes.
10. Il écrit un roman macabre.

2. Immediate future aspect

The combination of the present or imperfect of the verb **aller** (to go) + infinitive may be used to form the equivalent of the English expression *"(to be) going to"* to refer to what is, or was, going to happen next.

Ces avions vont partir bientôt.
Those planes are going to leave soon.

Note: Aller + infinitive may be used only with the present or imparfait of aller. If the meaning of the main clause requires the subjunctive, use the subjunctive of devoir with a progressive meaning.

Il n'est pas certain **que je doive partir** tout de suite.
It's not certain that I am going to leave immediately.

Exercise 7

Answer the following questions with a form of aller followed by the infinitive. Then translate your sentence into English.

1. Je voyage en Europe; et vous?
2. Je finis mon travail; et lui?
3. Vous avez mangé du caviar; et eux?
4. Elle a repris ses études; et nous?
5. Le professeur parle aux étudiants; et le directeur?
6. Cet auteur écrit un beau roman; et sa femme?
7. Nous habitons a New York; et toi?
8. Les enfants dansent le rock-and-roll; et leurs parents?
9. Vous avez rendu visite au musée d'art; et vos frères?
10. Nous prendrons un verre de champagne; et vous?

3) Immediate Past

The expression **venir de + infinitive** may be used to make it clear that something just happened or had just happened.

Nous venons d'arriver.   We've just arrived.
Il venait de terminer ses devoirs.   He had just finish his homework.

Note: Venir de + infinitive may be used only in the present, subjunctive, and imparfait.

Exercise 8

Rewrite the following sentences to indicate that the events happened in the immediate past. Then translate your sentence into English.

1. Se sont-ils fiancés?
2. Elle avait fermé la porte de sa chambre.
3. A-t-il pris l'avion en destination de Paris?
4. Jean a téléphone.
5. J'ai terminé le roman.
6. J'ai commencé un nouveau livre.
7. Ils avaient complètement rénové leur voiture.
8. Nous sommes retournés d'Italie.
9. Est-ce qu'ils ont consulté un avocat?
10. J'avais posé une question.

4) Terminal aspect

The idiomatic expresson **finir par + infinitive** may be used to indicate the terminal aspect of an event or situation. It is translated in the sense of finally.

Il a fini par terminer ses devoirs.
He has finally finish his homeworks.

Note: Finir par + infinitive may be in all tenses.

Exercise 9

Tell what finally happened or happens in each instance.

1. S'il cuisinait, on mangerait bien ce soir.
2. Elle reussira, si elle fait un peu d'effort.
3. Nous sommes alles au musee, mais le musee etait ferme.
4. Nous achèterons une machine ordinateur, mais elle est en panne.
5. On le ferait, mais on se tromperait.

7. Causative Verb Phrases

The verb **faire, laisser**, or **envoyer** before an infinitive forms a causative verb phrase and means to have, make, let, send, or cause someone (to) do something. These causative phrases act as single verbs in respect to their various subjects and objects.

A. Single subject causative sentences

If a causative precedes an infinitive that has a direct and/or an indirect object, but no explicit subject, the objects of the infinitive function as the objects of the entire verb phrase.

Il a fait laver sa voiture.	He had his car washed.
Il l'a fait laver.	He had it washed.
Il a fait construire une maison.	He had a house built.
Il l'a fait construire.	He had it built.

Le professeur a fait réciter les élèves un beau poème.
The teacher had (made) the students recite a beautiful poem.

Notes: a) In the last sentence the direct object of faire is construire. **Faire**, therefore, does not agree with the direct object.

b) In the affirmative imperative, the direct object noun follows the infinitive, but the direct object prounoun preceded the infinitives.

Faites nettoyer la nappe.	Have the tablecloth cleaned.
Faites-la nettoyer.	Have it cleaned.

B. Two-subject causative sentences

1) If the infinitive in a causative verb phrase has an explicit subject different from that of the main verb, the infinitive subject functions as the direct object of the entire verb phrase.

Ne laisse pas mourir cette plante.   Don't let this plant die.

Ne la laisse pas mourir.   Don't let it die.

Note: If there is one object, it is a direct object.

If it is a noun, it follows the infinitive. If it is a pronoun, it precedes faire in the negative imperative and in declarative sentences.

2. If the infinitive in a causative phrase has both a subject and a direct object, the subject becomes the object of a preposition:

a) **par** - if the person in question is performing a task.

Il a fait laver la voiture par les garçons du quartier.
He had the car washed by the boys in the neighborhood.

Elle a fait construire la maison par la compagnie Nativel.
She had the house built by the company Nativel.

b) **à** - if he/she is actually having something done for him/her.

Le professeur a fait réciter un poème aux étudiants.
The teacher made the student recite a poem.

Le professeur le leur a fait reciter.
The teacher made them recite it.

Notes: a) The preposition "a" makes the second subject an indirect object.

b) The preposition, par simply makes the second subject the object of a preposition.

Il a fait laver la voiture par les garçons.
He had the car washed by the boys.

Il l'a fait laver par eux.
He had it washed by them.

3) Faire and the infinitive it governs form a unit. Consequently, all nouns whether subject or object of the infinitive, must follow it; all pronouns, whether subject or object of the infinitive, must precede faire, except in the affirmative imperative where object pronouns follow the verb. (They are attached to the command with hyphens.) Otherwise, the only other words that may separate faire from its infinitive are the second part of a negation (in simple tenses), certain adverbs or a reflexive pronoun.

Faites venir l'enfant dans mon bureau.
Have the child come to my office.

Je l'y **ferai venir** immediatement.
I shall have him come (there) immediately.

Avez-vous **fait réparer** votre montre?
Did you have your watch repaired?

Non, Je ne **la ferai pas** réparer.
No, I shall not have it repaired.

a) Whether a direct object is present, be it a pronoun, a noun or a clause, the subject of the infinitive is expressed by an indirect object pronoun.

Je lui ferai voir ce document.
I shall have him see this document.

Je le lui ferai voir.
I shall have him see it.

Les documents que je lui ai fait voir sont très importants.
The documents (that) I had him see are very important.

b) When in the English sentence the subject of the infinitive is a noun, and a direct object is present, the subject in the French sentence is expressed by **à + noun** or by **par + noun**, i.e., an agent. In those cases the infinitive has a passive meaning in French.

Vous devriez faire voir ces documents **à votre femme**.
You ought to show these documents to your wife.

J'ai fait écrire **à ma femme** une lettre d'invitation à nos amis, les Durand.
I had my wife write a letter of invitation to our friend, the Durands.

c) If **à + noun** can be confused with an indirect object, **par + noun** must be used. In the preceding sentences, **à votre femme** may be used because it is unlikely that the documents will be seen *"to"* the wife. **A nos amis** is used because the context makes clear that the letter of invitation can be written only by the wife, not to the wife. However, at times the distinction must be made to avoid ambiguity.

J'ai fait écrire une lettre **par Marie**.
I had Marie write a letter.

J'ai fait écrire une lettre **à Marie**.
I had a letter written to Marie.

Note: In doubtful cases, it is usually safer to use **par + noun**.

d) **Lui, leur, me, nous,** etc. are used whether the antecedent is **à + noun** or **par + noun**. Normally, the context will make the meaning clear, and it is only in rare cases that it should be necessary to use **par + a disjunctive pronoun**.

Je la lui ferai envoyer.
I shall have it sent to (or by) him.

Je leur en ferai envoyer.

I shall have some given to (or by) them.

e) Most of the adverbs that are placed between the auxiliary and the past participle may be placed between faire and the infinitive.

Tu me fais toujours rire.

You always cause me to laugh.

Notes: a) When the infinitive is a reflexive verb, it is treated as if it were an ordinary verb.

Faites-le se brosser.

but:

Faites lui se brossser les cheveux.

b) With a few verbs, the reflexive pronoun may be omitted. However, it is never incorrect to retain the reflexive pronoun because it is clearer.

Faites-le (s') asseoir.

4. **Caution:** The causative faire cannot be used if it would require an impossible juxtaposition of pronouns, subject or object of the infinitive: two indirect object pronouns, three pronoun objects, or me, te, nous, vous, used with one another or with lui, leur. In such cases, **demamder (de), dire (de)** are used instead of faire.

Je lui demanderai de leur envoyer une lettre.

NOT:

Je lui leur ferai envoyer une lettre.

I shall have him send them a letter.

Je lui dirai de vous payer immediatement.

NOT:

Je vous lui ferai payer immediatement.

I shall have him pay you immediately.

Note: The past participles, **laissé** and **envoyé** agree in number and in gender with a preceding direct object, if that object is the logical subject of the following infinitive.

Nous **l'avons envoyée** promener.

We sent her walking.

BUT

La voiture? Nous l'avons envoyé **chercher**.

The car? We sent for it.

5) The past participle **fait** is invariable in causative sentences.

J'ai fait écrire la lettre.   Je l'ai fait écrire.

6) The past participles **laissé** and **envoyé** agree in number and gender with a preceding direct object, if that object is the logical subject of the following infinitive.*

Nous l'avons **envoyée** promener.   We sent her walking.
BUT

La voiture? Nous l'avons envoyé **chercher**.
The car? We sent for it.

C. Laisser and verbs of perception + infinitive.

Some of the constructions which are mandatory with the causative **faire + infinitive** are or may be used with laisser, and particularly with the verbs of perception **voir, entendre, regarder, écouter, sentir,** and **apercevoir.** The constructions given below are not all compulsory but are quite customary.

1. When the subject of the infinitive is a noun or an indefinite pronoun, it usually follows the infinitive of an intransitive verb, provided the latter has no complement.

Je vois **venir** *un avion*.
I see a train coming.

Ne lasissez pas **sortir** *vos enfants*.
Don't let your children go out.

However:

Avez-vous vu une *femme blonde* **sortir** de l'avion?
Did you see a blond woman get off the airplane?

2. With the intransitive verb, the noun used as the subject precedes the infinitive in accordance with the general rule.

Madame Dupont regarde *son mari* **manger.**
Mrs. Dupont watches her husband eat.

Notes: a) Following the infinitive of a transitive verb, a noun can only be its object if there is no subject or if the subject is expressed by **par + noun** (agent). The French infinitive has a passive meaning and is used to translate an English past participle.

Nous avons vu arrêter un voleur.
We saw a thief being arrested.

Nous avons entendu louer votre œuvre par nos amis.
We have heard your work praised by our friends.

b) When the object of an infinitive having a passive meaning is a pronoun, it precedes the main verb.

Le voleur? Oui, nous l'avons vu **arrêter.**
The thief? Yes, we saw him being arrested.

Votre oeuvre? Oui, nous l'avons entendu **mentionner** par nos amis.
Your work? Yes, we have heard it mentioned by our freinds.

c) When both the subject and the direct object of the infinitive are pronouns, either one of these two constructions is possible:

1) Both pronouns may precede the main verb, in which case, an indirect object pronoun is used as the subject.

2) The pronoun may be used in the regular manner, i.e., subject before the infinitive; object before the main verb, in which case a direct object pronoun is used for the subject. The first construction is the more usual, particularly with laisser, and when the object is a thing. The second construction must be used if the first would result in an impossible juxtaposition of pronouns.

La pomme? Nous la leur laisserons pas manger.
The apple? We shall not let them eat it.

La lettre? Je la lui ai vu lire.   (rather than: Je l'ai vu la lire.)
The letter? I saw him read it.

However:
Je l'ai entendu vous saluer.
NOT:

Je vous lui ai entendu saluer.
I heard him greet you.

b) When **y** and **en** are adverbs, a direct object pronoun is used, whatever the construction.

Nous **lui** avons laisse prendre deux cravates.
(There is no adverb **y** or **en**. An indirect object is used.)

Nous **l'**avons laisse en prendre deux.
We let him take two (of them).

Je **l'y** ai vu aller.

OR:

Je l'ai vu **y** aller.
I saw him go there.

Nous **lui** avons laisse prendre la voiture.
(There is no **y** or **en** an indirect object is used.)
We let him take the car.

3) With **laisser**, and sometimes with **voir** and **entendre**, when the direct object of the infinitive is a noun or a clause, an indirect object pronoun is used for the subject.

Je *lui* ai laissé **voir** mon trouble.
I let him see my anxiety.

Je *lui* ai laissé **voir** que j'étais trouble.
I let him see that I was worried.

Je *lui* ai entendu **dire** que vous aller vous marier.
I heard him say that you are going to get married.

Note: Lui and **leur** are almost always used with the idiomatique expression **entendre dire que**.

4) With **laisser + voir, croire, entendre** (to hear/ understand), **faire** and a few other verbs (which must be learned from observation), the noun subject is expressed by **à + noun** if a direct object is present.

Ne laissez pas voir votre souffrance **à vos enfants**.
Don't let your children see your suffering.

Ne laissez pas voir **à vos enfants** que vous êtes souffrant.
Don't let your children see that you are suffering.

5) When the infinitive has an indirect object or both a direct and an indirect object or when the infinitive is a reflexive or a reciprocal verb, the regular construction is used.

Avez-vous vu le garçon **leur donner** leur addition?
Did you see the waiter give them their bill?

Oui, je l'ai vu **le leur donner**.
Yes, I saw him give it to them.

Nous **les** avons entendu **se disputer** amèrement.
We have heard them arguing bitterly.

Ne **les** laissez pas **s'en aller** de si tot.
Don't let them go so early.

Exercise 10

In the following sentences replace the direct object pronoun by le poème and the direct object pronoun by Marie. Two possibilities exist; give both.
Example: Je *le lui* **fais lire**.
Je fais lire **le poème à Marie**.
Je fais lire **le poème par Marie**.

1. Nous le lui faisons réciter. _____
2. Vous le lui faites donner. _____
3. Tu le lui fais envoyer. _____
4. Ils le lui font écrire. _____
5. Je le lui fais dicter. _____

Exercise 11

In the following sentences replace the object by pronouns.

Example: Je fais lire **le poème à Marie**.
     Je **le lui** fais lire.

1. Il a fait recopier la lettre par son fils.
2. Avez-vous fait venir le docteur chez nous.
3. Nous avons fait voir la voiture a Paul.
4. Fais etudier ces etudiants.
5. Le professeur a fait remarquer leurs fautes aux étudiants.

6. Faites dire a ces clients d'attendre un moment.

7. Elle a fait donner du lait à son bébé.

8. Faites donner des medicaments à ces malades.

9. Fais comprendre à Marie qu'elle ne peut pas sortir.

10. Je ferais savoir cela à mes enfants.

Exercise 12

In the following sentences, replace the pronoun **les** by **les étudiants**.

Example: Je les ai vus arriver à l'école.
           J'ai vu les enfants arriver à l'école.

1. Le professeur les laisse partir.
2. Nous les avons entendu gronder par leurs parents.
3. Nous les voyons revenir.
4. Nous les regardons descendre de l'autobus.
5. Nous les entendons parler à voix basse.
6. Nous les avons entendu appeler par leur professeur.
7. Nous les avons vu reciter leur leçon.
8. "Ne les laissez pas partir," je me suis dit.
9. Pendant la recreation, je les regarde jouer.
10. Je les laisse courir commes des gazelles.

8. Reflexive and reciprocal verbs

A. Reflexive verbs are generally used as in English to denote an action performed and borne by the subject.

The reflexive pronouns me, te, se, nous, vous, se precede the verb (the auxiliary, in compound tenses) except in the affirmative, when they follow.

Elles s'amusent.	They are having fun. (amusing themselves.)
Il se rase.	He shaves (himself).
Asseyez-vous!	Sit (yourself) down!

Notes: a) Sometimes the reflexive pronoun is understood in English. However, it must always be expressed in French.

b) The reflexive pronouns, *"myself," "himself,"* etc. should not be confused, when used as reflexive pronouns, with the same words used for emphasis. The latter are called stress pronouns and are translated in French as **moi-même, lui-même**, etc.

B. When an action is performed by the subject on a part of his own body, a reflexive verb is used in French and the definite article is used instead of a possessive adjective.

Ils *se* lavent *les* mains.   They wash their hands.

Notes: a) However, if the part of the body is modified by an adjective, except for droit (right) and gauche (left), the reflexive pronoun is not used, and the possessive adjective is used, as in English.

Ils lavent *ses mains sales*.	They wash their dirty hands.
Il s'est cassé la jambe droite.	He broke his right leg.

b) There is no agreement between the subject and past participle of a reflexive verb (**brossé**) when the direct object is expressed. She did not brush herself. She brushed her hair.

Elle s'est brossé ses cheveux.	She brushed her hair.

C. **Reflexive verbs used idiomatically in French.**

1) Certain verbs are essentially reflexive, i.e., they are always used with the reflexive pronoun, such as, se moquer de (to make fun of), se souvenir (to remenber).

2) A few verbs, when used reflexively, change their meaning to a greater or lesser extent and become essentially reflexive, such as: agir (to act) and s'agir de (to deal with), servir (to serve), and se servir de (to use), etc.

3) A number of direct transitive verbs are used reflexively when the action remains within the subject, such as **se laver, se lever, se preparer, se hâter, s'imaginer**, etc.

Il a lavé le chien avec de l'eau froide.
He has washed the dog with cold water.

Il s'est lavé avec de l'eau froide.
He washed himself with cold water.

Elle a preparé la nourriture avant le dîner.
She prepared the food before dinner.

Elle s'est préparée avant le dîner.
She got ready (prepared herself) before dinner.

Notes: a) Some verbs correspond to the English form, "*to become + past participle or adjective.*" For example, **s'inquiéter**, to get worried and **s'endurcir**, to get (to become) hard.

b) With the idiomatically reflexive verbs the reflexive pronoun is considered a direct object. **Exceptions: se rendre compte, se plaire, s'imaginer**, where the reflexive pronoun is an indirect object.

D. Reciprocal verbs in French are identical in form to the reflexive verbs. L'un l'autre (each other) or les uns les autres (one another) are added after the verb only to avoid ambiguity, when the nature of the verb does not show clearly whether the action is reciprocal or reflexive.

Elles se téléphonent souvent.   They telephone each other often.
Ils s'accussent les uns les autres.   They accuse one another.
Ils s'accusent.   They accuse themselves.

Note: With verbs requiring a prepositional complement, the preposition is inserted between **l'un** and **l'autre** or **les uns** and **les autres; à** and **de** contract with the article in the usual manner.

Elles se parlent l'un a l'autre.   They speak to each other.

Exercise 13

Restate the following sentences, making them reciprocal. Add l'un l'autre accordingly when necessary to avoid ambiguity.

Example: Il lui écrit / elle lui écrit. —> Ils s'écrivent.
Elle le blâme / il la blâme —>
Ils se blâment l'un l'autre.

1. Il l'aime/ elle l'aime.
2. Elle lui fait du mal / il lui fait du mal.
3. Il lui fait de la peine / elle lui fait de la peine.
4. Il lui téléphone / elle lui téléphone.
5. Il lui parle / elle lui parle.
6. Il la félicité / elle le félicité.
7. Il la présente a ses parents / elle le presente a ses parents.

9. **Reflexive causatives.** If one of the objects of a causative phrase is identical to its subject, it is referred to with a reflexive pronoun.

Ils se font couper les cheveux.   They get (have) haircuts.

Note: Se faire + infinitive is used to show that the subject will have, had, or is having something done form himself or to himself.)

Ils se laissent tomber.
They let themselves fall.

Les voleurs se sont laisses attrapper.
The thieves let themselves get caught.

Les Dupont se sont fait batir une nouvelle maison.
The Duponts had a new house built (for themselves).

Exercise 14

Replace the main verb in the following sentences with the appropriate causative verb.

1. Dans ce restaurant on ne permet pas aux clients de fumer.
2. Le garçon a demandé aux clients d'attendre.
3. Le patron avait ordonne a ses employes de decorer les tables.
4. Il disait aux serveuses de repasser les nappes?
5. Il demandait aux garçons de netoyer les vitres.

6. Il disait aux employés de faire attention.
7. Il ne permettrait pas à sa femme de travailler.
8. Il a demandé a son maitre-d d'arranger les chaises.
9. Il lui a demandé de servir du champagne de France.
10. Il dit a son coiffeur de lui couper les cheveux.

10. **Reflexive Passives**. To say that something is done without specifying who does it, usually requires a reflexive verb in French. The three following sentences are synonymous in meaning although example (1), the structure closest to English usage, is the least natural in French.

(1) Le français est parlé a la Martinique.
(2) On parle français a la Martinique.
(3) Le français se parle a la Martinique.
French is spoken in Martinique.

A. Personal reflexive passives

1) If the meaning of a transitive verb, (a verb requiring a direct object), demands that the subject and object be two different persons, but the true subject is omitted, use a reflexive pronoun.

Je m'appelle Jean. My name is John.
(They call me John. I am called John.)

2) When a verb has a reflexive meaning that makes sense when the subject is a person or persons, the **on** form is clearer in meaning.

Il s'est trouvé devant le musée.
He found himself in front of the museum.

On l'a trouvé devant le musée.
They found him in front of the museum.
(He was found in front of the museum.)

B. Impersonal reflexives

For a verb whose reflexive makes little sense when the subject is not a person, the reflexive passive structure may be used.

Notre hôtel se trouvait en face de l'église.
Our hotel was located (was found) across from the church.

Ici, les bicyclettes ne se louent pas, elles s'achètent.
Here, bicycles aren't rented; they are bought. (or)
Here we do not rent bicycles; we sell them.

Exercise 15

Make passive reflexive sentences from the following active sentences. If the reflexive form seems to have more than one meaning, write another sentence with on as its subject.

1. Ils ont fermé les portes du restaurant.
2. Vous ne gagnez rien en mentant.
3. Les gens lisaient les journaux le soir.
4. Personne ne disputera cette idée.
5. Vous trouvez New York nord est des Etats-Unis.
6. Ils choisiront le nouveau gouverneur en Novembre.
7. Rien ne contredit les faits.
8. On a vendu les meubles.
9. On servait le dîner.
10. Aucun évènement ne changera son avis.

11. Si and the imperfect tense

Si and the on or nous form of the verb in the imperfect tense can be used as a type of imperative to make a wish or suggestion.

Si on allait au cinéma.	How about going to the movies?
Si nous jouions au bridge.	Suppose we play bridge?

Exercise 16

Madame Dupont complains that she and Monsieur Dupont don't do much together. Monsieur Dupont proposes the following. Write M. Dupont's suggestion to the complaint given.

Example: (Mrs. Dupont) Nous n'allons jamais a la campagne.

Si nous allions a la campagne?

1. Nous ne dînons jamais au restaurant.
2. Nous n'achetons jamais de meubles neufs.
3. Nous n'allons jamais au théâtre.
4. Nous ne voyageons jamais.
5. Nous ne visitons jamais le musée.

12. Si and the conditional sentences

A conditional sentence consists of two parts: the condition or "si" clause, and the main or result clause.

Either clause may come first in the sentence.

A. The tense used in the main clause is the same in both languages. When the verb in the main clause is in the future, present, or imperative, the present indicative is used in the *"si"* clause.

S'il neige, nous ne sortirons pas.	If it snows, we shall not go out.
S'il neige, nous ne sortons pas.	If it snows, we do not go out.
S'il neige, ne sortez pas.	If it snows, do not go out.

B. When the main clause is in the present conditional, the imperfect is used in the "si" clause.

S'il neigeait, nous ne sortirions pas.
If it snowed (were to snow), we would not go out.

C. The same sequence of tenses applies in compound tenses, with the auxiliary considered as the verb.

Thus, if the past conditional is used in the main clause, the pluperfect is used in the "si" clause.

S'il avait neigé, nous ne serions pas sortis.
If it had snowed, we would not have gone out.

Notes: a) In conditional sentences, si always means if. The **-i** of si is dropped only before **il** and **ils**.

b) The imperfect tense after **si** is translated by a simple past tense or by **were to**.

Si vous commenciez   =   if you began, if you were to begin

c) The only tenses used in **"si"** clauses are the present indicative, the imperfect, and the pluperfect.

D. **Summary of the Sequence of Tenses**

Si clause	Main or Result Clause
present	future
present	present
present	imperative
imperfect	present conditional
pluperfect	past conditional

Note: When si means whether, it may be followed by any tense, just as in English.

Savez-vous si elle viendra a la fête?
Do you know whether she will come to the party?

Nous ne savions pas si elle connaissait Katia.
We didn't know whether she knew Katia.

Je ne sais pas si elle l'a fait.
I don't know whether she did it.

Exercise 17

Complete the following sentences with the correct form of the verb.

1. (faire) Nous irions a la plage s'il _____ beau.
2. (fermer) Si vous sortez _____ la porte.
3. (aider) si vous aviez voulu repare la voiture, je vous _____
4. (mourir) Si son mari _____ cette femme aurait été veuve.
5. (plaire) Si le film vous _____ , faites -le moi savoir.

6. (parler) Si elle me mentait, je ne lui _____ jamais.
7. (acheter) si les crvavates ne me plaisent pas, je ne les _____ pas.
8. (être) Si elle etait malade, elle _____ absente.
9. (aller) _____ vous sisiter Versailes si vous etiez en France.
10. (travailler) S'il _____ dur il sera fatigue.
11. (recevoir) S'ils _____ la lettre, ils y répondront immediatement.
12. (rester) Si l'hotel avait été climatise, je _____ une semaine entiere.
13. (arriver) Si elles avaient couru, elles y_____ à l'heure.
14. (comprendre) Si elle m'avait écoute, elle_____ mon point de vue.
15. (prêter) Si nous lui _____ l'argent, nous le rendrait-il?

13. Quand / lorsque / aussitôt que / des que / après que and the future tense

After **quand** (when), **lorsque** (when), **aussitôt que** (as soon as), **dès que** (as soon as), and **après que** (after), if the action refers to the future, in French the future or, less frequently, the future perfect tense is used.

Dites-lui bonjour de ma part **lorsque vous le verrez.**
Say hello to him for me when you see him.

Aussitôt qu'ils arriveront, nous nous mettrons a table.
As soon as they arrive, we will sit down at the table.

Ma mère ne sera plus ici **quand vous arriverez.**
My mother will no longer be here when you arrive.

Je partirai **dès que** j'aurai mange.
I shall leave as soon as I (shall) have eaten.

Notes: a) *"Shall"* or *"will"* is often omitted in English although the sense has a future meaning.

b) In all other cases, the tense used after these conjunctions is similar to the English tense. A customary action or a permanent general truth must be described in the present indicative. Otherwise, these conjuctions follow the time frame of the action.

Quand elle a soif, elle boit un verre d'eau.
When she is thirsty, she drinks a glass of water.
(customary action, present tense)

Je l'ai remarquée dès que je suis entré.
I noticed her as soon as I came in.
(brief action in the past. passe compose)

Quand j'étais petit, j'allais à la messe tous les dimanche.
When I was a child, I used to go to Mass every Sunday.
(repeated action, imperfect)

Exercise 18   Choose the correct response.

1. (Combien de temps, Depuis quand) a-t-il neige?
2. As-tu besoin d'un stylo lorsque tu (écris, ecriras)?
3. Vos cousins habitent a Paris? (Combien de temps, Depuis quand) y habitent-ils?
4. Ils y habitent (depuis, pendant) longtemps.
5. Ou habiteront-ils après qu'on (vend, vendra) la maison?
6. Portez-vous un pardessus quand il (neige, neigera)?
7. J'ouvrirai mon parapluie (s'il, quand il) pleut.
8. Depuis quand (a-t-il plu, pleuvait-il)?
9. J'habite New York (pendant, depuis) trois ans.
10. (Depuis quand, Combien de temps) faites-vous des exercices physique chaque jour?
11. (Combien de temps, Combien de temps y a-t-il que) vous faites du judo?
12. Aussitôt que vous (êtes, serez), pret nous nous mettrons en route.
13. Giselle étudiait le français (depuis, pour) trois ans quand elle a decidé d'aller en France.
14. M. et Mme. Dupont iront a Canne (pendant, pour) une semaine au mois d'août.
15. (Il y a, Il y avait) un quart d'heure qu'il se reposait.

Exercise 19   Compléter chaque phrase avec la forme convenable du verbe.

1. (voir) Tournez à gauche des que vous _____ le bâtiment blanc.
2. (causer) Marie et moi, nous _____ hier pendant plusieurs heures.
3. (mourir) Voulez-vous dîner? Oui, je _____ de faim depuis une heure.
4. (rencontrer) Elle ne me reconnait jamais lorsqu'elle me _____.
5. (réflechir) Il y a déjà vingt minutes que je _____.
6. (descendre) Ils _____ dîner lorsqu'ils changeront de vêtements.
7. (se sentir) Venez chez moi aussitot que vous _____ mieux.
8. (aller) Quand j'etais jeune, j' _____ à la plage.
9. (chercher) Combien de temps y avait-il que vous _____ le magasin de chaussures?
10. (faire) Il le _____ quand il aura le temps.

14. The verbs: **devoir, falloir, pouvoir, savoir, connaître ,vouloir.**

A. **Devoir** - to owe / must / should / ought to

Although the forms of devoir are irregular, its meanings in the different tenses are predicatble from its basic meaning combined with its tense endings. We perceive the different translations as irregularities because there is no equivalent English verb with a complete set of tenses.

1. Uses of **devoir**, to owe:

a) The verb devoir means owe(d) in all tenses — when it is used with a noun or pronoun direct object:

> Mon ami me doit cent dollars. (Il me doit cent dollars.)
> My friend owes me a hundred dollars.

b) **Devoir** followed directly by an infinitive:

1) The present tense of **devoir** is translated as *"must..."* in both the certain and conjectural senses, or *"have to..."*

> Je dois écrire à mes parents.   I must write to my parents.
> Ça doit être intéréssant.   It must be interesting.

2) The passé composé of **devoir** is translated as *"must have..."* , in the conjectural sense, or *"had to..."*

> Le directeur a dû le renvoyer.   The principal had to dismiss him.

3) Translate the imparfait of **devoir** as was(were) supposed to ... not specifying that the action was ever undertaken.

> Je n'avais pas le choix, je devais partir.
> I did not have a choice, I had to go.

4) In the conjectural sense, the imparfait of devoir means *"was probably..."*

> Il devait être fatigue quand il a eu l'accident.
> He must have been tired (he probably was tired) when he had the accident.

5) The future tense of devoir is translated as "will have to..."

> Nous devrons recommencer à zéro.
> We'll have to begin all over again.

6) The conditional of devoir is translated as "should..." or "ought to..." - implying "probably will not."

> Vous devriez manger quelque chose.
> You should (ought to) eat something.

7) The past conditional of **devoir** is tranlated as *"should have..."* or *"ought to have..."* , implying *"probably did not."*

> La direction aurait dû faire quelque chose.
> The people in charge should have done something.

8) The past participle of **devoir** has a circumflex accent *only in the masculine singular*: **dû, due, dus, dues.**

Exercise 20   Complete with the correct form of **devoir**.

1. Vous _____ changer d'école, mais vous ne le ferez jamais.
2. Mes amis _____ quitter New York l'année dernière. Leur permis de séjours à expiré.
3. Mon frère me _____ dix dollars.
4. Le gouvernement _____ annuler toutes les taxes un jour!
5. Tout le monde _____ obéir a la loi.
6. Les Haitiens _____ faire une revolution pour avoir leur independance.
7. Vous _____ obtenir votre passeport avant votre depart.
8. Le mécanicien _____ réparer le carburateur, mais il n'avait pas le temps.
9. Ma fiancée m'attendait devant le restaurant ou nous ... dîner.
10. Ma soeur _____ être malade pour appeler le médecin.
11. Je _____ vous appeler cet après-midi parce que je suis trop occupée en ce moment.
12. Ces enfants _____ étudier, mais ils préfèrent regarder la télévision.
13. Si elle a refusé de répondre elle ne _____ pas être seule.
14. Nous_____ les voir ce soir. Nous avons un rendez- vous.
15. J'_____ porter un pardessus ce matin. Il neigeait.

B. **Falloir** - to be necessary

Falloir, an impersonal verb, is most frequently followed by a dependent clause with the verb in the subjunctive, but it may also be followed by an infinitive. **Falloir** expresses a necessity or a compulsion, but it may also express an obligation or a duty and its meaning overlaps with that of **devoir**.

However, **falloir** must be used when a necessity or a compulsion is implied, when the obligation or duty is stressed, or when the used of **devoir** would be ambiguous.

1. Uses of the impersonal verb **falloir**:

a) with the infinitive in a statement in direct address, provided there is no ambiguity as to who is concerned.

Mon enfant, **il ne faut pas** déranger votre père.
My child, you must not disturb your father.

Il ne faut pas vous fâcher.
You must not get angry.

b) with an indirect object pronoun and the infinitive.

Il lui faut le dire puisque c'est la vérité.
He must say it since it is the truth.

Il me faudra partir tout de suite.
I will have to leave at once.

Notes: a) **Falloir** with an indirect object pronoun and a partitive or an expression of quantity is used instead of **avoir besoin de** to stress need.

The indirect object corresponds to the subject of need in the English sentence.

Il leur faudra beaucoup d'energy pour ce travail.
They will need a lot of energy for this work.

Certainement, **il leur en faudra** beaucoup.
Certainly, they will need a lot.

b) **Falloir** is used to translate *"to take"* followed by an expression of time, or when *"to take"* is used to mean "to require" or *"to need."* It usually introduces an infinitive phrase with **pour**.

Combien de temps **lui faudra-t-il** pour achever ce travail.
How long will it take him to do this work?

Il en faudra beaucoup.
It will take (need) a lot.

3. **Falloir** may be used as a complement.

Jeanne, avez-vous fait **tout ce qu'il a fallu**?
Jeanne, have you done all that was necessary
(all that you should/all that was needed)?

Je sais que vous tenez pas a travailler le samedi, mais **il le faut**.
I know you do not want to work Saturdays, but you must.

c) in an impersonal statement, frequently expressed by the passive in English.

Il faut éviter les accidents.   Accidents must be avoided.

Notes: a) The negative of the present and future of falloir can only mean *"must not." "Not to have to,"* meaning *"to be obliged to,"* or *"not to need to,"* is translated by ne pas **être obligé de, ne pas avoir besoin de**.

Vous n'êtes pas obligé de travailler après cinq heures.
You do not have to work after 5 o'clock.

Vous n'êtes pas obligé de lui répondre.
You do not have to answer him.

Vous n'avez pas besoin de hausser la voix.
You do not have to raise your voice.

2. **Falloir** in the conditionnal tenses, both present and past, is used to translate impersonal statements and English passives.

Il aurait fallu le terminer plus tôt.
It ought to have (should have) been finished sooner.

d) with the subjunctive.

Il faut qu'il le dise puisque c'est la vérité.
He must say it since it is the truth.

Il faudra que je parte tout de suite.
I will have to leave at once.

Il faudra qu'il prouve son innocence.
He will have to prove his innocence.

Faut-il que tu ailles a Moscou sans moi, ma chérie?
Must you (do you have to) go to Moscow without me, my darling?

Note: Although in principle a past tense of **falloir** should be followed by the imperfect subjunctive, modern usage permits the present subjunctive, except in formal writing.

Il aurait fallu que nous tombions (tombassions) malade si nous n'avions pas pris soin de notre santé.
We would have fallen sick if we had not taken care of our health.

e) Reminders.
1) **Falloir** shows necessity. It is stronger than devoir.
2) **Falloir** and **devoir** often express the same idea.
You must work. ——> **Vous devez travailler.**
Il faut que vous travailliez.   **Il vous faut travailler.**

3. When followed by a noun, **devoir** means "to owe," falloir, "to need."

Mon cousin me doit dix dollars.
My cousin owes me ten dollars.

Il me faut l'argent qu'il me doit.
I need the money (that) he owes me.

Il lui faut un travail.
He needs a job.

C. **Pouvoir**: to be able (physically)/be permitted to. **Pouvoir** may be translated by *"can," "to be able to," "may,"* or *"have permission to."*

Il ne peut pas faire du ski; il s'est casse la jambe.
He cannot ski; he has broken his leg.

Vous pouvez entrer.
You may come in.

Puis-je te voir demain?
May I see you tomorrow?

Je ne peux rien promettre.
I cannot promise anything.

Vous pourrez le faire demain.
You can (may do it) tomorrow.

Auriez-vous pu le faire sans moi?
Could you have done it without me?

Nous n'avions pas pu trouver un taxi.
We have been unable(could not) find a taxi.

Notes: a) *"Could,"* according to the case, may be translated by the conditional present or by a past tense of the indicative. *"Might"* and *"could/might have"* are translated by the present and past conditional, respectively.

b) "May," meaning "it may be that" is translated by **il se peut que + the subjunctive.**

Il se peut qu'elle vienne me voir.
She may come to see me.

Il se pourrait qu'elle vienne de bonne heure.
She might come early.

Il se peut qu'elle soit déjà arrivée.
She may have arrived already.

c) **Pouvoir** may express possibility.

Elle peut être en retard.
She may be late.

Ils auraient pu le perdre.
They might have lost it.

D. **Savoir** - to be able (mentally)/to know how.

1. **Savoir** is used when *"to know"* means *"to know through the mind,"* *"to know about,"* *"to be aware of,"* *"to know thoroughly,"* *"to know by heart or through study."* Savoir is not used when *"to know"* has as a direct object a person, an animal or a concrete object. In such cases connaitre is used.

Je said qu'elle est arrivée.
I know that she has arrived.

Savez-vous ou elle habite? Oui, je le sais.
Do you know where she lives? Yes, I know (it).

2. **Idiomatic use of the conditional.**

Sauriez-vous me dire ou elle demeure?
Can you tell me where she lives?

Je ne saurais vous le dire.
I cannot tell you.

E. Connaître - (to know)

Connaitre is used when *"to know"* means *"to be acquainted or familiar with,"* *"to know by sight,"* *"to recognize."* **Connaitre** must have a noun or a pronoun as direct object; it cannot be followed by a subordinate clause.

Je ne connais pas cette rue.
I do not know this street.

Qui est cette jeune fille? La connaissez-vous?
Who is this young lady? Do you know her?

Connaissez-vous cette église?
Do you know (recognize) this church.

Notes: a) When *"to know how + an infinitive"* means *"the ability to do something,"* *"how"* is not expressed in French.

Elle sait faire la cuisine.
She knows how to cook. (can)

Elle sait s'occuper des enfants.
She knows how to care fo children.

2. When "to know how" means *"in what way/manner,"* *"by what means,"* *"for what reason,"* or when it is followed by a verb in a finite form, *"how"* is expressed by **comment**.

Je sais *comment* **elle m'a trompé.**
I know how (in what manner) she cheated on me.

Je ne sais pas *comment* **me débarrasser de cette malaise.**
I do not know how to get rid of this illness.

F. Vouloir - to wish / want / will

The much used English idiomatic expression *"would (should) like"* in which *"like"* has the meaning of *"wish,"* or *"want,"* is translated in French by some form of **vouloir** or **desirer**.

"Would (should) like," used to express a desire politely or to attenuate a request, is translated by the present conditional of **vouloir** or **vouloir bien** (more emphatic), or by the present conditional of desirer (more formal).

The form **je veux** (the present indicative of **vouloir**) generally shows strong will, similar to a command. Thus, the conditional, **je voudrais,** a courteous form, often replaces the present indicative.

Je veux voir le directeur.
I want to see the principal.
(This is harsh. The conditional, **je voudrais,** is more polite.)

Je voudrais voir le directeur.
I would like to see the principal.
(More polite still is the conditional of **desirer:**

Je desirerais voir le directeur.)
I would like to see the principal.

Je voudrais lui parler.
I wish (would like) to speak to him.

Je voudrais (bien) savoir qui est cette jolie jeune fille.
I would like (very much) to know who that charming young lady is.

Je voudrais encore un peu de viande, s'il vous plait.
I would like a little more meat, please.

Ma mère voudrait que je lui écrive plus souvent.
My mother would like me (wishes that I would) write more often.

Notes: a) Vouloir requires the subjunctive in the subordinate clause.

b) Vouloir bien, *"to be willing," "to like," "to want,"* is used only in positive statements.

In the negative, and usually in the interrogative, vouloir alone is used.

Elle n'a pas voulu venir a la soirée.
She would not (was unwilling to) come to the party.

Viendras-tu ce soir? Je voudrais bien, (Je veux bien), mais je ne me sens pas bien.
Will you come tonight? I will/would be willing to, but I do not feel well.

c) In questions and answers "would (should) like" is often the English translation for the verb vouloir.

Que voulez-vous (désirez-vous)?
What would you like?

Voulez/Desirez-vous une tasse de thé?
Would you like/wish/want a cup of tea?

Voudriez-vous parler personellement au président?
Would you like (want) to speak to the president personally?

Je voudrais bien, si c'est possible.
I would (like to), if it is possible.

d) The imperative form veuillez is used with the infinitive to express polite command.

Veuillez fermer la porte, s'il vous plait.
Kindly close the door, please.

Veuillez nous excuser, madame.
Please excuse us, madame.

Exercise 21   Complete each sentence in English.

1. Nous devons nous dépêcher. _____ hurry.
2. Il lui faut du courage. _____ courage.
3. Pourra-t-elle oublier sa tristesse? _____ to forget her sadness?
4. Veuillez vous asseoir. _____ sit down.
5. Il ne faut pas regarder cette pinture. _____ look this drawing.
6. Sais-tu jouer au tennis? _____ play tennis?
7. Je ne pouvais pas comprendre le dialogue du film. _____ understand the dialogue of the film.
8. Ils ont dû être très fâché. _____ very angry.
9. Il faudra que nous lui envoyions un télégramme. _____ send him a telegram.
10. Sauriez-vous nous indiquer le musée? _____ point out the museum?

Exercise 22

Write an equivalent sentence using the verb in parenthesis.

    Example: **(devoir): Ils sont sans doute sinceres. —->**
                   Ils doivent êtres sincères.

1. **(falloir):** Nous avons besoin du temps.
2. **(pouvoir):** Est-il possible que vous m'aidiez?
3. **(devoir):** Après cette longue promenade, tu es probablement très fatiguée.
4. **(falloir):** Simone devra faire un effort pour se débarrasser de son rhume.
5. **(vouloir):** Je refuse de suivre la foule.
6. **(devoir):** Serez-vous obligés de partir de bonne heure?
7. **(falloir):** Je dois travailler ce soir.
8. **(pouvoir):** Ont-ils la permission de vous accompagner?
9. **(vouloir):** Asseyez-vous, s'il vous plait.
10. **(falloir):** Est-il necessaire de téléphoner pour retenir une place dans l'avion?

Exercise 23

Write in English.

1. Je ne veux pas me taire!
2. Il leur faut suivre un cours de musique.
3. Ceux qui gouvernent peuvent se tromper.
4. Je ne saurais vous le dire.
5. Il lui fallait de lunettes pour pourvoir lire.
6. J'ai recu l'argent qu'il m'avait dû.
7. Veut-il bien partager la vie de famille?
8. Ou peut-elle être? Elle peut être en ville.
9. Il faut que je vous rende votre roman.
10. L'avocat a du abandonner la cause; il ne pouvait pas faire autrement.

IDIOMS

Ideas common to all languages are often expressed in different ways. Idioms are expressions unique to the structure of a particular language. French idioms reflect the thinking and the culture of the French people. Idioms must be studied until their use is learned and applied naturally in both written and spoken French.

IDIOMS WITH AVOIR

1. **avoir...ans,** to be...years old
2. **avoir beau + infinitive,** to do (something) in vain
3. **avoir besoin de,** to need
4. **avoir envie de,** to feel like (doing something)
5. **avoir honte (de),** to be ashamed (of)
6. **avoir lieu,** to take place
7. **avoir mal à (+ part of the body),** to have a pain in, have a/an ... -ache
8. **avoir peur (de),** to be afraid (of)
9. **avoir quelque chose,** to have something wrong
10. **avoir de la chance,** to be lucky
11. **avoir de quoi (+ infinitive),** to have the means (materials, enough) to
12. **avoir l'air (+ adjective),** to seem, look
13. **avoir l'air de (+ infinitive),** to seem to, look as if
14. **avoir l'habitude de,** to be accustomed to
15. **avoir l'idée de,** to have a notion to
16. **avoir l'intention de,** to intend to
17. **avoir l'occasion de,** to have the opportunity to
18. **avoir le temps de,** to have (the) time to
19. **avoir la parole,** to have the floor (as a speaker)
20. **avoir chaud,** to be warm (of persons)
21. **avoir faim,** to be hungry
22. **avoir raison,** to be right
23. **avoir froid,** to be cold (of persons)
24. **avoir soif,** to be thirsty
25. **avoir tort,** to be wrong
26. **avoir sommeil,** to be sleepy

IDIOMS WITH FAIRE

1. **faire (with il)**, used in expressions of weather
2. **faire + infinitive**, to have something done
3. **faire à sa tête**, to do as one pleases
4. **faire attention à**, to pay attention to
5. **faire de la peine à**, to grieve, distress, trouble
6. **faire de son mieux** ⟶

   faire son possible ⟶ to do one's best
7. **faire des achats** ⟶

   faire des emplettes ⟶ to go shopping
8. **faire des progrès**, to make progress
9. **faire exprès**, to do on purpose
10. **faire la connaissance de**, to become acquainted with, meet
11. **faire la queue**, to stand on line
12. **faire la sourde oreille**, to turn a deaf ear, prétend not to hear
13. **faire mal à**, to hurt
14. **faire peur à**, to frighten
15. **faire plaisir à**, to please, give pleasure to
16. **faire savoir (a quelqu'un)**, to let (someone) know
17. **faire semblant de**, to prétend to, make believe
18. **faire ses adieux**, to say good-bye
19. **faire une partie de**, to play a game of
20. **faire une promenade**, to take a walk, a ride
21. **faire poser une question (à)**, to ask a question
22. **faire un voyage**, to take a trip
23. **faire venir**, to send for

REFLEXIVE EXPRESSIONS

1. **s'agir de (used impersonally with il)**, to be a question of, to be about
2. **s'approcher de**, to approach
3. **s'attendre à**, to expect
4. **se casser le bras (la jambe)**, to break one's arm (leg)
5. **se charger de**, to take charge of, undertake
6. **se demander**, to wonder
7. **se douter de**, to suspect
8. **s'en aller**, to go away
9. **s'étonner de**, to be astonished (surprised) at
10. **se fâcher contre**, to get angry with
11. **se faire mal**, to hurt oneself, get hurt
12. **se fier à**, to trust

13. **se marier avec,** to marry
14. **se mettre à,** to begin with
15. **se mettre en colère,** to get angry, lose one's temper
16. **se mettre en route,** to start out
17. **se moquer de,** to make fun of, laugh at
18. **s'occuper de,** to attend to, look after
19. **se passer de,** to do without
20. **se rendre à,** to go to
21. **se rendre compte de (or que),** to realize, understand
22. **se servir de,** to use
23. **se souvenir de** ⟶

se rappeller ⟶ ⟶ to remember

24. **se tirer d'affaire,** to get along, manage

OTHER VERBAL IDIOMS

1. **adresser la parole à,** to address, speak to
2. **aller,** to feel, be (of health)
3. **aller à,** to fit, suit
4. **aller à la pêche,** to go fishing
5. **aller à la rencontre de** ⟶

aller au-devant de ⟶ ⟶ to go to meet

6. **apprendre par coeur,** to memorize
7. **assister à,** to attend, to be present
8. **changer de,** to change (one thing for another of its kind)
9. **demander quelque chose à quelqu'un,** to ask for something
10. **donner sur,** to face, look out on
11. **éclater de rire,** to burst out laughing
12. **entendre dire que,** to hear that
13. **entendre parler de,** to hear of
14. **en vouloir à,** to have a grudge against, be angry with
15. **envoyer chercher,** to send for
16. **être à,** to belong to
17. **être bien aise de,** to be very glad to
18. **être d'accord (avec),** to agree (with), to be in agreement (with)
19. **être de retour,** to be back
20. **être en train de,** to be busy (doing something), be in the act of
21. **être enrhumé,** to have a cold
22. **être sur le point de,** to be about to
23. **féliciter de,** to congratulate on
24. **finir par (+ infinitive),** to end by, finally do (something)

25. **jouer à,** to play (a game)
26. **jouer de,** to play (an instrument)
27. **jouir de,** to enjoy (what one possesses)
28. **manquer de (+ noun),** to lack
29. **manquer de (+ infinitive)**
    faillir (+ infinitive) ⟩ almost (do something)
30. **monter à cheval,** to go horseback riding
31. **n'en pouvoir plus,** to be exhausted
32. **penser à**
    songer à ⟩ to think of
33. **penser de,** to think of (+ to have an opinion of)
34. **pleuvoir à verse,** to rain hard, pour
35. **prendre garde de,** to be careful not to
36. **prendre le parti de,** to decide to, make up one's mind to
37. **prendre un billet,** to buy a ticket
38. **profiter de,** to profit by, take advantage of
39. **remercier de,** to thank for
40. **rendre visite à (quelqu'un),** to pay (someone) a visit, visit (someone)
41. **ressembler à,** to resemble, look like
42. **rire de,** to laugh at
43. **sauter aux yeux,** to be evident
44. **savoir bon gré à quelqu'un de quelque chose,** to be grateful to someone for something
45. **tarder à,** to be long (late) in
46. **tenir à,** to insist upon, be anxious to, value
47. **valoir la peine de,** to be worth while
48. **valoir mieux,** to be better
49. **venir à,** to happen to
50. **venir à bout de,** to succeed in, manage to
51. **venir de,** to have just (used in the present and imperfect tenses)
52. **vouloir bien,** to be willing, to do (something) kindly
53. **vouloir dire,** to mean
54. **y être,** to understand, see the point

IDIOMS INTRODUCED BY à

1. **à** (with characteristic), with
2. **à** (when one is on the means of transportation), on, by
3. **à** (with time expression), good-bye until
4. **à cause de,** because of, on account of
5. **à côté de,** next to, beside
6. **à force de,** by, by means of, by dint of (repeated offers)
7. **à partir de,** from...on, beginning (with)
8. **à propos de**
   à sujet de about, concerning
9. **à droite,** on (to) the right
10. **à gauche,** on (to) the left
11. **à demi**
    à moitié half, halfway
12. **à jamais,** forever
13. **à merveille,** wonderfully well, marvelously
14. **à part,** aside
15. **à peine,** hardly, scarcely
16. **à présent,** now, at present
17. **à travers,** through, across
18. **à haute voix,** aloud, out loud
19. **à voix basse,** in a low voice
20. **à peu près,** nearly, about, approximately
21. **à quoi bon (+ infinitive)?** what's the use of?
22. **à son gré,** as one pleases, to one's liking
23. **à tout prix,** at any cost
24. **à vrai dire,** to tell the truth
25. **à la bonne heure!** Good! Fine! (About time!)
26. **à la campagne,** in (to) the country
27. **à l'école,** in (to) school
28. **à l'étranger,** abroad
29. **à la fin,** finally
30. **à l'heure,** on time
31. **à cette heure,** at this (that) time
32. **à la fois,** at the same time
33. **à temps,** in time
34. **à la main,** in one's hand
35. **à la maison,** at home, home
36. **à la mode,** in style, **l'occasion de,** at the time of
37. **à l'occasion de,** at the time of, on the occasion of

38. **à la page...,** on page...
39. **au contraire,** on the contrary
40. **au loin,** in the distance
41. **au moins,** at least
42. **au bas de,** at the bottom of
43. **au bout de,** at the end of, after
44. **au courant de,** informed of
45. **au-dessous de,** below, beneath
46. **au-dessus de,** above, over
47. **au fond de,** in the bottom of
48. **au haut de,** at the top of
49. **au lieu de,** instead of
50. **au milieu de,** in the middle of
51. **au pied de,** at the foot of

IDIOMS INTRODUCED BY DE

1. **d'abord,** first, at first
2. **D'accord.** Agreed. O.K.
3. **d'ailleurs,** besides, moreover
4. **d'avance,** in advance, beforehand
5. **de bon appétit,** heartily, with a good appetite
6. **de bon coeur,** willingly, gladly
7. **de bonne heure,** early
8. **de l'autre côté (de),** on the other side (of)
9. **de côté de,** in the direction of, toward
10. **de mon côté,** for my part, as for me
11. **de jour en jour,** from day to day
12. **plus en plus,** more and more, -er and -er
13. **de temps en temps**

    de temps à autre } from time to time, occasionally
14. **de nouveau**

    encore une fois } again
15. **d'ordinaire,** usually
16. **de parti pris,** deliberately
17. **de la part de,** on behalf of, from
18. **de quelle couleur...?** what color...?
19. **De rien**

    Je vous en prie } **Il n'y a pas de quoi** You're welcome. Don't mention it.
20. **de rigueur,** (socially) obligatory, required
21. **du matin au soir,** from morning till night
22. **du moins,** at least

IDIOMS INTRODUCED BY OTHER PREPOSITIONS

1. **autour de**, around
2. **chez (+ person)**, to (at) the house (place) of (the person)
3. **en (when one is inside the means of transportation)**, by
4. en **arrière**, backward(s), behind
5. **en bas**, downstairs
6. **en haut**, upstairs
7. **en effet**, (yes) indeed, as a matter of fact
8. **en face de**, opposite
9. **en famille**, as a family, within (in the privacy of) the family
10. **en même temps**, at the same time
11. **en plein air**, in the open air, outdoors
12. **en retard**, late (= not on time)
13. **en tout cas**, in any case, at any rate
14. **en ville**, downtown, in (to, into) town
15. **par conséquent**, therefore, consequently
16. **par exemple**, for example
17. **par hasard**, by chance
18. **par ici**, this way, in that direction
19. **par là**, that way, in that direction
20. **par jour (semaine, mois, etc.)**, a (per) day (week, month, etc.)
21. **sans doute**, without doubt, undoubtedly

MISCELLANEOUS IDIOMS AND EXPRESSIONS

1. **bien entendu**, of course
2. **bon gré mal gré**, whether one wants to or not
3. **bon marché**, cheap **meilleur marché**, cheaper
4. **bon pour**, good (kind) to
5. **Cela m'est égal.** That makes no difference to me. That's all the same to me.
6. **Cela ne fait rien.** That does not matter. That makes no difference.
7. **c'est-à-dire**, that is to say
8. **C'est entendu.** It's agreed. All right.
9. **en huit jours**, in (= during) a week **en quinze jours**, in two weeks
10. **et ainsi de suite**, and so forth
11. **faute de**, for the lack of
12. **grâce à**, thanks to
13. **Il y a...,...ago**
14. **Il y avait une fois...,** Once (upon a time) there was (were)...
15. **Jamais de la vie!** Never! Out of the question!
16. **le long de**, along
17. **n'importe**, never mind, no matter
18. **peu à peu**, little by little, gradually

19. **Plaît-il?** What did you say? Would you mind repeating? I beg your pardon?
20. **quant à**, as for
21. **que** ⟶ how (in exclamations)
    comme ⟶ how (in exclamations)
22. **tant bien que mal**, rather badly, after a fashion, so-so
23. **tant mieux**, so much the better
24. **tant pis**, so much the worse
25. **tous (les) deux**, both
26. **tout à coup**, suddenly
27. **tout à fait**, entirely, quite
28. **tout à l'heure**, just now, a little while ago (referring to the immediate past), in a little while, presently (referring to the immediate future)
29. **toute de même** ⟶ just the same
    quand même ⟶ just the same
30. **toute de suite** ⟶ immediately, at once
    à l'instant ⟶ immediately, at once

9

Vocabulary

ENGLISH - FRENCH

*T*his vocabulary list omits the following elementary items: articles; personal and relative pronouns; interrogative, demonstrative, and possessive pronouns; numerals; common negations; and the more common prepositions. Many of the more common prepositions form part of an English verb or idiomatic expression. "Attempt to," for example, will be found under attempt; "go up" will be found under go; "by train" under train, and so on.

Words ending in -ion are not generally listed in this vocabulary if the spelling and meaning are identical in both languages. These words are feminine.

The following abbreviations and special symbols are used: (f) feminine; (m) masculine; (pl) plural;(prep.) preposition; (pron.) pronoun; (conj.) conjunction; (adj.) adjective; (adv.) adverb; - repetition of the entry word; * following a verb indicates that it is conjugated irregularly.

A preposition without parentheses, following either an English or a French entry, indicates that the preposition is part of the verb or expression, for example, "to **look for**," chercher.

If a preposition is enclosed in parentheses following an entry, it indicates that this preposition is required when a component follows, for example, "to **obey**," obeir (a).

If a preposition and a plus sign (a +), (de +) are enclosed in parentheses following an entry, it indicates the preposition required before an infinitive.

abandon, to abandonner
able, capable; to be - pouvoir
about environ; (concerning) au sujet de
abroad à l'étranger
abruptly brusquement
absence une absence
absent; absent-minded distrait
absolutely absolument
academy une académie
accept, to accepter (de+)
accident un accident
acclaim, to acclamer
accompany, to accompagner
accused un accuse
accustomed, to be être accoutumé à,
 - avoir coutume de
acquire, to acquérir*
across; de l'autre côté de;
- ; to walk, ride, etc. - traverser
act, to agir;
- up faire le malin
actor; un acteur
add, to ajouter
address une adresse
admire, to admirer
admit, to admettre*
adore, to adorer
advance, to avancer
adventure une aventure
advice le(s) conseil(s)
advise, to conseiller (a, de+)
afraid, to be - avoir peur (de)
after après
afternoon l'après-midi (m)
afterward par la suite
again encore; de nouveau; re + verb
against contre
age un âge
ago il y a
agree, to consentir (à);
- on convenir de;
- with être de l'avis de
air un air; -port un aéroport
alas hélas
alarm une alarme
alarming alarmant
algebra l'algèbre (f)
alive en vie
all tout; at- du tout

A

ancient ancien(ne)
angry fâché, en colère;
-, to get; se fâcher se mettre en colère
animal un animal, une bête
announce, to annoncer
annoy, to ennuyer
annoying ennuyeux
another un autre, encore un
answer la réponse
answer, to répondre à
anyhow n'importe
anymore ne ... plus
anyone quelqu'un, n'importe qui
anything n'importe quoi, quelque chose, tout
anxious, to be tenir* à (desirous)
apartment un appartement;
- house un immeuble
apologize (for), to s'excuser (de);
- to faire des excuses a
appear, to (seem) paraîitre,* sembler;
- ; (become visible) apparaître
appetite un appétit
appointment le rendez-vous
approach, to s'approcher (de)
approve, to approuver
argue, to discuter
aristocratic aristocratique
arithmetic l'arithmétique (f)
arm le bras
arm, to armer
armchair le fauteuil
army une armée
around autour de; (about) environ; (time) vers
arrangement make -s prendre des dispositions
arrest une arrestation
arrest,to arrêter
arrival une arrivée
arrive, to arriver
as comme; -...- aussi ... que ; - for quant à;
- soon as aussitôt que; dès que;
- much autant; - early - dè s le ...
ashamed honteux;
- to be - avoir honte (de), être honteux (de)
aside from en dehors de
ask, to demander (a, de+); - for demander
asleep endormi; to fall - s'endormir
assure, to assurer
attempt to, to tenter de, chercher à
attend, to (be present) assister à

to allow permettre* (a, de+)
almost presque; **to -** faillir,* manquer de
alone seul
aloud a haute voix
already déjà
also aussi
alternative une alternative
although quoique, bien que
always toujours
American américain
ambassador un ambassadeur
among parmi; chez
amusing amusant

bad (adj.) mauvais, méchant;**-ly** (adv.) mal;
- , it is too c'est dommage (de+)
baggage les bagages
balance l'équilibre
bandage le bandage
bandage, to bander
bandit le bandit
bang, to claquer
bank la banque
bargain une occasion;
- day le jour de solde
bark, to aboyer
bath le bain;
- room la salle de bains; **- tub** la baignoire
to be être;* avoir;* faire;*
- am to, was to, etc. devoir;*
- (of health) aller,* se porter
beard la barbe; **-ed** barbu
beautiful beau (bel), belle
because parce que; **-** of a cause de
become, to devenir*
bed le lit; **to go to -** se coucher, aller se coucher
bedroom la chambre à coucher
beer la bière
before (prep. of time) avant (de+);
- (prep. of place) devant;
- hand d'avance; (previously) auparavant
begin, to commencer (a+), se mettre à;
- again se remettre à
beginning le commencement, le début;
   in the **-** au début
behave, to se conduire;* être sage
behavior la conduite
believe, to croire*
belong, to appartenir*

- to - to s'occuper de
attention une attention; **to pay -** faire attention
attentively attentivement, avec attention
audience une assistance, les auditeurs (m)
author un auteur
authorize, to autoriser (a+)
automobile une auto(mobile)
available disponible
avoid, to éviter (de+)
await, to attendre
awaken, to (s')eveiller, (se) réveiller
aware, to become s'apercevoir
away *see under the verb*

B

birthday un anniversaire (de naissance)
blame (for), to blâmer (de)
block to bloquer
blue bleu
blush, to rougir
boast, to se vanter
boat le bateau
bonus la gratification
book le livre
bookseller le libraire
bored, to be s'ennuyer
boring ennuyeux
born, to be naître*
borrow, to (from) emprunter (a)
boss le patron
both tous (toutes) les deux
bottle la bouteille
bowl le bol
box la boite, le carton; **-seat** le coffre
boy le garçon
bread le pain **to break -** casser
breakfast le petit déjeuner
bridge le pont; **(cards)** me bridge
bridle la bride
bring, to apporter, amener; **-up** monter;
- down descendre; **- up** monter;
 - up (a child) élever; **- back** rapporter
brother le frère
brown brun
brush, to brosser
budge, to bouger
build, to bâtir, construire*
building un batiment;
- un immeuble (**apartment house**)
bureau la commode

bedside auprès de
(the) best le mieux (adv.); le meilleur (adj.)
better mieux (adv.); meilleur (adj.);
- to be - valoir mieux, **(health)** aller mieux
between entre
bicycle la bicyclette
big grand
bill la note; **(banknote)** le billet
binding la relivre
biography la biographie

cake le gâteau
call un appel; téléphone - un appel téléphonique
call, to appeler, faire venir,* téléphoner;
- on faire une visite, rendre visite;
- attention faire remarquer
calm(ly) calme(ment), tranquille(ment)
to calm down (se) calmer
camera un appareil (photographique)
can pouvoir,* savoir*
Canada le Canada
candy le bonbon; **(collectively)** les bonbons
car la voiture
care le soin; **take -** prendre garde;
   take - of se charger de, prendre soin de
careful soigneux; **-ly** soigneusement;
   to be - faire attention
carriage la voiture
to carry porter; **- up** monter; **-down** descendre;
- out executer; **- away** emporter
case le cas; **in any -** en tout cas
case (packing) la caisse
cat le chat
catastrophe la catastrophe
catch, to prendre,* attraper; **- up with** rattraper
cathedral la cathédrale
Catholic catholique
cause la cause
cause, to causer; **to - to** faire
cautious prudent
cavalcade la cavalcade
cease, to cesser (de+)
cell la cellule
century le siècle
ceremony la cérémonie
certain(ly) certain(ement)
chair la chaise
chance la chance; **by (any) -** par hasard
change le changement; la monnaie

burglar le cambrioleur
burn, to brûler
burst, to éclater; **- out laughing** éclater de rire
bus un autobus
business une affaire, les affaires
busy occupe (a+); **- (doing)** en train de (faire)
but mais
buy, to acheter
by par
bye bye au revoir, salut!

C

coat le manteau; **(of a suit)** le veston
coffee le café
cold froid; **to be (feel) -** avoir froid
   (weather) faire froid
college une université
colonel le colonel
color la couleur
come, to venir;* **(of thing)** arriver;
- back revenir; **- into** entrer; **- out** sortir;*
- up monter; **- down** descendre;
- to (toward, near) s'approcher de;
- home rentrer (chez soi); **-to get** venir chercher;
- to meet venir à la rencontre
comfortable comfortable, bien, à l'aise
comforting la consolation
comical comique
commander le commandant
communicate, to communiquer
company la compagnie
compare, to comparer
complain, to (of, about) se plaindre (de)
compliment le compliment;
   to pay a - faire un compliment
compliment, to on complimenter de
composition le thème; **(original)** la composition
compromising compromettant
conclude, to conclure*
condition la condition; **(state)** un etat
conduct la conduite
conductor le conducteur
conference la conférence
confess, to avouer
consent le consentement
consent, to consentir (a+)
consider, to considérer
considerable considérable
consist, to consister
consoling consolant

change, to changer; **- one's mind** changer d'avis
Channel (English) la Manche
chapter le chapitre
charming charmant, ravissant
chase, to chasser
chat, to bavarder
chauffeur le chauffeur
cheap bon marché
cheerful(ly) gai(ement)
check room (railroad) la consigne
chief le chef
child un(e) enfant
childhood une enfance
choice le choix
choose, to choisir
Christmas Noel
cigarette la cigarette; **- lighter** le briquet
circus le cirque
citizen le (la) bitoyen(ne)
city la ville
claim, to prétendre
class la classe;
classmate le(la) camarade de classe
classics les classiques (m)
clean propre
clean, to nettoyer
clever adroit, habile, **intelligent**
clock la pendule; une horloge **(large)**
close (to) près de
close, to fermer
closet le placard
clothes les vêtements
coachman le cocher
custom la coutume

dangerous dangereux
dare, to oser
dark sombre, noir
darkness une obscurité
date le rendez-vous
daughter la fille
dawn l'aube (f)
day le jour, la journée; **the - before** la veille (de);
the following - le lendemain;
   two -s later deux jour après, le surlendemain
deaf sourd
deal, a great beaucoup, bien
dealer le marchand; antique **-** un antiquaire
dean le doyen, la doyenne

consult, to consulter
contain, to contenir*
content le contenu
continue, to continuer (a+)
contradict, to contredire*
contrary le contraire; **on the -** au contraire
convince, to convaincre (de),* persuader (de)
cook le cuisinier, la cuisinière
copper le cuivre
corner le coin
corridor le corridor
cost, to coûter; **- much** coûter cher
could see pouvoir
country le pays; **(rural district)** la campagne;
   in the - à la campagne; **open -** la pleine campagne
course le cours
course, of - bien entendu
cousin le (la) cousin(e)
cover la couverture
cover (with), to couvrir* (de)
crazy fou (folle)
creature la créature
crippled infirme
crop (riding) la cravache
cross, to traverser, passer
crowd la foule
cruel cruel(le)
cry le cri
cry (weep), to pleurer; **(shout)** crier
cup la tasse
curiosity la curiosité
curious curieux
cut, to couper; **- down (of trees)** abattre
cute mignon

D

direct, to diriger
direction la direction; **in the - of** du côté de
director le directeur
dirty sale
disappear, to disparaître*
disappointed desappointé, déçu
discover, to découvrir;
   (become aware) s'apercevoir*
discourage, to décourager
discuss, to discuter
disdainfully dedaigneusement
dish le plat; **-es (collectively)** la vaisselle
dislike, to ne pas aimer, détester
disobey, to désobeir (a)

decide, to decider (de+), se decider (a+)
decision la décision
declare, to déclarer
decorate, to décorer
decrepit en ruine
defeat, to vaincre*
delay le délai, le retard
delighted enchanté
deny, to nier
department (govt.) le ministère;
 - store le grand magasin
derail, to dérailler
desert le désert
deserted désert
deserve, to mériter (de+)
desire le désir, une envie
desk le bureau
despair, to désesperer (de+)
despise, to mépriser
destroy, to détruire*
detail le détail
detain, to retenir
determined, to be to être décidé à
devote, to consacrer
dictate, to dicter
dictionary le dictionnaire
die, to mourir*
different différent; -ly différemment, autrement
difficult difficile
dining room la salle à manger
dinner le dîner; to have - dîner

each chaque (adj.); chacun (pron.)
early tôt, de bonne heure, en avance
earn, to gagner
easy facile; easily facilement, aisément
eat, to manger
economize, to économiser
education une éducation
egg un oeuf
elder ainé
elegant élégant
else autre
emotion une émotion
empty vide; - handed les mains vides
encourage, to encourager
endd la fin, le bout
end, to finir, (se) terminer
enemy un ennemi

disorder le désordre
dispatch la dépêche
displease, to déplaire a
dispose, to disposer
distinguished distingué
distressed, to be avoir de la peine
distressing lamentable
distrust, to se méfier de
ditch le fosse
dive, to plonger
dizzy, to make donner le vertige
do, to faire;* - over again refaire;
- without se passer de
doctor le docteur; (M.D.) le médecin;
 (direct address) Docteur
document le document
dog le chien
domain le domaine
door la porte; front - la porte d'entrée
doubt, to douter (de)
doubtful douteux
down see under the verb; - cast abattu
dozen la douzaine; half a - une demi-douzaine
dress la robe
dress, to (s')habiller
dressmaker le couturier, la couturière
drink, to boire*
drive, to conduire,* aller (venir) en voiture
during pendant, durant
dust la poussière
duty le devoir

E

eve la veille
even même
evening le soir, la soirée
eventful mouvemente
every chaque, tout; -body, -one tout le monde;
 -thing tout; -where partout
exactly exactement;
 (of time) précis, juste examine, to examiner
except auf
exceptional exceptionnel
exchange, to échanger
exclaim, to s'écrier
excuse une excuse
exercise un exercice; to take - faire de l'exercice
exhaust, to épuiser
exile un exil
existence une existence

engage, to engager
English anglais
English expedition une expédition
enjoy, to jouir de, aimer, se plaire
enough assez (de); **- to** de quoi
enter, to entrer (dans)
entire entier; **-ly** entièrement, **(quite)** tout à fait
entrance l'entrée
entrust, to confier
episode un épisode
error une erreur
escape, to s'évader
especially surtout
essential essentiel

face le visage, la figure;
    to make -s faire les grimaces
fail, to échouer (à); **failing to** faute de;
    not to - to ne pas manquer de
fairly assez
faithful fidèle
fall la chute
fall, to tomber; **- asleep** s'endormir*
false faux
family la famille
famous célèbre
far loin; **as - as** jusqu'à
fast rapide (adj.); vite (adv.);
    to be - (of a timepiece) avancer
fat, to get fat(ter) engraisser
father le père
fault la faute
favorite favori(te)
fear la crainte, la peur; **for -** de crainte (de+)
fear, to craindre* (de+), avoir peur (de)
fearful épouvantable
feel, to sentir; **(experience)** éprouver;
    to - like avoir envie de; **- + adj.** se sentir
few peu; **a -** quelques, quelques-uns
fight, to se battre* frais (fraîche)
finally finalement, enfin; **(end by)** finir par
find, to trouver, retrouver
fine fin; beau
finish, to finir (de+); (se) terminer
fire le feu
first premier; **(in the first place)** d'abord
fit, to aller* (bien)
flee, to fuir
floor (story) un étage; **(flooring)** le plancher;

expect, to s'attendre à, compter, attendre
expenses les frais
expensive cher (chère)
experience une expérience
explain, to expliquer
explanation une explication
exploit une exploit
explorer un explorateur
express, to exprimer
exquisite exquis
extinguish, to (s')éteindre
extraordinary extraordinaire
Europe l'Europe (f)
eye(s) un oeil, les yeux

F

fly, to voler
fog le brouillard
follow, to suivre;* **-ing** suivant;
    -ing day le lendemain
fond, to be - of (like) aimer
foot le pied; **on -** à pied
football le football
footstep le pas
for (destination, purpose) pour;
    (time) depuis, il y a, pendant, pour; **(because)** car
forbid, to défendre (à, de+)
foreign étranger(-ere)
foresee, to prevoir*
forest la forêt
forget, to oublier (de+)
forgive, to (for) pardonner
former ancien; **the -** celui-là
formerly autrefois
fortunately heureusement
fortune la fortune
found, to fonder
fountain pen le stylo
free(ly) libre(ment)
freedom la liberté
friend un(e) ami(e), le(la) camarade
frighten, to effrayer;
    be (become) -ed s'effrayer
from de; dès le
front, in - of devant
full plein
fun la distraction, un amusement
fun, to make - of se moquer de;
    have - s'amuser (bien)
furious furieux

on the - par terre,
   on the first - au premier (U.S. second floor)
flower la fleur
fluently couramment

gaily gaiement
gait une allure
galop, break into a - prendre le galop
game le jeu; **a - of** une partie de, **(formal)** un match
gaping beant
garden le jardin
gathering le rassemblement
general le general
generous genereux
gentleman le monsieur
geography la géographie
German allemand
Germany l'Allemagne (f)
gesticulate, to gesticuler
get, to (become) devenir;*
   (obtain) obtenir; - + adj. or past part.: use
   refl. verb (*see under the adjective or verb*);
   -into monter dans; **-off** descendre de;
   -up se lever; **-along** s'en tirer
gift le cadeau
girl (daughter) la fille;
   (young person) la jeune fille
give, to donner; - **back** rendre; **-up** renoncer à
glad content
glass le verre

habit une habitude
hair (a) un cheveu; **hair** les cheveux;
   by a -'s breadth d'un cheveu
half la demie; **-way a** mi-chemin
hallway le vestibule
hand la main; **on the other** - d'autre part;
   second -d'occasion
handsome beau
handwriting une écriture
happen, to arriver, se passer
happy heureux
harbor le port
hard dur (adj. or adv.); difficile (adj.)
hardly à peine, ne...guère
hat le chapeau
have voir (a+); prendre; **- to** devoir,* falloir; faire*
head la tête; **the - ache** le mal de tête;

fur la fourrure
furniture les meubles; **a piece of** - un meuble
further davantage; **without** - sans autre
furthermore de plus

G

glove le gant
go, to aller;* **- away** s'en aller; **- back** retourner;
   - down descendre; **to be -ing on** se passer;
   - by passer, **(of time)** se passer;
   - forward s'avancer;
   - into entrer dans; **- home** rentrer;
   - the wrong way se tromper de chemin;
   - to get aller chercher; **- to bed** se coucher;
   - out s'avancer; sortir; **- up** monter
good bon(ne); **to do** - faire du bien à
gown, dressing - un peignoir
grandmother la grand-mère
grant, to accorder
great grand
green vert
greet, to saluer; **(welcome)** accueillir
grieve, to (someone) faire de la peine à
grocer un épicier
groom le groom
ground le sol; **on the** - par terre
grumble, to grommeler
guard le garde
guess, to deviner
guest un invité
gun le fusil

H

hold, to tenir*
holiday la fête, le jour de fête;
   summer - les grandes vacances
home la maison, un intérieur; chez;
   at - chez (soi); **go, come back** - rentrer
homework le(s) devoir(s) (m)
honest honnête
hope un espoir
hope (for), to espérer
horror une horreur
horse le cheval; **on - back** à cheval
horsemanship une équitation
hospitable hospitalier
hospital un hôpital
hot chaud; **to be (feel)** avoir chaud,
   (weather) faire chaud
hotel un hôtel

have a - ache, to avoir mal à la tête
health la santé
hear, to entendre; entendre dire, entendre parler;
  - from recevoir des nouvelles de
heart le cœur; **by -** par cœur
heat la chaleur
heat, to chauffer
heaven le ciel
heavy lourd
help, to aider (a+)
here ici; **- is** voici
hesitate, to hésiter
hesitation une hésitation
hide, to (se) cacher
high haut; **(price)** élevé
hill la colline, la côte
history l'histoire (f)
hit, to heurter, se heurter contre; **- (with)** frapper (de)

idea une idée
identical identique
ill malade
imagine, to s'imaginer
immediately immediatement,
   à l'instant, tout de suite;
   -after aussitôt après
impatience une impatience
impetuosity la fougue
impolite impoli
imprisonment un emprisonnement
improve, to améliorer
in dans, en, à
incident un incident
incredible incroyable
induce (someone) to, to décider quelqu'un à
inexpensive bon marché
inform (of), to informer (de),
   faire savoir, faire part (de), renseigner
information le renseignement
injury, internal la lésion interne

jewel le bijou
job la situation
joke la plaisanterie
joke, to plaisanter
joy la joie; **-ful** joyeux
judge, to juger

hour une heure
house la maison; **to (at) the -** of chez
household le ménage; (adj.) ménager(-ère)
how comment; **how...!** comme, que;
  - long combien de temps, depuis quand;
  - much many combien
however cependant, pourtant; **- + adj.** si...que
howl, to hurler
humiliate, to humilier
humor une humeur
hungry, to be avoir faim
hunter le chasseur
hunting la chasse; **to go -** aller a la chasse
hurry, to se dépêcher
hurry la hâte; **to be in a -** être pressé (de+)
hurt, to faire* mal (a), blesser;
  - the feelings of faire de la peine a
husband le mari

I

inquire, to about (someone)
   prendre des nouvelles de (quelqu'un)
inside en dedans; **- it, them** dedans
insist (on), to insister (sur + noun),
   (pour + inf.) (que, pour que + clause)
instead of au lieu de
intellectual intellectuel
intend, to avoir l'intention (de+)
interest, to intéresser; **to be -ed in** s'intéresser a
interesting intéressant
interrupt, to interrompre
interview une entrevue
intimidate, to intimider
into dans; **in(to) it** dedans
introduce, to présenter, introduire*
invade, to envahir
invader un envahisseur
invite, to inviter (a+)
irritate, to agacer, irriter
irritating agaçant, irritant
isle une île

J

July juillet (m)
jump (out of), to sauter (de)
jury le jury
just justement; **to have -** venir* de;
  - as au moment ou;
  -the same quand même

keep, to garder
key la clef
kind aimable, bon
kind la sorte
kitchen la cuisine
knee le(s) genou(x)

lack, to manquer de
land, to atterrir
language la langue
large grand; **(voluminous)** gros(se)
last dernier; **at** - enfin
late tard, en retard; **it is getting** - il se fait tard
latter, the - celui-ci
laugh, to rire*
laundry le blanchissage
lawyer un avocat
lead, to conduire
least, the le moindre (adj.);
- le moins (adv.); **at** - au moins
lecture (in class) le cours;
 (formal) la conference
left gauche
left, to have (something) rester
leg la jambe
lend, to prêter
less moins (de); - **and** - de moins en moins
lesson la leçon
let see, to imperative; **(allow)** laisser;
 - **into** faire entrer
letter la lettre
library la bibliothèque
lid le couvercle
lie le mensonge
lie (down), to se coucher
life la vie
lift, to soulever
light la lumière; (adj.) léger

magistrate police - le commissaire (de police)
maid la bonne
mainly principalement, surtout
make faire;* rendre, donner; gagner
man un homme
manage, to conduire; s'en tirer; - **to** arriver à
manner la manière;
 in such a - de manière que

K

knock, to down renverser
know, to savoir,* connaître*;
- **to let** - faire savoir;
- **all about** être au courant de
knowledge les connaissances (f);
 not to my - pas que je sache

L

light, to allumer
like, to aimer, plaire,* vouloir*
likely probable
limp, to boiter
line la ligne
liner le paquebot
listen (to), to écouter
literature la littérature
little petit (adj.); peu (adv.)
live, to vivre;* **(inhabit)** habiter, demeurer
living room le salon
load, to charger
loaf of bread un pain
lock, to fermer a clef; - **up** enfermer
London Londres
long long(ue), longtemps;
 how - ? depuis quand? combien de temps?
longer, no ne...plus, ne pas... plus longtemps
look la mine
look - **at, to** regarder; -**for** chercher;
 - **(seem)** avoir l'air (de+); - **well**
(badly) avoir bonne (mauvaise) **mine;**
 - **after** soigner; - **like** se ressembler
lose, to perdre
lot le sort; a- beaucoup
love un amour
love, to aimer
luck la chance
lucky, to be avoir de la chance
lunch le déjeuner; **to have** - déjeuner
luxury le luxe

M

mind l'esprit (m);
 change one's - changer d'avis;
 make up one's - se décider (a+)
minute la minute
misadventure la mésaventure
miss, to manquer
mistake la faute
mistaken, to be se tromper

manuscript le manuscrit
many beaucoup
map la carte
marble le marbre
marry, to marier, se marier, épouser
master le maître
matter, to be a - of s'agir de
mattress le matelas
may pouvoir*; **maybe** peut-être
May mai (m)
meal le repas
mean, to vouloir* dire
means le moyen; **(resources)** les moyens
medical médical
meet, to rencontrer,
   faire* la connaissance de, retrouver
meeting la réunion, la rencontre
member le membre
memory (mental faculty) la mémoire; le souvenir
mention, to mentionner
merely simplement
meter le mètre
middle le milieu
midnight minuit (m)
might see pouvoir
mighty puissant
mile le mille
milk le lait
milky lactée, **- Way** Voie lactée
mill moulin
   wind - moulin à vent

name le nom; **what is the - of** comment s'appelle
name, to **nommer**
narrow étroit
navy la marine
near près (de); **-ly** à peu près;
   the -est le plus proche
necessary nécessaire
need le besoin
need, to avoir besoin de; falloir*
needle une aiguille
needless inutile. superflu
negligence la négligence
neighbor le voisin
neighborhood le voisinage, le quartier
nephew le neveu
never jamais
nevertheless néanmoins

mistress la maîtresse
modern moderne
modify, to modifier
moment le moment, un instant;
   any - d'un instant à l'autre
money l'argent; la monnaie
month le mois
more plus (de), davantage
moreover de plus, en outre
morning le matin, la matinée;
   next - le lendemain matin
most (of) la plupart (de),
   la plus grande partie (de)
mother la mère, la maman
motorcycle la mortocyclette
mount la monture
mountain la montagne
moustache la moustache
move, to (intrans.) bouger; **(trans.)** remuer;
   (from one residence to another) déménager;
   -away s'éloigner; **-in** emmenager;
- forward s'avancer
mover le déménageur
moving le déménagement
movies le cinéma
much beaucoup
museum le musée
music la musique
must devoir,* falloir*
mysterious mystérieux
mystery mystère

N

new nouveau (nouvelle); neuf (neuve)
   news (one item) la nouvelle;
(several items) les nouvelles
newspaper le journal
next prochain; **- day** le lendemain
night la nuit; **last -** hier soir, la nuit dernière
nightmare le cauchemar
nobody personne, nul, aucun
noise le bruit; **noisy** bruyant
nosey curieux
note la note; **(short letter)** un billet
notice, to apercevoir,* s'apercevoir, remarquer
notify, to prevenir,* avertir
now maintenant
nowadays aujourd'hui, de nos jours, actuellement
nowhere nulle part
nul nulle, invalide, **- and void** nul et non avenu

obey, to obeir (a)
object un objet
occur (happen), to arriver
o'clock heure (f)
offer une offre
offer, to offrir* (de+)
office le bureau; **(doctor)** le cabinet;
   (lawyer) l'étude
officer un officier
often souvent
old vieux (vieil, vieille);
   to be ... years avoir ... ans
older, oldest ainé

pace une allure
package le paquet
pain la douleur
paint, to peindre;* **hand -ed** peint à la main
painter le peintre
painting la peinture, le tableau
pale pale; **to turn (become)** palir
panic-stricken affolé; **to get panicky** s'affoler
paper le papier; **(news) -** le journal
paradox le paradoxe
park le parc
particular(ly) particulier(-èrement)
passage le passage
passenger le voyageur, le passager
path le chemin
patience la patience
patient le malade; **(adj.) patient; -ly** avec patience
pay (for), to payer; **- attention** faire* attention;
- a visit faire (une) visite, rendre visite
peaceful paisible
peach la pêche
people les gens, le monde, les personnes;
   young - (youth) les jeunes gens
perfect(ly) parfait(ement)
performance la représentation
perhaps peut-être
period une époque; **during the -** à l'époque
permit permettre* (a, de+)
persist (in), to persister (a+)
person la personne
personally personnellement
pharmacist la pharmacien
pharmacy la pharmacie
phonograph le phonographe

O

on (upon) sur; **- it, them** dessus
once une fois; **(all) at -** à la fois
only ne ... que, seulement, seul
open ouvert
open, to ouvrir*
opinion un avis; **to have an -** être d'un avis
order un ordre
order, in - to afin de, pour
otherwise autrement
ought devoir*
overcoat le pardessus
owe, to devoir*
own propre

P

police la police
policeman un agent de police
   un agent **(for short)**
polite poli
poor pauvre; **-ly** pauvrement, mal
porter le porteur
position la position; **(job)** la situation
possessions le bien
post (assignment) le poste
post card la carte postale
post office la poste, le bureau de poste
postpone, to remettre,* ajourner
pound la livre
poverty la pauvreté
power la puissance
practical pratique
prance, to danser
predict, to prédire*
prefer, to aimer mieux, préférer
prepare, to préparer; **-to** se préparer a
present (adj.) présent; **to be - at** assister a
president le président
press la presse
pretend to, to faire* semblant (mine) de,
   affecter de
pretty joli
prevent, to empêcher (de+)
price le prix
priest le prêtre
prison la prison
prisoner le prisonnier
printed imprimé
probably probablement, sans doute
problem le problème

piano le piano
pick, to cueillir; **-up** ramasser
picture une image; **(painting)** le tableau
picturesque pittoresque
piece le morceau
pillow un oreiller
pitiful pitoyable
pity la pitie; **it is a** - c'est (grand) dommage;
   what a - ! quel dommage!
place la place; **(location)** un endroit;
   in your - à votre place;
   to take - avoir lieu
plan le plan
plane un avion; **by** - en avion, par avion
platform (railroad) le quai
play (theatrical) la pièce
please s'il vous plaît, je vous prie (de+)
please, to plaire, faire* plaisir
pleased content
pleasure le plaisir
pocket la poche
pocketbook le portefeuille
pole le poteau;
   telegraph - le poteau télégraphique

qualifications les qualités
quarrel, to se quereller
question la question; **to be a - of** s'agir de
question, to interroger

radio la radio
rain la pluie; **in the** - sous la pluie
rain, to pleuvoir*
raise une augmentation
raise, to soulever; **(bring up)** élever;
   (eyes, hand, etc.) lever
rank le rang
rascal le scélérat
rather plutôt, assez; **- than** plutôt que (de+)
reach, to atteindre*
read, to lire*
ready prêt (a+)
real(ly) vrai(ment)
realize, to se rendre compte de
reason la raison; **- able** raisonnable
recall, to (se) rappeler, se souvenir* de
receive, to recevoir;* **(welcome)** accueillir
recognize, to reconnaître*

proceed, to avancer
professional professionnel
professor le professeur
promise, to promettre* (a, de+)
propose, to proposer (de+)
proposal la proposition
protest, to protester
Protestant protestant
proud fier
prove, to prouver
provided that pourvu que
province la province; **in the -s** en province
publisher un éditeur
punish, to punir
punishment la punition
purchase un achat
purpose le but; **on** - exprès
purse le porte-monnaie
pursue, to poursuivre*
push, to pousser
put, to mettre;* **- down** poser;
   - back remettre; **- on** mettre;
   - away mettre de côté
puzzle l'énigme, le mystère

Q

quick rapide; **-ly** vite, rapidement
quiet tranquille; **to keep** - se taire*
quiet, to - down (se) calmer
quite tout; **- (emphatic)** tout à fait

R

repeat, to répéter
replace, to remplacer
reply, to répondre (a)
report le rapport
republic la république
request, to demander (a, de+)
require, to exiger, falloir
requirement une exigence
resignation la résignation;
   (from job) la démission
response la réponse
responsibility la responsabilité
responsible responsable
rest le repos; **(remainder)** le reste
rest, to se reposer
restaurant le restaurant
result le résultat
resume, to reprendre

recommend, to recommander (de+)
record (phonograph) le disque
recount, to raconter
recover (from), to se remettre* (de);
   (roof) recouvrir; **- from illness** se rétablir
red rouge
reference la référence
refreshments les raffraîchissements (m)
refrigerator la glacière
refuse, to refuser (de+)
regret, to regretter (de+)
reign la règne
relate, to raconter
relatively relativement
relief le soulagement
relieve, to soulager
remain, to rester
remedy le remède
remember, to se souvenir* de, se rappeler
remind, to rappeler (de+)
remove, to enlever, retirer
rent, to louer
repair, to réparer
repeal, to!abroger, annuler

sad(ly) triste(ment)
saddle la selle; **to get into the** - se mettre en selle
safe le coffre-fort; (adj.) en sureté;
   - from a l'abri de
salary les appointements (m)
same même; **it's all the - to me** cela m'est égal
satellite le satellite
satisfy, to satisfaire;*
   to be -ed with se contenter de
say, to dire*
scare, to faire* peur (à)
scarcely à peine, ne ... guère
scatter, to éparpiller
scene la scène
sceptical sceptique
school une école; **riding** - le manège
scissors les ciseaux
scold, to gronder
seamstress la couturière
search la recherche; **house** - visite domiciliaire
search, to fouiller
sea sickness le mal de mer;
   to be sea sick avoir le mal de mer
seat la place

return, to revenir,* retourner, rentrer, rendre
reunite, to (se) reunir
revolution la révolution; **-ary** revolutionnaire
Rhine le Rhin
rich riche
rid, get - of, to se débarrasser de
ride, to monter (a), aller*
rider le cavalier
right droit; juste; **to be -** avoir raison (de+);
   - away out de suite; **all -** très bien, bon
ring, to give a - donner un coup de téléphone
rock le rocher
roof le toit
room la pièce, la chambre, la salle;
   -mate le (la) camarade de chambre
rose la rose
royalist le (la) royaliste
rubber (bridge) la partie
rudeness la grossierete
rug le tapis
rule la règle; **slide** - la règle a calcul
run, to courir;* **- away** se sauver
   (escape) s'échapper;
- over écraser; **-away (horse)** emballé

S

slumped affaisée
small petit
smoke, to fumer
so (adv.) si, aussi; (conj.= thus) ainsi;
   that de sorte que
sofa la canapé
soldier le soldat
some (adj.) quelques; (pron.) quelque-uns
somebody quelqu'un
someone quelqu'un
something quelque chose
sometimes quelquefois, parfois
somewhere quelque part
son le fils
song la chanson
soon bientôt; **-er** plus tôt;
   as - aussitôt que, dès que
sorry, to be regretter (de +)
sort la sorte
sort, to trier
South America l'Amerique (f.) du Sud
speak, to parler; **-to (address)** s'adresser a
special special
spectacle le spectacle

secret le secret; (adj.) secret(-ète)
secretary le (la) secrétaire
see, to voir;* **- again** revoir;*
 - to it that veiller a ce que
to seem sembler
seldom rarement
sell, to vendre
semester le semestre
send, to envoyer; **to - for** envoyer chercher
sensible sense, raisonnable
sensitive sensible
serious (lit.) sérieux; (fig.) grave;
 -ly sérieusement, gravement;
 -ly wounded grièvement blessé;
 -ly ill gravement malade
servant le(la) domestique; la servante
serve, to servir; *- as servir de
service le service
settle (down), to s'installer
several plusieurs
shake hands(se), to serrer la main
shaken, quite - tout tremblant
sham, to simuler
shave, to raser
shelf le rayon
shelter un abri; **to take -** se refuger
ship le bateau; (navy) le vaisseau
shirt la chemise
shiver, to grelotter
shop, to faire des achats
short court
should devoir
shout, to crier
show, to montrer, faire voir;
 (evince) témoigner
shriek le cri
shriek, to pousser des cris
shut, to fermer
sick malade
side le côté
sigh, to soupirer
sign le signe
sign, to signer
signal le signal
silk la soie
simple simple, elementaire;
 simply simplement
since (prep.) depuis; (conj.) puisque
single seul
sink, to (ship) couler

speculation la spéculation
speech le discours
speed la vitesse
spelling l'orthographe (f.)
spend, to dépenser, passer
spite in - of malgré; **in - of all** quand même
sport le sport
spread, to éparpiller
square (le) carré; la place
stable une écurie
stairs (stairway) un escalier
stamp (postage) le timbre (-poste)
stand, to être debout, se tenir debout;
 - up se lever, se mettre debout
start, to commencer (a +);
 (to set about) se mettre à
state un état
station (RR) la gare
stay, to rester,
 - at someone's house demeurer chez
steal, to voler
still (adv.) encore, toujours (emphatic)
stirrup un étrier
store le magasin;
 department - le grand magasin
storm un orage, la tempête
story une histoire; **short -** le conte
straight directment; droit
strange étrange
stranger un étranger, un inconnu
street la rue
strike la grève; **on -** en grève
student (college) un(e) étudiant(e);
 school un(e) élève
study une étude; le bureau
study, to étudier
stunned étourdi
stupid stupide, sot
style le style
succeed (in), to réussir (à, à +)
such si, tel
sudden soudain;
 all of a - tout à coup; **-ly** soudain
suggest, to suggérer (a, de +)
suit, to convenir à
suitcase la valise
summer un été
sing, to chanter
suppose, to supposer
sure sur, **to make -** s'assurer

sister la sœur
skate le patin
skid (of a car), to déraper
sleep, to dormir; **go to -** s'endormir
sleepy, to be - avoir sommeil
slipper la pantoufle
slow(ly) lent(ment) **to be (timepiece)** retarder
slow, to down ralentir
slumber le sommeil

table la table; **- cloth** la nappe
tact le tact
tail la queue
take, to mener, porter, prendre; falloir
- (away) emporter;
- out sortir
- off enlever
talent le talent
talk, to (about) causer (de);
 stop - ing se taire
tall grand
taste le goût
taxi le taxi
tea le thé; **- spoon** la cuillère à thé
teach, to apprendre, enseigner
teacher le maître, la maîtresse, le professeur
teaching l'enseignement (m)
tear la larme
tear, to déchirer; **- off** arracher
tease, to taquiner
telegram le télégramme, la dépêche
telephone le téléphone
telephone, to téléphoner
telescope le téléscope
tell, to dire, raconter
temper le caractère
tenant le locataire
tennis le tennis
terrace la terrasse
terrify, to terrifier
terror la terreur
text le texte
thank (for), to remercier (de);
 - you merci, je vous remercie
thanks les remerciements; **- to** grace a
theater le théâtre
then (so, at that time) alors; **(next)** puis
there, -is il y a, voilà
thick épais(se)

surprise la surprise, un étonnement
surprise, to surprendre, étonner
suspect un suspect
suspect, to se douter de
suspicious soupconneux
swarm, to with fourmiller de
swim, to nager; **swimming** la nage;
 to go swimming - se baigner
sympathy la compasssion

T

throw, to (away) jeter
Thursday jeudi (m)
thus ainsi
ticket le billet
tie (neck-) la cravate
tight serré
time l'heure, le temps, la fois,
in - a l'heure; **from -to-** de temps en temps;
 on - a temps; **a long -** longtemps
timid(ly) timide(ment)
tip le bout
tire (auto) le pneu
tired fatigue, las(se)
to (toward) vers
today aujourd'hui
together ensemble
tomorrow demain
tonight ce soir, cette nuit
too trop
tooth la dent
touch, to toucher
toward vers
towel la serviette (de toilette)
town la ville; **down -** en ville
toy le jouet
traffic la circulation
train le train; **by -** par le train
translate, to traduire
translation la traduction
trash les ordures;
 (a piece of) une saleté (colloquial)
travel le voyage
travel, to voyager; **take a -** être en voyage
tree un arbre
tremble, to trembler
trip le voyage; **take a -** faire un voyage
tropics les tropiques
trot le trot
trouble la difficulté, un ennui

thief le voleur
thin maigre
thing la chose
think, to penser, croire, reflechir trouver, songer
thirst la soif; **to be -y** avoir soif
though, as - comme si
thread le fil
threat la menace
thrifty économe
through à travers

ugly laid; (emphatic) affreux
ultimately finalment, à la fin, par la suite
umbrella le parapluie
unable to be - to ne pas pouvoir
under sous
understand, to comprendre
undress, to (se) déshabiller
unfortunate infortune, malheureux
unhurt indemne
uniform un uniforme

vacation les vacances (f)
vague(ly) vague(ment)
vain vain; **in -** en vain, avoir beau
vase le vase
veil le voile
very très
vestibule le vestibule
victim la victime

wages les gages (**servants**)
wait (for), to attendre
wake (up), to (se) réveiller
walk la promenade;
   to take a- faire une promenade;
   to go for a- aller se promener,
   aller faire une promenade
walk, to marcher, aller a pied
want, to vouloir
war la guerre
warm chaud; **to be (feel)-** avoir chaud,
  (weather) faire chaud
wash, to laver
watch, to regarder
water l'eau (f)
way le chemin; la manière, la façon;
  on the - back au retour

truck le camion
trunk la malle
truth la verité
try, to essayer (de +), s'efforcer (de +);
  - on essayer
turn, to tourner
tutor le precepteur
twice deux fois
type, to taper
typewriter la machine à écrire

U

university une université
unknown inconnu
unless à moins que or de +
until jusqu'à
unwise peu sage
upset ému, contrarié
use, to se servir de; **be - d for** servir à;
  be of no - ne servir à rien,
  be -d to être habitué, accoutumé à
utensil un ustensile

V

view la vue
village le village
violent voilent; (of pain) vif, vive
violin le violin
visit la visite
visit, to (a place) visiter;
  (**a person**) aller voir, rendre visite
voice la voix

W

whole, the tout(e) le (la)
why pourquoi; ... mais...
wife la femme
wild sauvage
will vouloir
willing, to be - vouloir bien
window la fenêtre; **shop** - la vitrine
wine le vin
winter un hiver
wipe essuyer
wire la depêche
wish, to vouloir, desirer, souhaiter
without (prep.) sans; (conj.) sans que
woman la femme
wonder, to se demander
wonderful merveilleux, étonnant
word le mot

to get under - se mettre en route
weak faible
wear (clothes), to porter
weather le temps
week la semaine a - from... de ... en huit;
    week-end la fin de la semaine or le week- end
well bien; to be- aller bien;
    well-known bien connu; Well! Eh bien!
whatever quelconque, n'importe quel, tout ce que
when quand, lorsque
whenever toutes les fois que
where où
whereas tandis que
whether si
while (conj.) pendant que, tandis que, (prep.) en;
    once in a- de temps en temps
whimper, to geindre
white blanc, blanche
whoever quiconque, qui que

year un an, une année
yellow jaune

work le travail; (literary, artistic) une œuvre;
    (handwork) ouvrage
work, to travailler
world le monde
worn used
worried inquiet, inquiète
worry, to (s')inquiéter
worse, worst pire,
    plus mauvais (adv.) plus mal, pis
worth, to be - valoir,
    to be - while valoir la peine
wound, to blesser
wrap, to envelopper
wretched pitoyable, triste
write, to écrire
writer un écrivain
writing une écriture
wrong, to be - avoir tort;
    take the - way se tromper de chemin

Y

yet, not ... - ne ... pas encore
young jeune

VOCABULAIRE FRANÇAIS-ANGLAIS

abaisser to lower
abat-jour (m) lampshade
abattreto knock down, pull down
abbaye (f) abbey, monastery
abeille (f) bee
abîme (f) abyss, chasm
abonner s'abonnerto subscribe
aborderto land, approach, accost
aboyerto bark
abri (m) shelter
abriterto shelter, protect
abuserto deceive; misuse, take advantage of
accablerto overwhelm
accrocherto hang up, hook
accueillirto receive, greet, welcome
acharné eager, stubborn, desperate
achat (m) purchase
acheverto complete, finish, conclude
acier (m) steel
actualités (f pl) current events, newsreel
actuel present, current
actuellement now, at the present time
adresse (f) address, skill
adversaire (f) opponent, rival
affaiblirto weaken, lessen
affamé starving, hungry, famished
affectueux affectionate
affiche (f) poster, bill
afficherto post, display
affligerto afflict, distress
affreux dreadful, frightful, horrible
agacerto annoy, irritate
agenouiller s'agenouillerto kneel (down)
agité restless, excited, troubled
agiterto wave, shake, disturb
agneau (m) lamb
aieul (m) ancestor (pl.= aieux)
aigle (m) eagle
aiguille (f) needle, hand (of watch or clock)
ail (m) garlic
aile (f) wing
ailleurs elsewhere; **d'ailleurs** besides, moreover
aimant (m) magnet
aîné elder, eldest
aise (f) ease, **comfort**

A

angoisse (f) anguish, distress, anxiety
anneau (m) ring
année, année bissextile leap year
annuaire (m) directory
annuaire du téléphone telephone
apaiserto appease, calm
apercevoirto see, perceive, notice
apogée (m) height, climax
appareil (m) apparatus, appliance, set
appuyer, s'appuyerto lean, rest
araignée (f) spider
arbitre (m) umpire, referee
arc-en-ciel (m) rainbow
ardoise (f) slate
argent (m), argent comptant cash
argile (f) clay
argot (m) slang
armoire (f) closet, wardrobe
arracherto pull out, snatch (away), uproot
arrêt (m) stop, stopping
abat-jour (m) lampshade
arroserto water, sprinkle
artichaut (m) artichoke
as (m) ace
asile (m) refuge, asylum, retreat
asperge (f) asparagus
aspirateur (m) vacuum cleaner
assistant (m) bystander
astre (m) star, heavenly body
atelier (m) studio, workshop
atteindre to reach, attain
atterrirto land
attirerto attract, lure
attrait (m) attraction
attraperto catch, trap
aube (f) dawn
auberge (f) inn
audace (f) daring, boldness
auditoire (m) audience
augmenterto increase
aumône (f) charity, alms
auparavant before, beforehand, previously
auprès (de) near, close (to)
aussitôt immediately, at once
autel (m) altar

aliment (m) food
allure (f) walk, gate, pace, speed, aspect
alouette (f) lark
alpinisme (m) mountain climbing
âme (f) soul
améliorerto improve
amer bitter
amertume (f) bitterness
ameublement (m) furniture
amoureux in love, loving
ampoule (f) bulb (light)
ananas (m) pineapple
âne (m) donkey, ass
ange (m) angel

bac (m) ferry
bague (f) ring
baignoire (f) bathtub
baillerto yawn
baisserto lower
balai (m) broom
balayerto **sweep**
balbutierto stammer
banlieue (f) suburbs, outskirts
baraque (f) hut, shanty
barrage (m) dam
basse-cour (f) farmyard, barnyard
bavard talkative, loquacious
bavarderto chat, chatter, gossip
bénirto bless
béquille (f) crutch
bercerto rock, lull
berger (m) shepherd
besogne (f) work, toil, task, job
bêtise (f) stupidity, foolishness, nonsense
béton (m) concrete
betterave (f) beet
biens (m, pl) goods, possessions, belongings
bienvenue (f) welcome
bière (f) beer
bifteck (m) beefsteak
bis twice, encore
bizarre strange, odd, peculiar
blague (f) humbug; joke
blé (m) wheat
blessure (f) wound
boisson (f) beverage, drink
boîte (f) box, can; **boîte de nuit** nightclub;
  boîte à musique jukebox

autoroute (f) superhighway, expressway
auto-stop (m) hitchhiking
autrement otherwise
autrui others, other people
avalerto swallow
avant-garde (f) vanguard
avare (m) miser
avènement (m) advent, coming
avenir (m) future
averse (f) shower, downpour
avertirto warn, notify
aveu (m) confession
aveugle blind
avouerto admit, confess

B

bonhomme (m) simple man,
  good soul, old fellow
bornerto limit, restrict, bound
botte (f) boot, bunch (of vegetables)
boucherto cork, stop up, obstruct
bouchon (m) cork
boucle (f) buckle, bow, curl
boucle d'oreille earring
boue (f) mud
bouffon comical, farcical
bougerto move,s stir, budge
bouillirto boil
bouleverserto upset, overthrow
bourdonnerto buzz
bourg (m) small town
bourreau (m) executioner
bourse (f) purse, scholarship
Bourse (f) Stock Exchange
bousculerto shove, jostle, upset
bouton (m) button,
  bud, pimple, door knob
boutonnerto button, bud
brasserie (f) beerhouse, restaurant
brebis (f) ewe, sheep
bref (adv) in short, in a word
brevet (m) patent
brique (f) brick
brise (f) breeze
briserto break
bronzé suntanned
brouillard (m) fog, mist
brouille on bad terms, **-e** scrambled
brume (f) thick fog, haze, mist
bruyant noisy

boiteux lame
bond (m) jump, leap
bondé crammed, overcrowded

cacahuete (f) peanut
cache-nez (m) muffler
cachet (m) cachet d'aspirine aspirin tablet
cadavre (m) corpse
cadet younger, youngest
cadran (m) dial
cadre (m) frame
caillou (m) pebble
caisse (f) case, chest, cashier's desk;
    caisse d'épargne savings bank
calendrier (m) calendar
camion (m) truck
canard (m) duck, drake
canot (m) small boat
cantique (m) hymm
caoutchouc (m) rubber
caporal (m) corporal
carafe (f) decanter
carnet (m) notebook, book
carré square
carrefour (m) crossroads, intersection
carton (m) cardboard
caserne (f) barracks
casquette (f) peaked cap
casserole (f) saucepan, pan
cauchemar (m) nightmare
céder to yield, give up
ceinture (f) belt, waist
célibataire single, ummarried
cendre (f) ash
cendrier (m) ashtray
censé supposed
cerise (f) cherry
cerveau (m) brain, mind, intellect
cervelle (f) brain(s) (as matter)
chair (f) flesh
chaleur (f) heat, warmth
chameau (m) camel
champignon (m) mushroom
chandail (m) sweater
chandelle (f) candle
charbon (m) coal
charcuterie (f) pork butcher's shop, delicatessen
charrue (f) plough
chasse (f) hunting, hunt

buisson (m) bush
but (m) goal, aim, purpose
buvard (m) blotter

C

coller to glue, paste, stick
collier (m) necklace; collar
comble (m) height, acme, summit
combustible (m) fuel
comédien (m) actor
comestible edible
commandant (m) commander, major
commerçant (m) merchant, dealer tradesman
commode convenient, suitable
compris, y compris including
compter to count, **to rely,** compter sur **to count on**
concitoyen (m) fellow citizen
concours (m) competition; contest
confection (f) ready-made clothing
conférencier (m) lecturer
confiance (f) confidence, trust
confidence (f) secret
confiture (f) jam
confondre to confuse, mistake
congédier to dismiss, discharge
connaissance (f) acquaintance;
    knowledge; consciousness
conquérir to conquer, win (over)
conseiller (m) adviser
consommation (f) consumption; drink
constater to ascertain, find out; state
contenu (m) contents
contrainte (f) constraint; restraint
convaincre to convince
convenir to suit, fit
copain (m) pal, buddy
coquille (f) shell
corail (m) coral
corbeille (f) basket
corne (f) horn
cornet (f) cone
cornichon (m) gherkin, pickle
corsage (m) waist, blouse
côte (f) coast, shore; rib
coucher (m), coucher du soleil sunset
coude (m) elbow
coudre to sew
couler to flow, run, slip by
coup (m) blow; **coup de coude** nudge;
coup de couteau stabbing;

chasseur (m) hunter; hotel porter
chatouiller to tickle
chauffage (m) heating
chaussée (f) road, middle of the street
chausette (f) sock
chauve bald
chef-lieu (m) chief town (of a department)
cheminée (f) fireplace; chimney smokestack
chêne (m) oak
chevaleresque chivalrous
chevelure (f) (head of) hair
cheville (f) ankle
chèvre (f) goat
chiffon (m) rag
chiffre (m) figure, number
chimie (f) chemistry
chirurgien (m) surgeon
choeur (m) chorus, choir
choix (m) choice, selection
chomage (m) umemployment
chou (m) cabbage
choucroute (f) sauerkraut
chou-fleur (m) cauliflower
chuchoter to whisper
chute (f) fall
cigogne (f) stork
cil (m) eyelash
cîme (f) top, summit
cimetière (m) cemetery
circulation (f) circulation; traffic
cire (f) wax
cirer to wax, polish
ciseaux (m pl) scissors
citoyen (m) citizen
citron (m) lemon
claquer to slam, bang, snap, click
cligner, cligner de l'oeil to wink
climatisé air-conditioned
clocher (m) belfry, steeple
clou (m) nail
cœur (m) heart
coiffeur (m) hairdresser
coiffure (f) hairdo, headdress
coin (m) corner
coincer to jam
col (m) collar, pass (in mountains)
colère (f) anger
collage (m) sticking, gluing
collant (m) body stocking, leotard
collègue (m) colleague

coup d'épée sword thrust;
coup d'état overthrow of government;
coup de feu gunshot;
coup de grace decisive blow, finishing stroke;
coup de main helping hand; coup d'oeil glance;
coup de pied kick; coup de poing punch;
coup de soleil sunburn; coup de sonnette ring;
coup de téléphone telephone call;
coup de tonnerre peal of thunder;
coup de vent gust
courant (m) current;
courant d'air draft of air/wind
courbe (f) curve
couronner to crown
courrier (m) mail
cours (m) course; cours d'eau river, stream
course (f) race; errand
coussin (m) cushion
couture (f) sewing
couvent (m) convent
couvert cloudy, overcast
couvert (m) cover; place setting
couverture (f) cover; blanket
cracher to spit
craquer to creak, squeak, crackle
créer to create
crêpe (f) pancake
crépuscule (m) twilight
creuser to hollow (out), dig (out)
creux hollow, empty
crever to burst, split
crevette (f) shrimp
cric (m) jack (for lifting)
crise (f) crisis; crise de nerfs attack of nerves
croître to grow, increase
cru raw
cruche (f) pitcher
cueillir to gather, pick
cuiller (f) spoon
cuir (m) leather
cuire to cook
cuisinière (f) cook; stove
cuisse (f) thigh
cuisson (f) cooking
cuivre (m) copper
culotte (f) panties, knickers
culte (m) creed, cult, worship
cure (f) treatment, cure; presbytery
curé (m) parish priest
cygne (m) swan

dactylo(graphe) (m & f) typist
dames (f pl) checkers
davantage more
dé (m) thimble; die
débarquerto land
déborderto overflow
début (m) beginning
décernerto award, bestow
déçu disappointed
dedans inside, within
défaireto undo
défaut (m) defect, failing, fault
défilé (m) parade, procession
dégouterto disgust
dégusterto taste
dehors outside
déménagerto move (out)
dentifrice (m) tooth paste, tooth powder
dépense (f) expense
déraperto skid
déroberto steal, rob;
    se déroberto escape, slip away
dès from, since, as early as
désespéré hopeless, desperate
désespoir (m) despair
désolé grieved, distressed
désormais henceforth, from now on
dessein (m) scheme, plan, purpose
dessin (m) drawing, sketch, design
destin (m) destiny, fate
destinée (f) destiny, fate
détroit (m) strait
détruireto destroy, demolish

eau-de-vie (f) brandy
éblouirto dazzle
ébranlerto shake
écarterto set aside, move apart
échantillon (m) sample
échecs (m pl) chess
échelle (f) ladder; scale
échine (f) spine
éclair (m) flash of lightning
éclaircirto clear up, clarify
éclairerto light, illuminate; enlighten
éclat (m) glare, lustre; glamor; burst
éclaterto burst, explode
écorce (f) bark; rind

D

dette (f) debt
deuil (m) mourning
devanture (f) store window
devinerto guess
devise (f) motto
dévoué devoted
diamant (m) diamond
digérerto digest
digne worthy, deserving
digue (f) dike
diminuerto reduce, decrease diminish
dirigerto direct, manage
discours (m) speech, talk
disque record
distrait absentminded
divertirto amuse, entertain
dompterto tame, subdue
don (m) gift, talent
doré gilded
dos (m) back
dossier (m) back (of seat); file
dot (f) dowry
douane (f) customs (on imports)
doublerto pass (a vehicle on the road);
    to line (clothing)
doublure (f) lining
douche (f) shower (bath)
doué gifted, endowed
douleur (f) pain, grief
drap (m) cloth; sheet
drapeau (m) flag
dresserto set up, raise; train;
    se dresserto stand up, rise

E

entrainerto drag along, carry away;
    involve; train
entreprendreto undertake
entrevoirto catch sight of
    catch a glimpse of
entrevue (f) interview
envahirto invade
envelopperto wrap
épargnerto spare, save
épatant terrific
épée (f) sword
épice (f) spice
épinards (m pl) spinach
épine (f) thorn

écran (m) screen
écraserto crush, run over
écrevisse (f) crayfish
écriteau (m) sign, notice
écriture (f) writing
écume (f) foam, froth, lather
écureuil (m) squirrel
écurie (f) stable
édredon (m) quilt
effets (m pl) belongings
effleurerto touch lightly, graze
efforcer, s'efforcerto strive, exert oneself
effrayerto frighten, scare
effroyable dreadful, frightful
égard (m) respect, consideration, regard
égarer, s'egarerto lose one's way
égoût (m) sewer
élan (m) impetus, dash
élireto elect
éloge (m) praise
éloigné distant, remote, far
émail (m) enamel
emballerto pack, wrap
embonpoint (m) stoutness
embouchure (f) mouth; mouthpiece
émission (f) broadcasting
emmenerto take along, take away
emparer, s'emparer deto take hold of, take possession of, seize
empêcherto prevent
emporterto take away, carry off
ému moved touched
encadrerto frame
endroit (m) place, spot
enfer (m) hell
enfermerto close in, confine, lock up
enflerto sell, puff up
enfoncerto drive, thrust in
énoncerto state, express
enseigne (f) sign
enseignement (m) teaching
ensemble together
entendreto hear
entente (f) harmony, understanding
enterrerto bury
entêté headstrong, stubborn
entier -ière whole, full
entourerto surround
entracte interval, interlude, intermission

épingle (f) pin
éponge (f) sponge
époque (f) period, time, epoch, era
épouse (f) wife
épouvantable dreadful, frightful, awful
époux (m) husband
épreuve (f) test, trial
éprouverto test, try; feel; experience
épuiserto exhaust
épurerto purify
équipe (f) team
érable (m) maple
ère (f) era
escargot (m) snail
esclave (m & f) slave
escrime (f) fencing
espace (m) space; interval
éleverto raise, bring up
esprit (m) spirit, mind, wit
esquisse (f) sketch, outline
essence (f) gasoline
estomac (m) stomach
étang (m) pond, pool
étendreto spread, stretch (out)
étendue (f) expanse
éternuerto sneeze
étincelerto sparkle, glitter
étiquette (f) label, tag
étoffe (f) cloth, material
étoufferto choke, stifle, suffocate
étourdi scatterbrained; stunned, dazed
être (m) being, creature
étrennes (f pl) New Year's presents
évanouir, s'evanouirto vanish; faint
éventail (m) fan
évêque (m) bishop
exalterto glorify, extol
exemplaire (m) copy
exigerto demand, exact, require
exotisme (m) exoticism
expédierto send, dispatch
experience (f) experience; experiment
expirant, -e dying
expliquerto explain
exposerto display, exhibit, show
exprès on purpose, deliberately
exprimerto express
extase ecstasy, rapture
extensible stretch, expanding

fabricant (m) manufacturer
fabrication (f) manufacturing
fabriquerto manufacture
fâcheux troublesome, annoying, trying
facture (f) bill (of sale)
fade tasteless, insipid
faience (f) pottery, crockery
faillir (+ inf)to come near, almost (do something)
fainéant (m) idler, slacker, lazybones
faisan (m) pheasant
falaise (f) cliff
fanerto wilt, wither
fantôme (m) phantom, ghost
farcirto stuff
farine (f) flour
farouche wild, fierce
fée (f) fairy
feindreto pretend
fendreto split, cleave
feodal feudal
fermeture (f) closing; **fermeture éclair** zipper
feu (m) fire; **feu rouge,** red light;
   feu d'artifice fireworks
feutre (m) felt
fiançailles (f pl) engagement
ficelle (f) string, twine
fiche (f) slip (of paper), index card
fierté (f) pride
fièvre (f) fever
figue (f) fig
fil (m) thread; wire
filerto spin; run away, take off
filet (m) net; rack (for baggage)
fils (m) son
fixerto fasten, make firm
flacon (m) flask, bottle
flan (m) custard
flânerto stroll, saunter
fléau (m) plague, scourge
flèche (f) arrow; spire
fléchirto bend
flétrirto wither, fade
fleur (f) flower
fleuve (m) river
flic (m) policeman
flocon (m) flake
floraison (f) flowering, blossoming

F

flot (m) wave
flotte (m) fleet
foi (m) wave
foie (m) liver
foin (m) hay
foire (f) fair (carnival)
foncé dark
fondre dark
forgeron (m) blacksmith
formidable terrific, tremendous
fossé (m) ditch
fossette (f) dimple
foudre (f) thunderbolt, lightning
fouet (m) whip
fouillerto search; dig
foule (f) crowd
four (m) oven
fourmi (f) ant
fourneau (m) stove; furnace
fournirto furnish, supply
fourrure (f) fur
fraise (f) strawberry
framboise (f) raspberry
franchirto clear,
   jump over, cross, surmount
frein (m) brake
frêle frail, weak
frémirto tremble, shake
fréquenterto frequent,
   associate with, visit, haunt
friandises (f pl) sweets
frireto fry
frôlerto touch lightly
froncerto wrinkle;
   froncer les sourcilsto frown
front (m) forehead
frotterto rub
fuirto flee, run away, escape
fuite (f) flight
fumerto smoke
fumier (m) dung, manure
funèbre funereal, dismal, gloomy
funérailles (f, pl) funeral, obseques
funeste disastrous, grievous
fureur (f) fury, rage
fusée (f) rocket
fusil (m) gun, rifle

gagerto bet, wager
gages (m pl) wages
gamin (m) "kid," urchin
gamme (f) scale; range
gare beware
garerto park, put into the garage
gargouille (f) gargoyle
garnirto furnish, stock
gaspillerto waste
gâterto spoil
gazon (m) lawn
géant (m) giant
gelerto **freeze**
gémirto moan, groan
gendre (m) son-in-law
gênerto hinder, be in the way, annoy, bother
génie (m) genius; engineering
genre (m) kind, sort; style; gender
gentilhomme (m) nobleman
gibier (m) game (wild animals)
gilet (m) vest
glisserto slip, slide
gomme (f) eraser
gonflerto inflate, blow up, swell
gorge (f) throat; gorge
gosse (m & f) "kid," youngster

habile skillful, able, clever
+hache (f) axe
+hacherto chop, mince
+haine (f) hate, hatred
+hairto hate
haleine (f) breath
+halle (f) (covered) market
+hardi bold, daring
+haricot (m) bean; **haricot vert,** string bean
+hasard (m) chance, risk, luck
+hâte (f) haste, hurry
+hausserto raise, lift up;
   +hausser les épaulesto shrug one's shoulders
+hautain haughty, proud
+haut-parleur (m) loud speaker
hebdomadaire weekly
hélas alas
hélice (f) propellor
hériterto inherit
héritier (m) heir
heure (f), heure d'été daylight saving time

G

goudron (m) tar
gourmand greedy; fond of good food
goût (m) taste
goûterto taste, relish, enjoy
goutte (f) drop
grange (f) barn
grappe (f) cluster, bunch
gratte-ciel (m) skyscraper
gratterto scrape, scratch
gratuit free
gravirto climb
grêlerto hail
grenier (m) attic, garret
grenouille (f) frog
grève (f) strike; beach
gréviste (m & f) striker
griffe (f) claw; talon
grimperto climb
grossier coarse, vulgar, rude
guéridon (m) small round table
guérison (f) recovery, cure
guerrier (m) warrior
gueule (f) mouth (of animal)
gui (m) mistletoe
guichet box office, ticket window
guillemet (m) quotation mark

H (+ indicates aspirate h)

+heurterto knock against, bump into
+hibou (m) owl
+hisserto pull, hoist
+hocherto shake, toss, nod
+homard (m) lobster
+honte (f) shame, disgrace
+honteux ashamed, shameful
+hoquet (m) hiccup
horaire (m) timetable
horloger (m) watchmaker, clockmaster
+hors de out(side) of
hôte (m) host; guest
hotel (m) hotel de ville town hall
+houille (f) coal
+houle (f) swell, surge
huile (f) oil
hui, a huis clos behind closed doors
huître (f) oyster
humeur (f) mood, temper
humour (m) humor
+hurlerto howl, yell

ignorer notto know, be unaware of
immeuble (m) building, apartment house
impératrice (f) empress
impitoyable pitiless
importerto matter
importunerto bother, pester **impot (m),** tax
imprévu unforeseen, unexpected
imprimerie (f) printing; printing house
incendie (m) fire
inconvenient (m) disadvantage, inconvenience
incroyable unbelievable, incredible
indigène native
individu (m) individual, fellow, person
infirmière (f) nurse

jadis formerly, of old
jalousie (f) jealousy; Venetian blind
jaloux jealous, envious
jambon (m) ham
jeterto throw, fling, hurl
jeu (m) game; **plaz; jeu de mots** pun;
   vieux jeu "old hat"
joindreto join, connect
joue (f) check

kiosque (m) stand, newspaper stand

labourerto plough
lacet (m) shoelace; hairpin curve
lâche (m) coward
lâcherto loosen, release
là-dessus thereupon
laiterie (f) dairy
laitue (f) lettuce
lame (f) blade; wave
lancerto throw, hurl, toss; launch
lapin (m) rabbit
lard (m) bacon
larme (f) tear
las, lasse tired, weary
lasserto tire, exhaust
laurier (m) laurel
lavabo (m) wash basin
lécherto lick
lévier (m) lever
libraire (m) bookseller

I

infligerto inflict, impose
ingénieur (m) engineer
injure (f) insult
innombrable countless, innumerable
inouï unheard of, extraordinary
inquiéterto worry, disturb
interdireto forbid, prohibit
intitulé entitled
intrigue (f) plot
introduireto admit, insert; usher in
invraisemblable unlikely, improbable
ivre drunk, intoxicated
ivresse (f) drunkenness, intoxication
ivrogne (m) drunkard

J

jouet (m) toy
joujou (m) toy
journalier daily
journaliste (m & f) reporter
jumeau (m) twin
jumelle (f) twin
jumelles (f pl) binoculars
jupe (f) skirt
jus (m) juice

K

kyste (m) cyst

L

lime (m) file
linge (m) linen
lisible legible
littoral (m) coastline
livrerto deliver, hand over;
   se livrer àto devote oneselfto
locataire (m & f) tenant
location (f) hiring, renting; reservation
locution (f) expression, phrase, idiom
logement (m) lodging, quarters, housing
logis (m) dwelling, house
lointain distant, far-off
loisir (m) leisure
louange (f) praise
loup (m) wolf
loyer (m) rent
lueur (f) glimmer, gleam
lugubre dismal, mournful
luireto shine, gleam

librairie (f) bookstore
lien (m) bond, tie
lierto tie, bind, fasten
lièvre (m) hare

mâcherto chew
mâchoire (f) jaw
magie (m) magic
magnétophone (m) tape recorder
maigre thin, lean, meager
maigrirto grow thin, lose weight
maillot (de bain) swimming trunks, swim suit
maint many a, many
mairie (f) town hall
maïs (m) corn
majeur major, of age
maladif sickly
maladroit clumsy, awkward
malaise (m) discomfort, uneasiness
male (m) male
malin, maligne smart, clever shrewd, mischievous
malpropre dirty, slovenly, untidy
manche (m) handle
manche (f) sleeve
mansarde (f) attic, garret
marais (m) marsh
marbre (m) marble
marche (f) step, stair, walk, progress
mare (f) pool, pond
marée (f) tide
marin (m) sailor
marine (f) navy
marmite (f) pot, saucepan
marque (f) mark; brand, make
marron (m) chestnut
marteau (m) hammer
mastiquerto chew
matelas (m) mattress
matelot (m) sailor
matière (f) matter, material subject matter;
   matières premières raw materials
matinal (adj) morning, early
maudire curse
méchancetée (f) wickedness, malice
médaille (f) medal
médicament (m) medicine
méfier, se méfier (de)to distrust, mistrust
mégarde, par accidentally, by mistake, inadvertently
mélange (m) mixture, blend

lutte (f) struggle
lutterto struggle, wrestle
luxe (m) luxury
lys (m) lily

M

ménagère (f) housewife, housekeeper
mendiant (m) beggar
mensonge (m) lie
mensuel monthly
menuisier (m) carpenter
mépris (m) contempt, scorn
mépriserto despise, scorn
méridional southern
messe (f) mass (religious service)
méteo (f) weather, forecast
mets (m) dish (of food)
metteur (m), metteur en scène director
meurtre (m) murder
miel (m) honey; lune de miel honeymoon
miette (f) crumb
mignon cute, darling, dainty
mine (f) look, appearance
mineral (m) ore
misère (f) misery; poverty
modiste (f) milliner
moeurs (f pl) customs, manners
moine (m) monk
moisson (f) harvest, crop
mondain worldy
mondial worldwide
montagnard (m) mountaineer
mordreto bite
morne dismal, gloomy
morue (f) cod
mou, molle soft
mouche (f) fly
moucher, se moucherto blow one's nose
moue (f) pout
mouette (f) seagull
mouillé wet damp
moule (f) mussel
moulin (m) mill; moulin à vent windmill
moustique (m) mosquito
moutarde (f) mustard
moyen, moyenne average, middle
moyen (m) means
moyenne (f) average
mugirto roar, bellow
muguet (m) lily of the valley

mêlerto mix, mingle
ménagerto save, be sparing of, treat with respect

nain (m) dwarf
nappe (f) tablecloth
narine (f) nostril
natal native
natation (f) swimming
naufrage (m) shipwreck
navet (m) turnip
navire (m) ship, vessel
néanmoins nevertheless
néant (m) nothingness
négociant (m) merchant, trader
nerf (m) nerve
net clean, neat
nettement clearly, distinctly
nettoyage (m) cleaning;
    nettoyage à sec dry cleaning

obéissant obedient
obligeance (f) kindness
obséderto obsess, haunt
occasion (f) opportunity, occasion, chance;
    d'occasion second-hand, used
odorat (m) sense of smell
œillet (m) carnation
œuvre (f) work
oie (f) goose
oignon (m) onion
oisif idle; lazy
ombrelle (f) parasol
onde (f) wave
ondulerto ripple, wave
ongle (m) nail
onguent (m) ointment, salve
opiniâtre obstinate, stubborn
opprimerto oppress
or now, well then
or (m) gold

paille (f) straw
paisible peaceful
paix (f) peace
paletot (m) overcoat
palier (m) landing
pamplemousse (m or f) grapefruit
pancarte (f) placard

mûr ripe
muraille (f) high thick wall

N

nid (m) nest
nierto deny
niveau (m) level
noce (f) wedding
noeud (m) knot; bow
noisette (f) hazelnut
noix (f) walnut, nut
nonne (f) nun
nouerto knot, tie
nourriture (f) food, nourishment
nouveauté (f) novelty, newness
noyer, se noyerto drown, be drowned
nuage (m) cloud
nue (f) cloud
nuireto harm, be injurious
nuisible harmful

O

orage (m) storm, thunderstorm
ordonnance (f) prescription
ordure (f) garbage, refuse
oreiller (m) pillow
orgueil (m) pride, arrogance
ornerto decorate
orphelin (m) orphan
orteil (m) toe
orthographe (f) spelling
os (m) bone
ôterto take away, take off, remove
ou, ou bien or else
ouïe (f) sense of hearing
ouragan (m) hurricane
ours (m) bear
outil (m) tool, implement
outre beyond, in addition to;
    en outre besides, moreover
ouvrage (m) work
ouvreuse (f) usher

P

pis worse
piscine (f) swimming pool
piste (f) track, trail, runway
placard (m) poster; closet
plaie (f) wound
plaireto please
plaisant amusing, funny

panier (m) basket; **panier à linge** hamper
panne (f) breakdown (car)
pantoufle (f) bedroom slipper
paon (m) peacock
papillon (m) butterfly
paquebot (m) steamer, ocean liner
paravent (m) screen
parcourir to go over, cover, peruse
parcours (m) distance, length
parer to adorn, decorate; ward off
paresse (f) laziness
pari (m) bet
parier to bet
parvenir à to succeed in, attain
passage (m) passage **à niveau** railroad crossing
passant (m) passer-by
passerelle (f) gangway
pastèque (f) watermelon
patinage (m) skating
pâtisserie (f) pastry; pastry shop
patron (m) boss, owner, employer
patte (f) paw, leg
paupière (f) eyelid
paysage (m) landscape
peau (f) skin
pêche (f) fishing; peach
péché (m) sin
peignoir (m) bathrobe, dressing gown
pélerin (m) pilgrim
pélerinage (m) pilgrimage
pelouse (f) lawn
pencher, se pencher to bend, lean
pendre to hang
pénible painful, arduous
pente (f) slope
perroquet (m) parrot
pesant heavy
peste (f) plague
petit-fils (m) grandson
phare (m) lighthouse; headlight
physicien (m) physicist
pic (m) peak
pic (m) woodpecker
piège (m) trap
piéton (m) pedestrain
pilule (f) pill
pin (m) pine tree
pincer to pinch, nip
pique-nique (m) picnic
piquer to sting, stick

plaisanterie (f) joke
planche (f) board
plat flat
plateau (m) tray
pli (m) fold, crease
plier to fold, bend
plomb (m) lead
pneu (m) tire
poids (m) weight
poignet (m) wrist
poil (m) hair
poilu hairy
poing (m) fist
poitrine (f) chest
poivre (m) pepper
pompier (m) fireman
pondre to **lay (eggs)**
porte-feuille (m) wallet
portière (f) door (of vehicle)
poste (m) job; station; set;
poste émetteur broadcasting station;
poste d'essence gas station
poubelle (f) garbage can
pouce (m) thumb; inch
poule (f) hen
pouls (m) pulse
poumon (m) lung
pourrir to rot
poussière (f) dust
pré (m) meadow
précieux precious; affected
précurseur (m) forerunner
prénom (m) first name
presqu'île (f) penisula
pressé hurried, in a hurry
presser, se presser to hurry
prétendant (m) suitor
prétendre to claim
prêtre (m) priest
preuve (f) proof
prévenir to notify, warn
prière (f) prayer
proie (f) prex
propreté (f) cleanliness
protéger to protect
prune (f) plum
pruneau (m) prune
puce (f) flea
puissance (f) power
puits (m) well

pire worse

quai (m) wharf, pier; platform
quelconque any (whatever)
quelquefois sometimes, occasionally, at times

raccommoderto mend, repair, darn
racine (f) root
radeau (m) raft
radis (m) radish
rafale (f) squall; gust of wind
ragoût (m) stew
raide stiff
raillerto make fun of, ridicule
raisin (m) grape; **raisin sec** raisin
ralentirto slow down
rampe (f) banister
rang (m) rank, row
rangerto put in order, tidy, arrange
ravirto delight
rayon (m) ray; shelf; department (of store)
réaliserto carry out, achieve, realize
recette (f) recipe; receipt
rechercherto look for, search for, look up
récipient (m) receptacle
réclamerto claim, demand; complain
récolte (f) harvest, crop
recueil (m) collection
reculerto move back
rédacteur (m) editor; writer
rédaction (f) editing; writing
rédigerto edit, draw up, compose
redouterto dread, fear
réduireto reduce
réfectoire (m) lunchroom
régime (m) system of government; diet
règlement (m) regulation
releverto raise again; point out
relierto connect, bind
remettreto put back; hand over; postpone
remonter to date, back to; wind
remords (m) remorse
remorquer (m) tugboat
remplaçant (m) substitute
remporterto carry off;
remporter une victoireto win a victory

sable (m) sand

pupille (f) pupil (of eye)

Q

queue (f) tail; line
quiconque whoever, anyone
quotidien daily

R

renommé renowned, famous
renommée (f) fame, renown
renoncer (à)to give up
renseignement (m) piece of information
rente (f) income
renverserto upset, overturn
répandreto spread, scatter
repasserto review; iron
répétiton (f) rehearsal
repousserto repel
représentation (f) performance
réseau (m) network
résoudreto solve; resolve
ressentirto feel, experience
ressort (m) spring
retenirto hold back, detain;
    retain, reserve; contain
réussite (f) result; success
revanche (f) revenge
    en revanche on the other hand; in return
réveille-matin (m) alarm clock
rez-de-chaussée (m) ground floor
rhume (m) cold
ride (f) wrinkle
ride wrinkled
rivage (m) shore, bank
riz (m) rice
robinet (m) faucet
roche (f) rock
rocher (m) rock, boulder, crag
romancier (m) novelist
romanesque romantic
ronflerto snore
rongerto gnaw, nibble
roseau (m) reed
rosée (f) dew
rossignol (m) nightingale
roue (f) wheel
rouillerto rust
royaume (m) kingdom

S

sinon otherwise; except

sabot (m) wodden shoe; hoof
sagesse (f) wisdom
saignant rare (of meat)
saignerto bleed
sain healthy, wholesome;
   sain et sauf safe and sound
saint holy, sacred
salerto salt
salirto dirty, soil
salut (m) safety; salvation; greeting
sang-froid (m) poise, composure
sanglant bloody
sanglot (m) sob
sangloterto sob
sapin (m) fir tree
Sarrasin (m) Saracen
saucisse (f) sausage (fresh or wet)
saucisson (m) sausage (dry)
sauf except
saule (m) willow
saumon (m) salmon
sauterto jump, leap
savant (m) scholar, scientist
saveur (f) taste, flavor
sceau (f) seal
scène (f) stage; scene
scierto saw
séance (f) session, meeting
seau (m) pail
!sécherto dry
sécheresse (f) dryness, drought
secouerto shake
secourirto help
secours help
séduisant attractive, fascinate
seigle (m) rye
seigneur (m) lord
sein (m) breast, bosom
séjour (m) stay; abode
selon according to
semblable similar
semblable (m or f) equal, fellow-creature
semerto sow
sensible sensitive; perceptible
sentier (m) path
sergent (m) sergeant
série (f) series
serrerto press, squeeze, tighten
serrure (f) lock
serviette (f) napkin; towel briefcase

sirop (m) syrup
société (f), société anonyme corporation
soi-disant so-called
soignerto take care of
sol (m) ground, soil
somme (m) nap
sonnette (f) bell
sort (m) destiny, fate
sottise (f) foolish act; silliness, stupidity
souci (m) worry, care
soucoupe (f) saucer
soufflerto blow, breathe; prompt
soufflet (m) slap
souffrance (f) suffering
souffrant ailing, sick
souhait (m) wish
soulagerto relieve
souleverto lift up, raise
souligner underline; stress, emphasize
soupçon (m) suspicion
soupçonnerto suspect
soupir (m) sigh
soupirerto sigh
source (f) spring, origin
sourcil (m) eyebrow
souris (f) mouse
sous-sol (m) basement
soutenirto support, maintain
souterrain underground
spirituel witty
sportif athletic, sporting
squelette (m) skeleton
stade (m) stadium
station (f), station balnéaire seaside resort, spa
stationnerto park
store (m) shade (for window)
subirto undergo, submitto
subtil subtle
subventionnerto subsidize
succursale (f) branch (of a firm)
sucrerto sugar, sweeten
suerto sweat
sueur (f) sweat
suite (f) continuation, result, series
suivant accordingto
superficie (f) area, surface
supplice (m) torture, torment
supplierto beg, implore
supprimerto suppress, abolish
sur on, over; out of

seuil (m) threshold
siège (m) siege; seat
sifflet (m) whistle
signaler to point out
signaler to indicate
signer to sign
singe (m) monkey

tablier (m) apron
tabouret (m) stool
tache (f) spot, stain
tâche (f) task, job
tacher to spot, stain
tâcher to try
talon (m) heel
tambour (m) drum; drummer
tant, tant que as long as
tantôt presently; just now
taquiner to tease
tarder to delay; tarder à to put off, be long in;
tarder de to long to
tarif (m) tariff, rate, fare
tas (m) heap, pile
tâter to feel, touch
tâtonner to grope
taureau (m) bull
taux (m) rate (of pay, discount, etc.)
teint (m) complexion
teinte (f) tint, shade, hue
teinturerie (f) dyeing
témoigner to testify; show
témoin (m) witness
tempête (f) storm
tendre to stretch, extend
ténèbres (f, pl) darkness, shadows
tenter to tempt; try
terrain (m) piece of land, ground
tête-à-tête (m) private conversation
têtu stubborn
thon (m) tuna
tiède lukewarm
tige (f) tem
tire-bouchon (m) corkscrew
tissu (m) cloth, material

unique only, sole;
    rue à sens unique one-way street
user to consume, wear out

sur-le-champ immediately
surlendemain (m) two days later
surnom (m) nickname
sympathique congenial, likable
syndicat (m) trade union;
syndicat d'initiative chamber of commerce
    tourist office

T

tombe (f) tomb, grave, tombstone
tombeau (m) tomb, tombstone
tonne (f) ton
tonner to thunder
tonnerre (m) thunder
tordre to twist
toucher (m) touch
tourbillon (m) whirlwind
tourne-disque (m) record player
tournedos (m) filet, mignon
tournoyer to whirl, swirl
tousser to cough
toutefois yet, nevertheless, however
toux (f) cough
trahir to betray
traineau (m) sled, sleigh
traire to milk
trait (m) feature, characteristic
traître (m) traitor
trajet (m) journey, way
tranche (f) slice
trancher to cut
transpirer to perspire
trèfle (m) clover; club (in cards)
tremper to dip, soak, drench
trésor (m) treasure
tressaillir to start, shiver, shudder
tribu (f) tribe
tricher to cheat, trick
tricot (m) knitting; sweater
tricoter to knit
trombe (f) waterspout
trottoir (m) sidewalk
trou (m) hole
troupeau (m) herd, flock
truite (f) trout

U

usine (f) factory
ustensile (m) utensil, implement
utiliser to use

vacarme (m) uproar
vague (f) wave
vaincreto conquer, defeat
vaisseau (m) vessel, ship
vaisselle (f) dishes
valeur (f) value
valse (f) waltz
vanter, se vanterto boast, brag
vapeur (f) steam
vaurien (m) good-for-nothing, scoundrel
veau (m) calf; veal
vedette (f) star (of stage or screen)
veille (f) eve, day before
veillerto keep watch, stay awake
vélo (m) bike
velours (m) velvet
vente (f) sale
ventre (m) belly
ver (m) worm
verger (m) orchard

wagon (m) railway car

V

veston (m) jacket (man's)
vêtirto dress, clothe
veuf (m) widower
veuve (f) widow
viderto empty
vieillirto grow old
vigne (f) vine
vinaigre (m) vinegar
virerto turn
vis-à-vis opposite; with respect to, towards
viserto aim
vitrail (m) stained glass
vitre (f) window pane
vitrine (f) store window, showcase
vœu (m) vow
voie (f) way, road, track
voisinage (m) neighborhood, vicinity
vol (m) flight; theft
volaille (f) poultry, fowl
volant (m) steering wheel

W

10

Answers to Exercises

EXERCISE 1

1. la page (F)
2. la sœur (F)
3. le régrigerateur (M)
4. le gratte-ciel (M)
5. l'hibou (M)
6. la chimie (F)
7. la chinoiserie (F)
8. la fleur (F)
9. la bicyclette (F)
10. la valise (F)
11. la solitude (F)
12. le médecin (M)
13. l'homme (M)
14. l'haine (F)
15. le comptoir (M)
16. la cigarette (F)
17. la fraise (F)
18. la biologie (F)
19. la patience (F)
20. l'invitation (F)

EXERCISE 2

M	1. anglais	l'anglais
F	2. image	l'image
M	3. danseur	le danseur
F	4. jeunesse	la jeunesse
M	5. lapin	le lapin
M	6. lion	le lion
M	7. tiroir	le tiroir
F	8. capitale	la capitale
F	9. église	l'église
F	10. histoire	l'histoire
M	11. professeur	le professeur
F	12. machine	la machine
F	13. question	la question
F	14. maison	la maison
M	15. ordinateur	l'ordinateur
F	16. chimie	la chimie
F	17. bouche	la bouche
M	18. chemise	la chemise
M	19. négoce	le négoce
M	20. musée	le musée

EXERCISE 3

1. classroom	la salle de classe
2. fashion	la mode
3. pound	la livre
4. cup	la tasse
5. sister	la sœur
6. fork	la fourchette
7. musician	le musicien
8. dryer	le séchoir
9. skirt	la jupe
10. necktie	la cravate
11. bike	le velo
12. show	le concours
13. flower	la fleur
14. beginning	le début
15. bull	le taureau
16. habit	l'habitude
17. kitchen	la cuisine
18. oil	la huile
19. jewelry	la bijouterie
20. wallet	le portefeuille

EXERCISE 4

1. le cahier les cahiers
2. le travail les travaux
3. la chemise les chemises
4. le pardessus les pardessus
5. le stylo les stylos
6. le bureau les bureaux
7. le journal les journaux
8. le chandail les chandails
9. le casse-noisette les casse-noisettes
10. le chapeau les chapeaux
11. la fête les fêtes

12. le festival les festivaux
13. la bouteille les bouteilles
14. le tire-bouchon les tires-bouchons
15. le petit-fils les petits-fils
16. le lycée les lycées
17. le hors-d'euvre les hors.d'œuvres
18. le gâteau les gâteaux
19. le coup de grace les coups de grace
20. le cheval les chevaux

EXERCISE 5

1. l'arc-en-ciel les arcs-en-ciel rainbows
2. le pou les poux lice
3. le hibou les hiboux owls
4. madame mesdames ladies   rendez-vous rendez-vous meetings
5. le prisonnier les prisonniers prisonniers le trou les trous holes
6. le chou-fleur les choux-fleurs cauliflowers
7. le travail les travaux jobs
8. le réveille-matin les réveille-matins
9. la grand-mère les grands-mères grandmothers le grand-père les grands-pères grandfathers le petit-fils les petits-fils grandchildren

EXERCISE 6

1. (le beau-frère) Les beaux-frères avaient promis de se rejoindre pour un grand diner en famille.
2. (un après-midi) Les dames passaient des après-midi a causer de leurs maris.
3. (cache-nez de laine) Quand nous faisons du ski, nous portons toujours les cache.nez de laine de notre clubs.
4. (l'abat-jour) Comment trouvez-vous les abat-jour?
5. (le prix du repas) Les prix du repas n'ont pas été changés.
6. (pneu) Ce matin ils ont dû changer les pneus?
7. (l'animal) Où sont les animaux?
8. (le gâteau) Les enfants ont mangé les gâteaux.
9. (le bal) Les bals ont eu lieu hier.
10. (le matelas) Les matelas sont faits aux Etats Unis.

EXERCISE 7

1. (le genou) Il essaya de se baisser sans plier les genoux
2. (le cheveu) Si j'ai le temps aujourd'hui, j'irai me faire couper les cheveux.
3. (l'œil bleu) Tous leurs enfants ont les yeux bleus.
4. (le timbre-poste) Nous cherchons un bureau de tabac pour acheter les timbres-poste étrangers.
5. (le cerf-volant) Mon père s'amusait plus que moi a jouer avec les cerfs-volants.
6. (le tire-bouchon) Il a enlevé les tires-bouchons.
7. (le taureau) Le jardinier approche les taureaux.
8. (le chemin de fer) M. Dupont aime les chemins de fer.
9. (le bateau) Le millionnaire a acheté les bateaux.
10. (le chandail) Madame Dubois donne les chandails de laine à sa mère.

EXERCISE 8

1. Le garçon achète la chemise blanche.
   The boy buys the white shirt.
2. La banane est sur la table.
   The banana is on the table.
3. Les boîtes sont dans le tiroir.
   The boxes are in the drawer.
4. Monsieur Dupont, aimez-vous le thé avec ou sans le lait?
   Mister Dupont, do you like tea with or without milk?
5. Vas-tu manger les pommes?
   Are you going to eat the apples?
6. La jeune-fille aime la petite voiture.
   The young girl likes the small car.
7. Les cerises coûtent 20 francs le kilo.
   The cherries cost 20 francs per kilo.
8. Madame Dupont voyage en été.
   Mrs. Dupont travels in the summer.
9. Elle est allée à Mouscou l'année dernière.
   She went to Moscow last year.
10. Les œufs coûtent 10 francs la douzaine.
    The eggs cost 10 francs per dozen.
11. Les enfants couvrent le livre?
    Do the children cover the book?
12. Mademoiselle se lave les cheveux.
    Miss washes her hair.
13. Elle achète les tomates à 10 francs la livre.
    She buys the tomatoes at 10 francs per pound.
14. Mardi est le deuxieme jour de la semaine.
    Tuesday is the second day of the week.
15. La Martinique est une île charmante.

EXERCISE 9

1. Je visite la musée le mardi.
2. Elle se brosse les dents le matin et la nuit.
3. Nous aprenons le russe maintenant.
4. J'aime les pommes.
5. Le sucre coûte 10 francs la livre.
6. Les livres sont dans ses bras.
7. Racontez-moi l'histoire en français.
8. C'est aujord'hui lundi.
9. J'aime aller au cinéma le dimanche.
10. Madame Dubois a les cheveux longs.
11. J'ai visite l'université vendredi.
12. Veux-tu ton café sans ou avec le sucre?
13. Je vais chez moi.
14. Elle aime New York au printemps.
15. L'Afrique est un immense continent.

EXERCISE 10

1. Pierre va au aéroport.
2. Je parle au garçon.
3. Qui est allé à la bibliothèque?
4. La jeune fille va au cinéma.
5. Nous voulons aller au parc.
6. Elle porte la lampe sur la table.
7. Ils sont alles au lycée.
8. Le professeur dit bonjour aux élèves.

9. J'ai parlé avec le professeur.

10. Je pose une question aux écrivains.

EXERCISE 11

1. J'ai les cahiers des enfants.
2. Elle admire l'architecture du musée.
3. Monsieur Dupont revient de la gare.
4. Madame Dupont mange de la salade.
5. Le président du Méxique aime la démocracie.
6. La couleur de la chemise est blanche.
7. Qui veut du thé?
8. On ne parle que des évènements récents.
9. Elle ne parle que de la Guadeloupe.
10. Pierre est arrivé au restaurant.

EXERCISE 12

1. un crayon: a pencil
2. une craie: a chalk
3. un musée: a museum
4. une école: a school
5. une image: a picture
6. une écriture: a document
7. des idées: some ideas
8. des hommes: some men
9. une pêche: a peach
10. une chaise: a chair
11. une cravate: a tie
12. des chemises: some shirts
13. des Anglais: some Englishmen
14. un couteau: a knife
15. une fourchette: a fork
16. des enfants: some children
17. des restaurants: some restaurants
18. des fiancés: some fiancés
19. une photo: a photograph
20. une invitation: an invitation

EXERCISE 13

1. Veut-elle un sandwich?
2. Elle a une vaiselle et des cerises.
3. Voici un stylo et un crayon.
4. Il est un très bon avocat.
5. Je mange des fruits et des legumes.
6. Elle porte des lunettes de soleil.
7. Ils ont des messages pour Jean.
8. Elle a besoin d'un voiture neuve.
9. Je voudrais un verre de lait, s'il vous plaît.
10. C'est un travail difficile.

EXERCISE 14

1. Monsieur Dupont n'a pas de patience.
2. Tous les matins, il boit du café sans sucre.
3. A midi, il mange des haricots verts.
4. Il mange des pommes frites avec de la viande.
5. Il mange aussi de bons petits pains et du beurre.
6. Toute de suite après le repas, il aimerait avoir de la confiture.
7. Il laisse toujours de la monnaie sur la table.
8. Avant de rentrer chez lui, il prend des billets de théâtre.
9. Parfois, il achète des fleurs pour sa femme.
10. A la maison, il ne mange pas de gâteau.

EXERCISE 15

1. Madame Dupont ne peut pas se passer de nourriture.
2. Au petit déjeuner, elle mange du pain et de la confiture.
3. Elle mange aussi des œufs.
4. Elle boit du jus d'orange.
5. Elle boit aussi du café avec du sucre et de la creme.
6. Au déjeuner, elle mange de la soupe et de la salade verte.
7. Elle boit un verre de vin.
8. Au dîner, elle mange du poulet et des légumes.
9. Elle mange aussi du riz blanc et des petits pois.
10. Elle ne fume jamais de cigarettes.

EXERCISE 16

1. Monsieur Dupont travaille au bureau.
2. Madame Dupont reste a la maison.
3. Elle adore faire les emplettes.
4. Il y a plusieurs supermarchés dans son quartier.
5. Monsieur Dupont n'aime pas de pommes.
6. Elle achète toujours une douzaine de pommes.
7. Monsieur Dupont n'aime pas de beurre.
8. Elle achète toujours une livre de beurre.
9. Elle a quelques amis qui aiment de bonnes pommes.
10. Ils aiment aussi du beurre sur une tranche de pain.

Mastery Drills

EXERCICE 1

A. 1. un, une 2. des 3. des
B. 1. les, le 4. l' 6. la 8. les 2. la 5. le, l' 7.le 9. les 3. l'
C. 1. de la 3. de la 5. du, du, de l' 7. des 2. du 4. du 6. de l'

EXERCICE 2

A. 1. du 3. l' 5. des 7. l' 2. la 4. des 6. du
B. 1. au 3. l' 5. aux 7. l' 2. la 4. aux 6. l'

EXERCICE 3

1. ...au professeur...
2. ...du syndicat.
3. Le résultat de l'examen sera affiché demain
4. ... à l'enfant.
5. ...au mur ...à la fenêtre
6. ...du dernier film...
7. ...de l'autre dictionnaire

EXERCICE 4

1. un, un 3. un 5. un
2. du 4. du 6. du

EXERCICE 5

1. une, la 5. les 8. un
2. le 6. le, au 9. les, des, aux
3. une, le 7. un 10. les, des, des,
4. des des, des, des

EXERCICE 6

A. 1. le 2. du 3. un 4. l' 5. de l' 6. un 7. le 8. du 9. un 10. un 11. du 12. le

EXERCICE 7

1. article défini contracté
2. article défini contracté
3. article partitif
4. article défini contracté
5. article indéfini
6. préposition + article défini
7. article indéfini

8. article défini contracte
9. article partitif

EXERCICE 8

un. le, de la, les, du. un, la, un, des.
le, les, la/une, les/des.

EXERCICE 9

A. 1. Il n'y a pas de lampe sur la table.
2. On ne voyait pas de lumière aux fenêtres.
3. Je n'ai pas acheté d'œufs au marché.
4. Les Berger n'ont pas de jardin.
5. Les étudiants n'avaient pas de questions à poser.
6. On n'a pas trouvé d'uranium dans cette région.
7. Il n'avait pas de travail à faire.

B. 1. Ce n'est pas du thé de Ceylan.
2. Ce n'est pas un film en version originale.
3. Ce ne sont pas des touristes étrangers.
4. Ce n'est pas de l'or pur.
5. Ce ne sont pas des bonbons à la menthe.

EXERCICE 10

1. Non, je n'ai pas d'ordinateur chez moi.
2. Non, je ne regarde pas régulièrement le journal télévisé.
3. Non, ils ne peuvent pas boire de vin.
4. Non, je ne fais pas la cuisine tous les jours.
5. Non, il n'y a plus de feuilles sur les arbres en décembre.
6. Non, je n'ai pas peur des araignées.
7. Non, je ne mets pas de sucre dans mon café.
8. Non, elle ne s'occupera plus de la bibliothèque de l'école l'an prochain.
9. Non, je ne porte pas de lentilles de contact.
10. Non, ce ne sont pas des fleurs naturelles.
11. Non, il n'y a pas de distributeur automatique de billets de banque dans la quartier.
12. Non, personne ne s'est servi des ciseaux.

EXERCICE 11

A. 1. des affiches
2. de belles affiches
3. des amis américains
4. de très bons amis américain.
5. de nouveaux quartiers
6. d'anciens camarades d'école.

B. 1. des petits amis.
2. des jeunes gens.
3. des petites annonces.
4. des petites filles.
des jeunes filles très sympathiques.
5. des petites cuillères.
6. des gros mots intéressantes 7. des petits pois

EXERCICE 12

1. Il y a trop de vent.
2. Jean-Christophe a plus de temps...
3. ... un peu de crème...
4. Combien d'enfants les Forestier ont-ils?

5. Y a-t-il assez de verres pour tout le monde?
6. ... beaucoup d'étudiants étrangers.
7. Jean-Michel a peu d'amis.

EXERCICE 13

1. un litre de lait.
2. deux kilos de pêches
3. cinq mètres de tissu
4. une livre de beurre
5. deux heures de tennis

EXERCICE 14

1. de cigarettes
2. de cafe au lait
3. de tulipes
4. de confiture
5. de vin
6. de jambon
7. d'eau
8. d'aspirine
9. de sucre en poudre
10. de pain
11. de dentifrice

EXERCICE 15

1. cristal
2. soie
3. velours
4. paille
5. cuir
6. métal argenté

EXERCICE 16

1. des clefs de voiture
2. Les clefs de la voiture
3. les dates des vacances
4. vos dates de vacances.
5. les arrêts d'autobus
6. L'arrét de l'autobus 63
7. une histoire de la France
8. Ce livre d'histoire de France.

EXERCICE 17

1. sa carte d'identité
2. un livre de grammaire.
3. une maison de campagne.
4. ton maillot de bain.
5. un acteur de cinema
6. un billet de théâtre.
7. Dans un magasin de sport.

EXERCICE 18

1. des enfants / d'enfants handicapés.
2. d'actrices / des actrices qui viennent
3. de crayons feutres / des crayons
4. de piles neuves
5. de maux de tête.
6. des noms de ces personnes.

EXERCICE 19

1. d'un mur
2. d'eau.
3. de photographes.
4. d'une nappe blanche.
5. de livres et de documents.
6. de neige.
7. de photos.
8. de la mort.
9. d'arbres.
10. de la preposition "a."
11. d'un complément

EXERCICE 20

1. outils
5. ongles
2. main
6. dents
3. . papiers
7. lettres
4. lèvres
8. pain

EXERCICE 21

1. Du café au lait
2. Une tarte aux pommes
3. Un croissant au beurre
4. Une glace a la vanille
5. Un poulet à la crème

Chapter 2

EXERCISE 1

1. Nous marchons vite.
2. Tu parles trop.
3. Vous dînez au restaurant.
4. Ils chantent bien, ces garcons.
5. Elle aide sa mère, cette fille.
6. On parle espagnol à Porto-Rico.
7. Nous causons au téléphone.
8. Moi, je porte un chapeau sur la tête.
9. Elles fument beaucoup, ces belles dames.
10. Elle habite à Paris avec son mari.

EXERCISE 2

1. Vous fermez la fenêtre. You close the window.
2. Nous arrivons en retard. We arrive late.
3. Ils expliquent la leçon. They explain the lesson.
4. Nous restons à la maison. We stay at home.
5. Ils tombent sur le trottoir. They fall on the sidewalk.
6. Vous quittez la maison à sept heures. You leave the house at seven o'clock.
7. Nous dansons mal. We danse poorly.
8. Elles commencent le travail. They begin the work.
9. Vous demandez le billet d'avion. You ask for the plane ticket.
10. Nous aimons les pommes frites. We like potato chips.

EXERCISE 3

1. enseignent
2. racontes
3. coûtent
4. accompagnez
5. trouvent
6. habitent
7. gagne
8. invite
9. traversons
10. ramasse

EXERCISE 4

1. Paul et Jacques, ils mangent au restaurant.
   Nous mangeons au restaurant.
   Qui mange au restaurant?
2. Nous aidons le docteur.
   Les etudiants aident le docteur.
   J'aide le docteur.
3. Voyagez-vous souvent?
   Est-ce que je voyage souvent?
   Le bebe, voyage-t-il souvent?
4. On ne fume pas beaucoup.
   Vous ne fumez pas beaucoup.
   Tu ne fumes pas beaucoup.
5. Ne causez-vous pas avec eux?
   Ne cause-t-elle pas avec eux?
   Vos amis, Ne causent-ils pas avec eux?

EXERCISE 5

1. Ma mère proteste quand je sors le soir.
2. Une femme porte une robe.
3. Oui, je travaille beaucoup.
4. Je déteste la guerre.
5. Je regarde la page 66 maintenant.
6. Elles étudient a l'ecole.
7. Oui, j'écoute la musique classique en travaillant.
8. J'étudie chez moi.
9. Non, ils passent l'été a la ville.
10. Non, je demeure aux Etats-Unis.

EXERCISE 6

1. Je cherche
2. Monte-t-il
3. Nous ne causons pas
4. Ils apportent
5. Elle ne chante pas
6. Empruntes-tu
7. Le boucher coupe
8. Ne dinez-vous pas
9. Marche-t-on
10. Nous aimons

EXERCISE 7

1. Ils quittent la maison de campagne.
2. Nous n'arrivons pas en retard à la gare.
3. Vous remarquez les fautes.
4. Rencontrent-elles l'avocat?
5. Les enfants tombent par terre.
6. Elles marchent vite.
7. Nous parlons anglais.
8. Vous fumez trop.
9. Ils achètent des souvenirs de Paris.
10. Nous voyageons souvent au Canada.

EXERCISE 8

1. Tu réussis toujours.
2. Nous remplissons le verre.
3. Qui choisit ce beau vase?
4. Elles finissent le livre.
5. Punissez-vous le chien?
6. Obéis-tu à la loi?
7. Les enfants grandissent bien.
8. Guerissez la maladie.
9. L'architecte bâtit un bel hôpital.
10. Réfléchissent-ils avant de parler?

EXERCISE 9

1. Que bâtissent-ils?
   Qui bâtit ce beau musée?
2. J'obéis au lieutenant.
   Nous obéissons à ses ordres.
3. Punissons-nous les voleurs?
   Qui punit-elle?
4. Les touristes remplissent l'hôtel.
   Pourquoi remplissez-vous cette boîte?

5. Quel sport choisissez-vous?
Combien de cartes choisis-tu?

EXERCISE 10

1. Non, nous choisissons ces vases.
2. Oui, nous la remplissons.
3. Oui, il lui obéit.
4. Oui, vous lui obéissez.
5. Oui, je la choisis.
6. Oui, vous en choisissez un.
7. Non, je ne lui obéis pas.
8. Non, ils ne le remplissent pas.
9. Non, elles choisissent les jupes.
10. Non, je remplis les tasses.

EXERCISE 11

1. bâtissons
2. punissent
3. choisit
4. bâtit
5. finis
6. réussit
7. guérissent
8. Remplis
9. réussit
10. obéissent

EXERCISE 12

1. Est-ce que je finis le roman?
2. J'aime finir mon travail.
3. Finissiez-vous les devoirs?
4. Je finis le dîner.
5. Nous ne finissons pas le livre.
6. Il finit la page.
7. Est-ce je ne finis pas tous les exercices?
8. Ne finissent-elles pas la soupe?
9. Elle finit la leçon.
10. Ils finissent l'histoire.

EXERCISE 13

1. vous
2. Elles
3. ils
4. Vous
5. tu
6. Elle
7. Il
8. Je
9. Nous
10. Je

EXERCISE 14

1. Nous perdons la clef de sa chambre d'hôtel.
Ils perdent la clef de sa chambre d'hôtel.
Je perds la clef de sa chambre d'hôtel.
2. Les enfants ne rendent pas l'addition.
Nous ne rendons pas l'addition.
Tu ne rends pas l'addition.

3. Je descends du train.
Il descend du train.
Elles descendent du train.
4. Attend-elle M. Dupont?
Attendez-vous M. Dupont?
Attendent-ils M. Dupont?
5. Paul entend l'oiseau.
J'entends l'oiseau.
Vous entendez l'oiseaux.

EXERCISE 15

1. Oui, j'entend les voitures dans la rue.
2. Non, je ne rends pas livres que j'emprunte.
3. Nous descendons à la salle à manger à huit heures.
4. Oui, je defends ma patrie.
5. Oui, ils attendent une lettre de leurs parents.
6. Jean répond aux questions en classe.
7. Le boucher vend de la viande.
8. J'attends mes amis.
9. On vend du pain à la boulangerie.

EXERCISE 16

1. M. et Mme. Dupont descendent.
2. La dame vend le journal à l'homme.
3. Qui rend la carte?
4. Ils perdent ses temps.
5. Attend-il toujours les filles?

EXERCISE 17

1. Madame Dupont never loses her time.
2. The grocer sells sugar.
3. Mr. Dupont doesn't like to wait.
4. When she gets up, she doesn't go back down.
5. The soldiers defend their country.
6. Doesn't he answer the question?
7. The boy waits for the command.
8. We answer the letter right away.
9. Do you hear the baby?
10. Do you return the books to the library?

EXERCISE 18

1. Je dors le weekend.
2. Elles lisent tous les romans de Stephen King.
3. Les enfants attendent le petit déjeuner.
4. Nous écrivons à ses parents.
5. Tu veux sortir malgré la neige. (tu)
6. Ils éteignent la lumière avant de sortir.
7. Croyez-vous a cette histoire?
8. Vous nous conduisez à travers le jardin.
9. Elles nous accueillent le bras ouvert.
10. Nous devons arriver à l'heure.
11. Vous buvez du café noir le matin.
12. Pierre et Jean, ils ne savent pas de danser.
13. Les jardiniers cueillent les pommes.
14. Prenez-vous du sucre?
15. Je fais de la bonne cuisine.
16. Nous convainquons les clients.
17. Tu as beaucoup d'argent.

18. Nous sommes en bonne santé.
19. Ils ouvrent la porte pour la dame.
20. Pourquoi ne résolvez-vous pas le problème?

EXERCISE 19

1. Nous envoyons une carte postale à notre amie.
2. Que voulez-vous?
3. Les artistes peignent des portraits de valeur.
4. Elles veulent acheter une robe neuve.
5. Ayez la bonté de fermer la porte en sortant.
6. Les étudiants prennent ses cours au sérieux.
7. Vous lisez le journal en mangeant votre petit déjeuner.
8. Souffrez-vous souvent de maux de tête?
9. Nous n'en pouvons plus. Nous sommes crevés.
10. Elles connaissent bien cette route.

EXERCISE 20

1. Elle admet d'avoir menti.
2. Qu'est-ce qu'ils construisent là-bas?
3. Nous buvons du jus d'orange chaque matin.
4. L'enfant s'endort tout habile.
5. Le film ne lui plait pas.
6. Le garçon sert la salade.
7. Vous recevez une lettre importante.
8. Ils prennent un grand repas.
9. Ont-ils encore de l'appétit?
10. Etes-vous prêts mes amis?
11. Nous connaissons bien ce peintre.
12. Les enfants sortent sans la permision.
13. Où vont-ils?
14. Vous éteignez la lumière avant de vous coucher.

EXERCISE 21

1. Voyons les images.
2. N'oublions pas!
3. Mangeons de la glace.
4. Réussissons!
5. Faisons les devoirs.
6. Ne cassons pas la tasse.
7. Ouvrons la porte.
8. Partons!
9. Buvons le thé.
10. Soyons raisonnable!

EXERCISE 22

1. Bring the book to school.
2. Run to the store.
3. Let's leave at once.
4. Fill that bottle.
5. Don't blush, children.
6. Learn this proverb.
7. Let's wash the floor.
8. Be more active!
9. Let's not laugh so much.
10. Do not break the plate.

EXERCISE 23

1. Réfléchissez bien.
2. N'attendez pas l'avion.
3. Ne riez pas.
4. Parlez moins haut.
5. Traduisez le paragraphe.
6. Apprenez le poème.
7. Dépêchez-vous!
8. Dites la vérité.
9. Ouvrez les fenêtres.
10. Dormez bien

EXERCISE 24

1. Traverse le jardin.
2. Tais-toi!
3. Bois le lait.
4. Sois sage!
5. Obéis à sa sœur.
6. Joue a la balle.
7. Reviens vite.
8. Remplis la tasse.
9. Va a l'école.
10. Prends un taxi.

EXERCISE 25

1. Ecris la lettre.
2. Voyons la télé.
3. Ne vendez pas votre billet.
4. Choisissez une de ces chemises.
5. Ne croyez pas cette histoire.
6. Disnous son point de vue.
7. Cherchez le travail.
8. Envoies la lettre.
9. Ne mange pas si vite, mon enfant.
10. Traduisons la phrase.

EXERCISE 26

1. se levent
2. Se réveillent
3. me couche
4. se porte
5. Se dépêchent
6. se promène
7. nous habillons
8. appelez-vous
9. vous trouvez
10. s'ennuie

EXERCISE 27

1. D'habitude, je me lève avant neuf heures.
2. Je ne me souviens votre adresse.
3. Je me promène tous les soirs.
4. Ne te brosse pas dans la salle de séjour.
5. Se sent-elle mieux?
6. Je ne veux pas me lever.
7. Dépêchons-nous pour y arriver.
8. Je me couche si je suis fatigue.
9. Lavez-vous tout de suite!
10. Ils se blèsseront s'ils y restent.

EXERCISE 28

1. A quelle heure vous levez-vous le matin?
2. Vous lavez-vous rapidement?
3. Pourquoi vous dépêchez-vous?
4. Votre père, comment s'appeletil?
5. Le New York, ou se trouve-t-il?
6. Quand vous reposerez-vous?
7. Vous endormez-vous tôt?
8. Votre mère, comment se sent-elle?
9. Estce vous vous ennuyez facilement?
10. Est-ce vous vous trompez?

EXERCISE 29

1. I am located in front of the department store.
2. I think that you are mistaken.

3. Do the students get up before six?
4. Don't they have fun on weekends?
5. We wake up at seven.
6. You brush your hair.
7. I don't get bored in Paris.
8. They wash themselves before eating.
9. They never hurry.
10. Suddenly, the teacher gets angry.
11. Aren't you feeling well?
12. The patient takes a walk when it is nice.
13. I shave with cold water
14. She washes her face.
15. They brush their teeth.

EXERCISE 30

1. Nous nous amusons bien ce matin-là.
2. Nous allons nous brosser les dents.
3. Se promenerontils autour du lac?
4. Non, nous n'appelons pas Durand.
5. Couche-toi ici, Pierre.
6. Elles se sentent mieux.
7. Attention! Ne vous blessez pas.
8. Je m'habille à sept heures chaque matin.
9. Lave-toi, Pierre!
10. Levons-nous vers huit heures!

EXERCISE 31

1. laisse
2. su
3. venue
4. dormi
5. tu
6. défendu
7. retournés
8. ravi
9. assis
10. pu

EXERCISE 32

1. Haven't they returned from Canada?
2. We stayed in the waiting room.
3. The kitchen pleased him.
4. I had enough of it.
5. You arrived on time.
6. She became a nurse.
7. Didn't it rain last night?
8. He didn't want to enter all alone.
9. The peasant lived for a long time.
10. Did you bring your credit card?

EXERCISE 33

1. J'ai du partir toute de suite.
2. A-t-il épousé son amie d'enfance?
3. Nous avons saisi l'occasion de lui envoyer une note.
4. Qu'avez-vous craint?
5. Sa grand-mère a meurt l'année dernière.
6. Avez-vous connu sa nouvelle adresse?
7. Les enfants, sont-ils tombés?

8. Il a fallu écrire la lettre en vitesse.
9. La mère a conduit son fils au musée.
10. Le peintre a découvert sa nouvelle peinture.
11. Elles ont fait un voyage en Californie.
12. Bien entendu, nous sommes arrivés en retard.
13. Cette église a valu une visite.
14. Les plantes ne sont pas mortes.
15. A quelle heure êtes vous rentrée, Marie?

EXERCISE 34

1. Ou sont elles allées?
2. Elles sont allées a Paris.
3. J'ai eu son billet d'avion.
4. Qui est entré au restaurant?
5. J'ai mis les clefs de voiture sur le bureau.
6. Quel livre as-tu pris?
7. Nous avons ouvert la fenêtre.
8. Combien ontils compris?
9. Comment l'a-t-il fait?
10. Quand sont-ils alles au café?
11. Pourquoi n'avez vous pas couru hier soir?
12. A quelle heure est-il sorti?
13. Pourquoi ne sont-elles pas allés au cinéma?
14. Nous n'avons pas vu l'indice.
15. Le prêtre, qui a-t-il béni?

EXERCISE 35

1. J'ai bu du lait ce matin.
2. L'élève a écrit les phrases sue cette feuille de papier.
3. Oui, la nuit est déjà tombée.
4. Non, je n'ai pas suivi les nouvelles à la télé.
5. Ils ont reçu l'argent hier soir.
6. Oui, j'ai couvert le lit.
7. Non, nous ne sommes pas sorti hier soir.
8. Je suis né(e) aux Etats Unis.
9. J'ai quitté la maison à huit heures ce matin.
10. Non, on n'a pas ri quand le comédian a raconté une histoire amusante.

EXERCISE 36

1. J'étais chez moi pendant qu'il neigeait.
2. Oui, quand j'étais jeune, j'obéissais à mon père.
3. Les étudiants lisaient Cyrano de Bergerac.
4. Ils faisaient ses devoirs.
5. J'allais au théâtre, hier soir.
6. Oui, il y avait beaucoup de gens dans le théâtre.
7. Non, on ne pouvait pas croire tout ce que je racontais.
8. Il faisait beau ce matin lorsque j'ai quitté la maison.
9. Nous dormions parce-que nous étions fatigués.
10. Je regardais la télévision pendant que tu écrivais la lettre.

EXERCISE 37

1. It was time.
2. She couldn't return on time.
3. We always followed our attorney's advice.
4. Was he writing a second novel?
5. They had a good tape recorder.

6. Was it necessary to drink this old bottle of wine?
7. He often lost his portfolio.
8. This country produced a lot of wheat.
9. We were were chatting when the teacher arrived.
10. Madame Dupont wanted to meet this lady?

EXERCISE 38

1. Il mettait la lettre dans la boîte a lettre.
2. N'avait-il pas un nouveau stylo?
3. Les étudiants causaient beaucoup.
4. Etudiiezvous tout seul?
5. Nous recevions la réponse de notre dernière lettre.
6. Ne connaissais-tu pas cette rue?
7. Qu'est-ce que tu faisais?
8. Je la tenais dans mes bras.
9. Monsieur Dupont portait un belle cravate en soie.
10. Ils buvait l'eau mineral.

EXERCISE 39

1. ils attendaient   6. nous choississions
2. lisait-elle?   7. tu voyais
3. tu devais   8. il ne traduisait pas
4. nous riions   9. n'apprenaient-ils pas?
5. qui envoyais?   10. je ne réussissais

EXERCISE 40

1. Vous aidiez
2. Tout le monde savait
3. Ils accomplissaient
4. écrivais-tu
5. on pouvait
6. Nous croyions
7. ils couraient
8. était-il
9. elle rougissait
10. il ne pleuvait pas

EXERCISE 41

1. Je parlais au moment elles sont rentrées.
2. Le chien aboyait quand des visiteurs sont arrivés.
3. Ils lisaient et nous regardions la télé.
4. Je dormais et puis le téléphone a sonné.
5. Il faisait froid quand il a commencé à neiger.
6. La dame a regardé le titre du livre que je lisais.
7. Quand ils sont partis je mangeais le petit déjeuner
8. Comme il fasait beau nous sommes allés à la pêche.
9. Je mangeais et je regardais la télé.
10. Madame Dupont nettoyait la chambre, son fils dormait.

EXERCISE 42

1. Jean portait un parapluie parce qu'il pleuvait.
2. Monsieur Dupont a bu de la bierre parce qu'il avait soif.
3. Elle se dépêchait parce qu'elle était en retard.
4. L'enfant est allé chez le médecin parce qu'il était malade.
5. Il a ouvert la fenêtre parce qu'il avait chaud.

6. J'ai visité mon ami parce-que je lui ai du un livre.
7. Renée restait à la maison parce qu'elle ne se sentait pas bien.
8. Je suis allé à la gare parce que mes amis y attendait.
9. Elle avait chaud parce-qu'elle est allée à la plage.
10 Elle a rougi parce-que le garçon la regardait.

EXERCISE 43

C'était le trois janvier. Il a été sept heures du matin. Il faisait froid. J'allait à l'école pour la première fois apres les vacances de noël. J'ai pris le metro. Il ne marchait pas bien. Il faisait chaud à l'interieur des wagons. Les gens se bousculaient. Le train s'est arrêté plusieurs fois.

J'ai changé le train. J'ai pris un autre train. J'ai fait la correspondance à Manhattan. Malgrés tous mes efforts je suis arrivé quand même à l'école en retard. Je passait une journée désagréable.

EXERCISE 44

1. Vous saurez sa réponse.
2. Ils recevront le candidat.
3. Tu courras avec moi.
4. Colette ne sera pas en retard.
5. Nous n'aurons pas tort.
6. Elle lui enverra une carte postale.
7. J'irai en France.
8. Elles feront des achats.
9. Nous verrons la pièce.
10. Les acteurs ne jouerons pas.

EXERCISE 45

1. Dans quel pays demeurera-t-il?
2. Vous me devrez mille francs.
3. Saurons-nous son opinion?
4. Il y aura plusieurs statues dans le village.
5. Ils verront les étoiles du drapeau.
6. Quand finiras-tu le roman?
7. Elle vous invitera à la soirée.
8. Je lirai le conte.
9. Cela lui fera plaisir.
10. Il ne pleuvra pas.
11. N'iront-ils pas en ville?
12. Quel collège choisiront-ils?
13. Il prendra le petit déjeuner a huit heures.
14. Répondrez-vous à la question?
15. Qui coupera la viande?

EXERCISE 46

1. Pourquoi serez-vous absent demain?
2. Qui vous accompagnera à la gare?
3. Elles enverront leurs billets aujourd'hui.
4. Je ne pourrai pas le terminer.
5. Ils ne vendront pas leur appartement.
6. Que ferons-nous ce soir?
7. Je voudrai voir la chambre.
8. Le médecin guerira le garçon.
9. Quand aurez-vous la nouvelle voiture?

10. Il faudra partir à sept heures du matin.

EXERCISE 47

1. Je demanderai un sandwich et une bière.
2. Estce que je vous verrai ce weekend?
3. Nous n'aurons pas assez d'argent pour ce voyage.
4. Qui retournera mon stylo?
5. Viendront-ils nous voir a dimanche?
6. Elle remplira votre verre.
7. Enverrez-vous les cravates de soie a M. Dupont?
8. Ils ne feront jamais le travaille à l'heure.
9. Les dames ne seront-elles prêtes à midi?
10. Quand est-ce j'arriverai a Paris?

EXERCISE 48

1. Il croyait que je ne verrais pas sa bague.
2. Où est-ce qu'on bâtirait la nouvelle église?
3. Si je vous envoyais la lettre ce matin, quand la recevriez-vous?
4. Son père pensait qu'elle deviendrait avocate.
5. Y aurait-il assez de café pour tout le monde?
6. Nous ne savions pas qu'elles reviendraient bientôt.
7. Pourquoi faudrait-il cacher l'addition?
8. Saurais-tu réparer cette machine?
9. Nous devrions encourager les jeunes artists.
10. On a dit qu'il neigerait ce soir.

EXERCISE 49

1. He wouldn't have enough sugar.
2. We would sell the car.
3. I would like a cup of coffee, please.
4. You should leave right away.
5. We would come to the house early.
6. What would you do this weekend?
7. We would send him a postcard.
8. I would run quickly to the post office.
9. We could try to see the room.
10. Would you know them?

EXERCISE 50

1. vous pourriez
2. Elles nageraient
3. Je voudrais
4. Nous irions
5. Tu assierais
6. Vous auriez
7. Nous recevrions
8. Il payerait
9. Nous ferions
10. Nous mourrions

EXERCISE 51

1. Nous irions au théâtre.
2. Auriez-vous le temps de le faire?
3. Qui recevrait le grand prix?
4. Qu'est-ce que vous écririez?
5. Il voudrait vous accompagner.
6. Ne dîneraient-ils pas au restaurant?

7. Pourquoi le feraient-ils?
8. Vous ne seriez pas impoli.
9. Nous choisirions la meilleure bouteille.
10. Elle tiendrait la tête haute.
11. Elle pourrait se défendre.
12. Sauriez-vous l'heure?
13. Que verraient-ils?
14. Nous prendrions un bon repas.
15. Tu devrais réflechir.

EXERCISE 52

1. Elle le ferait
2. Enverriez-vous
3. Nous réussirions
4. je viendrais vous voir.
5. elle rirait.
6. N'aideraient-ils pas
7. J'irais
8. nous ne nous tromperions pas.
9. vous verriez son point de vue.
10. il pleuvrait

EXERCISE 53

1. écrivit
2. regardâmes
3. chercha
4. racontèrent
5. quittas
6. demandai
7. mourut
8. devinrent
9. fîtes
10. coururent

EXERCISE 54

1. Ils réussirent à la faire.
2. Je remarquai sa beauté.
3. Nous vîmes l'ennemi.
4. Ils burent le vin rouge.
5. Qui lui donna les fleurs?
6. Les soldats perdirent la bataille.
7. Les nobles firent la guerre.
8. L'actrice naquit en Italie.
9. Elle lut le conte.
10. Je le reconnus immediatement.
11. Ce soir-la, il plut.
12. Les feuilles tombèrent.
13. Il tint le chapeau sous le bras.
14. Il rit en voyant mon expression.
15. Qui sut le faire?

EXERCISE 55

1. passa
2. fut
3. fis
4. vint
5. prirent
6. écrivîmes

7. traversai
8. dit
9. voulurent
10. eut
11. parla
12. finirent
13. traduisis
14. partit
15. virent

EXERCISE 56

1. elle craignit
2. nous suivîmes
3. il plut
4. elle ajoutera
5. nous courûmes
6. ils conduisirent
7. je m'assis
8. il reconnut
9. ils marchèrent
10. je tins
11. je sus
12. tu connus
13. qui traduisit?
14. elle se tut
15. on plaignit
16. il plut
17. je ramassai
18. vous allates
19. il valut
20. je construisis

EXERCISE 57

1. Suddenly, she opened her eyes.
2. The workers received the new offer joyfully.
3. They entered into the forest.
4. I had to stay at my house.
5. The queen did not want to accept the reforms.
6. The thief put the jewels in the box.
7. There were forty-five years of war.
8. We didn't believe a single word.
9. Molière was born in 1633 and died in 1673.
10. We chatted with our cousins.
11. He took his umbrella and left.
12. The enemies arrived under the walls of Paris.
13. Francois the First was one of the best kings of France.
14. They heard the noise of the crowd.
15. Rouget de Lisle composed "la Marseillaise."
16. They helped the country to win its independance.
17. Pasteur did a lot to help humanity.
18. You did not tell the truth.
19. Someone led me into a big room.
20. Napoléon gave France a good legal system.
21. She saw a child who was looking at her.
22. You could not see your faults.
23. Paris became the center of French culture.
24. A lot of people learned to read.
25. In the 16th century, people built many beautiful mansions in France.

EXERCISE 58

1. J'emploie un transistor. J'emploierai un transistor.
2. Vous appelez le coiffeur. Vous appellerez.
3. Nous ne répétons pas ce qu'il a dit.
Nous ne repèterons pas ce qu'il a dit.
4. Tous ces chemins mènent à la ville.
Tous ces chemins mèneront à la ville.
5. Tu jetes la balle. Tu jeteras la balle.
6. Tout le monde prefère une maison comfortable.
Tout le monde prefèrera une maison comfortable.
7. Nous corrigeons ce que nous avons écrit.
Nous corrigerons ce que nous avons écrit.
8. Ils n'enlèvent pas nos privilèges.
Ils n'enlèveront pas nos privilèges.
9. Nous nettoyons bien les escaliers.
Nous nettoierons bien les escaliers.
10. Vous possédez un bon système de communication.
Vous possèderez un bon système de communication.

EXERCISE 59

1. Ils annoncaient, ils annonca
2. Je partageais, je partageai
3. Nous prononçons, nous prononçâmes
4. Ces conditions changeaient, ces conditions changèrent
5. M. Leger avançait, M. Léger avanca

EXERCISE 60

1. Elle achetait la maison.
2. Je préfère des croissants.
3. Ils levaient la table.
4. Effaçons la phrase entière.
5. Jettent-ils les pierres?
6. Elle nettoiera la lampe.
7. Qui m'appellera demain?
8. Cela m'ennuie.
9. On emploierait du bois.
10. Ses parents voyageaient souvent.

EXERCISE 61

1. Nous jetons
2. Nous essayons
3. Vous effacez
4. Vous n'esperez pas
5. Ils voyagerent
6. Nous commencons
7. Achetez
8. Elles corrigeaient
9. Nettoyez-vous
10. Nous menons

EXERCISE 62

1. Nous effaçons le tableau noir.
2. Non, le président la jette.
3. Oui, je les emploie.

4. Oui, vous la payez.
5. Les messieurs commencèrent chanter.
6. Les annonciez-vous?
7. Bien entendu, j' espère y aller.
8. Je m'appelle Berthe.
9. Oui, vous nagiez très bien.
10. Non, nous ne l'achèterions pas.

EXERCISE 63

1. Combien de temps
2. lis
3. Depuis quand
4. Pendant
5. vendra
6. pleut
7. quand il
8. pleuvait-il
9. pendant
10. Combien de temps
11. Combien de temps y a-t-il que
12. laverez

EXERCISE 64

1. Depuis quand travailles-tu? Je travaille depuis trois semaines.
2. Combien de temps étudient-ils? Ils étudient pendant deux heures.
3. Combien de temps est-il resté en Europe? Il est resté pendant six mois.
4. Depuis quand chante-t-elle? Elle chante depuis dix minutes.
5. Combien de temps nagera-tu? Je nagerai pendant une demie heure.

EXERCISE 65

1. J'écrivais depuis un quart d'heure quand la cloche a sonné.
2. Quand les grandes vacances seront arrivées j'irai chez ma grandmère pour un long séjour.
3. Le mécanicien répare mon automobile depuis un mois.
4. Mon père lui dira la mauvaise nouvelle quand il reviendra.
5. Elles ont parlé pendant une heure au téléphone hier soir.
6. Cette jolie infirmière travaille depuis deux semaines dans cet hôpital.
7. Après que vous partirez j'irai au restaurant.
8. Vous pourrez garder ce livre pendant un mois.
9. Le soleil se lève quand la journée commence.
10. Je l'attendais depuis vingt minutes lorsqu'elle est rentrée.

EXERCISE 66

1. Depuis quand écoutent-ils la radio chaque matin?
2. Est-ce qu'ils écoutent la radio depuis une demi-heure?
3. Y a-t-il une demi-heure qu'ils écoutent la radio?
4. Est-ce qu'ils écoutaient la radio depuis une demi-heure?
5. Ont-ils écouté la radio pendant une demi-heure?

EXERCISE 67

1. Depuis combien de temps y a-t-il que vous lisez le journal?
2. Il y avait une heure depuis que nous mangions.
3. Il y a quinze jours depuis que je suis ici.
4. Voilà depuis longtemps que les deux garçons patinent.
5. Depuis combien de temps y avait-il qu'ils suivaient cette route?

Chapter 3

EXERCISE 1

1. he had stayed
2. I will have begun
3. you broke
4. she had died
5. I would have gotten up
6. we had known
7. they would have entered
8. we shall have prepared
9. she had had a good time
10. you would have preferred

EXERCISE 2

1. Elle est restée chez elle.
   Elle s'est ennuyé chez elle.
2. N'aurait-il pas mort?
   N'aurait-il pas bu?
3. Nous nous sommes fâchés ce soir-là.
   Nous sommes sortis ce soir-là.
4. Je m'étais habillé de bonne heure.
   J'avais écrit de bonne heure.
5. Je serais entre dans la rue.
   J'aurais été dans la rue.
6. Est-ce que nous ne nous sommes pas blessés?
   Est-ce que nous ne sommes pas revenus?
7. Ils se seront finis avant six heures.
   Ils seront arrivés avant six heures.
8. Elles se seront déjà réveillées.
   Elles auront déjà oublié.
9. Avez-vous étudié au cinéma, Julie?
   Vous êtes-vous amuses au cinéma, Julie?
10. Elles ne seraient pas retournées.
    Elles ne se seraient pas ennuyées.

EXERCISE 3

1. j' avais emprunté.
2. il est né.
3. il était né.
4. ils se sont fâchés
5. il aura fait
6. elles étaient restées
7. elle serait venue
8. elles se sont levées

9. nous avions eu
10. je serai sorti
11. tu étais retourné
12. elle s'était amusée
13. elles auraient répondu
14. vous vous étiez lavé
15. je me serais dépêche

EXERCISE 4

1. Which car would he have driven?
2. She had not brushed her teeth again.
3. The day so waited for happened.
4. He would have become an engineer.
5. Where are the neckties that you bought?
6. What would he have said of me?
7. When you arrive, they will have left.
8. The waiter had kept the change.
9. How many animals would have died?
10. Would you have been able to do it?

EXERCISE 5

1. Les soldats marchèrent dans les rues désertés. ont marché
2. Nous répondîmes aussi honnêtement que possible. avons répondu
3. Le roi alla à la messe. est allé
4. Les musiciens voulurent jouer devant l'assemblée. ont voulu
5. Elle prit toutes les precautions nécessaires. Elle a pris
6. Les espions furent attrapés par les soldats du roi. ont été attrapés
7. On vendit les biens du baron. a vendu
8. Les cardinaux choisirent le nouveau Pape. ont choisi
9. Les invités vinrent nombreux. sont venus
10. Nous dûmes remercier notre protecteur. Nous avons dû
11. La petite fille vit la procession a vu
12. Le comte tint sa promesse au roi. a tenu
13. Qui furent ses ministres? ont été
14. Napoléon fit construire l'Arc de Triomphe. a fait
15. On brûla Jeanne d'Arc en 1431 à Rouen. a brûlé
16. Elle mourut sans reprendre conscience. est morte
17. Les messagers annoncèrent la mauvaise nouvelle. ont annonce
18. Nous sûmes que la reine était morte. avons su
19. La Fayette et Washington furent amis. ont été
20. L'actrice naquit en Italie. est née

EXERCISE 6

1. Dès que les révolutionnaires . a . . ouvert les portes de la Bastille, les prisonniers se sauverent.
2. Aussitôt que les Anglais . a . . brûlé Jeanne d'Arc, elle devint un symbole de patriotisme.
3. Les nobles s'arrangeaient pour augmenter les taxes dès que les récoltes . ont . . été bonnes.
4. Lorsque une croisade .fut . . annoncée les églises commençaient toutes à demander de l'argent aux fidèles .

5. Aussitôt que les colonies américaines se .furent . . déclarées independantes, la France les reconnut.
6. Quand les armées . ont . . chassé les Anglais de France, le peuple se réjouit.
7. Henri IV fut monté au pouvoir lorsque ses ennemis ont . . été répudiés.
8. Quand Balzac . a . . fini un roman, il en commençait tout de suite un autre.
9. Aussitôt que le Roi s'est . . levé, le public dût se lever aussi.
10. Tous les matins, pendant Napoleon surveillait les travaux, ses maréchaux furent consultés.

EXERCISE 7

1. Il n'eut jamais admis son erreur. n'a jamais admis
2. Il fallut que nous vissions ce spectable. Il a fallu que nous ayons vu
3. Leurs parents ne permettaient pas qu'ils vécussent ensemble. qu'ils aient vécu
4. Elle cherchait un mari qui sut faire la cuisine. savait
5. Il fut impossible que nous acceptassions ces conditions. Il était impossible que nous ayons accepté
6. La princesse était contente que son père fit cette célébration. ait fait
7. Le capitaine ordonna que les soldats revinssent en arrière. a ordonné que les soldats soit revenus
8. Les propriétaires n'étaient pas contents bien qu'ils s'enrichissent. se soient enrichis
9. S'il comprenait tout cela il se résignat. il se resignait
10. Les prêtes refuserent que les impots fussent diminués. ont refusé que les impôts soient dimuniés

EXERCISE 8

1. L'archevêque douta qu'elle se fut compromise dans l'affaire. a douté qu'elle se soit compromise
2. Elle ne voulait rien entendre, quoiqu'il eut fait tout son possible. quoiqu'il ait fait
3. Si vous nous aviez invités, nous eussions accepté avec plaisir. nous aurions accepté
4. Nous aurons voulu qu'elle eut dit franchement son opinion. qu'elle ait dit
5. Avait-il été certain que vous eussiez rejeté son offre? que vous ayez rejeté

EXERCISE 9

1. Je pris la liberté de m'asseoir.
2. Nous écrivîmes mainte fois au sénateur.
3. Monsieur Dupont tint sont chapeau sous le bras.
4. Les officiers donnèrent preuve d'une grande intelligence.
5. Ils agirent avec précaution.
6. Les armées du gouvernement conquèrent les envahisseurs.
7. Les fournisseurs fournirent des marchandises.
8. Le senateur fut élu.
9. Ce soir-là, il plut à verse.
10. Nous dîmes toutes nos pensées.
11. Finalement l'auteur arriva.

EXERCISE 10

1. Vous apprenez bien une langue pratiquant beaucoup.
2. Les valises arrivent sur des tapis roulant.
3. En cherchant je trouve une bonne réponse.
4. En chantant et sifflant il s'en va sur la montagne
5. Je n'ai jamais vu une soucoupe volant.
6. J'écoute en pensant d'autre chose.
7. Elle n'est pas contente d'être une femme obéissant!
8. Ne parle pas en mangeant.
9. Tu deviens bronze en restant au soleil.
10. Ils arrivent en criant parce qu'ils ont gagné.

EXERCISE 11

1. On a offert une cigarette à la dame.
2. On a vendu le journal dans la rue.
3. On a vu ces films à la télévision.
4. On a fermé les fenêtres a causé de la pluie.
5. On a peint les murs en blanc.
6. On a sert les clients comme il faut.
7. On a pris ces photos comme souvenir.
8. On a écrit souvent ces mots incorrectement.
9. On a mis cette lettre à la poste.
10. On a conduit l'auto pour lui.

EXERCISE 12

1. A school will be built near the church.
2. Cake is made with flour.
3. She was astonished at what she saw.
4. Nothing was added to the soup.
5. That is explained easily.
6. The soup is served.
7. The plates were put on the table.
8. The money due was payed.
9. Can this disease be cured?
10. It forbidden to park in front of the hotel.

EXERCISE 13

1. Comment prononce-t-on ce nom?
2. On n'a pas condamné l'assassin.
3. On prépare les repas dans la cuisine.
4. On guérira les malades.
5. On ne lira jamais ces romans.
6. Quelle langue parle-t-on au Méxique?
7. On a placé le papier sur le bureau.
8. On doit mettre cette lettre à la boîte à lettre.
9. On ne dit pas cela en publique.
10. On a servi la viande avec une salade verte.

EXERCISE 14

1. Les Antilles avait été découvertes.
2. Votre temps n'aurait pas été gaspille.
3. Par qui ce château a-t-il été construit?
4. La fenêtre avait été fermée par le professeur.
5. Ces cravates seront vendu dans tous les magasins.

EXERCISE 15

1. On dit que la ville de New York ne s'endort jamais.
2. On a donné un pourboire à la serveuse

3. Dans ce restaurant, on porte une cravate.
4. On offrira un prix au meilleur étudiant.
5. On a été divise le jambon en six tranches.

EXERCISE 16

1. Oui, il tâche de compléter ses devoirs.
2. Oui, je jure d'aider mes parents.
3. Oui, nous acceptons d'accompagner Marc.
4. Non, on oublie d'annoncer le dpart.
5. Oui, nous finissons de manger a midi.
6. Oui, il risque à manquer son autobus.
7. Oui, je décide de voter pour votre partie.
8. Non, elle refuse de travailler des heures supplementaires.
9. Oui, je promets d'employer la voiture de mon père.
10. Non, ils évitent à assister aux courses samedi.

EXERCISE 17

1. Il commande à la serveuse d'apporter une bouteille de champagne.
2. Ils ne permettent pas à Jeanne de passer la nuit dehors.
3. Le médecin ordonne à la malade de rester une semaine au lit.
4. Elle dit a son ami de regarder la première page du journal.
5. Nous écrivons à nos cousins de venir à New York par le prochain avion.

EXERCISE 18

1. Il est surprenant de remarquer toutes ces erreurs.
2. Elle est enchantée de voyager en première classe.
3. J'ai le plaisir de présenter mes amis à mes parents.
4. Elles sont vraiment contentes de finir leurs études.
5. Il est nécessaire de payer ses taxes.
6. Nous sommes bien obligés de remercier nos clients.
7. Henri-Roger n'a pas le temps de déjeuner.
8. Je n'ai vraiment pas envie de préparer le dîner.
9. Il est impossible d'arriver à l'heure.
10. Mon médecin a l'habitude de soigner les malades.

EXERCISE 19

1. Oui, mais il hésite à critiquer ses amis.
2. Oui, nous reussissons à finir ces exercices.
3. Oui, mais je tarde à demander mon passeport.
4. Oui, elle continue à étudier le russe.
5. Oui, nous commençons à profiter du beau temps.

EXERCISE 20

1. Je descends tout de suite pour manger maintenant!
2. Joue-t-elle au tennis? Tout le monde la regarde.
3. Il faut étudier le grammaire!
4. Je désire voyager en Europe.
5. Ils viennent à annoncer la bonne nouvelle.
6. J'entends sonner quelqu'un a la porte.
7. Elles aiment parler au téléphone.
8. Il prefere dîner seul au restaurant.
9. On entend arriver le train.
10. Je déteste de travailler à la jardin.

Chapter 4

EXERCISE 1

1. ce roman interessant
2. une blessure mortelle
3. la prononciation italienne
4. le bel homme
5. la gentille carte
6. cette sucrerie delicieuse
7. les pommes fraiches
8. la belle peinture ancienne
9. cet histoire médievale
10. des plans généraux
11. son frère ainé
12. la leçon difficile
13. cet eau fraiche
14. un vieil argument
15. une personne calculatrice
16. un portrait flatteur
17. une lettre discrète
18. cette actrice célèbre
19. votre meilleure amie
20. une position sérieuse
21. le nouveau velo
22. cette chemise bleue
23. l'exercice complet
24. un club actif
25. notre première leçon

EXERCISE 2

1. C'est un formidable écrivain!
2. Ce sont mes superbes romans!
3. Ce sont des émouvants poèmes!
4. C'est une magnifique peinture!
5. Voila le sensationnel gâteau!

EXERCISE 3

1. C'était une fille curieuse.
2. Je regarde un mauvais film.
3. Tous les jeunes gens dansent.
4. Ce cruel assassin a été condamne.
5. Elle a choisi une longue chanson.
6. C'est un beau bijou.
7. Aucune personne n'est venue.
8. Je vois toutes les roses.
9. J'ai acheté un bureau ancien.
10. Il mangeait trois pommes.

EXERCISE 4

1. These naughty boys play in the street.
2. I have some good friends.
3. I have some friendly neighbors.
4. He paints with a distinct style.
5. He paints with a sure style.
6. I have some dear souvenirs from California.
7. The unfortunate writer became famous.
8. I see a single person.
9. I see a person who's alone.
10. She arrived last week.
11. She arrived the final week.
12. This is a great man.
13. This is a tall man.
14. The school is in a former building.
15. The school is in an old building.
16. These buffeting storms hit the countryside.
17. The good banker loves poor children.
18. There is my own bed.
19. There is my clean bed.

EXERCISE 5

1. Non, ils font de la bonne cuisine.
2. Non, il est temps de voir des amis nouveaux.
3. Non, c'est un cher frère.
4. Non, elle sort avec un beau garçon.
5. Non, elle a la même modele de voiture.
6. Non, il prend le même train tous les jours.
7. Non, c'est une petite composition.
8. Non, c'est une ancienne bague.
9. Non, il est un garçon gentil.
10. Non, mon anniversaire tombe toujours à une même date.
11. Non, elle lit l'autre poème.
12. Non, il est un homme laid.
13. Non, elle est une personne jeune.
14. Non , il a des chaussures chères.
15. Non, il est notre ancien professeur.

EXERCISE 6

1. Il achète une voiture noire anglaise.
2. Prenez de ces pommes vertes delicieuses.
3. Qui va écouter cette musique moderne et ennuyeuse.
4. Nous nous asseyons à une table solide et lourde.
5. Vous offrez votre aide financière considérable.
6. Ils préfèrent les costumes chics et chers.
7. Je fréquente des amis étrangers intéressants.
8. Il a des leçons difficiles et compliquées.

EXERCISE 7

1. Oui, il est jeune sportif.
2. Oui, je pense a une sure profession certaine.
3. Oui, il est pauvre et malheureux.
4. Oui, il est gros et gras.
5. Oui, elle est charmante riche.
6. Oui, elle est petite et économique.
7. Oui, elle est blonde jolie.
8. Oui, il est bete méchant.
9. Oui, il est gentil et patient.
10. Oui, elle est belle et élégante.

EXERCISE 8

1. Ils sont des bons plans.
2. Elles sont des idées nouvelles.
3. Oui, ils sont des photos jolies intéressantes.
4. Oui, nous faisons des bons exercices physique.
5. Oui, il y a des anciens bijoux dans le musée.
6. Oui, elle a fait des biscuits petits.
7. Oui, nous avons des jeunes amies chinoises.

8. Oui, le Louvre a des beaux tableaux modernes.
9. Oui, il y a des grandes fleurs dans le jardin.
10. Oui, Jean a des vieilles peintures.

EXERCISE 9

1. L'eau est plus froide que le lait.
2. La lune est moins brillante que le soleil.
3. La crème est aussi nourissante que le lait.
4. Un livre n'est pas si léger qu'une plume.
5. Février a moins de jours que mai.
6. Les costumes sont plus chers que les cravates.
7. Un tyrant est plus cruel qu'un dictateur.
8. L'arithmétique est plus difficile qu'algebre.
9. L'eau n'est pas si solide que la glace.
10. Le New York est moins grand que Texas.
11. L' avion est plus rapide que le train.
12. Les hommes sont plus intelligents que les chiens.
13. Une annee est plus longue qu'un mois.
14. Le sucre est plus doux que les bonbons.
15. La pluie est moins froide que la glace.

EXERCISE 10

1. Le Texas est le plus grand état des Etats-Unis.
2. L'été est la plus agréable saison de l'année.
3. C'est le plus petit de mes soucis.
4. L'eau est la moins chère boisson du monde.
5. Ce sont les plus impressionnants édifices de notre ville.

EXERCISE 11

1. Elle nous a donné la plus mauvaise excuse.
2. Je pense que notre médecin est le plus habile.
3. Il a mis la plus vieille cravate.
4. Elle est sortie portant le plus élégant chapeau.
5. Le printemps est la plus belle saison.
6. Madame Dupont a la plus bonne idée.
7. Elle fait parfois des remarques les moindre originales.
8. C'est la plus ancienne école du pays.

EXERCISE 12

1. L'avocat a rendu visite à son client.
2. Mme Dupont va repasser ses robes.
3. Ne jouez pas avec votre santé.
4. Les paysans ont coupé la laine de leurs moutons.
5. J'ai dit bonjour en enlevant mon chapeau.
6. Fais-tu ta derniere année d'études?
7. Nous avons joui d'un beau temps pendant nos vacances.
8. Elle voudrait vivre sa propre vie.
9. Avez-vous amené vos amis au cinéma?
10. Les femmes n'ont pas encore fini son thé.

EXERCISE 13

1. Personne n'a oublié la plume.
2. Il a levé sa main.
3. Ma voiture est en panne.
4. Ils lisent leur journal.
5. Votre mère m'a écrit.
6. Elle brosse ses cheveux.
7. Il a sa main sur la table.

8. Leon et Andre ont écrit à leurs parents.
9. Tu as ta chemise.
10. Pierre et Andre a teleponé à leur mère.
11. Elle adore son père.
12. Mes amies sortent souvent avec moi.

EXERCISE 14

1. Ces faits sont importants.
2. Elle aime ce roman.
3. Elle a écrit cette pièce.
4. Cette automobile est dans le garage.
5. Ces amies arrivent ce soir.
6. Parlez à cet enfant.
7. Ce garçon arrive toujours en retard.
8. Sur cette page j'écris mon nom.
9. Cet homme défend son honneur.
10. Nous allons déjeuner dans ce restaurant.
11. Cette route va à Paris.
12. Cet artiste travaille bien.

EXERCISE 15

1. Quel sera le menu?
2. Quelles serait les objections?
3. Quels était les vins?
4. Quelle était la réponse?
5. Quelle est l'atmosphère?

EXERCISE 16

1. Quels livres!
2. Quel paysage!
3. Quelle peinture!
4. Quel arbre!
5. Quels animaux!

EXERCISE 17

1. Quel tableau est grand?
2. Quels restaurants sont bons?
3. Quelle est votre adresse?
4. Quelles robes sont dans l'armoire?
5. Quelles peintures aimez-vous?

EXERCISE 18

1. Jeanne a quelques mouchoirs.
2. Paul a plusieurs copains.
3. La jeune fille a quelque temps.
4. Certaines décisions sont difficiles.
5. Elle a vu diverses personnes.
6. Toute peine mérite salaire.
7. Avez-vous d'autres pommes?
8. Nous avons visité toutes les maisons.
9. Il y a aucun de verre dans la cuisine.
10. L'enfant mangé tous les bonbons.
11. Même son père le déteste.
12. Je n'ai jamais entendu telles bétises.
13. Telle est mon opinion.
14. Nous avons toute confiance en lui.
15. Des autres robes sont chères.
16. Nous avons parcouru quelques cent mètres.

17. Ils sont arrivés en toute hâte.
18. Prenez une cravate quelconque.
19. Il a perdu toute envie de vivre avec sa femme.
20. Toute l'équipe était prête.

EXERCISE 19

1. activement, plus activement, le plus activement
2. plus naturellement que, moins naturellement que
3. aussi pôliment que, le moins pôliment
4. plus pôliment que, moins pôliment que
5. très cruellement, trop cruellement, si bien
6. plus de cinq, moins de dix
7. vraiment, aussi, peut être
8. plus lentement que, aussi beaucoup que
9. aussi doucement que, le moins doucement
10. beaucoup, plus, le plus

EXERCISE 20

1. demain
2. seulement
3. tout de suite
4. de
5. bien
6. ensemble
7. que
8. parfaitement
9. lentement
10. malheuresement

EXERCISE 21

1. Non, j'écris peu.
2. Oui, il est bien
3. Oui, elle dépense beaucoup d'argent dans les grands magasins.
4. Non, il parle davantage de ses étudiants.
5. Non, il est plus intelligent que son collègue.
6. Oui, le climat devient de moins en moins agréable.
7. Oui, il est de plus en plus difficile.
8. Oui, elle a une si jolie robe.
9. Oui, il fait de si beaux cadeaux aux employés.
10. J'ai peu de devoirs à l'école.

EXERCISE 22

1. It will be winter soon.
2. They visited me more than ten times.
3. They got up immediately; then they left.
4. John got dressed quicker than we did.
5. Marianne goes to the movies as often as possible.
6. There were flowers almost everywhere in the garden.
7. How are your parents? They are much better.
8. Do the students study enough? They study too much, especially John.
9. The best students don't always write best.
10. He is the most brilliant of all the senators.

EXERCISE 23

1. Ils ont beaucoup voyagé au travers d'Europe.
2. Il y a plus de trente passagers dans cet autobus.

3. Lisez-vous autant de votre ami?
4. Ils ont souvent parlé de vous.
5. Il a fait moins de cinq erreurs dans sa composition.
6. Jean a dit rarement la vérité?
7. Nous le cherchait partout.
8. Pierre étudie plus qu'Andre mais moins que Jean.
9. Henri n'est pas encore sorti.
10. Qui travaille le moins? Pierre, André ou Jean?

Mastery Drills

EXERCICE 1

1. c', il   5. c', il   9. c', elle, c'
2. c', il, il   6. c', elle 10. c', elle
3. c', elle, elle   7. ce, ce, ils 1 1. c', il, il
4. c', il   8. c', il, il

EXERCICE 2

A. 1. C'est un compositeur français.
2. C'est Pasteur.
3. C'est un homme qui répare les chaussures.
4. C'est Descartes.
5. C'est Chagall.
6. C'est Louis XVI.
7. C'est un homme qui ne pense qu'a lui.
8. C'est....
9. Ce sont...
10. Ce sont les Belges, les Québecois, etc.
B. 1. C'est un bateau plat qui sert au transport des marchandises sur les rivières et les canaux.
2. C'est l'Organisation des Nations Unies.
3. C'est un lieu de culte israelite.
4. C'est un instrument de musique.
5. C'est un sport.
6. C'était le palais des rois de France.
7. C'est le...
8. Oui, c'est un vin mousseux.
9. Ce sont la vue, l'ouie, l'odorat, le toucher et le goût
10. C'est "grossir."
11. C'est "j'enverrai."
12. C'est le lapin.

EXERCICE 3

1. Elle est petite.
2. Elles sont hautes.
3. Oui, elles sont plus hautes.
4. Non, ils sont acides.
5. Il est très dur et brillant.
6. Elle est en or.
7. Elles sont en marbre, en bronze, etc.
8. Il a été froid.

EXERCICE 4

1. Ils sont bruns.
2. Ils sont bleus.
3. Il était américain.
4. Je suis...
5. Elle est gothique./ Elle est de style gothique.

6. Il est classique./ Il est de style classique.

EXERCICE 5

1. Il est dentiste.
2. Il est informaticien.
3. Non, il est architecte.
4. Non, elle est professeur.
5. Je veux être journaliste.
6. Il était pilote.
7. Il était cultivateur.

EXERCICE 6

1. Il est très beau.
2. C'est très beau.
3. Il est intéressant.
4. C'est très emouvant.
5. Elle est grande.
6. C'est très grand.
7. Il est agréable.
8. C'est pittoresque.

EXERCICE 7

1. C'   2. Elle   3. c'   4. il   5. ce   6. Elle
7. Il   8. c'   9. C'   10. Il

EXERCICE 9

A.   1. Elle est dans ma poche.   4. Il est à Rome.
2. Il est dans mon sac.   5. Elles sont à la bibliothèque
3. Il sont dans leur pays.
B.   1. C'est en Suisse.
2. C'est dans l'Ouest de la France.
3. C'est en Europe du Nord.
4. C'est en Afrique.
5. C'est au nord de l'Angleterre.
6. C'est dans l'Est de la France.
7. C'est au sud de la France.
8. C'est dans le mer des Caraibes.

EXERCICE 10

A.   1. La longuer de l'avenue des Champs Elysées est
de 1880m. Elle a 1880m de long./ Elle mesure
1880m. Elle fait 1880m de long.
2. La largeur de ma rue est de 15m./ Elle a 15m de large.
Elle mesure 15m./ Elle fait 15m de large.
3. La hauteur de l'Everest est de 8880m./ Il a 8880m de
haut./ Il mesure 8880m./ Il fait8880m de haut.
4. La largeur d'un lit d'une personne est de 90cm et sa
longeur est de 1,90m./ Il a 90cm de large et 1,90m
de long./ Il mesure de 90cm de large et 1,90m de
long. Il fait 90cm de large et 1,90m de long.
B.   1. L'épaisseur de mon livre est de 2cm./ Il a 2cm
d'épaisseur./ Il fait 2cm d'épaisseur.
2. La profondeur d'un réfrigérateur est de 80cm./ Il a
80cm de profondeur./ Il fait 80cm de profondeur.
3. La profondeur du petit bain est de 70cm./ Il a 70cm
de profondeur./ Il fait 70cm de profondeur.
4. L'épaisseur d'une belle moquette est de 3cm./ Elle a
3cm d'épaisseur./ Elle fait 3cm d'épaisseur.

EXERCICE 11

1. Je mesure 1,70m./ Je fais 1,70m.
2. Je chausse du 40./ Je fais du 40.
3. Je pese 60kg./ Je fais 60kg.
4. Je fais du 42.

EXERCICE 12

1. La température est de 30.
2. La distance de Paris à Munich est de 800km.
3. La population de la France était de 54,8 millions.
4. La durée des vacances de Noel est generalement de
deux semaines.
5. Mon salaire est de 10000 francs par mois.
6. La valeur du yen était de 3,85F.
7. L'augmentation du prix de l'essence sera de 3%.
8. La production de café de la Colombie a ete de 724 il-
lions de tonnes.
9. Le loyer de mon appartement est de 3000F par mois.
10. La consommation de cette voiture est de 10 litres au cent.

Les Adverbes - Mastery Drills

EXERCICE 1

A. Doucement, premièrement, nettement, facilement,
complètement, sérieusement, certainement, franchement, vivement, exceptionnellement.
Evidemment, constamment, couramment, violemment,
suffisamment, fréquemment, inconsciemment,
patiemment, bruyamment, récemment.

EXERCICE 2

1. confortable, confortablement
2. gratuitement, gratuit
3. objectif, objectivement
4. brièvement, bref
5. rapide, rapidement
6. sec, sèchement

EXERCICE 3

1. bons, bon
2. cher, chères
3. haute, haut
4. dur, dur
5. fortes, fort
6. faux, fausses
7. droite, droit

EXERCICE 4

1. Il a déjà neige.
2. Il a beaucoup plu.
3. Elle a toujours porté des lunettes.
4. Ce plombier a très bien travaillé.
5. Vous n'avez pas assez mangé.
6. J'ai mal compris votre explication.
7. M. Girodet a peu parlé.
8. Cet enfant a vite appris à lire.
9. J'ai mieux dormi.
10. Il est sûrement arrive a 8 heures.

11. Cet expert s'est rarement trompe...
12. Il a enfin avoué la vérité.

Chapter 5

EXERCISE 1

1. Mettons les dans la voiture.
2. Je lui ai explique le problème.
3. Me montreront ils leur chef d'uvre?
4. Prenez ce journal et portez le chez vous.
5. Nous ont ils vus?
6. Je crois qu'elle vous dit la vérité.
7. Ne leur parlons pas maintenant.
8. Donnez moi une livre de jambon, s'il vous plaît.
9. Sa mère lui lit un conte.
10. Habille toi vite, Theodore.

EXERCISE 2

1. Non, elle ne l'a pas encore lu.
2. Les voici.
3. Le professeur leur a enseigne le français.
4. Achetons une pomme et mangeons la.
5. Oui, il m'a montre le tableau.
6. Ils les ont rencontrés à la gare.
7. Philippe va le couper.
8. Oui, je t'aime.
9. Ils se portent bien.
10. Oui, il nous a guéris.

EXERCISE 3

1. He refuses to answer them.
2. Let's have fun tonight.
3. When one is sick, one sends for the doctor.
4. We were invited to the dance.
5. We didn't give them a gift.
6. How does one translate this proverb?
7. He made a mistake, but he corrected it.
8. Give him back the soap; he wants to wash himself.
9. In France, people eat well.
10. Didn't they give you the computer?

EXERCISE 4

1. Oui, elle les a déjà terminé ses études.
2. Non, on ne le comprend pas aux Etats Unis.
3. Oui, je leur téléphone souvent.
4. Oui, je veux les aider.
5. Oui, je peux les entend.
6. Oui, on l'a fermé a clef.
7. Oui, il lui fait attention.
8. Oui, je t'écouté.
9. Oui, ils vont me répondre tout de suite.
10. Elle s'est levée à huit heures.

EXERCISE 5

1. Je ne peux pas vous oublier.
2. Il se lave.
3. Nous avons nous brossé les dents.
4. Nous avons nous brossé(e)s.
5. Ils le font.
6. Ils ne l'ont pas fait.
7. Ne l'ont ils pas fait?
8. Faites le.
9. Ne le faites pas.
10. Je la connais.
11. Elle me connait.
12. Je lui ai parlé.
13. Me parlera-t-elle?
14. Elle veut me parler.
15. Ne lui a-t-elle pas parlé?
16. Je vais leur parler.
17. Regarde-la.
18. Ne la regardons pas.
19. Attendez moi.
20. Attendons-les.

EXERCISE 6

1. Quand il a commencé à neiger, je me trouvais au cinéma.
2. Pierre, où tu te promenerais s'il faisait beau cet après midi?
3. Ne vous en allez pas si tôt.
4. Françoise et moi, nous nous voyons souvent.
5. Mme Lejeune, je ne me fâcherai pas si vous vous trompez.
6. Ne te portes tu pas bien aujourd'hui?
7. M. Martin, vous vous marierez en juin ou en juillet?
8. Vous ennuyez-vous quand il n'y a rien a faire?
9. Tais toi quand le professeur parle.
10. Je me dépêcherais si j'étais en retard.

EXERCISE 7

1. Vous souvenez-vous de ce qu'il vous a dit?
2. Ne se rasait-il pas chaque matin?
3. Je m'en irai tout à l'heure.
4. Cette femme se plaint sans cesse.
5. Tu t'ennuierais si tu étais tout seul.
6. Elle se regarda dans la glace.
7. Dépêchez-vous, mes enfants!
8. Nous nous habillerons vite.
9. Elle ne se rappelle pas le nom du livre.
10. Repose-toi avant de te laver.

EXERCISE 8

1. Je me sens heureux aujourd'hui.
2. Les Etats Unis se trouvent en Amerique du Nord.
3. Je prefère me promener en ete a l'ombre.
4. L'eleve paresseux se plaindrait des devoirs.
5. Oui, je me souviens de la date de la pris de la Bastille.
6. Oui, tu t'amuseras si tu vas en France.
7. Je me brosse les dents avant le petit dejeuner.
8. Elle s'appelle Mme Dupont.
9. Le soleil se couche à dix neuf heures.
10. Nous nous dépêchons parce que nous sommes en retard.

EXERCISE 9

1. What was happening?

2. The old man sits in the arm chair to rest.
3. Do you wash your hands with warm water and soap?
4. They won't hurt themselves if they don't fight.
5. It seems to me that you are wrong.
6. Go away, naughty boy!
7. We would get up early if the weather was nice.
8. The child undressed, lay down, and fell asleep immediately.
9. I used to stop each day in front of the newsstand.
10. Why were the two sisters scolding each other?

EXERCISE 10

1. Ne vous fâchez pas.
2. Je me levais.
3. Comment s'appele-t-elle?
4. Ne se promenent-ils pas?
5. Amusez-vous.
6. Il ne se tromperait pas.
7. Ne nous arrêtons pas.
8. Ne te blessé pas.
9. Elle se lavait la figure.

EXERCISE 11

1. Oui, il y va.
2. Non, je n'en aurai pas besoin.
3. Oui, ils y vont la semaine prochaine.
4. Oui, je m'en sers.
5. Bien entendu, il s'en souvient.
6. En avez-vous?
7. Non, elles n'y sont pas allées.
8. Il en parle quatre.
9. Prenez en.
10. Oui, ils y étaient.
11. Mon frère y frappait.
12. Oui, j'en ai assez pris, merci.
13. Non, il n'y demeure plus.
14. Je vais en acheter une douzaine.
15. Oui, elles y sont.

EXERCISE 13

1. How many of them are there?
2. Yes, she chose several of them.
3. No, he's going there by bicycle.
4. Do you need it?
5. If you have so many pencils, lend some to your friends.
6. Yes, Dad, we're there.
7. Answer it immediately, please.
8. There are less than a hundred of them!
9. No, I don't come from there.
10. Yes, it's there.
11. Here are some.
12. Yes, they have gone there.
13. What do you think of it?
14. She recited five of them.
15. Yes, I remember some of it.

EXERCISE 14

1. Parlons en.
2. Vous en avez tant.
3. N'en ont ils pas vendu?
4. Achetez en.
5. N'en emprunté.
6. J'en ai besoin.
7. Il en a trouvé.
8. Nous en parlerons.
9. En as tu?
10. J'en ai vingt.
11. Nous n'en avons pas un.
12. Mange en.
13. N'en mange pas.
14. Je n'en veux pas.
15. Choisissez en trois.
16. Est-il né en Espagne? Oui, il y est né.
17. Est Jean chez lui? Oui, il y est.
18. Répondez-vous aux questions? Oui, j'y reponds.
19. Je vais au parc. N'y reste pas long.
20. Est il allé au cinéma? Oui, il y est allé.

EXERCISE 15

1. J'en ai vingt trois.
2. Oui, j'y vais souvent.
3. J'en sors à sept heures.
4. Non, je n'y réponds pas.
5. Oui, j'y marche.
6. J'en ai besoin quand il pleut.
7. Non, je n'en mange pas trop parfois.
8. Oui, j'y vais quand j'ai mal aux dents.
9. Oui, elle y sera cette année.
10. Oui, j'en viens.

EXERCISE 16

1. L'agent l'y a arrêté.
2. Lisez le leur.
3. Je t'en félicité.
4. La domestique nous les a apportés.
5. Envoyons le lui.
6. Le journaliste s'en souvient il?
7. Porte-les y.
8. Voulez-vous bien me le réciter?
9. La Garonne s'y jette.
10. Donnez-nous en un demi kilo.

EXERCISE 17

1. Vendez la lui.
2. Envoyez les nous.
3. Va t'en.
4. Dites-la moi.
5. Rendons-les leur.

EXERCISE 18

1. Prête-le moi..
2. Ne les lui prêtez pas.
3. Je vous les prêterai.

4. Ne leur en prêtez pas.
5. N'y en a-t-il pas?
6. Prêtez-lui en.
7. Je ne peux pas vous en prêter.
8. Prêtez les nous.o us.
9. Ne nous le prêtez pas.
10. Je te les ai prêtes.

EXERCISE 19

1. Oui, je lui en ai offert.
2. Oui, le professeur la leur enseignera.
3. Mon père les y accompagnes.
4. Il m'en a emprunté dix?
5. Je vais vous l'expliquer demain.
6. Oui, il y en a assez pour réaliser le projet.
7. Non, nous ne voulons pas que vous nous l'écriviez.
8. Robert le lui a donné.
9. Je t'y attendais depuis vingt minutes.
10. On me les enverra aujord'hui.

EXERCISE 20

1. That man sleeps less than you.
2. It's not you that I'm looking for.
3. Do you remember them?
4. It is they who deserved it.
5. You and I, we will buy the castle.
6. She is going home.
7. Is it you who speak English?
8. Who is going pick them up at the airport? I am.
9. You are a good student!
10. The museums were in front of us.

EXERCISE 21

1. Ils ont reçu des lettres de nous.
2. C'est lui qui devrait travailler dur.
3. Mon ami est plus gentil que toi.
4. Qui va nous l'expliquer? Moi, je vous l'expliquerai.
5. Cette clef est pour vous, monsieur.
6. Sortirez-vous avant votre fiancée? Oui, je sortirai avant elle.
7. Toi et moi, nous paierons l'addition.
8. La jeune fille parle mieux que moi.
9. Qui l'a entendu? Nous.
10. Leurs amis jouent au tennis, mais eux, ils étudient.
11. Elle chante; nous, nous dansons.
12. Ils courent vers elles.
13. Vous êtes arrive avant eux.
14. Elle demeure loin de lui.
15. C'est eux que nous avons rencontrés à la gare?

EXERCISE 22

1. Oui, elle demeure près de moi.
2. Oui, c'est elle.
3. Non, ils sont moins riches que nous.
4. J'irai chez elle demain.
5. Pierre et moi, nous allons au cinéma chaque vendredi.
6. Oui, c'est à vous.
7. Naturellement, je pense souvent à eux.

8. Je voudrais bien dîner avec toi.
9. Oui, nous sommes arrivés après elles.
10. Moi, je ne l'oublierai jamais, le jour de mon premier baiser.

EXERCISE 23

1. Est-ce elle?
2. Il est plus riche que toi.
3. Ils ont été assis devant nous.
4. Qui vient d'arriver? Lui.
5. Faites-le pour elle.
6. Jean mange plus que toi et moi ensemble.
7. Est-ce vous, madame?
8. Venez avec moi, s'il vous plaît.
9. C'est eux qui ont acheté la maison à côté.
10. Eux, ils sont tristes; mais moi, je suis heureux.
11. Moi, je ne fume pas!
12. Lui et moi, nous travaillons ensemble.
13. Il y a une sortie près de vous.
14. Il ne sort jamais sans elle.
15. Ce n'est pas moi.

EXERCISE 24

1. Oui, je me souviens de vous.
2. Non, ce n'est pas moi qui parle si fort dans la classe.
3. Je rendrai visite à eux aujord'hui.
4. Oui, le train est arrivé avant nous.
5. Oui, j'irais en Europe sans eux.
6. Oui, je pourrai jouer au tennis avec vous demain.
7. Non, elle n'est pas a moi.
8. Oui, c'est lui qui n'aime pas parler en public.
9. L'equipe de football de New York était plus fort qu'elle.
10. Je pense plus souvent a toi.

EXERCISE 25

1. Ce sont les siens.
2. C'est le tien.
3. Ce sont les notres.
4. C'est la mienne.
5. C'est le sien.
6. Ce sont les miens.
7. C'est la notre.
8. Ce sont les siennes.
9. C'est le votre.
10. C'est le leur.

EXERCISE 26

1. Il préfère ma solution à la sienne.
2. Ces avenues sont plus larges que les notres.
3. J'ai pris mon ordinateur et le sien.
4. Vos enfants travaillent ils aussi dur que les leurs?
5. Tu as mes lunettes de soleil et les tiennes.
6. Cherchez votre route et nous chercherons la nôtre.
7. Votre mère et la mienne travaillent bien ensemble.
8. Voici mes bagages. Où sont les vôtres?
9. Parlez vous de nos photos ou des siennes?
10. Mon père est aussi jeune que le leur.

EXERCISE 27

1. Leur chambre et la nôtre sont sur le premier étage.
2. Ses chansons et les nôtres ont recu un prix.
3. Ce château est à son père et le mien.
4. Mes amis et les tiens sont allés au cinéma.
5. Son chat et le nôtre se battent souvent.
6. Leurs enfants et les miens sont retournés du long voyage.
7. Mon voisin et le vôtre parlent beaucoup.
8. Notre ville et la leur sont propres.
9. Vos billets et les siens sont chers.
10. Sa bonne reputation et la mienne ont aide nos enfants.
11. Le directeur parle bien de tes sœurs et des leurs.
12. Remplissez ma tasse et la sienne, s'il vous plait.
13. Son lycée et le vôtre offrent un bon programme d'été.
14. Ses lettres et les miennes n'ont pas été très longues.
15. Leur famille et la nôtre toujours passent ensemble l'été.

EXERCISE 28

1. Oui, je répondrai aux vôtres.
2. J'ai pris les miennes.
3. Ils ont acheté les leurs.
4. Oui, j'ai vu les nôtres.
5. Non, je n'ai pas les miennes.
6. Oui, notre maison est plus belle que la vôtre.
7. La mienne donne aussi sur la rue.
8. Oui, je peux vous prêter le mien.
9. Oui, je te montrerai les miennes.
10. Non, ma voiture est moins économique que la tienne.

EXERCISE 29

1. Celle-là a choqué ses parents.
2. C'est un systeme politique.
3. C'est mon seul rêve.
4. Il déteste cela (ça).
5. C'est très impressionant.
6. C'est faux.
7. Il lui a donne celle-ci.
8. C'est due demain.
9. Cela (ça) me rend fou de tristesse.
10. C'était suprennant.
11. Ce sont des étudiants intelligents.
12. Celle-là est une avocate douée.
13. Elle attend cela.
14. C'est une des grandes puissances du monde.
15. Il ne voulait pas accepter cela.

EXERCISE 30

1. Qui t'a suggéré celle-là?
2. Regarde ce que j'ai.
3. Cela met en relief le même point.
4. Marie verra celles-ci et elle m'écrira.
5. Celle-là n'est plus bonne à boire
6. Ce sont les plus longues de l'Afrique.
7. Qui aurait pensé qu'il aurait acheté celles-ci.
8. Donnez-moi ce que vous m'avez promis.
9. Celui-ci décolle à 15 heures et celui-là part à 20 heures.
10. Celles-ci sont a bon marché.

EXERCISE 31

1. Cela (ça) va bien
2. Non ceci ne me plaît pas
3. Cela va très bien
4. Cela est formidable
5. Cela (ça) me dit rien

EXERCISE 32

1. Il est Péruvien
2. C'est une maison de campagne
3. Ce sont des hommes d'affaire habiles
4. Ils sont jeunes
5. C'est une bonne amie
6. C'est une belle ville
7. C'est un médecin excellent
8. Il est secrétaire
9. Elle est avocate
10. C'est une américaine noire

EXERCISE 33

1. C'est trop bon marché.
2. Cela doit être facile.
3. Ce sera cher.
4. Cela m'est égal.
5. Cela dépend d'elle.

EXERCISE 34

1. (that) Partira-t-il malgré cela?
2. (It) Ce n'est pas une méthode nouvelle.
3. (They) Ils sont en guerre.
4. (They) Ce sont des bateaux a moteur.
5. (it) Est-ce un aliment qui donne des forces?
6. (This) Cela vous donnera la même impression.
7. (These) Ce sont les miens.
8. (She) C' est la seule qui reçoive tant de lettres.
9. (She) Elle est actrice.
10. (It) C'est mon tour.
11. (that) Qu'est ce que cela prouve?
12. (He) C'est un savant illustre.
13. (they) Achetez ces roses; Elle sont très jolies.
14. (That) Ce n'est pas de la science fiction.
15. (this) Regardez cela.
16. (It) C'est New York.
17. (They) A qui sont ces gants? Ils ne sont pas à moi.
18. (This) C'est la plus difficile des questions.
19. (It) C'est la fête de maman.
20. (Those) Ce sont les résultats de plusieurs années de recherches.

EXERCISE 35

1. C'est le musée d'histoire naturelle.
2. Elles sont revenues tard.
3. C'est lui qui le fera.
4. Il est écrivain.
5. Ce sont des climats froids.
6. C'est Henri.

7. Ce n'était pas sa faute.
8. C'est probable qu'elle m'a reconnu.
9. C'est du sable blanc.
10. Est-ce une machine à laver?
11. Connaissez-vous Albert? Il est très timide.
12. C'est celui de l'avocat.
13. Ce sont les meilleurs du monde.
14. Il est utile de savoir nager.
15. C'était la marine française.
16. Elles sont toujours heureuses.
17. L'Etat, C'est moi.
18. C'est cela.
19. La paix est précieuse. Oui, C'est précieuse.
20. C'est le Rhône.
21. Ce sera demain vendredi.
22. Tout le monde aime le beau temps. C'est vrai.
23. C'était M. Sorel.
24. De quelle couleur sont les arbres? Ils sont verts.
25. C'est le dos du livre.
26. Il est neuf heures et demie.
27. Il est le plus intelligent de la classe.
28. Quel est cet oiseau? C'est un aigle.
29. Où sont vos fils a present? Ils sont en Europe.
30. C'est un projecteur de cinéma sonore.

EXERCISE 36

1. C'est une violette.
2. IL est très beau.
3. Ce sont des œufs qu'elle bat.
4. Ils sont dans le réfrigerateur.
5. C'est possible.
6. Elle est un peu sourde.
7. C'est la lune qui tourne aotour de la terre.
8. Elles sont fortes en mathematiques.
9. Il est coiffeur.
10. C'est une glace à la vanille que je mange.
11. Ce sont les nôtres.
12. C'est impossible.
13. C'est le gratte ciel le plus haut de la ville.
14. Ce sont des langues faciles à comprendre.
15. Ce sont nos voisins qui frappent à la porte.
16. C'est une pièce de Molière.
17. SIl est midi précis.
18. Ce sont les Pyrenées.
19. Elle est construite pour durer.
20. Elle la sœur de Bernard.

EXERCISE 37

1. She is my grandmother.
   C'est ma grande mère.
2. Who gave you this?
   Qui vous a donné cela?
3. He is a sculptor.
   Il est sculpteur.
4. He is a well known sculptor.
   C'est un sculpteur bien connu.

5. Today is June 10th.
   C'est aujourd'hui le 10 juin.
6. Those are beautiful leaves.
   Ce sont de belles feuilles.
7. He came back? That's interesting!
   Il est revenu? C'est intérressant!
8. Do you prefer this or that?
   Preférez vous ceci ou cela?
9. It is easy to read that.
   Il est facile de lire cela
10. That is easy to read.
    C'est facile a lire.

EXERCISE 38

1. qui	2. ce qui	3. lesquelles
4. que	5. ce que	6. qui
7. qu'	8. ce qu'	9. dont
10. laquelle	11. que	12. dont
13. ce qui	14. qu'	15. qui

EXERCISE 39

1. The eggs that I ate were very fresh.
2. Here is the bottle of wine I was talking about.
3. Who is the person to whom you are writing?
4. Tell us what they did.
5. Give me the things that I need.
6. That's the boat in which I took a long trip.
7. Here are the notebooks in which I write my homework.
8. There are many Europeans who English.
9. Where is the child whose father has just arrived?
10. Do you know what I forgot?

EXERCISE 40

1. Un boulanger est un homme qui vend du pain.
2. Voici l'atelier dans lequel l'artiste travaille.
3. Le lait que j'ai bu était delicieux.
4. Voici ce qu'elle m'a envoyé.
5. Montre moi les chapeaux que vous avez achetés.
6. La ville à laquelle nous sommes arrivés était tout a fait moderne.
7. Avez vous lu l'anecdote dont nous avons parlé?
8. C'est mon oncle qui est avocat.
9. Dites-moi qui est dans la voiture.
10. La femme avec laquelle elle est partie est ma mère.
11. C'est l'ingénieur dont j'ai fait la connaissance.
12. Où est la lampe qu'il a cassée?
13. C'est la porte par laquelle ils sont sortis.
14. Je comprends ce que vous avez dit.
15. Voilà l'église dont la cloche a sonné.

EXERCISE 41

1. Le bureau où il y a une règle est a moi.
2. Ce que j'ai reçu est très cher pour moi.
3. La mère dont fils a réussi est mon amie.
4. Le Français auquel j'ai parle est impoli.
5. La viande qui était sur la table était chère.
6. Son chien n'est pas un Saint Bernard.

7. Ceux que nous avons choisis n'étaient pas chers.
8. L'homme qui est parti est un écrivain célèbre.
9. La maison qu'ils ont construite a trois étages.
10. Ce qui est sur le toit ne tombera pas.
11. Le restaurant dont tout le monde parle se trouve à Rue Saint Honoré.
12. Le chapeau que vous porterez est très elegant.
13. Les amis avec qui j'étudie demeurent downtown.
14. Ce qu'elle a acheté ne la plaît pas.
15. Le train qui part arrivera à l'heure.

EXERCISE 42

1. Prenez l'argent que vous avez gagné.
2. J'ai écouté le poète qui parle bien.
3. Nous avons manqué le train qui est parti.
4. Voila l'appartement où Pierre demeure.
5. Ouvrez le sac dans lequel j'ai mis mes pierres.
6. C'est notre cousin dans chez qui nous avons diné.
7. Voici les romans qu'elle a lus.
8. Elle nous montrait les vêtements dont elle avait parlé.
9. Donnez lui les timbres qui sont sur le bureau.
10. Jean est l'ami avec qui je joue chaque jour.

EXERCISE 43

1. quoi	2. Auquel	3. Que
4. A qui	5. Que	6. Qu'
7. Quelles	8. Qui	9. De qui
10. Quel	11. Qui	12. Qu'est ce qui
13. qui	14. Laquelle	15. qui

EXERCISE 44

1. Que cherchez-vous?
2. Avec qui est elle partie?
3. Qui sera à la fête?
4. Qui avez vous rencontré?
5. Qu'est ce qu'elle a trouvé?
6. Qu'est ce qui est tombé?
7. Duquel as tu peur?
8. Qu'est ce qu'il a demandé?
9. Qui est ce qui s'est blessé?
10. Auquel donneront ils le cadeau?

EXERCISE 45

1. Quel jour est le plus court?
2. De qui est elle la fille?
3. Laquelle de ces fleurs est la plus belle?
4. Quelle heure est-il?
5. Que buvez-vous?
6. Lequel est le plus court?
7. Qui savez vous?
8. Qui est entré?
9. Qu'est ce qu'elle a vu?
10. A quels enfants lisait-il?
11. Auxquels lisait il?
12. Pour qui travaille-t-il?
13. Qu'est ce qui est sur la chaise?
14. A qui est ce mouchoir?
15. Avec quoi coupera-t-il le gâteau?

EXERCISE 46

1. Que	2. Qui	3. De qui
4. A qui	5. Qu'est ce que	6. Quel
7. Qu'est-ce que	8. A qui	9. De quoi
10. Qu'est-ce qu'	11. Qui	12. De quoi
13. Chez qui	14. Lesquels	15. Qu'

EXERCISE 47

1. Of which ones were you speaking?
2. Whose aunt is she?
3. Who gave you this poodle?
4. What was he looking at?
5. In which country is he going to travel?
6. With what is she writing?
7. What fell?
8. Whose ticket is this?
9. What did you receive?
10. Which one do you wish to sing?

EXERCISE 48

1. N'importe qui peut faire une faute.
2. Quelqu'un viendra.
3. Tout le monde voudrait vivre en paix.
4. On peut manger dans ce restaurant.
5. Elle a fait quelque chose de bon à manger?
6. Nous n'avons pas tout entendu.
7. Les autres sont déjà partis.
8. Elles les a toutes écrit.
9. Oui, j'en ai quelques uns.
10. Ils partiront l'un et l'autre.
11. Nous ne voulons pas l'un ou l'autre.
12. Certaines d'entre elles aimeraient y aller.
13. Ce garçon fera n'importe quoi.
14. Veux tu quelque chose d'autre, ma chérie?
15. Tout ce que Jean dit est amusant.
16. Nous avons plusieurs voitures.
17. Oui, j'en ai quelques unes.
18. Chacun des enfants apportera quelque chose.
19. Quelqu'un d'autre m'accompagnera à la gare.
20. Quelques uns chantaient; les autres jouaient de la guitare.
21. Elles se téléphonent l'une a l'autre.
22. Vous avez deux crayons. Donnez-moi l'un ou l'autre.
23. N'importe qui peut obtenir un permis de conduire.
24. Non, c'est la même.
25. Aucune d'elles ne partira avant midi.
26. Personne ne sait le numero de téléphone de Jean.
27. Tout est charmant dans ce petit village.
28. Rien n'est absolu.
29. Allez voir Monsieur un tel.
30. Qui que ce soit qui sortira sans manteau, aura froid.
31. Il ne faut pas dire rien.
32. Ont ils n'importe quoi d'autre?

Chapter 6

EXERCISE 1

1. Madame Dupont est au bureau. Elle est dans la salle de conférence à dix heures du matin.
2. Elle est au lycée à midi. Elle est en classe. Elle est dans la classe de rédaction.
3. Elle sort de l'école à trois heures de l'après-midi.
4. Elle va en ville. Elle va chez le boulanger. Elle marche sur le boulevard Saint Michel. Elle rentre chez elle tard le soir.
5. Elle range ses achats sur le placard.
6 Elle met ses livres, et ses papiers dans un tiroir.
7. Monsieur Dupont va au bureau à six heures et il retourne à la maison à sept heures.
8. Lui aussi, il marche sur le boulevard Saint Michel. Souvent il y a beaucoup d'étudiants dans la rue.
9. Il va en ville pour faire des courses. Il rentre chez lui et il dine avec sa femme dans la salle de manger.
10. Le matin, Madame Dupont travaille au bureau; l'après-midi elle enseigne au lycée. Le soir elle prépare à manger dans la cuisine.

EXERCISE 2

1. Elle revient d'Italie.
2. Elle est passée en France.
3. Je suis à New York et ma femme est au Japon.
4. Mr Dupont est en Afrique et en Afrique du Nord.
5. Sa femme demeure à Paris.
6. Ils ont voyagé au Méxique et en Amérique du Sud.
7. En route pour l'Angleterre, ils ont passé par la Belgique.
8. L'accident a lieu en Espagne.
9. Pendant ses séjours aux Etats Unis Jean a demeuré en Floride, dans le Vermont et au Nouveau Méxique.
10. Le train part pour Bruxelles.
11. Il revient du Québec.
12. Ils sont débarqués au Havre.
13. M. Dupont va à San Francisco en Californie.
14. De Russie, ils sont allés en Israel.

EXERCISE 3

1. Les officiers paradent à cheval.
2. M. Dupont va au travail en metro.
3. Les enfants voyagent de Paris à Tokyo en avion.
4. Les enfants font à l'eglise à pied.
5. Les jeunes marriés voyagent par le train.
6. Les touristes américains aiment voyager en bateau.
7. Madame Célestin va en ville en voiture.
8. Son mari va au cinema en autobus.
9. Il n'aime pas voyager en bicyclette.
10. La compagnie va nous envoyer le colis par bateau.

EXERCISE 4

1. après
2. en
3. à
4. avant, après

EXERCISE 5

1. en 2. dans
3. dans 4. Dans
5. en 6. en
7. dans 8. en

EXERCISE 6

1. à 2. de
3. de, de 4. aux
5. aux, aux, au 6. de
7. à 8. de
9. aux 10. d'
11. en 1 2. de, de
13. de

EXERCISE 7

1. Il lui a parlé avec tendresse.
2. Elle lui a regardé d'un air curieux.
3. Quand elle lui parle, elle parle à haute voix.
4. Elle lui a questionné avec dureté.
5. Il a tenu le colis à la main. Enfin il le lui donne en pleurant avec de joie.

EXERCISE 8

1. Ce sont des voitures à louer.
2. Elle a honte d'avoir fait une bétise.
3. Ce probleme est difficile à résoudre.
4. Pourquoi hesitez vous à répondre?
5. Il n'est pas nécessaire de mentir.
6. Vous avez l'air d'ennuyer.
7. Ce travail est difficile à faire.
8. Ayez la bonté d'entrer.
9. C'est facile à laver.
10. Soyez sûr de le féliciter.

EXERCISE 9

1. un professeur de français
2. un appartement à louer
3. la dame aux cheveux rouges
4. une tarte aux pommes
5. la soupe au tomate
6. une tasse de thé
7. la glace à la vanille
8. une agence de voyage
9. une cravate en soie
10. une cravate de soie
11. un verre d'eau
12. un verre à eau
13. une tarte aux pommes
14. une cuiller à soupe

EXERCISE 10

1. au 2. le
3. et le 4. en
5. du 6. a
7. en 8. a
9. de 10. a
1nn1. à 1 2. dans

13. à 14. a
15. à 16. a
17. au 18. à la
19. sur 20. avec
21. aux 22. du
23. aux 24. au
25. de 26. dans
27. dans 2 8. de
29. à 30. d'
31. à 32. a
33. avant 34. en
35. de 36. en
37. Chez 3 8. d'

Chapter 7

EXERCISE 1

1. Non, quatre ne précède pas trois.
2. Non, il ne neige pas en été.
3. Non, nous ne mangeons pas le dessert avant la salade.
4. Non, je n'étudie pas le chinois ce semestre.
5. Non, nous ne fermons pas des fenêtres en juillet.
6. Non, nous ne déjeunons pas à quatre heures.
7. Non, on ne fume pas en attérrissant en avion.
8. Personne ne préfère pas échouer aux examens.
9. Je ne suis pas en retard à mes classes.
10. Non, les profs n'apprécient pas les erreurs des élèves.

EXERCISE 2

1. Non, je ne réponds jamais en français.
2. Non, je ne demeures plus ou je suis ne.
3. Non, il ne regrette point son crime.
4. Non, je ne fume jamais des cigarettes.
5. Non, elle ne travaille guère.

EXERCISE 3

1. Personne ne parle cinq langues dans votre famille.
2. Rien ne précède la lettre A dans l'alphabet.
3. Je ne regarde personne en ce moment.
4. Aucun pays n'est plus grand que la Russie.
5. On ne mange rien en parlant.
6. Aucune lettre ne précède la lettre A dans l'alphabet.
7. Je ne refuse rien dans un restaurant de luxe.
8. Personne ne proteste quand je sors le soir.
9. Je ne déteste personne.
10. Rien ne ressemble à Asterix.

EXERCISE 4

1. Il n'abandonne ni famille ni foyer.
2. Ni la mer ni le soleil ne suffisent.
3. On n'offre ni thé ni café.
4. Vous n'écoutez ni avec intérêt ni avec attention.
5. Les Américains ne prennent ni apéritif ni digestif.

Chapter 8

EXERCISE 1

1. vingt et unième
2. deux douzaines
3. François premier
4. cinq milles
5. la moitié
6. quatre vingt un
7. Milliers
8. une demi bouteille
9. une tasse et demie
10. cent dix

EXERCISE 2

1. en été
2. le premier avril, mille neuf cent vingt trois
3. en mille huit cent trente et un
4. le trente novembre, mille six cent soixante dix
5. seize heures et demie
6. vers deux heures du matin
7. minuit vingt cinq
8. à une heure précise
9. en février
10. le douze octobre

EXERCISE 3

1. Le jour qui suit dimanche est lundi.
2. L'été est la saison où il fait le plus chaud.
3. Ma montre retarde de quinze minutes.
4. Généralement il pleut beaucoup au printemps.
5. J'ai fini le travail à midi precis.
6. Le premier janvier, c'est le Nouvel An.
7. L'indépendance des Etats Unis a été déclaré le quatre juillet 1776.
8. Nous aimons faire du ski en hiver.
9. Je vous verrai jeudi prochain, c'est-à-dire, d'aujourd'hui une semaine.
10. Le trente et un décembre est le dernier jour de l'année.

EXERCISE 4

1. Oui, nous avons cette maison depuis un an.
2. Oui, il y a un mois que le magasin est fermé.
3. Oui, ils viennent régulièrement depuis plusieurs jours.
4. Oui, je les prends depuis je suis enrhumé.
5. Oui, personne n'habite cet appartement depuis longtemps.
6. Oui, il y a trois semaines qu'on ne voit plus ces gens.
7. Oui, ce film se joue en ville depuis quelques temps.
8. Oui, il y a un mois qu'il étudient le français.
9. Oui, il y a six mois que je suis fiancés.
10. Oui, ils se connaissent depuis longtemps.

EXERCISE 5

1. Oui, il y avait un mois qu'ils sont partis en vacances d'été. / Yes, it has been one month since they left on their summer vacation.
2. J'attendais cette lettre depuis longtemps./
I had been waiting for this letter for a long time.

3. Oui, ils voyagaient depuis quelques mois quand l'accident a eu lieu./ They had been travelling for a few months when the accident happened.
4. Oui, il y avait des heures que je mangeais quand le téléphone a sonné./ I had eaten a couple of hours ago when the phone rang.
5. Oui, elle dormait depuis longtemps quand on frappe à la porte./ She had beem sleeping for a long time when someone knocked on the door.

EXERCISE 6

1. Il était en train de mourir de faim.
2. Nous étions en train de dépenser tout notre energy.
3. Ils sont en train de raconter une histoire drôle.
4. Ce monsieur est en train de perdre son temps.
5. Les travailleurs étaient en train de transporter des marchandises sur leurs épaules.
6. Ils sont en train d'annoncer le départ de notre train.
7. Le pays était en train de subir de grands changements.
8. Pourquoi étaient-elles en train de faire toutes ces grimaces?
9. Les professeurs sont en train de resolver les problèmes.
10. Il est en train d'écrire un roman macabre.

EXERCISE 7

1. Moi aussi, je vais voyager en Europe.
2. Il va finir son travail.
3. Ils va manger du caviar.
4. Nous allons reprendre nos études.
5. Le directeur va parler aux étudiants.
6. Sa femme va écrire un roman.
7. Moi aussi, je vais habiter à New York.
8. Non, leurs parents ne vont pas danser le rock.
9. Mes frères allait rendre visite au musée d'art.
10. Merci, mais je ne vais pas prendre un verre de champagne.

EXERCISE 8

1. Viennent ils de se fiancer?
2. Elle venait de fermer la porte de sa chambre.
3. Vient-il de prendre l'avion en destination de Paris?
4. Jean vient de téléphoner.
5. Je viens de terminer le roman.
6. Je viens de commencer un nouveau livre.
7. Ils venaient de complètement renover leur voiture.
8. Nous venons de retourner d'Italie.
9. Est ce qu'ils viennent de consulter un avocat?
10. Je venais de poser une question.

EXERCISE 9

1. S'il cuisinait, on finirait par manger bien ce soir.
2. Elle finira par reussir, si elle fait un peu d'effort.
3. Nous sommes alles au musée, mais le musée finissait par être fermé.
4. Nous achèterons une machine ordinateur, mais elle finit par être en panne.
5. On le ferait, mais on finirait par se tromper.

EXERCISE 10

1. Nous faisons réciter le poème à Marie.
   Nous faisons reciter le poème par Marie.
2. Vous faites donner le poème à Marie.
   Vous faites donner le poème par Marie.
3. Tu fais envoyer le poème à Marie.
   Tu fais envoyer le poème par Marie.
4. Ils font écrire le poème à Marie..
   Ils font écrire le poème par Marie.
5. Je fais dicter le poème à Marie.
   Je fais dicter le poème par Marie.

EXERCISE 11

1. Il la lui a fait recopier
2. L'y avez vous fait venir?
3. Nous l'avons fait lui voir.
4. Fais les étudier.
5. Le professeur les lui a fait remarquer.
6. Faites le leur dire.
7. Elle lui en a fait donner du lait.
8. Faites leur en donner.
9. Fais lui comprendre qu'elle ne peut pas sortir.
10. Je le leur ferais savoir.

EXERCISE 12

1. Le professeur laisse partir les enfants.
2. Nous avons entendu les enfants gronder par leurs parents.
3. Nous voyons revenir les enfants.
4. Nous regardons descendre les enfants de l'autobus.
5. Nous entendons parler les enfants à voix basse.
6. Nous avons entendu les enfants appeler par leur professeur.
7. Nous avons vu réciter les enfants leur leçon.
8. "Ne laissez pas partir les enfants," je me suis dit.
9. Pendant la récreation, je regarde jouer les enfants.
10. Je laisse courir les enfants commes des gazelles.

EXERCISE 13

1. Ils s'aiment l'un l'autre.
2. Ils se font mal l'un l'autre.
3. Ils se font de la peine.
4. Ils se téléphonent.
5. Ils se parlent l'un à l'autre.
6. Ils se félicitent l'un l'autre.
7. Ils se présentent l'un l'autre aux leurs parents.

EXERCISE 14

1. Dans ce restaurant on ne se laisse pas de fumer.
2. Les clients se sont faits demander d'attendre.
3. Les employés se sont faits ordonner de decorer les tables.
4. Les serveuses se sont faites dire de repasser les nappes?
5. Les garçons se sont faits demander de nettoyer les vitres.
6. Les employés se sont faits dire de faire attention.
7. Sa femme ne se laisserait pas de travailler.

8. Le maître d se faisait demander d'arranger les chaises.
9. Il s'est fait demander de servir du champagne de France.
10. Son coiffeur se fait dire de lui couper les cheveux.

EXERCISE 15

1. Les portes du restaurant se sont fermées.
2. Rien ne se gagne en mentant.
3. Les journaux se lisaient le soir.
4. Cette idée ne se disputera pas par personne.
5. Le New York Nord se trouve aux Etats Unis.
6. Le nouveau gouverneur se choisira en Novembre.
7. Les faits ne se contredit pas.
8. Les meubles se sont vendus.
9. Le dîner se servait.
10. Son avis ne se changera pas par aucun évènement.

EXERCISE 16

1. Si nous dînions au restaurant.
2. Si nous achetions des meubles neufs.
3. Si nous allions au theatre.
4. Si nous voyagions.
5. Si nous visitions le musée.

EXERCISE 17

1. Nous irions à la plage s'il faisait beau.
2. Si vous sortez, fermez la porte.
3. Si vous aviez voulu répare la voiture, je vous aurais aidé.
4. Si son mari avait mort, cette femme aurait été veuve.
5. Si le film vous plaît, faites le moi savoir.
6. Si elle me mentait, je ne lui parlerais jamais.
7. Si les cravates ne me plaisent pas, je ne les achèterai pas.
8. Si elle etait malade, elle serait absente.
9. Iriez vous visiter Versailes si vous etiez en France?
10. S'il travaille dur il sera fatigue.
11. S'ils reçoivent la lettre, ils y repondront immediatement.
12. Si l'hôtel avait été climatisé, je serais resté une semaine entière.
13. Si elles avaient couru, elles y seraient arrivées à l'heure.
14. Si elle m'avait écoute, elle aurait compris mon point de vue.
15. Si nous lui prêtions l'argent, nous le rendrait-il?

EXERCISE 18

1. Combien de temps
2. écris
3. Depuis quand
4. depuis
5. vendra
6. neige
7. s'il
8. pleuvait-il
9. depuis
10. Combien de temps
11. Combien de temps y a-t-il que

12. serez
13. depuis
14. pour
15. Il y avait

EXERCISE 19

1. verrez
2. causait
3. meurs
4. rencontrait
5. réfléchis
6. descendront
7. vous sentirez
8. allais
9. cherchiez
10. fera

EXERCISE 20

1. Vous devriez changer d'école, mais vous ne le ferez jamais.
2. Mes amis ont dû quitter New York l'année dernière. Leur permis de séjours à expiré.
3. Mon frère me doit dix dollars.
4. Le gouvernement devra annuler toutes les taxes un jour!
5. Tout le monde doit obéir à la loi.
6. Les Haitiens ont dû faire une révolution pour avoir leur indépendance.
7. Vous devez obtenir votre passeport avant votre départ.
8. Le mécanicien devait réparer le carburateur, mais il n'avait pas le temps.
9. Ma fiancée m'attendait devant le restaurant ou nous devions dîner.
10. Ma sur doit être malade pour appeler le médecin.
11. Je devrai vous appeler cet après-midi parce que je suis trop occupée en ce moment.
12. Ces enfants devraient étudier, mais ils préfèrent regarder la télévision.
13. Si elle a refusé de répondre elle ne doit pas être seule.
14. Nous devrons les voir ce soir. Nous avons un rendez-vous.
15. J'devais porter un pardessus ce matin. Il neigeait.

EXERCISE 21

1. We must hurry.
2. He must have courage.
3. Will she be able to forget her sadness?
4. Kindly sit down.
5. We must not look at this drawing.
6. Do you know how to play tennis?
7. I could not understand the dialogue of the film.
8. They must have been very angry.
9. We will have to send him a telegram.
10. Can you point out the museum to us?

EXERCISE 22

1. Il faut que nous ayons du temps.
2. Peut-il que vous m'aidiez?
3. Après cette longue promenade, tu dois être fatiguée.
4. Il lui faut faire un effort pour se débarrasser de son rhume.

5. Je ne veux pas suivre la foule.
6. Devrez vous partir de bonne heure?
7. Il faut que je travaille ce soir.
8. Peuvent-ils vous accompagner?
9. Veuillez-vous asseoir.
10. Faut il téléphoner pour retenir une place dans l'avion?

EXERCISE 23

1. I will not shut up!
2. They have to take a music class.
3. Those who govern can make mistakes.
4. I cannot tell you.
5. He needed glasses to be able to read.
6. I received the money that he owed me.
7. Would he like to share in family life?
8. Where can she be? she can be in the city.
9. I must return your novel.
10. The lawyer had to abandon the case; he couldn't do anything else.

Index

Index